External Liberalization, Economic Performance and Social Policy

External Liberalization, Economic Performance, and Social Policy

edited by
Lance Taylor

OXFORD

UNIVERSITY PRESS

2001

OXFORD
UNIVERSITY PRESS

Oxford   New York

Athens   Auckland   Bangkok   Bogotá   Buenos Aires   Calcutta
Cape Town   Chennai   Dar es Salaam   Delhi   Florence   Hong Kong   Istanbul
Karachi   Kuala Lumpur   Madrid   Melbourne   Mexico City   Mumbai
Nairobi   Paris   São Paulo   Shanghai   Singapore   Taipei   Tokyo   Toronto   Warsaw

and associated companies in
Berlin   Ibadan

Library of Congress Cataloging-in-Publication Data
External liberalization, economic performance, and social policy /
edited by Lance Taylor.
p.   cm.
Includes bibliographical references and index.
ISBN 0-19-514546-1
1. Free trade—Social aspects—Developing countries.
2. Globalization—Economic aspects—Developing countries.
3. Globalization—Social aspects—Developing countries.
4. International economic relations.   I. Taylor, Lance.
HF2580.9 .E95   2000
337—dc21   00-049205

3 5 7 9 8 6 4 2
Printed in the United States of America
on acid-free paper

Contents

Contributors

Janine Berg
Center for Economic Policy Analysis, New School University, New York

Korkut Boratav
Faculty of Political Science, Ankara University, Turkey

Rob Davies
Department of Economics, University of Zimbabwe

Amitava Krishna Dutt
Department of Economics, University of Notre Dame, Indiana

Angela Ferriol Muruaga
Instituto Nacional de Investigaciones Económicas, Cuba

Roberto Frenkel
Centro de Estudios de Estado y Sociedad, Buenos Aires, Argentina

Martín González Rozada
Centro de Estudios de Estado y Sociedad, Buenos Aires, Argentina

Ahmet H. Köse
Faculty of Political Science, Ankara University, Turkey

John Langmore
United Nations, New York

Ju-Ho Lee
Korea Development Institute, School of International Policy and Management

Nora Lustig
Inter-American Development Bank, Washington, DC

José Antonio Ocampo
United Nations Economic Commission on Latin America and the Caribbean, Santiago, Chile

J. Mohan Rao
Department of Economics, University of Massachusetts at Amherst

Jørn Rattsø
Department of Economics, Norwegian University of Science and Technology

Jaime Ros
The Helen Kellog Institute for International Studies, University of Notre Dame, Indiana

Lance Taylor
Center for Economic Policy Analysis, New School University, New York

Camilo Tovar
United Nations Economic Commission on Latin America and the Caribbean, Santiago, Chile

Alexander Vorobyov
Institute of World Economy and International Relations, Moscow, Russia

A. Erinc Yeldan
Bilkent University, Turkey

Jong-Il You
Korea Development Institute, School of International Policy and Management

Stanislav Zhukov
Institute of World Economy and International Relations, Moscow, Russia

Foreword

JOHN LANGMORE
UN Division for
Social Policy and Development

Liberalization has been the dominant focus of economic policy change in most countries for at least the last two decades. Liberalization of international trade and finance has been amongst the principal forces for increasing global integration. The reviews of the experiences of nine developing countries and countries with economies in transition in this book are therefore timely. The issues are of great practical importance as well as being of intense theoretical and analytical interest, for while liberalization may have some intrinsic benefits, it can only be justified if it is an effective means to the end of improved human well-being.

There is considerable controversy about the consequences of the liberalization of international economic relations. Has global market integration stimulated economic growth—in some countries, in most, everywhere? Has financial liberalization intensified financial market volatility? What has been the impact on employment and on equity? Does increasing global integration constrain the capacity of governments to offset the damaging effects of liberalization through active social policy? There are many questions and the answers can be difficult to discern.

Yet all governments have to find answers and to decide on policies for maximizing benefits and minimizing costs. This is simple for some, for the benefits are clear. For example the United States has benefited especially from financial liberalization, for in the last years of the twentieth century it alone 'took in two thirds of the rest of the world's surplus saving.'[1] The net consequences are not at all clear for many other countries. For example those which

---

1. John Eatwell and Lance Taylor, *Global Finance at Risk; The Case For International Regulation*, The New Press, New York, 2000, p50.

consider themselves compelled to keep interest rates well above international norms in order to retain and attract funds are also therefore discouraging local entrepreneurs from borrowing and investing, and are therefore restraining their own economic development. Yet the preeminent approach to political economy during the last couple of decades has presumed that liberalization would be beneficial for all.

The fact that these issues are vigorously debated at international political forums adds to the rationale for their study. The World Summit for Social Development in Copenhagen in March 1995 was convened in part because of concern that liberalization had been receiving disproportionate attention and causing neglect of the central human and social priorities. There was a widespread perception that poverty was increasing, unemployment was high and many societies were in disarray and that these problems were not being adequately addressed by the prevailing economic orthodoxy.

An indication of the importance of the social issues is that more heads of state and government attended the Social Summit than any global meeting that had been held before. This may seem surprising, but social issues are of central political concern. Voters are preoccupied with the availability and quality of income earning opportunities, of schools and of health facilities and more generally with various aspects of the economic security and social cohesion of their societies. At the Social Summit the national leaders from developed, transitional and developing countries agreed on the Copenhagen Declaration on Social Development, which contains ten commitments and on a Programme of Action that outlines strategies aimed at their achievement. The central themes are commitment to eradicating poverty, achieving full employment and strengthening social integration.

The United Nations General Assembly held a Special Session in Geneva in June 2000 to evaluate progress in implementing the Copenhagen commitments, to identify constraints and to decide on further initiatives. During the five years between 1995 and 2000 international concern has multiplied about increasing inequality, marginalization, exclusion and the technological divide between the information rich and poor. The UN Division for Social Policy and Development offered support for the studies that are reported in this book to provide background material for that meeting.

Despite the conceptual and methodological difficulties in identifying and isolating the consequences of liberalization, the chapters here provide penetrating analysis and rigorous evaluation. The influence of Professor Lance Taylor's intellectual leadership of the project is demonstrated in the common framework and the analytical and empirical consistency of the chapters. As would be expected, the conclusions differ for each country, but it is clear that liberalization is not the panacea that its advocates have claimed. Skepticism about all panaceas, whether from right or left, should be one of the laws of human discourse!

The conclusions of these studies as well as the national assessments of progress (or, unfortunately, regress) since the Social Summit indicate the importance of achieving improved balance between public and private sectors.[2] Both sectors are prone to failure and both need the corrective influence of the other to be efficient and effective. Future policy prescriptions would do well to draw on the conclusions of this study and on the experience of more successful countries where there is a complex interplay of market and state, of freedom and opportunity on the one hand and public service provision and regulation on the other. This would require increased 'investment in the capability of the state' as suggested by Berg and Taylor, a decision comparable in importance to that which led to the spread of liberalization. Furthermore, in a globalizing world, some supportive and regulatory activities can only be efficiently provided globally: international cooperation in provision of global public goods must be increased.

The overarching theme of the Social Summit and the subsequent Special Session were that human well-being and social justice must be at the heart of global political priorities. This book shows that within that framework liberalization may sometimes be a useful tool but that it can also be misjudged and economically and socially damaging and that where governments decide to liberalize its timing and scope are crucial. Central issues are how to manage both national policies and the more integrated world so that efficiency and equity are simultaneously improved. Without strengthened social justice the durability of economic reform is at risk.

------

2. The national assessments are summarized and analyzed in the *Comprehensive Report on the Implementation of the outcome of the World Summit for Social Development*, A/AC.253/ 13 of 19 December 1999. This is available at www.un.org/socialsummit

1

Outcomes of External Liberalization and Policy Implications

LANCE TAYLOR

This book reports on a fundamental economic policy shift in transition and developing economies after the mid-1980s—the replacement of traditional regimes of widespread state controls and import-substituting industrialization by packages aimed at liberalizing the balance of payments, on both current and capital accounts. The new policy mix showed up throughout Latin America, Eastern Europe, Asia, and even in parts of Africa. Together with large but highly volatile foreign capital movements (often but not always in connection with privatization of state enterprises), this wave of external deregulation has been the central feature of "globalization" for the less industrialized world.

This thrust toward liberalization is analyzed herein on the basis of recent historical evidence from nine economies—Argentina, Colombia, Cuba, India, South Korea (hereafter simply "Korea"), Mexico, Russia, Turkey, and Zimbabwe. A companion volume edited by Ganuza, Taylor, and Vos (2000) focuses on the experiences of the four Latin American countries just mentioned, along with ten others. This chapter is an "executive summary" of the principal results. It draws heavily on material presented in Chapter 2, and ultimately on the country papers.

1. The Liberalization Debate

Through the mid-1980s, stabilization and structural adjustment efforts outside the industrialized economies had concentrated on fiscal and monetary restraint and realignment of exchange rates. Then in the late 1980s and early

1990s came drastic reductions in trade barriers and domestic and external financial liberalization, almost simultaneously in most countries. Complementary policies included restructuring domestic financial markets, tax systems, and labor markets. These steps toward liberalization mark close to a 180-degree shift in the course of development policy. It will take time before their full effects can by studied and understood, but one should surely expect large consequences.

The old policy model had been criticized for failing to promote efficient and competitive industrial production, for creating insufficient employment, and for failing to reduce income inequality. Its rapid abolition raises a new set of fundamental questions. Will the liberalization of trade and capital flows help countries meet social goals such as reductions in inequality and poverty, better provision of health and education, and social security? Will a world system in which national economies are highly integrated in commodity and capital markets (in terms of both increased transactions flows and tendencies toward price equalization) attain these goals of its own accord? Can social policies be deployed to ease the task?

The main official justifications for the reforms were the visible increases in economic efficiency and output growth that they were supposed to bring. Governments and international institutions promoting liberalization were less explicit about its distributional consequences. The predominant or "Washington Consensus" view is that deregulated markets are likely to lead to better economic performance, at least in the medium to long run. Even if there are adverse transitional impacts, they can be cushioned by social policies, and in any case after some time they will be outweighed by more rapid income growth.

Like all recent mainstream economic discourse, these conclusions rest on supply-side arguments. The purpose of trade reform is to switch production from non-tradable goods and inefficient import-substitutes towards exportable goods in which poor countries should have comparative advantage. Postulated full employment of all resources (labor included) enables such a switch to be made painlessly. Opening the capital account is supposed to bring financial inflows that will stimulate investment and productivity growth.

A second position is reflected in the annual *Human Development Reports* issued by the United Nations Development Programme and more technical underlying books and papers. It is more radical than the Washington consensus in arguing that social policies *should* be deployed to help the poor, on the implicit assumption that the forces determining the income distribution, the extent of poverty, and social relationships are largely independent of liberalization, globalization, and market processes more generally.

Finally, a third group believes that while there may be supply-side benefits from trade and capital market reforms one should not overlook aggregate demand, its potentially unfavorable interactions with distribution, and the impact of capital inflows on relative prices. The import-substitution model relied on expansion of internal markets with rising real wages as part of the strategy. Under the new regime controlling wage costs has come to center stage. So long as there is enough productivity growth and no substantial displacement of workers, wage restraint need not be a problem because output expansion could create space for real income growth. But if wage levels are seriously reduced and/or workers with high consumption propensities lose their jobs, contraction of domestic demand could cut labor income in sectors that produce for the local market. Income inequality could rise if displaced unskilled workers end up in informal service sector activities for which there is declining demand.

Rising capital inflows following liberalization tend to lead to real exchange rate appreciation (a "stronger" local currency), offsetting liberalization's incentives for traded goods production and forcing greater reductions in real wage costs. Appreciation in turn may be linked to high real interest rates, which add to production costs and penalize capital formation. Higher rates may also draw in more external capital, setting off a high interest rate/strong exchange rate spiral. Via the banking system, capital inflows feed into international reserves and domestic credit expansion. On the positive side, more credit may stimulate aggregate spending through increased domestic investment. However, credit expansion can also trigger a consumption boom (with purchases heavily weighted toward imports) or a speculative asset price bubble (typically in equity and/or real estate). The demand expansion may prove to be short-lived if the consequent widening of the external balance is unsustainable or if capital flees the economy when the bubble begins to deflate. Lack of prudential financial regulation makes the latter outcome all the more likely.

The thrust of these observations is that the effects of balance of payments liberalization on growth, employment, and income distribution emerge from a complex set of forces involving both the supply and the demand sides of the economy. Income redistribution and major shifts in relative prices are endogenous to the process. Nor is social policy a panacea for rising inequality and distributional tensions. Only a few countries such as Korea in 1998-99 and Chile and Colombia through much of the 1990s took advantage of strong fiscal positions to introduce large-scale programs to offset some of liberalization's adverse distributional effects. Cuba continued a strong tradition of social support, and introduced new programs to offset economic dualism induced by opening the capital and current accounts. Russia, Turkey, and Zimbabwe simply lacked fiscal capacity, and cut back social programs. To a large extent, Argentina and India left pre-existing systems (with at best partial coverage of the population) intact, and Mexico abandoned policies supporting the rural poor. In the rest of the Latin American sample, distributional shifts were allowed to cascade through the system.

2. Effects of Liberalization

An immediate conclusion from the country studies included in this volume is that the effects of globalization and liberalization have not been uniformly favorable. In a classification that is overly simplistic but still suggestive, outcomes can be summarized in the following fashion:

Social Impacts

Effect on growth	FAVORABLE	NEUTRAL	UNFAVORABLE
POSITIVE			Argentina (pre-1997–8) Mexico (post-1995)
NEUTRAL		Cuba Turkey	India Korea Mexico (pre-1995)
NEGATIVE		Colombia	Russia Zimbabwe Argentina (post-1998)

At least until 1997–98 when it fell into deep recession, Argentina was the only economy in the group with growth that accelerated for a substantial period after 1990. Mexico was a late-joining counterpart, with a rapid growth rate in the late 1990s that may not be sustainable when the United States, its largest trading partner, slips into recession. The "neutral" growth impacts in some cases are really slow-downs that can be explained by exogenous factors (e.g. Cuba's loss of support from the socialist bloc), while Russia and Zimbabwe have clearly been adversely affected by globalization. The "neutral" social impacts are in fact a mix of gains and losses, with losses dominating in the rest of the sample. Broadly similar observations apply to the Latin American case studies in Ganuza, et.al. (2000), but some country outcomes were more favorable. In the 1990s, Chile, Costa Rica, the Dominican Republic, and Peru all sustained fairly high growth rates with stable or falling indexes of inequality. The somewhat illiberal policy mix that supported these "success cases" (all of which rested on capital inflows) is described below.

3. Economic Performance over Time

To trace through the impacts of liberalization in more detail, the country papers deployed several decomposition techniques to trace economic changes over time.[1] One looked at how effective demand (and therefore the level of output) was influenced by partially offsetting pressures among national investment and saving, exports and imports, and government spending and taxes. Another decomposed sectoral employment growth in light of growth rates of

---

1. The analytical details are presented in Chapter 2 and the country papers.

demand and productivity, a third was an analysis of interactions across sectors of productivity growth per se, and finally some of the papers discussed shifts in the "functional" income distribution across sectors and recipient classes. Beginning with a broad analysis of growth and equity, the main results were as follows:

Growth and Equity

Apart from years of overt crisis, most countries achieved moderate growth rates of GDP in the 1990s. Russia and not quite so disastrously Colombia and Zimbabwe were the main losers. Except in Korea prior to its crisis, household per capita income growth was negative or not far above zero.

Capital inflows increased substantially to most countries (in some cases, only prior to their respective crises). As discussed above, incoming foreign capital tended to be associated with increases in international reserves, domestic credit expansion, and real appreciation. Stronger exchange rates were generally associated with higher interest rates and increasing spreads between borrowing and lending rates. Capital inflows, credit creation, and real appreciation together stimulated aggregate demand to increase more rapidly than GDP, with consequent widening of the current account deficit.

Inequality of primary incomes increased across both samples. Almost all countries' wage differentials between skilled and unskilled workers rose with liberalization and participation rates (or shares of populations that are "economically active") increased or were stable. As proportions of the economically active (following the standard definition), unemployment rates were stable or tended to rise.

Sources of Effective Demand

One of the principal justifications for external liberalization was its anticipated effect on trade performance. Due to efficiency gains induced by freer trade, "export-led" growth was supposed to be an immediate consequence. It did not happen, at least in terms of effective demand generation in the countries analyzed in this volume. As the country studies demonstrate, exports did tend to rise with liberalization but import leakages went up as well, especially when the local currency appreciated in real terms. Trade therefore held back or added weakly to effective demand. The export stimulus was present, but much less strongly than originally supposed by advocates of liberalization.

The public sector's contribution to demand varied across countries. It was positive in Columbia due to increases in social spending, Cuba as it recovered from external shocks in 1994-98, India where the consolidated government deficit has supported demand for many years, and Russia as plummeting demand was at least slowed by the fact that government spending did not decrease quite so rapidly as receipts from a failing tax system. Elsewhere, government's impact on demand was broadly neutral. Positive or "stop-go" public sector demand effects are a surprising outcome, given the rhetoric about downsizing the state that accompanied the drive towards liberalization.

Without strong contributions from the foreign and public sectors, private sector demand growth emerged as the major driving force in several of the country histories. In particular, import-led consumption booms following trade and financial liberalization were the rule rather than the exception. They were triggered by both cheapening of imported traded goods (import liberalization and real exchange rate appreciation) and expansion of domestic credit supply (fomented by the surge in capital flows and domestic financial liberalization). Private savings rates fell in consequence. Fewer cases were observed in which domestic demand was driven by expanding private investment, but it did occur in Argentina and Korea early in the 1990s. The rapid reduction in demand in Russia was provoked by an investment collapse in an economy that had historically been driven by high rates of accumulation. In Mexico late in the decade, higher private capital formation could give hope for a brighter future were it not for a setback due to global instability in 1998-99.

Productivity and Employment Growth

With Korea prior to its crisis as a notable outlier, only modest aggregate productivity increases were observed. Where data are available, they are broadly consistent with greater observed productivity growth in traded than non-traded sectors. The change in aggregate productivity is result of the sum of productivity changes by sectors (weighted by sectoral output shares) plus a positive reallocation effect if labor moves from low- to high-productivity activities. Findings from the country studies indicate that within-sector productivity shifts and output growth rates largely determined the aggregate outcomes. However, in some cases there was a negative reallocation effect as workers moved toward low productivity non-traded and/or agricultural sectors.

With Cuba and Russia as exceptions, the share of the economically active population (the participation rate) increased under liberalization. Except in Turkey, the unemployed as a proportion of the economically active went up as well, especially after crises and/or later in the decade. Given the modest growth of GDP noted previously, a lackluster employment performance under liberalization is scarcely surprising.

6. Developments in Social Policy

The macroeconomic conditions emerging from external liberalization—appreciation of the real exchange rate, high interest rates, domestic credit expansion, and an import boom—were scarcely favorable for an often outdated and "inefficient" industrial sector making the transition to a free trade environment.

In the nine countries surveyed, the transition typically meant labor shedding in industry. Productivity increased, yet output gains were usually not strong enough to offset employment and wage losses via other sectors of the economy.

In Korea, the severe austerity program following the 1997 financial crash led to a deep recession, causing output, employment, and wage contraction in the industrial sector. For all the countries studied, the result has been a loss of relatively high-paying jobs, replaced by underemployment and lower wages in the service sector, often in the informal economy. Skilled workers suffered the least and in some cases (Argentina, Mexico) benefited from the economic policy shift. This pattern, coupled with declining opportunities for the low-skilled, led to rising income inequality in all nine countries.

Social policy is an important tool that can in principle be used by governments to cushion some of the adverse effects of external liberalization. However, it is not always available. Governments facing inflation often have to restrain their deficits as a first step toward price stabilization; social policy programs may bear the brunt of reduced government spending. Besides deficit financing, raising taxes can provide revenue for social policy programs, but often the willingness to reform and increase the tax base does not exist. The nine countries can broadly be divided into three groups in terms of their social spending during liberalization: those that did increase spending, those that couldn't, and those that chose not to.

Colombia, Cuba, and Korea introduced social policy programs to offset some of the negative consequences of liberalization. Colombia broadened and increased its tax base, allowing expanded social security coverage as well as improved school attendance rates, access to drinking water, and housing. Poverty as measured by unsatisfied basic needs declined, despite a fall in the terms of trade and increased unemployment. Cuba, during the external shock of 1989–93, suffered output, productivity and real wage contraction as well as increased poverty. Pressed with the need to generate foreign exchange, the government restructured the economy. One consequence was rising inequality between people working in export sectors and the rest of the population. To lessen this divide, the government maintained and increased social policy programs, compensating workers not employed in exports. In Korea, the economic crisis provided momentum for expanding social services, an area historically neglected in favor of growth. Government outlays for social expenditures increased from 5% of GDP in the 1980s to 7.8% in 1997. Additional programs could be funded if a more progressive tax system were put in place.

Russia, Turkey and Zimbabwe faced fiscal resource constraints during external liberalization and were forced to cut back on social programs. Russia is the most acute example. Privatization of state-owned energy industries coupled with a lack of capital controls led to external capital flight in its principal foreign-exchange-earning sectors. The combination of capital flight and growing informalization of the economy meant the government did not have resources to compensate workers who lost their jobs because of liberalization. Funding of health, education, and other services deteriorated severely. Along with the hardships accompanying the transition, the funding cuts have contributed to an increase in the incidence of poverty and income inequality.

In Turkey and Zimbabwe, an unwillingness to raise taxes relates directly to the countries' inability to finance social programs. During the 1980s, Turkey expanded government spending on social programs via deficit finance. By 1993, this effort was no longer sustainable, leading to cutbacks. Unless taxes are increased, the government will be unable to finance social spending, as it will not risk a return to rising inflation. Similarly, in Zimbabwe, external liberalization has been accompanied with a tightening of government spending in an attempt to control inflation. Social programs instituted during the 1980s in an attempt to lessen inequality between racial groups have been cut back. This is unfortunate given that many Zimbabwean workers have been displaced as a result of liberalization, while those still employed have seen their real wages fall.

In Argentina, India, and Mexico, external liberalization has not been accompanied with increased social spending. Argentina responded to the increase in unemployment caused by liberalization by making the labor market more flexible. This led to an increase in underemployment, measured by a rise in part-time work, as well as lower wages. However, a state-subsidized employment program in the health and education sectors has enabled some, mostly female, workers to get jobs. With the removal of tariffs, India lost an important source of government revenue. The revenue loss helped cause a decline in government spending to the detriment of social programs in rural development, health, education, and housing. In Mexico, the government has not instituted social programs to help those hurt by the transition. In an extreme opposite example, the government dismantled long-standing support for the rural agricultural sector to the detriment of rural incomes.

The experience of the nine countries indicates that the negative effects accompanying external liberalization can be somewhat offset, if the state has the power and will to raise taxes and finance the needed spending. Deficit financing may be unsustainable, as in Turkey and Zimbabwe. In Russia, on the other hand, the state was too weak even to attempt to maintain social spending. Colombia, Cuba and Korea did attempt to cushion the transition, though their spending was also constrained by their ability to tax. In Argentina, India and Mexico, the negative effects of external liberalization could have been dampened had the governments sought recourse through taxation to fund social programs.

5. Policy Alternatives

The usual caveats about policy prescriptions apply. Given the diversity of country experiences that was observed, it is risky to generalize about lessons and conclusions. Of course, diversity of outcomes is a result in itself. It should negate the relevance of general sweeping statements about whether the reforms have been exclusively beneficial or exclusively costly in terms of growth, employment, and equity.

If one is to sing a sad song, however, the evidence certainly shows that in the post-liberalization era few if any of the countries considered seem to have found a sustainable growth path. Employment growth has generally been slow to dismal and rising primary income disparity (in some cases over and above already high levels of inequality) has been the rule.

Better performances such as those in Mexico and Korea after their financial crises (as of the year 2000, three years of sustained growth in Mexico and one in Korea) were associated with avoiding the macro price mixture of a strong real exchange rate and high domestic interest rates. Post-crisis effective demand was led by the foreign sector in Mexico and by private consumption and investment spending in Korea, suggesting that each recovering country may have its own particular demand path.

Similar conclusions apply to the handful of Latin American economies described in Ganuza, et.al. (2000) that combined adequate growth with improvement or stability of indexes of inequality. Their better performances were associated with a policy mix that combined (a) avoiding a macro price mixture of real exchange rate appreciation and high domestic interest rates, (b) maintaining a system of well-directed export incentives whether put in place at the national level or as part of regional integration agreements, and (c) having a system of capital controls and prudential financial regulation able to contain the negative consequences of capital surges.

For the other countries described in this volume, the news is less good. Among the historically capitalist economies, Turkey and Argentina continue to wander in a slow growth, falling employment, and increasing inequality wilderness. India's growth and equity performance has not improved with liberalization, and despite a strong effort on the social policy front, Colombia's is far worse. In part because of an explicit effort to cushion the liberalization shock, Cuba's growth and equity performances are mediocre. Zimbabwe's and especially Russia's are disasters.

Of the three views regarding liberalization mentioned at the outset, the first "market friendly" narrative is hard to discern in the countries analyzed here. To a certain extent, their distributional deterioration may *not* have been the result of liberalization and globalization—the second view—but one would have to strain to make the case. For most of the countries considered here (and in the Latin American sample as well), it is difficult to refute the third view that liberalization and deteriorating growth and equity performances can easily go hand-in-hand.

Finally, fundamental questions arise regarding social coherence and social policy. The mainstream view of liberalization emphasizes its likely positive effects on economic performance. Adverse transitional impacts can in principle be smoothed by social policies, and in any case after some time "a rising tide lifts all boats" (except, as is sometimes added, the ones that happen to sink). The much more disquieting possibility is that liberalization can unleash

dynamic forces leading not only to an unimpressive aggregate economic performance but also to long-term slow employment expansion and increasing
income concentration. In principle, governments could put countervailing
social policies into place. In practice, the evidence just reported suggests that
they may well lack the capacity to do so because of their own fiscal and administrative limitations.

Such constraints on social policy and burden-sharing can be reduced by
investment in the capability of the state, as experience in now industrialized
countries demonstrated in the 19th century and again after World War II in
the construction of welfare states. But an explicit political decision would be
needed before such investments could be undertaken. It would be comparable in scope to the one that led to the worldwide spread of liberalization in
the first place. Nevertheless, for the countries considered here, the initial outcomes of liberalization suggest that a move first toward and then away from an
extreme liberal policy stance could be forthcoming in the not-so-distant future. A deteriorating social performance from any economic policy line leads
ultimately to its reversal as society rallies to protect its own.

10. Acknowledgements

The country papers and other research efforts presented in this book were
made possible through grants made by the Division for Social Policy and Development of the United Nations and the John D. and Catherine T. MacArthur
Foundation to the Center for Economic Policy Analysis of the New School
University. Their support is gratefully acknowledged.

2

External Liberalization, Economic Performance, and Social Policy

JANINE BERG *and* LANCE TAYLOR

As seen from the year 2000, economic policy in developing and post-socialist economies during the preceding 10 to 15 years had one dominating theme. Packages aimed at liberalizing the balance of payments, on both current and capital accounts, showed up throughout Latin America, Eastern Europe, Asia, and even in parts of Africa. Together with large but highly volatile foreign capital movements (often but not always in connection with privatization of state enterprises), this wave of external deregulation was the central feature of "globalization" for the non-industrialized world.

This volume draws together recent historical evidence from nine developing and transition economies—Argentina, Colombia, Cuba, India, South Korea (hereafter simply referred to as "Korea"), Mexico, Russia, Turkey, and Zimbabwe—to study and assess these changes and their economic and social consequences. A companion book edited by Ganuza, Taylor, and Vos (2000) covers the experience of the four Latin American countries just mentioned, along with ten others. The discussion here concentrates on the sample of nine countries, with results from Latin America brought in where they add information.

This analytical introduction summarizes the results of the studies from several perspectives. It begins with a review of different ways of analyzing liberalization and globalization that appear in the literature. Then the basic approach of the country papers and their key results regarding growth and inequality are quickly presented. These points are elaborated in the form of a simple macroeconomic model that captures the flavor of liberalization on the ground. An initial application of the model is followed by a review of decomposition exercises for effective demand and employment and distributional changes that are presented in the papers. The results of the decompositions and other salient indicators of the effects of liberalization are displayed in a set of tables, which are used to construct vignettes summarizing the country experiences. Next comes a discussion of the social policy issues emphasized by the country authors. The chapter closes with a review of open questions regarding macroeconomic and external policy alternatives, and whether social policy can ameliorate the worst effects of globalization and balance of payments deregulation.

1. Views about Liberalization

Liberalization arrived abruptly. Stabilization and structural adjustment efforts through the mid-1980s had concentrated on fiscal and monetary restraint and realignment of exchange rates. Then in the late 1980s and early 1990s came drastic reductions in trade restrictions and domestic and external financial liberalization, almost simultaneously in most countries. Complementary steps were also taken toward restructuring domestic financial markets, tax systems, and labor markets.

All these changes are very recent. It will take time before their full effects on growth, employment, income distribution, and poverty can be fully assessed. But external liberalization marks a dramatic switch in development policy away from traditional regimes of widespread state controls and import-substituting industrialization. One would expect to see large consequences.

The old policy model had been criticized for failing to promote efficient and competitive industrial production, for creating insufficient employment, and for failing to reduce income inequality. Its rapid abolition raises a new set of fundamental questions. Will the liberalization of trade and capital flows help countries meet social goals such as reductions in inequality and poverty, better provision of health and education, and social security? Will a world system in which national economies are highly integrated in commodity and capital markets (in terms of both increased transactions flows and tendencies toward price equalization) attain these goals of its own accord? Can social policies be deployed to ease the task?

The main official justification for the reforms was stated in terms of visible increases in economic efficiency and output growth that they were supposed to bring. Governments and international institutions promoting them were less explicit about their distributional consequences. The predominant view is that liberalization is likely to lead to better economic performance, at least in the medium to long run. Even if there are adverse transitional impacts, they can be cushioned by social policies, and in any case after some time they will be outweighed by more rapid income growth.

This conclusion is fundamentally based on supply-side arguments. The purpose of trade reform is to switch production from non-tradable goods and inefficient import-substitutes towards exportable goods in which poor countries should have comparative advantage. Presumed full employment of all resources (labor included) enables such a switch to be made painlessly. Opening the capital account is supposed to bring financial inflows that will stimulate investment and productivity growth. In a typical mainstream syllogism, Londoño and Szekely (1998) postulate that equity is positively related to growth and investment. These in turn are asserted to be positively related to structural reforms, so the conclusion is that liberalization supports low-income groups.

A second position is more radical in that its proponents such as Rodrik (1998) and Sen (1999) argue that social policies *should* be deployed to help the poorest, on the implicit assumption that the forces determining the income distribution, the extent of poverty, and social relationships more generally are largely independent of liberalization and globalization.

Finally, others argue that while there may be supply-side benefits from trade and capital market reforms one should not overlook aggregate demand, its potentially unfavorable interactions with distribution, and the impact of capital inflows on relative prices. The import-substitution model relied on expansion of internal markets with rising real wages as part of the strategy. Under the new regime controlling wage costs has come to center stage. So long as there is enough productivity growth and no substantial displacement of workers, wage restraint need not be a problem because output expansion could create space for real income growth. But if wage levels are seriously reduced and/or workers with high consumption propensities lose their jobs, contraction of domestic demand could cut labor income in sectors that produce for the local market. Income inequality could rise if displaced unskilled workers end up in informal service sector activities for which there is a declining demand.

Rising capital inflows following liberalization tend to lead to real exchange rate appreciation, offsetting liberalization's incentives for traded goods production and forcing greater reductions in real wage costs. Appreciation in turn may be linked to high real interest rates, which add to production costs and penalize capital formation. Higher rates may also draw in more external capital, setting off a high interest rate/strong exchange rate spiral. Via the banking system, capital inflows feed into international reserves and domestic credit expansion. On the positive side, more available credit may stimulate aggregate spending through increased domestic investment. However, credit expansion can also trigger a consumption boom (with the new purchases heavily weighted toward imports) or a speculative asset price bubble (typically in equity and/or real estate). The demand expansion may prove to be short-lived if the consequent widening of the external balance is unsustainable or if capital flees the economy when the bubble begins to deflate. Lack of prudential financial regulation makes the latter outcome all the more likely.

The thrust of these observations is that the effects of balance of payments liberalization on growth, employment, and income distribution emerge from a complex set of forces involving both the supply and the demand sides of the economy. Income redistribution and major shifts in relative prices are endogenous to the process. Nor is social policy a panacea for rising in-equality and distributional tensions. Only two countries in the sample (Korea in 1998-99 and Colombia through much of the 1990s) took advantage of strong fiscal positions to introduce large-scale programs to offset some of liberalization's adverse distributional effects. Cuba continued its long tradi-tion of social support, and introduced new programs to offset economic dual-ism induced by opening the capital and current accounts. Russia, Turkey, and Zimbabwe simply lacked fiscal capacity, and cut back social programs. To a large extent, Argentina and India left pre-existing systems (with at best partial coverage of the population) intact, and Mexico abandoned policies support-ing the rural poor.

The bottom line is that there can be no facile conclusions about liberalization's effects, nor about how they can be contained. To date, costs in many countries have outweighed the benefits, and this situation may persist for an extended period of time.

2. The Approach of the Country Papers

To a greater or lesser extent, the authors of the country studies collected in this volume adhere to the third, "structuralist" worldview mentioned above. Structuralism is not accepted in all circles. But the strength of the papers is that their shared analytical stance eases the task of cross-country comparisons and points to coherent policy conclusions. The countries considered were selected on the basis of their economic importance and the ability of poten-tial authors to carry high quality studies through. The sample is not large enough to be "representative," but its analysis in depth is well able to support generalizations about likely outcomes of the globalization/liberalization policy mix in other national circumstances.

How did the authors separate effects of specific policy changes from other factors, such as external shocks and other policy initiatives? They addressed this standard problem in economic analysis with a mixture of the following approaches:

· Well-informed country "narratives" discussing policy changes and ob-served outcomes in a "before-and-after" approach. The country stories started with a basic set of questions and hypotheses and a simple analytical framework suggesting possible channels of causation as outlined below. Authors sub-divided their period of analysis into "episodes" with relatively homogeneous policy packages and economic circumstances. They could then trace the ef-fects of liberalization from one episode through another.

· Still within the realm of "before and after," standardized decomposition analyses of aggregate demand, factoral income distribution, employment, and productivity growth were applied wherever data availability made them possible. These decompositions (also described below) give essential compara-tive information on changes in output, employment, and inequality that actu-ally took place.

· Counterfactual policy simulations ("with and without") were incorporated in some case studies, based on country-specific models.

It could be argued that, ideally, an approach based on formal modeling for all countries would be a better method to verify the effects of the various exogenous shocks and policy changes. As just noted, some case studies incorporated results from such costly exercises, providing useful insights. But while models may permit a more rigorous isolation of the effects of different reform measures, they have important limitations due to their assumptions about directions of economic causality and specification of parameters, not to mention their inability to describe changes in behavior after liberalization and to take into account political economy. A combination of methods is better able to provide the ingredients needed to understand the underlying processes.

Initial Summary of Results

An immediate conclusion is that the effects of globalization and liberalization have not been uniformly favorable. In a classification that is overly simplistic but still suggestive, outcomes for the countries included in this study can be summarized in the following fashion:

	Social Impacts		
	FAVORABLE	NEUTRAL	UNFAVORABLE
Effect on growth			
POSITIVE			Argentina (until 1997–8) Mexico (post-1995)
NEUTRAL		Cuba Turkey	India Korea Mexico (pre-1995)
NEGATIVE		Colombia	Russia Zimbabwe

At least until 1997–98 when it fell into deep recession, Argentina was the only economy in the group with growth that accelerated for a substantial period after 1990. Mexico was a late-joining counterpart, with a rapid growth rate in the late 1990s that may not be sustainable when the United States, its largest trading partner, slips into recession. The "neutral" growth impacts in some cases are really slow-downs that can be explained by exogenous factors (e.g. Cuba's loss of support from the socialist bloc), while Russia and Zimbabwe have clearly been adversely affected by globalization. The "neutral" social impacts are in fact a mix of gains and losses, with losses dominating in the rest of the sample. Broadly similar observations apply to the Latin American case studies in Ganuza, et.al. (2000), but some country outcomes were more favorable. In the 1990s, Chile, Costa Rica, the Dominican Republic, and Peru all sustained fairly high growth rates with stable or falling indexes of inequality. The somewhat illiberal policy mix that supported these "success cases" (all of which rested on sustained capital inflows) is described below.

Finally, all the country histories reflect internal social and political developments that influenced economic performance. The seismic changes in Russia require no comment; although less dramatic, the breakdown of centralized planning in Korea is almost as significant. There was a strong political cycle in Turkey between redistributive and market-stabilizing policy regimes (at times under the auspices of the same government). Shifts in the other countries made fewer headlines, but may be equally as important for political economy in the medium run.

3. A Model of Liberalization

Along with the aggregate outcomes just summarized, liberalization had strong differential effects on prices and quantities in different sectors of the economy. For many but not all countries, an appropriate disaggregation of the non-financial, price/quantity side of the economy focuses on traded and non-traded goods. The key relative price is the real exchange rate or ratio of traded to non-traded goods price indexes. In more populous, less intrinsically open economies one also has to consider other price ratios such as the agricultural terms of trade (India, Turkey) or the relative price of energy products (Russia). In sub-Saharan African economies such as Zimbabwe's (not to mention primary product exporters in Latin America and the Caribbean), the terms of trade between an urban-industrial and rural-agricultural sector come to the fore. In all cases, a mixture of price and quantity adjustments to the liberalization experience is evident.

Since it is broadly applicable, the traded/non-traded separation is explored in the discussion to follow. Direct effects of removing barriers to trade and capital movements show up first in the traded (or tradable) goods sector but spillovers in both directions with non-traded goods have been immediate and substantial. Amadeo and Pero (2000) and Ros (1999) point out the major connections in similar fashions.

The framework is a "fix-price/flex-price" model à la Hicks (1965) and many others. Traded goods are assumed to be produced under imperfect competition. The simplest model involves a discriminating monopolist manufacturing goods that can both be exported and sold at home, as in Ocampo and Taylor (1998). Households at home buy both domestically made and imported consumer goods. Prior to liberalization, firms have established mark-up rates over variable costs in both their markets—the levels will depend on the relevant elasticities. Variable cost is determined by the market prices and productivity levels of unskilled labor and intermediate imports; skilled labor and physical capital are fixed factors in the short run. The traded goods price level P_t follows from the domestic mark-up over variable cost.

With stable mark-up rates, traded goods comprise a Hicksian "fix-price" sector, with a level of output X_t determined by effective demand. The level of production of non-traded goods is also determined by demand, but the sector may well have decreasing returns to unskilled labor in the short run. Higher production X_n is made possible by greater unskilled employment (or labor demand) L_n^d. However, cost-minimizing producers will hire extra workers only at a lower real product wage w/P_n, where w is the unskilled nominal wage (fixed in the short run but subject to adjustment over time as discussed below) and P_n is the price of non-traded goods. In other words, a higher price-wage ratio P_n/w is associated with greater non-traded goods production and employment, and (if there are decreasing returns) reduced labor productivity. If P_n/w is free to vary, then non-traded goods aggregate into a "flex-price" sector. With stable mark-up rates in the traded goods sector, the inter-sectoral price ratio P_t/P_n will fall as P_n/w rises, i.e. a rising price of non-traded goods is associated with real appreciation as measured by the ratio of traded to non-traded goods price indexes (a commonly used proxy is the ratio of wholesale to retail price levels).

Figure 1 gives a graphical presentation of the model.[1] The key quadrant lies in the extreme northeast. It shows how prices and output in the two sectors are determined. Along the schedule for "Non-traded goods equilibrium," a higher traded goods output level X_t is assumed to generate additional demand for non-traded goods. As it is met by an increase in supply, the non-traded price-wage ratio P_n/w will rise. In the market for traded goods, depending on income effects a higher level of P_n/w can be associated with either higher or lower demand. The "Traded goods equilibrium" schedule illustrates the former case—demand for X_t is stimulated by an increase in P_n/w. As drawn in the Figure, the short-run macro equilibrium defined by the intersection of the two curves is stable.

This equilibrium helps determine the status of several markets in the economy. For example, unskilled labor demand in the non-traded sector (L_n^d) is determined in the northwest quadrant. Employment in the traded goods sector is shown in the second quadrant from the top on the right. A lower employment level in traded goods liberates labor that can be used in the other sector, as shown in the second quadrant from the top on the left. As the figure is drawn, labor supply L_n^s exceeds demand L_n^d in the non-traded sector, i.e. there is open or disguised unemployment as measured by the difference ($L_n^s - L_n^d$). Finally, in the extreme southeast quadrant, bigger trade deficits are associated with higher levels of X_t and P_n/w.

---

1. See Taylor (1991) for an algebraic treatment of linkages like those described in the text in models closely related to the one illustrated in Figure 1.

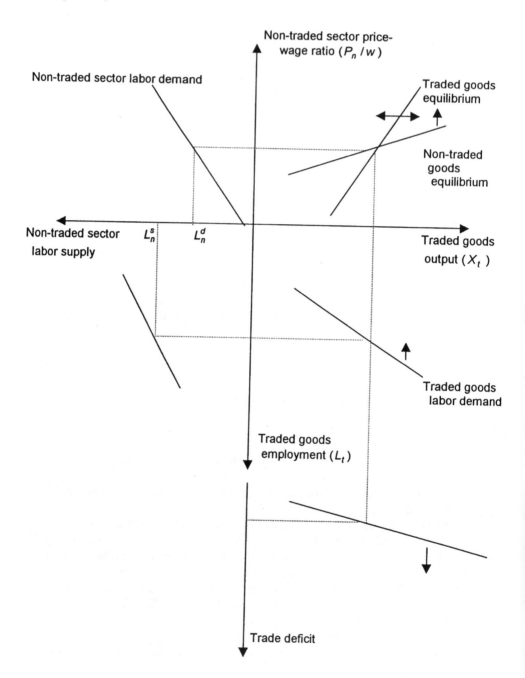

FIGURE 1: Initial equilibrium positions in traded and non-traded goods markets and probable shifts after current and capital account liberalization

4. Effects of Liberalization

As indicated above, in many developing economies both current and capital accounts of the balance of payments were liberalized nearly simultaneously in the late 1980s or early 1990s. Given this history, one has to consider the two policy shifts together. However, for analytical clarity it is useful to dissect them one at a time. In addition, effects of other reforms have to be considered as well, in particular domestic financial, tax, and labor market deregulation. We begin with the capital account, followed by the current account, to end with some comments regarding the other sets of reforms.

Capital Account Liberalization

Countries liberalized their capital accounts for several apparent reasons—to accommodate to external political pressures (Korea and many others), to find sources of finance for growing fiscal deficits (Turkey, Russia), or to bring in foreign exchange to finance the imports needed to hold down prices of traded goods in exchange rate-based inflation stabilization programs (Argentina, Mexico).

Whatever the rationale, when they removed restrictions on capital movements, most countries received a surge of inflows from abroad. They came in subject to the accounting restriction that an economy's net foreign asset position (total holdings of external assets minus total external liabilities) can only change gradually over time through a deficit or surplus on the current account. Hence, when external liabilities increased as foreigners acquired securities issued by national governments or firms, external assets had to jump up as well. The new assets typically showed up on the balance sheets of financial institutions, including larger international reserves of the central bank. Unless the bank made a concerted effort to "sterilize" the inflows (selling government bonds from its portfolio to "mop up liquidity," for example), they set off a domestic credit boom. In poorly regulated financial systems, there was a high risk of a classic mania-panic-crash sequence along Kindleberger (1996) lines—the famous crises in Latin America's Southern Cone around 1980 were only the first of many such disasters.

When the credit expansion was allowed to work itself through, interest rates could be low. However, other factors entered to push both levels of and the spread between borrowing and lending rates upward. One source of widening spreads is related to asset price booms in housing and stock markets, which forced rates to rise on interest-bearing securities such as government debt. Another source playing a role at times originated from central banks trying to sterilize capital inflows, and so pushing up rates as well. Finally, in non-competitive financial markets, local institutions often found it easy to raise spreads. High local returns pulled more capital inflows, worsening the overall disequilibrium.

Unsurprisingly, exchange rate movements complicated the story. In many countries, the exchange rate was used as a "nominal anchor" in anti-inflation programs. Its nominal level was devalued at a rate less than the rate of inflation, leading to real appreciation. In several cases, the effect was rapid, with traded goods variable costs in dollar terms jumping upward immediately after the rate was frozen.

The same outcome also showed up via another channel. As countries removed capital controls and adopted "floating" rates, they lost a degree of freedom in policy formulation. From standard macroeconomic theory we know that in a closed economy the market for bonds will be in equilibrium if the money market clears as well. When proper accounting restrictions (including a fixed level of net foreign assets in the short run) are imposed on portfolio choice in an open economy, this theorem continues to apply (Taylor, 1999). That is, an open economy has just one independent "asset market" relationship, say an excess supply function for bonds of the form

$$B - B^d[i, i^*, (\varepsilon/e)] = 0$$

In this equation, B and B^d are bond supply and demand respectively. The latter depends positively on the domestic interest rate i, and negatively on the foreign rate i^* and on expected depreciation ε as normalized by the current spot rate e.[2] Total bond supply B will change slowly over time as new paper is issued to cover corporate and (especially) fiscal deficits.

For given expectations, the formula suggests that the interest rate and spot exchange rate will be related inversely. If, for the reasons mentioned above, the domestic interest rate i tended to rise, then the exchange rate would appreciate or fall. Or, the other way 'round, if the exchange rate strengthened over time, then interest rates would be pushed upward. This tendency would be amplified if real appreciation stimulated aggregate demand in the short run—the other side of the coin of the well-known possibility that devaluation can be contractionary in developing economies (Krugman and Taylor, 1978). Abandoning capital controls made the exchange rate/interest rate trade-off far more difficult to manage. Some countries did succeed in keeping their exchange rates relatively weak, but they were in a minority.

Summarizing, capital account liberalization combined with a boom in external inflows could easily provoke "excessive" credit expansion. Paradoxically, the credit boom could be associated with relatively high interest rates and a strong local currency. These were not the most secure foundations for liberalization of the current account, the topic we take up next.

---

2. Scaling the expected change in the exchange rate by its current level puts the quantity ε/e—the expected rate of return from capital gains on foreign securities—on a comparable footing with the two interest rates.

Current Account Liberalization

Current account deregulation basically took the form of transformation of import quota restrictions (where they were important) to tariffs, and then consolidation of tariff rates into a fairly narrow band, e.g. between zero and 20%. With a few exceptions, export subsidies were also removed. There were visible effects on the level and composition of effective demand, and on patterns of employment and labor productivity.

Demand composition typically shifted in the direction of imports, especially when there was real exchange appreciation. In many cases, national savings rates also declined. This shift can partly be attributed to an increased supply of imports at low prices (increasing household spending, aided by credit expansion following financial liberalization), and partly to a profit squeeze (falling retained earnings) in industries producing traded goods. The fall in private savings sometimes was partially offset by rising government savings where fiscal policy became more restrictive. Many countries showed 'stop-go' cycles in government tax and spending behavior.

Especially when it went together with real appreciation, current account liberalization pushed traded goods producers toward workplace reorganization (including greater reliance on foreign outsourcing) and down-sizing. If, as assumed above, unskilled labor is an important component of variable cost, then such workers would bear the brunt of such adjustments via job losses. In other words, traded goods enterprises that stayed in operation had to cut costs by generating labor productivity growth. Depending on demand conditions, their total employment levels could easily fall.

The upshot of these effects often took the form of increased inequality between groups of workers, in particular between the skilled and unskilled. This outcome is at odds with widely discussed predictions of the Stolper-Samuelson (1941) theorem, according to which trade liberalization should lead to an increase in the remuneration of the relatively abundant production factor in low and middle income countries (unskilled labor) with respect to the scarce factor (capital or skilled labor). Of course, besides considering exchange rate and capital flow effects on remunerations, the model just presented departs from the standard Heckscher-Ohlin trade theory framework underlying Stolper-Samuelson by working with more than two production factors and allowing for open unemployment, factor immobility, and product market imperfections. These considerations along with changes in the sectoral composition of output, as emphasized in Figure 1, are important factors in determining the distributive effects of trade liberalization (Wood 1997). With liberalization stimulating productivity increases leading to a reduction of labor demand from modern, traded-goods production, primary income differentials widened between workers in such sectors and those employed in non-traded, informal activities (e.g. informal services) and the unemployed.

5. Graphical Illustration of the Effects of Liberalization

It is easy to trace through the implications of these changes in Figure 1, beginning with the Traded goods equilibrium schedule in the northeast quadrant.
The sector was subject to several conflicting forces:
    · By switching demand toward imports, current account liberalization
tended to reduce output X_t. This demand loss was strengthened by real appreciation and weakened or even reversed by devaluation. Removal of export
subsidies hurt manufacturing and raw materials sectors in some cases.
    · Domestic credit expansion and a falling saving rate stimulated demand
for both sectors, although high interest rates may have held back spending on
luxury manufactured items such as consumer durables and cars (in countries
where they were produced).
    The outcome is that the shift in the Traded goods equilibrium schedule
was ambiguous, as shown by the double-headed arrow in the diagram. The
contractionary forces just mentioned did not impinge directly on non-traded
goods; as shown, the corresponding market equilibrium schedule shifted upward. The likely results after both schedules adjusted were a higher non-traded
price-wage ratio P_n/w, a fall in the intersectoral terms-of-trade P_t/P_n, and an
ambiguous change in X_t. In some cases (notably Cuba, Russia, and Zimbabwe),
the increase in the "flex-price" P_n was associated with an inflationary process
shifting the income distribution away from wages and toward public revenues
or profits. The outcome was a reduction in effective demand through "forced
saving" by wage-earners with high propensities to consume, as analyzed by
Keynes and contemporaries in the 1920s and Kaldor after World War II.[3]
    Turning to employment and productivity changes, new jobs were typically
created in the non-traded sector, i.e. L_n^d went up along the demand schedule
in the northwest quadrant. With overall decreasing returns in the sector, its
real wage w/P_n and labor productivity level X_n/L_n^d could be expected to fall.
    In the traded goods sector, higher labor productivity meant that the labor
demand schedule in the middle quadrant on the right moved toward the origin. Regardless of what happened to their overall level of activity, traded goods
producers generated fewer jobs per unit of output. Reading through the lower
quadrant on the left, L_n^s or unskilled labor supply in non-traded goods tended
to rise. The effect on overall unemployment $(L_n^s - L_n^d)$ was unclear. Wage dynamics
appeared to be driven by institutional circumstances in partly segmented labor markets, with details differing country by country. In many cases, stable or
rising unemployment and unresponsive wages caused the overall income distribution to become more concentrated. The differential between skilled and
unskilled wage rates tended to rise.
    The final curve that shifted was the one setting the trade deficit in the
extreme southeast quadrant. Higher import demand and (typically) lagging

---

3. See Taylor (1991) for references and further discussion.

exports meant that it moved away from the origin—for a given output level, the deficit went up. The corresponding increase in "required" capital inflows fed into the shifts in the capital account discussed above.

Other Reforms

When assessing the effects hypothesized above in real country contexts, one has to take account of other measures that were implemented simultaneously in many places and which compounded the effects discussed above. We briefly mention three other major areas of liberalization:

Domestic financial sector deregulation: the effects of capital account liberalization have to be understood in conjunction with the domestic financial sector reforms that also took place in many countries before or around 1990. The lifting of interest-rate ceilings, lowering of reserve requirements, and easing of entry for new banks and other financial institutions were conducive to private credit expansion fuelled by foreign capital inflows. With inadequate bank regulation and supervision in most countries, these changes in regulatory policy exacerbated the risk of banking crises along the lines described above (Vos 1995).

Labor market liberalization: Typically, only small changes have occurred in this area. However, distributional outcomes can be strongly influenced by the degree of wage rigidity and labor market segmentation. In most cases institutional wage setting in modern sector firms continues to prevail (as assumed above), as well as regulations stipulating high severance payments in case of dismissal of employees. Strongly segmented labor markets are still a main characteristic in many countries. The bargaining power of organized labor may well have declined, reducing the political space for real wage adjustments.

Tax reforms: Broadly speaking, countries moved towards taxation of consumption through valued added taxes and away from direct taxation, roughly a shift away from taxing the wealthy and toward lower and middle income groups. Substantial lowering of marginal rates on income and corporate taxes has been common.

6. Decomposition Techniques

To trace through the sorts of changes described by the model in detail, the first step is to examine how major economic aggregates shift over time. To this end, the country papers deploy several simple time series decomposition techniques. The essentials are outlined in this section, beginning with effective demand and going on to employment, productivity growth, and the functional income distribution.

Effective Demand

Over the liberalization period, there have been substantial changes in demand-side parameters such as import coefficients and savings rates along with jumps in flows such as annual exports, investment, etc. It is illuminating to look at how output has responded to these shifts, using a simple decomposition of demand "injections" (investment, government spending, exports) versus "leakages" (saving, taxes, imports). The key point is that in macroeconomic equilibrium, totals of injections and leakages must be equal. Broadly following Godley (1999) this fact can be used to set up a decomposition methodology for effective demand.

At the one-sector level, aggregate supply (X) can be defined as the sum of private incomes (Y_p), net taxes (T) and imports (M):

(1) $X = Y_p + T + M$

The aggregate supply and demand balance can be written as:

(2) $X = C_p + I_p + G + E$

i.e., the sum of private consumption, private investment, government spending and exports. Leakage parameters can be defined relative to aggregate output, yielding the private savings rate as $s_p = (Y_p - C)/X$; the import propensity as $m = M/X$ and the tax rate as $t = T/X$. From this one gets a typical Keynesian income multiplier function:

(3) $X = \dfrac{1}{s_p + t + m} (I_p + G + E)$

which can also be written as:

(4) $X = \dfrac{s_p}{(s_p + t + m)} \cdot \dfrac{I_p}{s_p} + \dfrac{t}{(s_p + t + m)} \cdot \dfrac{G}{t} + \dfrac{m}{(s_p + t + m)} \cdot \dfrac{E}{m}$

in which I_p/s_p, G/t and E/m can be interpreted as the direct "own" multiplier effects (or "stances") on output of private investment, government spending, and export injections with their overall impact scaled by the corresponding "leakages" (respectively, savings, tax, and import propensities).

The country papers use equation (4) in several ways. The simplest is a diagram of stances and total supply over time. In Mexico before 1994, for example, I_p / s_p was substantially higher than X, as the private sector pumped demand into the system, while $(E/m) < X$ meant that high import levels were cutting into demand. The roles of the private and foreign sectors reversed sharply after the devaluation of 1994–95. Another representation involves the levels of $(I_p - s_p X)$, $(G - tX)$, and $(E - mX)$ which from (4) must sum to zero. Both such diagrams are helpful in identifying expansionary and contractionary factors in effective demand. Several papers apply discrete time "first differencing" techniques to (4) along the lines presented below. These show the contributions of shifting weights vs. shifting multiplier impacts in determining X.

From the above equation system one can also derive the economy's real financial balance as:

$$(5)\ \Delta P + \Delta Z + \Delta A = (I_p - s_p X) + (G - tX) + (E - mX) = 0$$

where ΔP, ΔZ, and ΔA stand respectively for the net change in financial claims against the private sector, in government debt, and in foreign assets. In continuous time, we have $dP/dt = I_p - s_p X$, $dZ/dt = G - tX$, and $dA/dt = E - mX$.

A couple of points can be made here. First, claims against an institutional entity (the private sector, government, or rest of the world) are growing when its stance with respect to X exceeds X itself. So when $E < mX$, net foreign assets of the home economy are declining, while $G > tX$ means that its government is running up debt. A contractionary stance of the rest of the world requires some other sector to be increasing liabilities or lowering assets, e.g. the public sector when $G > tX$. Because it is true that $dP/dt + dZ/dt + dA/dt = 0$, such offsetting effects are unavoidable.

Second, stock/flow disequilibrium problems threaten when ratios such as P/X, Z/X, or $-A/X$ (or P/Y_p, Z/tX, or $-A/E$) become "too large." Then the component expressions in (1) and the accumulation flows in (2) have to shift to bring the system back toward financial "stock-flow" or "stock-stock" equilibrium. Such adjustments can be quite painful.

Costs associated with the accumulation of net lending over time may imply important income redistribution effects between private and public domestic agents and the rest of the world. When taking such asset-related income transfers into account, we get the more familiar macroeconomic balances linked to expenditures and savings out of the disposable income of each institution, rather than from total supply as implied by equation (5) above, i.e.,

$$(6)\ \Delta Dp + \Delta Dg - (\Delta Fp + \Delta Fg) = (I_p - s_P X - iD_g + ei^* F_p) + (G - tX + iD_g + ei^* F_g)$$
$$+ (E - mX - ei^* F) = 0$$

where D_p, D_g and $F(=F_g + F_p)$ stand for, respectively, the stock of net private sector debt, net government debt, and net external liabilities, as accumulated through the financing of the three gaps (in parentheses on the right-hand side) "after transfers" over time. The level of $-F$ is the "after transfer" counterpart of net foreign assets A. The parameters i, i^* and e in equation (6) stand for the domestic interest rate, foreign interest rate and the nominal exchange rate. The formula permits detailed study of shifting patterns of effective demand.

Employment Decompositions

Next, we take up decompositions of employment shifts. To save algebra, the formulas are presented in continuous time. That is, they are not set up in terms of discrete changes of the variables that they contain, even though this is how the data are always presented. With enough patience in writing down discrete-time first difference expansions, the right- and left-hand sides of all the decomposition expressions that follow can be made equal by balancing beginning- and end-of-period terms—see Pieper (2000) for examples. Such refinement is omitted here in the interest of ease of presentation.

In terms of notation, we consider changes from time $t-1$ to t, or from time zero to time one. The difference operator is Δ, i.e. $\Delta X=X_t-X_{t-1}$, and we see $\hat{X}=DX/X_{t-1}$ to indicate a growth rate.[4] Let P be the population, E the economically active population, L the total of people employed, and U the total unemployed or $U=E-L$. The participation rate is $\varepsilon=E/P$ and the unemployment rate is $v=U/E$. The employment rate is $L/E=1-v=\lambda/\varepsilon$ with $\lambda=L/P$ as the employed share of the population. Evidently, we have $E=L+U$ dividing by P lets this expression be rewritten as $\varepsilon=\lambda+\varepsilon v$. Taking first differences and a bit of algebra show that

$$(7)\ 0=(1-v)(\hat{\lambda}-\hat{\varepsilon})+v\hat{v}=(1-v)\hat{\varepsilon}+v\hat{v}+(1-v)\hat{\lambda}$$

The first expression basically states that changes in the rates of employment and unemployment must sum to zero. The second further decomposes this condition in terms of the participation rate ε, the unemployment rate v, and the employed share of the population λ. In turn, the employment ratio, $\lambda=L/P$, provides a useful tool to analyze job growth across sectors. Let L_i be employment in sector i, with $L=\sum L_i$. Let X_i be real output in sector i, and $x_i=X_i/P$ or sectoral output per capita. The labor/output ratio in sector i can be written as $b_i=L_iX_i$, and let $\lambda_i=L_i/P$. Then we have $\lambda=\sum(L_i/X_i)(X_i/P)=\sum b_i x_i$. Taking first differences gives

$$(8)\ \hat{\lambda}=\sum\lambda_i\ (\hat{x}_i+\hat{b}_i)=\sum\lambda_i(\hat{x}_i-\hat{\rho}_i)$$

so that the growth rate of the overall employment ratio is determined as a weighted average across sectors of differences between growth rates of output levels per capita and labor productivity (with productivity defined as $\rho_i=X_i/L_i$, and $\hat{\rho}_i=-\hat{b}_i$). Combined with (7), equation (8) provides a framework in which sources of job creation can be usefully be explored. In expanding sectors (relative to population growth), productivity increases do not necessarily translate into reduced employment; in slow-growing or shrinking sectors, higher productivity means that employment declines. Under liberalization, the interaction of non-traded and traded sectors can be traced in this fashion, along with the behavior of sectors acting as "sources" or "sinks" for labor (agriculture has played both roles recently, in different countries).

Labor Productivity Growth

Formalizing a suggestion by Syrquin (1986), one can also decompose growth of overall labor productivity $\rho=X/L=\sum X_i/\sum L_i$. The first difference decomposition is

$$\begin{aligned}
&\hat{\rho}=\sum[(X_i/X)\hat{X}_i-(L_i/L)\hat{L}_i]\\
(9)\quad &=\sum(L_i/L)\hat{\rho}_i+\sum[(Xi/X)-(Li/L)]\hat{X}_i\\
&=\sum(X_i/X)\hat{\rho}_i+\sum[(Xi/X)-(Li/L)]\hat{L}_i
\end{aligned}$$

---

4. An alternative notation used in the literature and some of the papers is $X^*=\Delta X/X_{t-1}$.

The first line decomposes overall productivity growth into movements in output and employment, weighted by sectoral shares of these two variables. As discussed above, a common pattern under liberalization involved slow output growth and positive productivity growth in traded goods sectors, and faster output growth but low or negative productivity growth in non-traded. Across sectors, the outcome was fairly slow productivity growth overall.

The second and third lines show how overall productivity change can be written as a weighted average of sectoral productivity shifts plus a "correction" term involving weighted reallocations of output or employment across sectors. The reallocation weights $[(X_i/X)-(L_i/L)]$ reflect differing productivity levels in different sectors. An output or employment loss in a low productivity sector (agriculture, for example, with a negative value of $[(X_i/X)-(L_i/L)]$, will add to overall productivity growth, as will an employment or output gain in a sector with a relatively high output/labour ratio. In the country studies, such reallocation effects were observed everywhere, but were economically important in only a few cases.

Capital and Labor Productivity and Real Earnings

Assuming two labor skill or ascriptive classes, total value-added nationally or in a sector can be written out as $PX=\pi+w_1L_1+w_2L_2$, where P is an output price index, w_1 and w_2 are wage levels for the two sorts of labor, and π stands for other payment flows (profits in a broad sense, perhaps self-employment income, etc.) Let $\theta_i=w_iL_i/PX$. The first difference version of the decomposition of payments is then

$$(10) \quad 0=(1-\theta_i-\theta_2)\ (\hat{\pi}-\hat{P}-\hat{X})+\sum\theta_i[(\hat{w}_i-\hat{P})-(\hat{X}-\hat{L}_i)]$$

If a breakdown of value-added by components is available, (10) provides a useful means to think about productivity and payment shifts. If $\pi=rPK$, where r is the profit rate and K the level of capital stock, then $\hat{\pi}-\hat{P}-\hat{X}=\hat{r}+\hat{K}-\hat{X}$. With a rising capital/output ratio, a falling profit rate would be needed to open room for real (product) wage growth $\hat{w}_i-\hat{P}$ for labor type i to equal or exceed its productivity growth rate $\hat{X}_i-\hat{L}_i$. In the labor market itself, moderate wage and high productivity growth for skilled workers may combine with low or negative productivity and wage growth for the unskilled to maintain the equality in (10).

7. Summary of Liberalization's Outcomes

To trace through all the changes described in previous sections, the first step is to examine how major economic aggregates shifted over time. Tables 1 through 9 give overviews of the main country findings regarding growth, employment, productivity, inequality, sources of effective demand, and overall macroeconomic performance. Their periodization is based on the policy "episodes" identified by the country authors in their papers.

TABLE 1: Argentina

Growth, Employment and Inequality	1990-94	1995-96	1996-97
Growth rate	8.5	0.4	8.6
Real exchange rate (+=real app.)*	++	0	0
Employment rate (+=fall in unemp.)	-	–	+
Wage share in GDP	–	0	0
Real Wages	+	0	0
Income Inequality			
Per capita household income	-	-	+/0
Primary incomes (labor force)	+	-	+
Skilled/Unskilled	+	-	+
Formal/Informal	+	+/0	+/0
Employment Structure			
Traded/Non-traded	-	-	-
Skilled/Unskilled	+	+	+
Formal/Informal	-	-	-
Aggregate Demand Decomposition	**1990-94**	**1995-96**	**1996-97**
Aggregate Demand	9.6	0.5	10.1
Direct Multiplier Effects			
Investment/Savings	+	-	+
Govt/Tax	n.a.	n.a.	+/0
Exports/Imports	–	+	-
Effect of Leakages			
Savings	+/-	+	0
Taxes	n.a.	n.a.	-
Imports	-	+	-
Productivity and Employment	**1990-94**	**1995-96**	**1996-97**
Overall Productivity Growth	7.8	2.7	1.2
Overall Growth in Employment	0.2	-2.0	7.3
Emp. Sector reallocation effects	negative	negative	small
Labor Supply Changes			
Participation Rate	+	+	+
Unemployment Rate	++	++	-
Employment Rate	–	0/-	+/0
Macroeconomic variables	**1990-94**	**1995-96**	**1996-97**
Trade deficit	++	-	+
Domestic credit	–	+/0	+/0
Changes in reserves	+	–	0/-
Real Interest Rate	n.a.	+/-	+/0
Interest Rate Spreads	n.a.	+/-	-
Imports/GDP	++	0	+/0
Exports/GDP	–	+	0

*Real exchange rate as compared with US dollar. The real effective exchange rate of the Argentine peso appreciated during the 1990s along with the US dollar.

KEY: ++=strong increase, +=increase, +/0=slight increase, –=strong decrease, -=decrease, 0/-=slight decrease, +/-/+=fluctuating trend, +/-=up then down (or vice versa), 0=no change, n.a.=not available.

SOURCE: Country report; World Development Indicators, 1999; ILO, 1998.

TABLE 2: Colombia

Growth, Employment and Inequality	1992-95	1995-98
Growth rate	5.7	1.8
Real exchange rate (+=real app.)	+	+
Employment rate (+=fall in unemp.)	0	-
Wage share in GDP	++	+
Real Wages	++	+
Income Inequality		
Per capita household income	+	0
Primary incomes (labor force)	+/0	-
Skilled/Unskilled	++	++
Formal/Informal	+	+
Employment Structure		
Traded/Non-traded	-	-
Skilled/Unskilled	+	+
Formal/Informal	0/-	0/-

Aggregate Demand Decomposition	1992-95	1995-98
Aggregate Demand	9.6	2.1
Direct Multiplier Effects		
Investment/Savings	++	−
Govt/Tax	+	+/-
Exports/Imports	-	+
Effect of Leakages		
Savings	++	-
Taxes	-	-
Imports	−	-

Productivity and Employment	1991-95	1995-97
Productivity Growth		
Overall	2.6	2.1
Traded	3.0	2.8
Non-traded	2.7	2.0
Overall Growth in Employment	0.2	-1.5
Emp. Sector reallocation effects	small	negative
Labor Supply Changes		
Participation Rate	-	+
Unemployment Rate	0/-	++
Employment Rate	0	-

Macroeconomic variables	1992-95	1995-98
Trade deficit	++	0
Domestic credit	++	−
Changes in reserves	-/+	+/-/+
Real Interest Rate	++	-/+
Interest Rate Spreads	0	0
Imports/GDP	+	0/-
Exports/GDP	0	+

KEY: ++=strong increase, +=increase, +/0=slight increase, −=strong decrease, -=decrease, 0/-=slight decrease, +/-/+=fluctuating trend, +/-=up then down (or vice versa), 0=no change, n.a.=not available.
SOURCE: Country report; World Development Indicators, 1999; ILO, 1998.

TABLE 3: Cuba

Growth, Employment and Inequality	1989-93	1994-98
Growth rate	-8.5	4.4
Real exchange rate (+=real app.)	++	-/+
Employment rate (+=fall in unemp.)	+/0	0/-
Wage share in GDP	-	0/-
Real Wages	--	++
Income Inequality		
Per capita household income	+	-
Primary incomes (labor force)	+	-
Formal/Informal	+	-
Employment Structure		
Traded/Non-traded	+	-
Formal/Informal	--	--
Aggregate Demand Decomposition	**1989-93**	**1994-98**
Aggregate Demand	-13.7	7.0
Direct Multiplier Effects		
Investment/Savings	--	++
Govt/Tax	+	-
Exports/Imports	+	+/0
Effect of Leakages		
Savings	++	--
Taxes	+	-
Imports	-	0
Productivity and Employment	**1989-93**	**1994-98**
Productivity Growth		
Overall	-8.3	4.1
Traded	-13.7	11.1
Non-traded	-5.0	0.1
Overall Growth in Employment	-1.0	-1.7
Emp. Sector reallocation effects	none	none
Labor Supply Changes		
Participation Rate	-	0/-
Unemployment Rate	-	+
Employment Rate	+/0	0/-
Macroeconomic variables	**1989-93**	**1994-98**
Trade deficit	--	++
Imports/GDP	--	++
Exports/GDP	--	++
Imposition of export incentives	++	++

KEY: ++=strong increase, +=increase, +/0=slight increase, -=strong decrease, -=decrease, 0/-=slight decrease, +/-/+=fluctuating trend, +/-=up then down (or vice versa), 0=no change, n.a.=not available.
SOURCE: Country report; World Development Indicators, 1999; ILO, 1998.

TABLE 4: India

Growth, Employment and Inequality	1986-1991	1992-1996
Growth rate	5.9	5.3
Real exchange rate (+=real app.)	+	-/+
Employment rate (+=fall in unemp.)	+	+
Wage share in GDP	-	-
Real Wages	+	-
Income Inequality		
Per capita household income	+	-
Primary incomes (labor force)	+	-
Skilled/Unskilled	+	+
Formal/Informal	+	+
Employment Structure		
Traded/Non-traded	-	-
Skilled/Unskilled	+	+
Formal/Informal	-	-

Aggregate Demand Decomposition	1986-1991	1992-1996
Aggregate Demand	5.4	7.5
Direct Multiplier Effects		
Investment/Savings	0	-
Govt/Tax	++	+
Exports/Imports	-	-
Effect of Leakages		
Savings	-	-
Taxes	+	+/-
Imports	-	–

Productivity and Employment	1986-1991	1992-1996
Productivity Growth		
Overall	3.8	2.5
Traded	n.a.	n.a.
Non-traded	n.a.	n.a.
Overall Growth in Employment	2.0	2.0
Emp. Sector reallocation effects	none	negative
Labor Supply Changes		
Participation Rate	+	+
Unemployment Rate	-	+/0
Employment Rate	+/0	0/-

Macroeconomic variables	1986-1991	1992-1996
Trade deficit	-	++
Domestic credit	0	+
Changes in reserves	-	+
Real Interest Rate	+	+/-
Interest Rate Spreads	0	+/-
Imports/GDP	+/0	+
Exports/GDP	+	+
Imposition of export incentives	0	-

KEY: ++=strong increase, +=increase, +/0=slight increase, –=strong decrease, -=decrease, 0/-=slight decrease, +/-+=fluctuating trend, +/-=up then down (or vice versa), 0=no change, n.a.=not available.
SOURCE: Country report; World Development Indicators, 1999; ILO, 1998.

TABLE 5: Korea

Growth, Employment and Inequality	1980-88	1988-93	1993-97	1997-98
Growth rate	9.4	7.2	7.5	-5.8
Real exchange rate (+=real app.)	+/-/+	-	+/-	–
Employment rate (+=fall in unemp.)	+	0	+/0	–
Wage share in GDP	+/-/+	++	0/-	–
Real Wages	6.0	9.4	5.4	-9.3
Income Inequality				
Per capita household income	++	+	+/0	-
Primary incomes (labor force)	++	+	0	–
Skilled/Unskilled	–	0/-	0	++
Formal/Informal	-	0/-	0	++
Employment Structure				
Traded/Non-traded	++	+	+	–
Skilled/Unskilled	+/0	+/0	++	++
Formal/Informal	+	+	+	–
Aggregate Demand Decomposition	**1980-88**	**1988-93**	**1993-97**	
Aggregate Demand	8.3	6.9	9.6	
Direct Multiplier Effects				
Investment/Savings	+/0	+	++	
Govt/Tax	-	0	0	
Exports/Imports	+	0	0/-	
Effect of Leakages				
Savings	-	-	+	
Taxes	0/-	0/-	+/0	
Imports	+	0	-	
Productivity and Employment	**1980-88**	**1988-93**	**1993-97**	**1997-98**
Overall Productivity Growth	6.4	4.8	5.3	n.a.
Overall Growth in Employment	2.8	2.2	2.2	-6.2
Emp. Sector reallocation effects	large	large	small	negative
Labor Supply Changes				
Participation Rate	++	++	+	-
Unemployment Rate	–	0	0/-	++
Employment Rate	+	+	+	-
Macroeconomic variables	**1980-88**	**1988-93**	**1993-97**	**1997-98**
Trade deficit	–	0/-	++	–
Domestic credit	+/0	+	++	n.a.
Changes in reserves	++	++	+	–
Real Interest Rate	+	0/-	++	+
Interest Rate Spreads	+/0	0	+/0	+
Imports/GDP	-	0/-	++	–
Exports/GDP	+	-	+	–
Imposition of export incentives	++	+	0/-	–

KEY: ++=strong increase, +=increase, +/0=slight increase, –=strong decrease, -=decrease, 0/-=slight decrease, +/-/+=fluctuating trend, +/-=up then down (or vice versa), 0=no change, n.a.=not available.
SOURCE: Country report; World Development Indicators, 1999; ILO, 1998.

TABLE 6: Mexico

Growth, Employment and Inequality	1985-87	1988-94	1994-95	1996-98
Growth rate	-1.8	3.9	-6.2	5.8
Real exchange rate (+=real app.)	n.a.	++	−	+
Employment rate (+=fall in unemp.)	-	+/0	−	+
Wage share in GDP	-	++	-	0
Real Wages	0/-	++	−	-
Income Inequality				
Per capita household income	-	+	-	+
Primary incomes (labor force)	-	+	−	+/0
Skilled/Unskilled	+	+	+	0
Formal/Informal	0/-	+	-	+/0
Employment Structure				
Traded/Non-traded	0/-	−	+/0	+/0
Skilled/Unskilled	+	+	+	0
Formal/Informal	-	-	-	0
Aggregate Demand Decomposition	**1988-94**	**1994-95**	**1996-98**	
Aggregate Demand	5.5	-7.8	8.3	
Direct Multiplier Effects				
Investment/Savings	++	−	+	
Govt/Tax	+/0	0	+/0	
Exports/Imports	-	++	0	
Effect of Leakages				
Savings	++	-	-	
Taxes	0	+	0	
Imports	−	+	−	
Productivity and Employment	**1988-93**	**1994-97**		
Productivity Growth				
Overall	0.6	-0.8		
Traded	6.0	-0.2		
Non-traded	-0.5	-2.1		
Overall Growth in Employment	2.8	3.0		
Emp. Sector reallocation effects	small	small		
Labor Supply Changes				
Participation Rate	+	+		
Unemployment Rate	-	++		
Employment Rate	+	-		
Macroeconomic variables	**1985-87**	**1988-94**	**1994-95**	**1996-98**
Trade deficit	0	++	−	+/0
Domestic credit	+	-	+	-
Changes in reserves	-	+/-/+	−	+/0
Real Interest Rate	n.a.	n.a.	++	−
Interest Rate Spreads	n.a.	n.a.	++	−
Imports/GDP	+	++	0/-	+
Exports/GDP	+	+	++	+
Imposition of export incentives	−	0	0	0

KEY: ++=strong increase, +=increase, +/0=slight increase, −=strong decrease, -=decrease, 0/-=slight decrease, +/-/+=fluctuating trend, +/-=up then down (or vice versa), 0=no change, n.a.=not available.
SOURCE: Country report; World Development Indicators, 1999; ILO, 1998.

TABLE 7: Russia

Growth, Employment and Inequality	1990-92	1992-94	1994-97	1998
Growth rate	-9.75	-10.7	-2.2	-4.6
Real exchange rate (+=real app.)	-	++	++	-
Employment rate (+=fall in unemp.)	--	--	--	-
Wage share in GDP	--	+	-	0
Real Wages	--	+/-	--/+	-
Income Inequality				
Per capita household income	--	--	+/0	--
Primary incomes (labor force)	--	-	0	-
Skilled/Unskilled	--	+	+	-
Formal/Informal	0	--	-	0
Employment Structure				
Traded/Non-traded	0/-	-	-/+	0/-
Skilled/Unskilled	n.a.	+/0	+/0	n.a.
Formal/Informal	0	--	-	0
Aggregate Demand Decomposition	**1990-92**	**1992-94**	**1994-97**	
Aggregate Demand	2.4	-19.2	-3.0	
Direct Multiplier Effects				
Investment/Savings	--	--	--	
Govt/Tax	++	+	+	
Exports/Imports	+/0	-	-	
Effect of Leakages				
Savings	n.a.	+	+	
Taxes	+	++	++	
Imports	--	-	--	
Productivity and Employment	**1990-92**	**1992-94**	**1994-97**	**1998**
Productivity Growth				
Overall	-7.5	-8.5	-1.0	-3.0
Traded	-9.5	-11.0	9.0	-3.0
Non-traded	-5.5	-6.0	-5.5	-4.0
Overall Growth in Employment	-2.2	-2.5	n.a.	n.a.
Emp. Sector reallocation effects	negative	negative	none	negative
Labor Supply Changes				
Participation Rate	+/0	-	-	0
Unemployment Rate	++	++	++	+
Employment Rate	--	--	--	-
Macroeconomic variables	**1990-92**	**1992-94**	**1994-97**	**1998**
Trade deficit	+	++	+/0	-
Domestic credit	0/-	--	+	++
Changes in reserves	+	-	++	-
Real Interest Rate	--	++	+/-	--
Interest Rate Spreads	n.a.	n.a.	--	n.a.
Imports/GDP	++	--	0/-	+
Exports/GDP	++	--	0/-	+

KEY: ++=strong increase, +=increase, +/0=slight increase, −=strong decrease, -=decrease, 0/-=slight decrease, +/-/+=fluctuating trend, +/-=up then down (or vice versa), 0=no change, n.a.=not available.
SOURCE: Country report; World Development Indicators, 1999; ILO, 1998.

TABLE 8: Turkey

Growth, Employment and Inequality	1980-88	1989-93	1994	1995-97
Growth rate	5.4	4.8	-5.5	7.2
Real exchange rate (+=real app.)	--	++	--	+/0
Employment rate (+=fall in unemp.)	++	+	+/0	+
Wage share in GDP	--	++	--	-
Real Wages	-	++	--	+/0
Income Inequality				
Per capita household income	-	+	-	+
Primary incomes (labor force)	--	+	-	-
Skilled/Unskilled	+	++	+	++
Formal/Informal	+	++	-	-
Employment Structure				
Traded/Non-traded	+	-	-	-
Skilled/Unskilled	-	--	--	-
Formal/Informal	-	--	-	-
Aggregate Demand Decomposition	**1980-88**	**1989-93**	**1994**	**1995-97**
Aggregate Demand	6.2	5.2	-4.9	10.1
Direct Multiplier Effects				
Investment/Savings	+	+	+	+
Govt/Tax	--	++	-	+/0
Exports/Imports	-	-	-	--
Effect of Leakages				
Savings	+/-	+	-	+
Taxes	-	+/0	--	+/0
Imports	-	--	+	--
Productivity and Employment	**1980-88***	**1989-93**	**1994**	**1995-97**
Productivity Growth				
Overall	2.6	1.7	-7.5	3.5
Traded	-2.1	1.2	-13.1	3.2
Non-traded (Construction)	8.3	2.3	-0.6	3.9
Overall Growth in Employment	3.2	3.2	1.9	3.7
Emp. Sector reallocation effects	small	none	negative	none
Labor Supply Changes				
Participation Rate	+	+	0	+
Unemployment Rate	--	-	0/-	-
Employment Rate	++	+	+/0	+
Macroeconomic variables	**1980-88**	**1989-93**	**1994**	**1995-97**
Trade deficit	-	++	--	++
Domestic credit	+	-	+/0	+
Changes in reserves	--	-/+/-	+	--
Real Interest Rate	-	+	++	++
Interest Rate Spreads	-	+	++	++
Imports/GDP	+	+/0	+/0	+
Exports/GDP	++	-	++	+
Imposition of export incentives	++	0	-	0

*Data for non-traded are for 1983–1998.

KEY: ++=strong increase, +=increase, +/0=slight increase, –=strong decrease, -=decrease, 0/-=slight decrease, +/-+/-=fluctuating trend, +/-=up then down (or vice versa), 0=no change, n.a.=not available.

SOURCE: Country report; World Development Indicators, 1999; ILO, 1998.

TABLE 9: Zimbabwe

Growth, Employment and Inequality	1986-90	1991-92	1993-97
Growth rate	5.2	-1.8	3.6
Real exchange rate (+=real app.)	-	+	-
Employment rate (+=fall in unemp.)	+	0/-	0
Wage share in GDP	+	-	-
Real Wages	+	–	-
Income Inequality			
Per capita household income	+	–	0/-
Primary incomes (labor force)	+	-	-
Skilled/Unskilled	+	+	+
Formal/Informal	-	+	+
Employment Structure			
Traded/Non-traded	+/0	–	-
Skilled/Unskilled	0/-	+	+/0
Formal/Informal	+/0	-	-

Aggregate Demand Decomposition	1986-90	1993-97
Aggregate Demand	5.5	4.6
Direct Multiplier Effects		
Investment/Savings	+	+
Govt/Tax	+	-
Exports/Imports	+	++
Effect of Leakages		
Savings	+	+
Taxes	-	0
Imports	-	-

Productivity and Employment	1986-90	1991-92	1993-97
Productivity Growth			
Overall	1.5	-3.0	0.9
Traded	1.2	-6.8	-1.0
Non-traded	1.6	-0.2	2.4
Overall Growth in Employment	2.5	1.9	1.4
Emp. Sector reallocation effects	none	negative	negative
Labor Supply Decomposition			
Participation Rate	+/0	0	+/0
Unemployment Rate	-	+	0
Employment Rate	+	0/-	0

Macroeconomic variables	1986-90	1991-92	1993-97
Trade deficit	+/0	++	-
Domestic credit	+/-/+	+	++
Changes in reserves	-	++	-
Real Interest Rate	+/-	–	++
Interest Rate Spreads	+/0	–	++
Imports/GDP	0	++	+

KEY: ++=strong increase, +=increase, +/0=slight increase, –=strong decrease, -=decrease, 0/-=slight decrease, +/-+=fluctuating trend, +/-=up then down (or vice versa), 0=no change, n.a.=not available.
SOURCE: Country report; World Development Indicators, 1999; ILO, 1998.

Growth and Equity

Apart from years of overt crisis, most countries achieved moderate growth rates of GDP in the 1990s. Russia and not quite so disastrously Colombia and Zimbabwe were the main losers. Except in Korea prior to its crisis, household per capita income growth was negative or just above zero.

Capital inflows increased substantially to most countries (in some cases, only prior to their respective crises). As discussed above, incoming foreign capital tended to be associated with increases in international reserves, domestic credit expansion, and real appreciation. Stronger exchange rates were generally associated with higher interest rates and increasing interest spreads. Capital inflows, credit creation, and real appreciation together stimulated aggregate demand to increase more rapidly than GDP, with consequent widening of the current account deficit.

Inequality of primary incomes increased in most countries. Virtually without exception wage differentials between skilled and unskilled workers rose with liberalization, reflecting employment reallocation as suggested in Figure 1. More often than not, participation rates increased or were stable. Relative to the economically active population (following the standard definition), the unemployment rate was stable or tended to rise, again consistently with Figure 1.

Sources of Effective Demand

One of the principal justifications for external liberalization was its anticipated effect on trade performance. Due to efficiency gains induced by freer trade, "export-led" growth was supposed to be an immediate consequence. It did not happen, at least in terms of effective demand generation in the countries analyzed in this volume. As the country studies demonstrate, exports did tend to rise with liberalization but import leakages as well, especially when the local currency appreciated in real terms. As summarized in Tables 1–9, trade therefore held back or added weakly to effective demand. The export stimulus was present, but much less strongly than originally supposed by advocates of liberalization.[5]

The public sector's contribution to demand varied across countries. It was positive in Columbia due to increases in social spending, Cuba as it recovered from external shocks in 1994–98, India where the consolidated government deficit has supported demand for many years, and Russia as plummeting demand was at least slowed by the fact that government spending did not decrease quite so rapidly as receipts from a failing taxation system. Elsewhere, government's impact on demand was broadly neutral. Positive or "stop-go"

---

5. By way of clarification, effects of changes in saving, tax, and import parameters are reported with positive signs in the tables. For example, the saving rate dropped sharply in Mexico in 1988–1994, strongly stimulating aggregate demand.

public sector demand effects are a surprising outcome, given the rhetoric about downsizing the state that accompanied the drive towards liberalization.

Without strong contributions from the foreign and public sectors, private sector demand growth emerged as the major driving force in several of the country histories. In particular, import-led consumption booms following trade and financial liberalization were the rule rather than the exception. They were triggered by both cheapening of imported traded goods (import liberalization and real exchange rate appreciation) and expansion of domestic credit supply (fomented by the surge in capital flows and domestic financial liberalization). Private savings rates fell in consequence. Fewer cases were observed in which domestic demand was driven by expanding private investment, but it did occur in Argentina and Korea early in the 1990s. The rapid reduction in demand in Russia was provoked by an investment collapse in an economy that had historically been driven by high rates of accumulation. In Mexico late in the decade, higher private capital formation could give hope for a brighter future were it not for a setback due to global instability in 1998–99.

Productivity and Employment Growth

With Korea prior to its crisis as a notable exception, only modest aggregate productivity increases were observed. Where data are available, they are broadly consistent with greater observed productivity growth in traded than non-traded sectors. As observed above, the change in aggregate productivity is result of the sum of productivity changes by sectors (weighted by sectoral output shares) plus a positive reallocation effect if labor moves from low- to high-productivity sectors. Findings from the country studies indicate that within-sector productivity shifts and output growth rates largely determined the aggregate outcomes. However, in some cases there was a negative reallocation effect as workers moved toward low productivity non-traded goods sectors.

With Cuba and Russia as exceptions, the share of the economically active population (or the "participation rate") increased under liberalization. With the exception of Turkey, the unemployed as a proportion of the economically active went up as well, especially after crises and/or later in the decade. Given the modest growth of GDP noted previously, a lackluster employment performance under liberalization is scarcely surprising.

8. Country Experiences with Growth and Distribution

To complement the preceding discussion, it makes sense to consider what happened in detail in specific countries. Drawing heavily on the papers in this volume, the following sketches bring out the major points.

Argentina closely fits the results of the model presented above. After liberalization and imposition of an exchange rate freeze (the "convertibility plan") in 1991, the economy continued an expansion that had started the year before. In practice, convertibility turned the central bank into a currency board. Domestic credit creation was tied directly to foreign reserves, so that the level of economic activity was driven by the volume of capital flows.

In the first part of the decade, inflows were ample and the trade deficit widened. Growth continued until 1995 when the region was hit by the tequila crisis. Imports expanded rapidly until that crisis hit; exports jumped upward at mid-decade, stimulated by MERCOSUR and real appreciation in Brazil due to implementation of the Real anti-inflation plan. After the effects of the tequila shock dissipated, the economy started to grow again as capital inflows recovered, but then entered into sharp contraction in 1998-99 with slow growth and devaluation in Brazil cutting into exports.

Aggregate demand was led by an early investment boom and perhaps a fall in the saving rate (not estimated independently in Argentine national accounts). In labor markets, there was apparently a lagged adjustment to the wage and price realignments that took place rapidly after the exchange rate was pegged. In the industrial sector during the 1990-96 expansion, output grew at about 5% per year due to higher local consumption and exports, not fully offset by higher imports. There was rapid labor productivity growth of about 6.6% per year over the period, which forced industrial employment to fall despite the output expansion.

The drop in industrial employment spilled over into other sectors, with an increase over time in open unemployment and "involuntary underemployment" (the difference between the total employment rate and the rate for full-time jobs). Per capita incomes of employed people rose until mid-decade but then declined. Between 1991 and 1998, income per capita for economically active people grew by 12.2%. Without increased unemployment and labor market restructuring the total would have been 29.4%. Labor shedding in industry also took its distributional toll. Among the economically active population, the Gini coefficient rose from 0.471 in 1991 to 0.534 in 1998.

By 1999, the economy was in deep recession with unemployment steadily rising. Eight years of "convertibility" ended up generating future prospects substantially worse than they were when the scheme was started.

Colombia Economic performance also broadly followed the Figure 1 model. Import restrictions and export promotion schemes were reduced sharply in the early 1990s. Capital movements were liberalized, although cost-based impediments to inflows were retained. Government spending, much of it directed toward social programs, rose during the decade. The increase was largely financed by higher taxes, although the public sector did have a net expansionary effect on effective demand in the recession-plagued second half of the 1990s.

Macroeconomic performance was uneven—a "go" phase in the first part of the 1990s, then a prolonged "stop." Effective demand was led by the external sector in the late 1980s. The subsequent liberalization phase (1992–95) was accompanied by a jump in private investment and a fall in saving, exchange rate appreciation, and a demand boom for non-traded goods. Retrenchment began with monetary tightening in 1996. With some loosening in 1997, the monetary authorities held tight, provoking an open recession in 1998-99.

One result of these changes was that the capacity of the economy to generate jobs deteriorated notably. There was labor productivity growth in both traded and non-traded sectors, in the range of 2.0–2.5 percent per year. Demand growth for traded goods was negligible throughout the decade, while non-traded demand grew at 4.5% per year during 1991–95 and 2% per year during 1995–1997. As a consequence, overall employment growth was approximately zero during 1991–95, and –1.7% during 1995–97.

This poor employment performance hit workers with low levels of education the hardest. Nor did demand for their labor services appear to be sensitive to wage changes. The beneficial effects of liberalization appear to have been modest at best in terms of productivity growth, while tight money and capital inflows have been associated with an increasingly prolonged recession.

Cuba   The socialist model provided a basis for visible output growth through the mid-1980s—average rates were 6.5% in 1971–80, and 8.5% in 1981–85. Thereafter, a tightening external constraint and rising fiscal deficits were associated with only 0.7% growth per year between 1986 and 1989. The big external shock came between 1989 and 1993 when the import share of GDP fell from 29% to 12% while GDP per capita declined by 30%. The authorities chose to maintain both employment and nominal wages stable; as a consequence labor productivity and real wages declined in tandem with GDP per capita. With a basket of "essential" goods provided through the pre-existing rationing system, prices of freely traded commodities had to jump to force the real wage reduction. The price index for informal markets rose from 100 in 1987 to 510 in 1992 and 1553 in 1993. This inflation process was one of several in the sample involving forced saving.

After 1993 there was a strong push to develop export industries, along with relaxation of state controls over external transactions and opening up of markets within Cuba for foreign exchange. Greater access to foreign exchange through tourism and other exports along with (newly liberalized) flows of direct foreign investment and remittances from abroad permitted a gradual recovery of GDP after 1993. However, growth did not exceed 2.5% per year between 1994 and 1998. The government was the main support for effective demand during the adjustment period, with its spending substantially exceeding revenues. The private sector was the main beneficiary; hence its effect on demand was contractionary. Exports and imports have gone up together since the early 1990s, so their demand contribution has been neutral.

After 1993, productivity growth averaged 4% annually economy-wide, and 11% in traded goods sectors. These improvements took place in a rapidly evolving labor market. "Other labor incomes" (of people selling products in free markets) rose from less than 20% to 40% of GDP between 1989 and 1996, while the wage share fell from 60% to 45%. The overall profit share went up after 1993, especially for traded goods and services such as mining and tourism.

There is an income gap between wage earners and more informal workers, although it has declined recently. Nevertheless, overall inequality is was higher in the late 1990s than during the 1980s, with an increase in the Gini coefficient for primary incomes from about about 0.24 to about 0.38. Provision of social services probably pushed the coefficient for secondary income down to about 0.3.

India Like Argentina and Russia, India was forced into liberalization by an economic crisis in the early 1990s. There had been halting steps in a liberal direction since the 1970s, but the crisis gave orthodox reformers (both local and from the international financial institutions) a stronger hand. However, in a very populous country many segments of the economy remained delinked from international influences. Deregulation concentrated more on the current than capital account. The rupee remained unconvertible for capital transactions, a liberalization "failure" that offset the worst effects of the Asian crisis. Current account liberalization went together with dismantling an opaque and cumbersome industrial licensing system and relaxation of controls on technology imports. Despite some increase in cross-border capital movements, the exchange rate did not appreciate strongly. The real interest rate remained high (lending rates on the order of 15%), but declined a bit after the mid-1990s and spreads narrowed.

Trade liberalization was associated with increases in both exports and imports; the latter increased more as a share of GDP so the trade deficit widened. The contractionary effect of trade on output was offset by the government. Indeed, a fiscal deficit has been the main support for domestic demand since the 1970s. However, the fiscal position took a turn for the worse with liberalization, due to falling revenues from taxes on trade and an increasing interest burden on outstanding debt. Beginning in the mid-1990s, private investment increased, also offsetting the import drag on demand. More capital formation, however, did not translate into faster output growth. Nor did it stimulate productivity; the economy-wide growth rate slowed in the mid-1990s.

At the sectoral level, agricultural growth slowed markedly in the 1990s. The root causes were lack of rural infrastructure and the rigidity of the prevailing agrarian structure. The agricultural share of GDP declined sharply, despite a claim that liberalization would remove price biases against the sector. Since higher agricultural prices penalize the rural poor (who are net food consumers), changes in the terms of trade carry significant social and political implications.

As in other countries, the labor force has experienced increased informalization. Employment in the "organized" urban manufacturing sector has declined, probably signaling job losses in household and non-factory manufacturing as well. In the early 1990s, poverty and inequality both increased, in part because of policy-induced increases in food prices and cutbacks in public expenditure. These initiatives were subsequently reversed, as policy responded to the political reaction that followed. Clearly, globalization has not served to reduce poverty and inequality. If anything, its main effect has been to slow down improvements on these fronts that had been occurring in the 1980s.

Korea began to move slowly toward liberalization after a financial crisis in 1979-80. The emphasis was on the current account and domestic financial system; both had been tightly regulated by the planning bureaucracy for the preceding three decades. Pressures for liberalization came from private sector interests (consumers wanting access to more imports and business seeking more financial freedom), the international community (US corporations and financial institutions seeking access to the tightly controlled Korean market), and the fact that hands-on bureaucratic control of a complex economy had become increasingly ineffective. Economic power was concentrated in the hands of the industrial conglomerates or chaebol, complemented by a poorly understood and unregulated financial system.

The liberalization process accelerated sharply in the early 1990s. Cross-border financial flows were decontrolled, at the behest of the chaebol. They were seeking cheaper funds abroad and the opportunity for outgoing direct foreign investment (or DFI). Between 1993 and 1996, short-term external debt of private enterprises rose from $8 billion to $22 billion; debt of financial institutions went from $11 billion to $39 billion. Outflowing DFI jumped from $1 billion to $5 billion, mostly in holdings which became worthless with the pan-Asian crisis of 1997.

The capital inflows came on the heels of a boom in the late 1980s, which had been sparked by depreciation of the won after the Plaza accord in 1985, improvements in the terms of trade (especially low oil prices), and falling international interest rates. The US forced strong appreciation in the late 1980s as its trade deficit with Korea widened. Incipient depreciation early in the decade reversed again as foreign capital moved in. Household savings rates declined in standard fashion with liberalization, strengthening the traditional pattern of private sector-led effective demand. In 1997, a collapse in export prices for memory chips, haphazard industrial policy decisions, a highly unbalanced external financial position, and lack of prudential regulation allowed the crisis in Southeast Asia to engulf Korea's far stronger economy. Recovery began in late 1998, with conflicting prospects for both the income distribution and further liberalization.

Tracing the distributional effects of two decades of liberalization is not easy. Through the 1980s, unemployment decreased, the wage share increased, wage inequality (Gini coefficient and the ratio of average wages in the top and bottom deciles) declined, skill premiums fell, and the wage differential between large and small enterprises went down. Rising wage and falling profit shares put distributional pressure on the traditional growth model, which had been led by investment demand supported by high corporate and household saving rates and a fiscal surplus. A transition toward growth led by consumption from wage income is as yet incomplete.

The favorable distributional trends petered out in the early 1990s, in part because of increased subcontracting by the *chaebol* to domestic suppliers with lower wage and productivity levels, in Korea's version of the shifts depicted in Figure 1. When the crisis hit, the IMF imposed an outlandishly intense austerity package that lasted through mid-1998. The unemployment rate rose by five percentage points and the real wage fell by 9%. Excepting the top decile which benefited from higher interest rates on its assets, average household incomes fell across the board, with the greatest reductions (on the order of 20%) in the bottom deciles. Government spending on social support was increased in 1998, and following relaxation of the IMF's demand restraints there was strong output growth (partly led by domestic demand) in 1999. Whether the crisis will provoke a long-term trend toward increasing inequality in Korea remains to be seen.

Mexico The liberalization process got underway in the 1980s as the economy was massively restructured after the 1982 debt crisis. It was largely complete by January 1994, when NAFTA went into effect. Financial liberalization had been completed a couple of years previously.

There were two separate stages in Mexico's adjustment to liberalization, punctuated by the financial crisis of 1994–95. Beginning in the late 1980 there was a consumption boom associated with falling saving rates, rising import coefficients, and capital inflows which fed into domestic credit creation. The strong exchange rate/high interest macro price tandem was very much in evidence. This phase ended with a 45% real devaluation between 1994 and 1995. Between 1994 and 1998, exports rose from 17% to 29% of GDP, while imports went from 22% to 29%. As a consequence, the economy is now very open, with generation of effective demand led in the late 1990s by foreign trade and investment (private saving rates having recovered).

The first phase featured rapid productivity growth in mining and manufactures. Agricultural employment grew at 5.8% per year during 1988-1993, while output grew at 1.9%; the sector thereby served as a labor sponge for workers displaced from the other traded goods sectors. Productivity growth in non-traded goods was –0.5% per year. In the second phase, the economy-wide rate of productivity growth fell from 0.6% per year in 1988–93 to –0.8% in 1993–97. Most sectors had negative rates, although employment growth stopped in agriculture as its productivity growth rate rose to 1.2%.

While these reallocations of the labor force were taking place, the distribution of earnings became more unequal, with a rapid increase in the wage premium for skilled labor. The skill mix shifted rapidly in traded goods sectors (except agriculture) with unskilled labor serving as a component of variable cost which had to be reduced in the face of a profit squeeze due to trade liberalization and a strong exchange rate. In manufacturing the wage spread grew more rapidly in subsectors in which displacement of unskilled labor was greater.

As the decade closed, the economy was growing at 5-6% per year, with low levels of unemployment (that is, there was slow productivity growth). The big devaluation after 1994 clearly removed a fundamental inconsistency between liberalized markets and macro policy. Another major factor supporting Mexico's growth has been the long American upswing of the 1990s. When the US finally stops growing, the adaptability of the new Mexican model will face a major test.

Russia The Russian transition doubtless has more acts to play. "Summarizing this yet unfinished drama is beyond anyone's individual capacity," the authors of the country paper rightly point out. Nonetheless, a few key scenes can be illustrated by appropriate reinterpretation of Figure 1.

The "flex-price" sector in Russia in the 1990s was energy production. In Soviet times, internal energy prices were held at fantastically low levels—on the order of 10% of world prices. But by the mid-1980s, per unit output costs were beginning to rise and available supplies to fall as easily accessible oil and gas fields ran out. To allow export sales to continue, internal energy consumption had to be cut. The mechanism in wake of the Soviet collapse was a rapid rise of domestic energy prices in a generally inflationary environment. By 1997, price indexes in energy-related sectors had gone from a value of 1 in 1991 to levels between 5 and 10 thousand; wage indexes were around 1 to 2 thousand, and other producing sectors' price indexes in the low thousands. If Figure 1's "Non-traded goods equilibrium" schedule is taken to refer to the energy sector, it shifted strongly upward during the decade.

The "Traded goods equilibrium" curve can be interpreted as referring to the rest of the economy. It shifted strongly to the left as investment demand collapsed and price increases held down consumption via forced saving as in Cuba. The final outcomes were big increases in relative energy prices and reductions in most other sectors' levels of employment and economic activity. Compression of internal energy demand allowed the schedule for the trade deficit in Figure 1 to remain in place or even shift toward the origin, but for reasons about to be discussed the economy at large derived no benefit.

Prior to its demise, the Soviet system had two main proto-classes, the nomenklatura in charge of the party/state governing apparatus and the rest of the population. The nomenklatura were the clear gainers from the transition, as in connection with the criminal "mafia" they seized control of the major productive assets in a blatantly rigged privatization process, and engaged in massive capital flight. The capital outflow largely offset any current account improvement from higher world prices or volumes of energy exports, leaving the economy in a difficult external position.

At the same time, the government's ability to collect tax and other revenues was systematically reduced, in part due to maneuvers of the ex-nomenklatura/emergent capitalist class. Fiscal spending was cut back with a lag, so that the public sector's contribution to effective demand lay above the generally falling trend line. Meanwhile, different entities in the public and private sectors built up massive totals of payments arrears with one another. This innovation certainly benefited the emergent capitalists but also helped the economy to sidestep some effects of highly contractionary monetary policy, and probably kept output reductions from being worse than they actually were.

Employment even increased in relatively successfully adjusting sectors such as energy, finance and credit, and public administration, and was held fairly stable elsewhere. As in Cuba after its external shock, job protection combined with falling output and real wage reduction due to forced saving led to negative apparent productivity growth in virtually all sectors. The only Russians (the so-called "new Russians") whose real earnings rose were people in upper income strata who benefited from forced saving and the rapid, corrupt privatization. In less than a decade, the Gini coefficient literally doubled, from around 0.3 to 0.6.

The rising fiscal deficit could not be financed internally. As in Turkey, the authorities turned to external borrowing to cover the fiscal gap and ratify the widening external gap (post-capital flight). Short-term government bonds were the chosen vehicle. As is well-known, their high interest rates and a spiraling stock market touched off booming capital inflows beginning at mid-decade. Together with an upward blip in export prices, the foreign money gave the population some respite from the bitter initial years of the transition. But the euphoria ended with the financial crisis of August 1998.

Newly rising world oil prices, increasing output in import-competing sectors stimulated by the post-crisis maxi-devaluation, and further expansion of arrears probably permitted positive GDP growth in 1999, and helped ease the worst effects of the crisis. But the income distribution remains strikingly unequal, four-fifths of the population are now poor or very poor according to the official poverty lines, overall output (even taking into account the shadow economy) is 30–40% below its level a decade previously, the production structure shows sharp duality between activities that may survive under the new economic regime and those that will not, and while Soviet-style industrial organization has been obliterated, a market-based system has not emerged in its place. At best, it will be many years before globalization and liberalization in Russia may produce happy results.

Turkey was an "early reformer," with a liberalization push coming on the heels of an external crisis in the late 1970s. Developments in the 1980s and 1990s make an interesting contrast, as initial current account and labor market deregulation set up a jerky transition toward liberalized external and internal capital markets. The early 1980s witnessed a major export push, facilitated by rapid demand growth in Turkey's major trading partners and pushed on the domestic front by devaluation, aggressive export subsidies, and policies aimed at cutting real wages and the agricultural terms of trade (in contrast to India, higher agricultural prices appear to benefit—not harm—low-income peasant proprietors in the countryside). Despite rapid export growth, investment in traded goods sectors did not increase, so that capacity limits helped choke off the boom later in the decade. Moreover, higher exports were matched by imports so that demand was not externally led.

More fundamentally, the model broke down as repression of wages and the terms of trade could no longer by sustained—there was a wage explosion in 1988 accompanied by a marked political shift toward "populism" à la Turk. However, the government was unwilling or unable to raise taxes to fund its higher expenditures. Liberalizing the capital account was the expedient adopted to permit higher public borrowing. The pattern was for the banking system to borrow in external markets, and then re-lend the money to the government with a handsome interest rate spread.

Real appreciation and a widening trade deficit led to another crisis in 1994. Real wages and the terms of trade were forced back down, along with real depreciation. But a new export boom did not follow, in part because interest rates and domestic credit creation remained high. Recovery after 1994 was led by private and public consumption, as saving and tax rates fell.

In general, effective demand has not been driven by the external sector, especially in the 1990s. Productivity growth has been slow, and fairly evenly balanced between traded and non-traded goods. Labor force participation has risen, accompanied by informalization and widening of wage spreads between skilled and unskilled labor. Although data are scarce, it is likely that poverty has increased. Shifts toward and away from populism on the political front were dramatic and the sequence of liberalization efforts was non-standard, but otherwise Turkey adhered quite closely to the model of Figure 1.

Zimbabwe The effects of liberalization are most easily visualized if the Non-traded goods equilibrium schedule in Figure 1 is taken to refer to a rural/agricultural export sector while the Traded goods curve refers to an urban/industrial sector. Removal of protection shifts the urban curve leftward and by stimulating exports may shift the rural curve up. Spillover effects from removal of rents to import quotas previously generated in the urban sector and shifts in savings rates may complicate the effective demand and income distribution story (Rattso, 1999; Taylor, 1991).

In practice, Zimbabwe entered into external liberalization in the early 1990s with an extremely closed economy. The urban/industrial sector was far stronger than in most sub-Saharan African economies, in part because of an import-restriction system built up in response to UN sanctions during the former Rhodesia's Unilateral Declaration of Independence period in the 1960s and 1970s. This control system was continued when the new Zimbabwen government took over in 1980. An initial boom (1980–82) was unsustainable on foreign exchange grounds. Subsequently, macro stability was maintained by using the controls to regulate the current account deficit. Liberalization got underway in the early 1990s, first with deregulation of intermediate imports and then of final goods. By mid-decade the capital account had been substantially decontrolled, although some restrictions were re-imposed following currency crises in 1998.

The overall liberalization experience during 1990–96 (the period covered by available numerical data) is difficult to evaluate because of a serious drought in 1992, the key transition year. The essential changes were output and investment contractions of 8–10%, a doubling of the inflation rate to 40%, a consumption boom fed by increased imports, and a tripling of the trade deficit. The latter two shifts can largely be attributed to liberalization, insofar as they replicate experience elsewhere. The inflation shock was related to several factors, including the agricultural drought, forced saving led by food prices as the supply curve shifted inward, and fiscal imbalance coming into the open.

Liberalization was clearly part of the explanation. Nominal wages proved to be highly inelastic to price increases. The cut in investment could have been an accelerator response to the fall in output induced by the drought.

Over the longer period, output and capital formation followed a stop-go pattern, but real GDP per capita in 1996 was below its 1992 level, and well below its gradually rising trend during the period 1985–1991. Imports and exports increased in tandem after liberalization, so external factors made a small positive contribution to effective demand. The main impetus came from reductions in the private saving rate.

During 1993–97, the real exchange weakened after appreciating in 1992. Real interest rates and the interest rate spread increased, perhaps due to the need to pay higher returns on the growing public debt. Real wages and the wage share fell, consistent with the inelasticity of labor earnings to inflation noted above. Partial survey results suggest that spreads between skilled and unskilled wage rates widened.

In sum, both growth and equity decreased in the wake of liberalization. This observation does not suggest that Zimbabwe should return to its previous regime of controls, since that was probably unsustainable. But it does leave open a major question about what sort of economic management can be successful in present circumstances.

9. Social Policy

Following upon the preceding discussion, in this section we review the main points that the country authors make regarding social policy during the liberalization period.

Argentina As already noted, the Argentine stabilization and market-friendly reforms of the 1990s produced "unfriendly" effects in the labor market. Unemployment rose from an average of 6.9% between 1990 and 1992 to 16.1% between 1995 and 1998. At the same time, the "involuntary underemployment" rate (as defined above) increased from 8.6% to 12.8%. Of the contraction in full-time employment, two-thirds of those affected were in manufacturing, two-thirds were male, and over half were heads of households.

The country authors discuss social policy largely in terms of the labor market. They raise the following points:

· A more flexible labor market did not alleviate unemployment, but rather contributed to underemployment and lower wages. There was a clear shift toward more intensive use of short-term contracts with lower labor costs as well as redefinition of traditional overtime work rules.

· Trade liberalization concomitant with an appreciated currency accelerated the adoption of new technologies, leading to restructuring in manufacturing. Two-thirds of the contraction in full-time employment took place in that sector. (During the expansionary phase, imports satisfied more than half of increased domestic demand for manufactures.) Workers at all schooling levels were negatively affected, but job losses among the unskilled were most severe.

· State-subsidized employment programs in 1997 led to a rise in female employment in health and education services. Female employment was also aided by a 1997 education reform.

· Income has followed a cyclical pattern although after 1994 wage income fell while non-wage income rose. Highly skilled employees have received the greatest increases in income.

Colombia combined liberalization with an ambitious social policy program. It achieved success in terms of improvements in basic needs indicators and social service coverage, but also caused the government deficit to increase. The policy package helped cushion low-skilled workers from the negative effects of trade liberalization and structural reforms.

The distributional and employment effects of the globalization process included the following:

· As in Argentina, liberalization and exchange rate appreciation caused severe contraction in manufacturing employment, an increase in low-skilled unemployment, and higher urban income inequality.

· Declining terms of trade for the agricultural sector following from real appreciation negatively affected rural rents, hurting both landowners and (low-skilled) agricultural workers

· Rising aggregate demand during the expansionary years, 1991–1995, alleviated some of the low-skilled employment loss by creating jobs in construction and transport. However, most of the employment increase was in services, benefiting higher skilled (secondary and tertiary education) workers. Overall, job creation was weak during the 1990s.

· Lower labor force participation helped reduce the unemployment rate in 1993–1995, but the participation rose after 1996. By 1998, the unemployment rate had reached the highest level in recorded history (15.3% in urban areas).

As noted above, significant social policy changes were implemented along with liberalization in Colombia. They included the following:

· The government increased the value-added tax rate, and at the same time broadened its base.

· Half of the increase in social spending went to expansion of social security coverage; the other half was transferred to regional and municipal governments for spending on education and health.

· Secondary school attendance rates improved, as did coverage of water and sewerage systems, dwelling characteristics, and health indicators.

· Poverty as measured by unsatisfied basic needs declined from 45.6% in 1985 to 37.2% in 1993.

· Social spending primarily benefited poor people and rural areas.

Cuba has traditionally maintained a wide range of social services, many of which continued into the globalization period. New policies were aimed at combating rising inequality between those working in sectors that generate foreign exchange and those who do not, with consequent segmentation of the labor market and income flows. The package included the following:

· Legalization of remittances and holding of foreign exchange; creation of publicly owned and operated stores (including food markets) for spending foreign exchange.

· Creation of public feeding services at subsidized prices for low-income people.

· Maintenance of social security coverage and benefits, including health and education.

· Maintaining the full-employment guarantee by not shedding all unnecessary public sector jobs; protecting those workers whose jobs were shed.

· Giving state-owned farmland to cooperatives and families for agricultural production.

· Allowing self-employment activities, particularly in the tourism sector.

India Liberalization in the 1990s was not accompanied by an expansion of programs aimed at meeting social needs. Social policy could be characterized as "business as usual." The government maintained the package put into place in the 1970s and 1980s, without significant modifications. Some effects of liberalization are clearly of social concern:

· Gains for rural workers that had been predicted by free-market reformers have not taken place. Despite an unprecedented string of favorable monsoons, the growth rate of food grain output declined in the 1990s as compared with the 1980s, implying a decrease in per capita supply.

· Liberalization of agricultural prices (a policy presently being discussed) could have a devastatingly negative impact on the poor. The government probably lacks the capability to compensate the poor if the policy is put in place.

· There is a new fiscal squeeze due to loss in tariff revenues from liberalization; customs revenue as share of total government revenues fell from above 33% in 1991 to 23% in 1995. Public capital formation slowed notably in the 1990s.

· Reforms have had an adverse effect on government spending in defense and economic services; expenditures on rural development and social (including health, education and housing) services have fallen slightly.

· There is ongoing public investment on the production side of agriculture, yet it has not helped rural (especially landless) labor because non-labor inputs and capital equipment have been subsidized. Labor absorption rates in Indian agriculture are very low.

· Manufacturing employment in the "formal" sector has continued a downward trend that began in late 1970s.

· Private sector employment was stagnant throughout the 1990s; formal sector job growth was limited to the public sector and was positive only until 1992. There is growing informalization of the labor market.

· There is no social security coverage for the 90% of the population not employed in formal, organized sector. No Western-style unemployment insurance is offered, although relief programs exist for areas suffering from drought. Some state-level programs have been notably successful.

· Public expenditure on education remains low. Free and compulsory education does not exist, literacy rates are low, and there is a strong bias against primary level education. A reduction in public spending on education caused the number of primary school teachers to drop, but this trend was partially reversed after 1994.

In designing social policy programs for future, it is important to keep in mind that poverty reduction in India has occurred fastest in those states that have experienced rapid rural growth with strong infrastructure development (Punjab, Haryana) and in those that relied on human resource development (Kerala).

Korea The 1998 financial crisis in Korea resulted in an increase in the unemployment rate to levels not seen since the 1960s, as well as a tripling of the poverty rate. However, the crisis provided momentum for expanding social expenditures. Although Korean social policy expenditures are low by international standards (even when compared to Malaysia and Thailand), the government has increased such outlays from 5% of GDP in the 1980s to 7.8% in 1997. Social changes related to liberalization and the financial crisis include the following:

· After 1992, wage inequality ceased to decline. The continued rise in the share of college graduates in the labor force stopped having a positive supply-side effect on wage differentials. The financial crisis caused a 20-year trend toward lower inequality to reverse. This occurred for four reasons: (1) 13% of production workers and laborers lost their jobs, while professional and managerial jobs increased by 1.3%; (2) wage cuts fell most heavily on the low-skilled; (3) the construction and manufacturing sectors, where lower-paid, less-skilled labor is employed, suffered the greatest job losses; and (4) wage differentials between the chaebol and small and medium enterprises have widened.

· The crisis has brought about flexibilization of the labor market; workers in large firms can no longer enjoy de facto lifetime employment.

Despite the increase in social policy expenditures due to the crisis, there are pressing needs for improved and expanded efforts:

· Presently most government spending goes to defense and subsidies to farmers.

· Only 10% of unemployed workers received unemployment assistance in 1998. There is a pressing need to expand coverage.

· There is no program aimed at helping unemployed workers find jobs. There are no programs to place workers graduating from government-established, but privately run, vocational schools.

· There is a strong need to modernize tax administration and institute a more progressive tax system.

· College admission procedures that rely on written examinations have encouraged the growth of private instruction to the detriment of poorer students.

· Health insurance, although universal, only covers limited medical expenses, typically for less serious ailments. The fee-for-service method of reimbursing doctors leads to unnecessary medical tests and rising health care costs. The government should improve monitoring of health insurance.

Mexico Neither the liberalization of the late 1980s nor the financial crisis of the mid-1990s was accompanied by government efforts to improve provision of social services. Most Mexicans have seen their real wages and employment opportunities fall over the decade, leading to an increase in the incidence of extreme and moderate poverty. The income of the top 10% of the population has significantly increased. The major developments on the social policy front in the 1990s include:

· Job creation has been sluggish, with employment losses in the manufacturing sector due to poor output performance coupled with productivity increases. Labor absorption has been in the low-productivity agricultural and non-traded sectors causing an overall slowdown in productivity growth for the economy, not to mention underemployment.

· Due to the flexibility of the labor market, real wages have fallen dramatically, to roughly 60% of the level reached in the early 1980s.

· The Gini coefficient of wage inequality has steadily increased to 0.53 in 1994 from 0.44 in 1984. High-skilled workers have benefited from increased employment opportunities and wage increases.

· Rural incomes have worsened. Government "modernization" of the agriculture led to the dismantling of long-established programs aiding the sector. Farmers and farm workers have suffered from the collapse in the real guaranteed price for major crops, high interest rates, and the loss of subsidies.

Russia As already noted, the political and economic transition has split the economy and society into two disparate sectors. From a quasi-egalitarian society during Soviet times, Russia today ranks among the most inequitable countries in the world, with a Gini coefficient of 0.56. The implications for social policy are profound.

· The transition benefited the top 10% of the population, especially high-level management of newly privatized resource-based industries and shadow-economy businesses.

· Resource-based and finance industries have increased their share of employment, while employment shares in import-competing industries (machinery and metalworking, food, production materials) have decreased. Manufacturing and construction have shed 1/3 of their labor force.

· There is significant unemployment for the first time since the 1930s, reaching 12% in 1998. Real average wages in the 1990s dropped by more than 50%, concomitant with a fall in the wage share of income.

· There has been a severe erosion of the tax base due to privatization of state enterprises, decentralization of foreign trade and expansion of the shadow economy (presently accounting for about one-third of GDP). The Russian federal budget in 1999 was $20 billion, making it impossible to support education, health and social services (in comparison, New York City's budget in 1998 was $38 billion).

· Because of the erosion of the tax base, the government has had to rely on external loans, leading to greater indebtedness and concern about the availability of future resources for social spending.

Without a tax base, the government has been unable to compensate its citizens for the negative effects of the transition. The end result has been significant deterioration in the living standards of the population at large.

Turkey When Turkey fully liberalized in 1988, it pursued social policy goals by increasing spending on public services. However, by 1993, this effort proved to be unsustainable, leading to fiscal austerity and cutbacks of social spending. The government's inability to sustain populist policies was directly related to its failure to broaden and increase taxes on the rich.

Liberalization has not had the extreme negative effects on tradable sector employment witnessed in other countries, but it has been accompanied by rising wage inequality. There has been growing informalization of the labor force. At the same time, there has also been a decline in public sector employment due to privatization. Those remaining in the public sector have seen their wages rise in comparison to the private sector.

Post-1993 adjustment costs fell mostly on urban workers and the peasantry. Real wages of formal sector workers dropped by 23% and rural incomes fell by 16%, both exceeding the proportionate macroeconomic costs of adjustment. The government's decision to privatize many health and education services led the private sector's share in total education and health investments to reach 50% by 1996–1997. However, this has not benefited the poor, but instead led to the emergence of elite private hospitals and schools.

Zimbabwe Liberalization has hurt its previously protected industries leading to deindustrialization, as consumers have switched to imported goods. Income distribution has widened since the reforms. High-skilled workers received real wage increases while the majority of wage earners suffered significant losses in real wages due to the inflation shock of 1992.

Another consequence of the reforms of the 1990s has been a tightening of government spending to the detriment of social policy. When Zimbabwe gained independence in the 1980s, it increased social policy spending and transfers in an attempt to narrow gaps between living standards of racial groups. The tax system was revised and made more progressive. Funds were used to expand the educational system and improve access to health care. Labor protection was increased and a national minimum wage was instituted, while farmers received agricultural support.

For a variety of reasons, including pressures on the deficit, funding of social policies began to erode in the late 1980s. The erosion has continued into the 1990s with the following results:

· User fees have been introduced for previously free education and health services.

· The value of the real minimum wage has fallen with inflation.

· Programs to alleviate poverty such as the 1991 Social Dimensions of Adjustment program and the 1994 Poverty Alleviation Action Plan have received inadequate funding and support, leading to scant success in reducing poverty.

In sum, liberalization and adjustment have hurt the Zimbabwean poor by (1) contributing to real wage and job losses and (2) forcing the government to cut social spending in an attempt to curtail the deficit during the adjustment process.

10. Policy Alternatives

The usual caveats about policy prescriptions apply. Given the diversity of country experiences just reported, it is risky to generalize about lessons and conclusions. Of course, diversity of outcomes is a result in itself. It negates general sweeping statements about whether the reforms have been exclusively beneficial or exclusively costly in terms of growth, employment, and equity.

If one is to sing a sad song, however, the evidence certainly shows that in the post-liberalization era few if any of the countries considered seem to have found a sustainable growth path. Employment growth has generally been slow to dismal and rising primary income disparity (in some cases over and above already high levels of inequality) has been the rule.

Better performances such as those in Mexico and Korea after their financial crises (as of the year 2000, three years of sustained growth in Mexico and one in Korea) were associated with avoiding the macro price mixture of a strong real exchange rate and high domestic interest rates. Post-crisis effective demand was led by the foreign sector in Mexico and by private consumption and investment spending in Korea, suggesting that each recovering country may have its own particular demand path.

Similar conclusions apply to the handful of Latin American economies described in Ganuza, et.al. (2000) that combined adequate growth with improvement or stability of indexes of inequality. Their better performances were associated with a policy mix that combined (a) avoiding a macro price mixture of real exchange rate appreciation and high domestic interest rates, (b) maintaining a system of well-directed export incentives whether put in place at the national level or as part of regional integration agreements, and (c) having a system of capital controls and prudential financial regulation able to contain the negative consequences of capital surges.

For the other countries described in this volume, the news is less good. Among the historically capitalist economies, Turkey and Argentina continue to wander in a slow growth, falling employment, and increasing inequality wilderness. India's growth and equity performance has not improved with liberalization, and despite a strong effort on the social policy front, Colombia's is worse. In part because of an explicit effort to cushion the liberalization shock, Cuba's equity has been maintained, despite mediocre growth performance. Zimbabwe's and especially Russia's are disasters.

Of the three views regarding liberalization mentioned at the outset, the first "market friendly" narrative is hard to discern in the countries analyzed here. In line with the second view, some might argue that their distributional deterioration was not the result of liberalization and globalization but they would have to strain to make the case. For most of the countries considered here (and in the Latin American sample as well), it is difficult to refute the third view that liberalization and deteriorating growth and equity performances can easily go hand-in-hand.

Finally, fundamental questions arise regarding social coherence and social policy. The mainstream view of liberalization emphasizes its likely positive effects on economic performance. Adverse transitional impacts can in principle be smoothed by social policies, and in any case after some time "a rising tide lifts all boats." The much more disquieting possibility is that liberalization can unleash dynamic forces leading not only to an unimpressive aggregate economic performance but also to long-term slow employment expansion and increasing income concentration. In principle, governments could put countervailing social policies into place. In practice, they probably lack the capacity to do so because of their own fiscal and administrative limitations.

Such constraints on social policy and burden-sharing can be reduced by investment in the capability of the state, as experience in now industrialized countries demonstrated in the 19th century and again after World War II in the construction of welfare states (Polanyi, 1944). But an explicit political decision would be needed before such investments could be undertaken. It would be comparable in scope to the one that led to the worldwide spread of liberalization in the first place. Nevertheless, for the countries considered here, the initial outcomes of liberalization suggest that a "double movement" á la Polanyi, first toward and then away from an extreme liberal policy stance, could be forthcoming in the not-so-distant future. Inadequate social performance of any economic policy line leads ultimately to its reversal as society organizes to protect its own.

REFERENCES

Amadeo, Edward J. and Valeria Pero (2000) "Adjustment, Stabilization, and the Structure of Employment in Brazil," *Journal of Development Studies*, forthcoming.
Ganuza, Enrique, Lance Taylor and Rob Vos (eds.) (2000) *External Liberalization and Economic Performance in Latin America and the Caribbean*, New York: United Nations Development Programme.
Godley, Wynne (1999) "Seven Unsustainable Processes," Annandale-on-Hudon, NY: Jerome Levy Economics Institute.
Hicks, John R. (1965) *Capital and Growth*, Oxford: Clarendon Press.
Kindleberger, Charles P. (1996) *Manias, Panics and Crashes* (3rd edition), New York: John Wiley and Sons.
Krugman, Paul, and Lance Taylor (1978) "Contractionary Effects of Devaluation," *Journal of International Economics*, 8: 445–456.
Londoño, Juan Luis and Miguel Székely (1998) "Sorpresas Distributivas después de una Década de Reformas," *Pensamiento Iberoamericano-Revista de Económica Política* (Special Issue).
Ocampo, José Antonio and Lance Taylor (1998) "Trade Liberalization in Developing Economies: Modest Benefits but Problems with Productivity Growth, Macro Prices and Income Distribution," *Economic Journal*, 108: 1523–1546.
Pieper, Ute (2000) "Openness and Structural Dynamics of Productivity and Employment in Developing Countries: A Case of Deindustrialization?" *Journal of Development Studies*, forthcoming.
Polanyi, Karl (1944) *The Great Transformation*, New York: Rinehart.

Rattsø, Jørn (1999) "Income Distribution, Growth and Protectionism in Sub-Saharan Africa and the Case of Zimbabwe," forthcoming in *Festschrift to George Waadenburg*, Rotterdam: Erasmus University.

Rodrik, Dani (1998) "Who Needs Capital Account Convertibility?" Cambridge: Harvard University (processed).

Ros, Jaime (1999) "La Liberalización de la Balanza de Pagos en Mexico: Efectos en el Crecimiento, el Empleo y la Desigualdad Salarial," paper presented at UNDP-CEPAL-IDB conference on the Effects of Balance of Payments Liberalization on Employment, Distribution, Poverty and Growth, Rio de Janeiro, February.

Sen, Amartya (1999) *Development as Freedom*, New York (NY): Alfred A. Knopf.

Stolper, Wolfgang F. and Paul A. Samuelson (1941) "Protection and Real Wages," *Review of Economic Studies*, 9: 58–73.

Syrquin, Moshe (1986) "Productivity Growth and Factor Reallocation," in Hollis B. Chenery, Sherwin Robinson, and Moshe Syrquin (eds.), *Industrialization and Growth*, New York: Oxford University Press.

Taylor, Lance (1991) *Income Distribution, Inflation, and Growth*, Cambridge (MA): MIT Press.

Taylor, Lance (1999) "The Exchange Rate is Indeterminate in the Portfolio Balance and Mundell-Fleming Models—Each Has One Fewer Independent Equation than People Usually Think," New School for Social Research, New York (processed).

Vos, Rob (1995) "Financial Liberalization, Growth and Adjustment: Some lessons from Developing Countries," in Stephany Griffith-Jones and Zdenek Drábek (eds.), *Financial Reform in Central and Eastern Europe*, London: Macmillan, pp. 179–220.

Wood, Adrian (1997) "Openness and Wage Inequality in Developing Countries: the Latin American Challenge to East Asian Conventional Wisdom," *World Bank Economic Review*, 11: 33–57.

3

Argentina: Balance-of-payments Liberalization: Effects on Growth, Employment and Income

ROBERTO FRENKEL *and* MARTÍN GONZÁLEZ ROZADA*

Introduction

In the first half of the nineties, Argentina witnessed an impressive process of market-friendly reforms, targeting the privatization of a large proportion of state-owned enterprises, as well as both trade and financial opening.

At the same time the country was emerging from a period of extreme instability in prices which had led to two brief hyperinflationary episodes in 1989 and 1990. This price stabilization was concurrent with a strong recovery in growth that had its dark side: unemployment grew significantly and inequality deepened.

One of the main structural reforms in the nineties was the opening of the economy to international trade. It was already in 1988 that notable inroads had been made in this direction. However, in the nineties the previous gradual approach was abandoned and the opening was accelerated. Average import tariffs were reduced from 26.5 percent in October 1989 to 9.7 percent in April 1991. In addition, specific duties were eliminated, as were quantitative restrictions on imports.[1]

*CEDES. The authors thank Carola Ramón for her collaboration and Lance Taylor for his comments on the draft. The authors also wish to thank the participants in the New York, Rio de Janeiro and San Salvador seminars for their comments on the draft.

1. Between 1987 and 1988 the average tariff dropped from 43 percent to 30 percent and quantitative restrictions were reduced. In October 1989, some 807 tariff lines were subject to "transitory additional duties," 122 to import licensing and 129 to specific duties. In April 1991 not one tariff line was subject to either specific duties, transitory additional duties or to import licences. Restrictions remained in effect for only 25 tariff items—those corresponding to motor

Privatizations, for their part, commenced in 1990 with the transfer of the telephone company and the national airlines. By late 1994 the major part of the state-owned firms producing goods and services had been sold, including the most important ones: the oil company (YPF) and the producers and distributors of electric power. This process covered a wide range of productive areas from iron and steel works to petrochemicals and gas. In some cases (oil fields, railways, ports, highways, waterworks and sewage, and television channels and radio stations) the government resorted to concession mechanisms.

Several legal norms marked the structural reform process. First was the Law of the State Reform (August 1989) which established the legal bases for the privatization of state-owned enterprises with the capitalization of public debt. Second, in order to improve the performance of the public accounts, the Law of Economic Emergency (September 1989) suspended several subsidy mechanisms, such as those that were implicit in the industrial and regional promotion regimes. This law established equal treatment for foreign and domestic capital invested in productive activities in the country. In this way, prior approval for direct foreign investment was no longer necessary. In addition, in November 1991, a Deregulation Decree eliminated a wide set of regulations encompassing diverse economic activities.

The most important legal instrument of the stabilization process was the Convertibility Law (March 1991) that established a fixed peso-dollar parity and validated contracts in any foreign currency. It also stipulated that the Central Bank must back 100 percent of its monetary base with foreign reserves. The new Central Bank Charter (September 1992) suppressed the official guarantee on deposits and fixed narrow limits whereby it could purchase public bonds and lend to commercial banks. The law also established the autonomy of the Central Bank.

In practice, the Convertibility Law transformed the Central Bank into a currency board and completed the deregulation of the capital account of the balance of payments. So that from early 1991, both trade and capital flows were fully liberalized.

This research paper gives a summary[2] analysis of the growth process, the performance of the labor market and the evolution of income and wages in the context generated by the structural reforms, as well as a discussion of the stabilization policies that were applied in the nineties. There are seven sections to the paper, following the introduction.

Section 1 presents some aspects of the macroeconomic dynamics, mainly in the form of graphs that facilitate the comparison between the eighties and

---

vehicles and auto parts—out of a total of 10,000. Special rates were also maintained for motor vehicles and electronics, which were subject to a 35 percent tariff. The tariff structure in April 1991 included three rates: zero for raw material, 11 percent for inputs and capital goods, 22 percent for final goods. See Damill and Keifman (1993). Since 1995 the Argentine staff structure has been that of the MERCOSUR (with some exceptions).

2. See Frenkel and González Rozada (1999a) for the complete version of the report.

the nineties and highlight the stylized facts of the latter. In this shorter version we have solely presented the most relevant features for the analysis of income and employment. Section 2 presents an econometric model that describes the macroeconomic performance in the nineties and summarizes the estimation results. Section 3 focuses on the behavior of the urban labor market at the national level and in Greater Buenos Aires (GBA). The presentation compares the eighties with the nineties and stresses the main stylized features of the latter. Section 4 includes the formulation and estimation of an econometric model of the aggregate urban labor market. In Section 5 GBA data are utilized to analyze variations in urban employment by sector of activity and socio-demographic characteristics. The manufacturing sector is by far the most important urban tradable activity. The analysis shows that the contraction in employment in this sector explains two-thirds of the fall in total full-time employment observed in the nineties. Section 6 studies the performance of production, employment and productivity in the manufacturing sector using data from the industrial survey. An econometric model of labor demand in this sector is presented. The econometric estimations, together with the trade information on the manufacturing sector, are utilized to separate and calculate the different effects on the employment contraction in this sector. Finally, Section 7 focuses on income and its distribution.

1. Stylized features of the macroeconomic dynamics.[3]

The short-run cycle and growth

Graph 1 shows the evolution of quarterly GDP (in logs) in both the eighties and nineties. The trend is obtained using the Hodrick-Prescott filter (with the conventional parameter). As can be seen, GDP in the eighties fluctuated cyclically on a stagnant trend while showing a clearly positive trend in the nineties. The HP filter in the graph indicates a new growth trend in the nineties, with an annual rate of 4.8 percent.

There is a first expansionary phase that lasted until 1994. This expansion begins before the Convertibility Plan was launched, in the second semester of 1990, and reached its peak in the second semester of 1994.[4] Between the second semester in 1990 and that of 1994 seasonally adjusted GDP grew by 35.7 percent (an average annual rate of 8%). The second phase marks a recession associated with the tequila effect in 1995, which produced a 6.8 percent contraction in GDP between the second semesters in 1994 and 1995. Recovery from the recession began in the second semester in 1996, with an activity level

---

3. Sections I and II are based on research carried out together with Mario Damill. More detailed analysis can be seen in Fanelli and Frenkel (1999) and in Frenkel, Fanelli and Bonvecchi (1998).

4. As data on employment are available only by semester, it is useful for the sake of the analysis to present GDP evolution in the same way.

GRAPH 1: Log GDP and Hodrick-Prescott trend

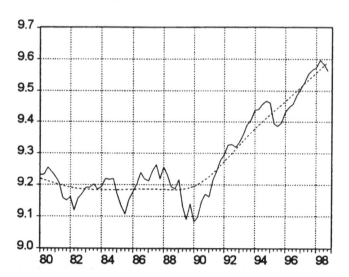

return to a level similar to that of the second semester of 1994. Finally, in late 1996, the country enters its most recent expansionary phase, with growth accelerating as a result of the large capital inflows. Between the second semesters of 1996 and 1997, GDP increased by 9.2 percent. However, the expansion decelerated after October 1997, following the Asian crisis. GDP has exhibited a recessionary trend since the second semester of 1998.

Foreign trade and the balance of payments

During the first expansionary phase, the export ratio at constant prices (Graph 2) remained practically stagnant. This ratio jumps between 1994 and 1995 but later shows a stagnant trend. On the other hand, the import ratio at constant prices sharply increases during the first expansionary phase, then decreases with the recession, only to steadily increase during the second expansion.

On observing trends in the foreign account at current prices, the dynamics of the balance of payments appears halted with the 1995 crisis (Graphs 3 and 4). During the first phase, capital inflows grow annually until 1993 and then show a decline in 1994, when the United States interest rates are raised. The country risk rate descends until 1993, then rises in 1994 (Graph 7). On the other hand, the current account deficit exhibits a growing trend in the first expansionary phase, and given that before 1994 capital inflows were mainly private and systematically larger than the current account deficit, reserves increase (Graphs 5 and 6). With the decline in private capital inflows in 1994, reserves tend to stagnate. This change in the trend was followed in the first quarter of 1995 by abrupt capital outflows and a contraction in reserves caused by the tequila crisis.

**GRAPH 2: Exports and Imports
as proportions of GDP at 1986 constant prices (%)**

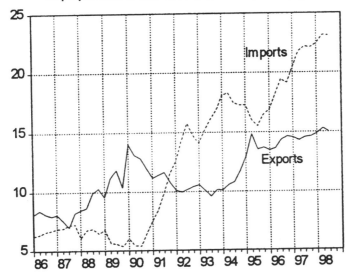

**GRAPH 3: Exports and Imports in current dollars.
Seasonally adjusted.**

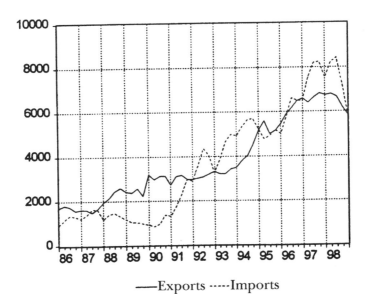

——Exports ·····Imports

GRAPH 4: The trade balance and the GDP fluctuation

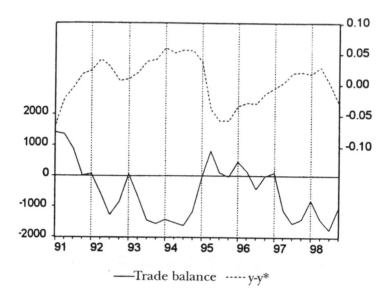

—Trade balance ·····y-y*

GRAPH 5: Current account, capital account and change in reserves

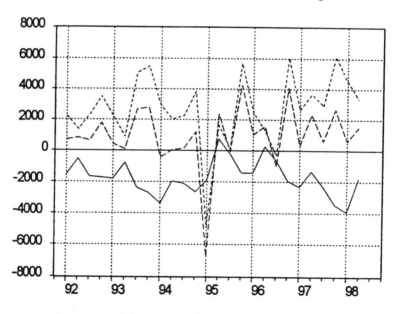

—— Current account ······Capital account ────Change in reserves

GRAPH 6: Government and private sector net inflows of capital

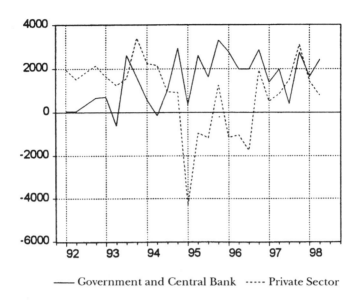

—— Government and Central Bank ----- Private Sector

GRAPH 7: Private sector capital inflows and country-risk premium

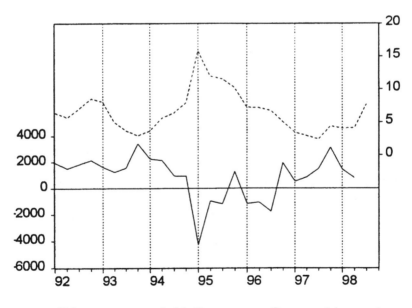

—— Private sector capital inflows ----- Country-risk premium

Following this crisis, there is a transition phase in the evolution of the balance of payments that extends to the third quarter of 1996. This is characterized, in the first place, by a transitory reduction in the current account deficit explained by the behavior of the trade balance. The above jump in export volume is mainly compounded by the impact of Brazil's Real Plan on Argentina and increasing prices in agricultural and oil commodities. On the other hand, the level of imports dropped as a result of the recession. Altogether, these effects made it possible to achieve a transitory trade balance. During this phase capital inflows correspond exclusively to the public sector, thanks to the rescue operation led by the IMF.

From late 1996 the evolution of the balance of payments once more shows similar features to that of the first expansionary phase of 1991–93. This recent expansionary phase extends from late 1996 to the Asian crisis. Net capital inflows, again mostly private, are similar to the maximum annual inflow registered before 1994. The current account deficit tends to increase swiftly, mainly because of the rise in imports. However, just as in the first expansionary phase, capital inflows surpass the deficit and reserves accumulate. The country-risk rate tends to fall after 1995 and reaches a minimum (similar to that of 1993) in the months preceding the Asian crisis. The deceleration in growth in late 1997 and the new recessionary phase in 1998, are associated with successive higher country-risk rates and lower private capital flows.

Sources of demand expansion, savings and investment

During the first expansionary phase not only consumption but also investment[5] contribute to the expansion in domestic absorption. The investment rate at the end of the eighties was at its lowest point ever and tended to increase rapidly in this first phase, thanks to the exchange rate appreciation which raised the purchasing power of (imported) capital goods for a determined savings rate. With the 1995 crisis the proportions of both consumption and investment were reduced. After the crisis, from 1996 on, both components of the absorption increased their participation in the product. Although the consumption rate remained lower than those in the first expansionary phase, the investment rate continued to climb.

Until 1994, in the first expansionary phase, consumption dominates aggregate demand increases, particularly in the first two years, and there is no export growth contribution. During the 1995 crisis, contractions in consumption and investment equally contribute to the fall in aggregate demand, while, for just this time, the increase in exports plays a significant counter-cyclical

---

5. Argentina's National Accounts system does not have an independent consumption estimate. The variable is a residual calculation based on the estimations of the other components of the Accounts. The estimated consumption thus includes inventory variations. The investment variable is the gross fixed investment.

role. The recovery from the post-tequila phase was again steered by consumption, but the contributions of investment and consumption tend to converge in 1997 when growth accelerated.

The savings rate in the nineties falls systematically below that of the eighties. The difference with the investment rate tends to widen in the first expansionary phase despite the tendency of the savings rate to rise in the second half of the phases. The rates converge in the 1995 crisis owing to the sharp reduction in investment, together with a fall in the savings rate. The adjustment mechanism was the contraction of the product along with a mainly exogenous increase in exports. The savings-investment gap tends to widen again in the post-tequila phase, reaching its 1994 level in 1997.

Inflation

The consumer price dynamics (a proxy for non-tradable goods) is most commonly observed in shock stabilization plans with an exchange-rate anchor (Graph 8). The «inertial inflation» persists for some time via the survival of price and wage indexation mechanisms. Given that inflation is gradually reduced in a context of strong money, credit and demand expansion, the process can only be attributed to the stabilizing role of the fixed exchange rate in a context of greater trade opening. Once the exchange rate is fixed,

GRAPH 8: Quarterly rates of inflation (%)

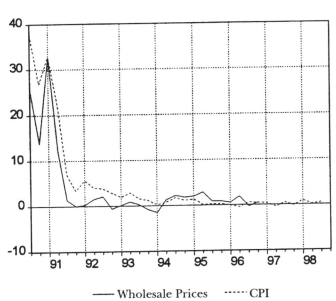

—— Wholesale Prices ······ CPI

the inflation rate of consumer prices gradually converged with the international inflation rate. This process took approximately three years.

In contrast, the appreciation of the exchange rate in the previous year contributed to the immediate convergence of tradable goods prices (approximated by the wholesale price index). In this way, international prices operated as a constraint on domestic tradable ones from the very moment the plan was launched.

Relative prices

Relative prices in the nineties differ greatly from those that characterized the previous decade. Trade and financial opening affected macroeconomic behavior and employment mainly via changes in relative prices.

Assuming the launch of the Convertibility Plan as the starting point of the new regime, the major part of the change takes place within relatively few months before and after the launch. The change in relative prices takes the form of a shock, so relative prices are determined from the very beginning. The changes that are produced from 1991 are of secondary importance to those that occurred upon the launch.

These considerations are clearly valid for the real exchange rate and wages valued at constant dollars[6] (Graphs 9 and 10). The following table shows the average values for the different periods.

	1986–90	1986–88	1990:4–1991:1	1991:2–1998	1994–98
Real exchange rate	1.22	1.16	0.62	0.50	0.49.
Wages in const. dollars	0.76	0.83	1.33	1.48	1.51

As can be seen, the changes in relative prices domestic producers of tradable goods faced were in full effect from the beginning of the period. The relative prices characterizing the period were determined as a shock from the first moment. Thus, it is reasonable to consider the transformations observed in the productive structure and in the technology and organization of the firms as adaptation processes to these new conditions rather than as gradual changes based on the gradual changes in relative prices.

Taking into account the behavior of inflation and relative prices and the focus of the paper, we can dichotomize without significant loss the analysis of prices and quantities and consider prices as exogenous in the macroeconomic model below.

---

6. The wage considered here is the industrial manufacturing wage published by FIEL, corresponding to a sample of large-sized firms. The dynamic in the nineties differs from that of the wage in INDEC's household survey, but this difference does not affect the point referring to the change in the eighties and the nineties.

GRAPH 9: Exchange rate of the USA dollar.
Base: second semester 1986=1

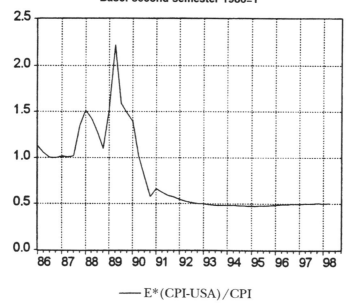

——— E*(CPI-USA)/CPI

GRAPH 10: Real wage and wage in constant USA dollars

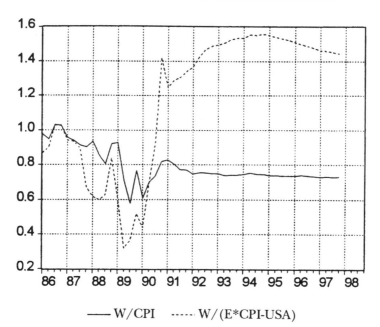

——— W/CPI   ·····W/(E*CPI-USA)

2. The macroeconomic model

This section presents a simple model of the macroeconomic performance under the convertibility regime. The model ignores sustainability conditions and external and/or financial crises in order to focus exclusively on the economy's short-run real dynamics and growth.

Capital flows, the country risk premium and exports are exogenous. The exogenous character of the capital flows and the country risk premium is a simplification intended to stress that both variables have been essentially determined by international conditions. The model determines the evolution of the balance of payments, the product, investment and employment.[7] This section does not include the equations for the labor market. These will be presented later.

Definitions and equations

$R=X-M+Z+CK$, where dR is the international reserves variation of the banking system (including the foreign currency denominated segment); X: exports; M: imports; Z: foreign factors service payments; CK: the capital account balance.

$CC=X-M+Z$ is the current account balance.

$dB=dR$. TC is the currency board rule. The monetary base variation equals reserves variation times the exchange rate.

$BR=B/P$ is the real value of the monetary base. P is the local price level (CPI).

$TCR=TC$. P^*/P is the real exchange rate. $TC=1$ (Convertibility Law). P^* is the USA price level (CPI).

$r = r^*+PRISK$. The relevant interest rate equals the international rate plus the country risk premium.

$Y=Y (BR, r)$ $Y_{BR}>0;$ $Y_r<0$, where Y is the GDP.[8]

$M=M (Y, TCR)$ $M_Y>0;$ $M_{TCR}<0$.

$I=I (Y, r)$ $I_Y>0;$ $I_r<0$, where I is investment.

$PRISK=PRISK (\theta, CC)$ $PRISK_{CC}<0$ and so $r_M>0$. θ is an exogenous vector representing the international financial markets conditions.[9]

$Z=-r^* \int CK(h) dh$ where $\int CK(h) dh$ is the accumulated stock of net capital flows between time 0 and time t.

As a short run dynamic model, the reduced equations express the activity level, investment and imports as functions of exports, capital flows and the country risk premium.

---

7. As the National Accounts system has no independent estimation of consumption, the models includes an aggregate product equation and an investment equation.

8. Xi X=X(Z, Y, . . .); X_Z=dX/dZ, X_Y=dX/dY, etc.

9. The sensitivity of the country risk premium to the current account balance only affects the speed of adjustment of GDP to the balance of payment variations.

The long-run dynamics implied by the model can be illustrated by the following exercise. Suppose there are balance-of-payments surplus initial conditions, exports grow on a linear trend, the international interest rate and the country risk premium are constant and there is a constant positive capital inflow. With these simplifying assumptions the model can be easily resolved in a differential equation in the reserves variation. This equation tells us that pushed by the capital inflows the economy is initially growing and accumulating reserves. The expansion induces increasing imports. The external debt interest payments and the foreign capital services also have growing trends, as the capital inflows accumulate in a growing stock of foreign liabilities. The current account deficit rises and the initial balance of payments surplus tends to fall, reducing the reserves and the economy rates of growth. The reserves, the monetary base and the GDP tend to linear trends. The slopes of those trends are positive or negative depending exclusively on the difference between the trend in exports and the trend in foreign factors payments ($X–r^*$ CK). This means that in a context of constant capital inflows the economy experiences an initial boom and a decelerating growth trend tending to a long term path which slope, positive or negative, depends exclusively on the rate of growth of exports.

The econometric estimations

Our econometric estimations of the model equations show[10] that the evolution of the balance of payments and the relevant interest rate tells quite accurately the convertibility period macroeconomic history. The balance of payments evolution strongly depends on capital inflows. The capital account variance explains 36 percent of the reserves variation variance. The one quarter lagged reserves rate explains 42 percent of the quarterly GDP rate. On the other hand, GDP and investment show a highly significant direct link with the international financial conditions confronted by the country. The relevant interest rate variance explains 40 percent of the GDP quarterly rate of growth variance. Quantity (capital inflows) and price (relevant interest rate) factors, mainly determined by the volatile international financial context, explain in a great deal the ups and downs of activity level and investment. This is not an extraordinary characteristic in times of financial globalization. Argentina's distinctive characteristic is the close connection with the international financial markets established by the Convertibility regime.

---

10. We estimated the product equation in quarterly rates of growth and in deviations with respect to the log trend. The imports and investment equations were estimated in quarterly rates of growth. All by OLS with heteroskedasticity consistent variances estimators. In all cases we obtained significant (5%) coefficients estimators and satisfactory usual fit tests. The estimations can be seen in the complete version of the paper.

3. The evolution of national urban employment

Graph 11 shows the evolution of the activity rates (NTPEAPOB), employment (NTASAN) and full-time employment[11] (NTASANPLE) from 1980 as proportions of the urban population. The graph also presents trends obtained using the Hodrick-Prescott filter.

The trend in the activity rate is upward sloping from the mid-eighties. The long-run trend estimated with the HP filter from the second half of the eighties is an annual 0.9 percent. Nevertheless, as can be seen in the graph, the nineties starts with an activity rate that falls below the long-run trend. The trend estimated on the series from the second semester of 1990 is slightly higher than one percent per year.

In the nineties the negative trend in full-time employment accentuates and the total employment trend turns negative, although the latter is cushioned by the rise in involuntary underemployment. The full-time employment curve in

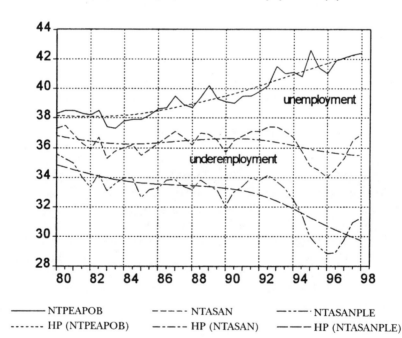

GRAPH 11: Country rates of activity, total employment and full-time employment as proportions of urban population (%)

———— NTPEAPOB   – – – – · NTASAN   — – · · — NTASANPLE
······· HP (NTPEAPOB)   – · – · – HP (NTASAN)   — – — HP (NTASANPLE)

11. Full-time employment includes those persons working 35 or more hours per week and those choosing to work less than 35 hours. Data utilized correspond to urban conglomerates covered by INDEC's Household Survey. These surveys are carried out twice a year in April and October. As these months are central to the first and second semester of the year, we present the analysis by semester.

the nineties shows a cycle with a peak in the second semester of 1992. From then until the second semester of 1996, full-time employment shows a steady decline, more so in the first semester of 1995 due to the recession resulting from the tequila effect. A recovery in the full-time employment rate can be observed in 1997, associated with the strong expansion mentioned above.

The areas between the activity and employment curves and between the total and full-time employment curves in Graph 11 are the unemployment rate (NTUNEMP) and the involuntary underemployment rate (NTASANSUB), respectively, as proportions of the urban population. The trends in the nineties and the importance the contraction in full-time employment had in explaining the rise in both unemployment and involuntary underemployment are highlighted.

The variation in these rates in the nineties, measured as percentages of the active population, are summarized in the following table:

	Average 1990–1992:1	Average 1995–1998:1	Difference
Unemployment (%)	6.9	16.1	9.2
Invol. underemployment(%)	8.6	12.8	4.2
Unemploy. + invol.underemploy.(%)	15.5	28.9	13.4

The contraction in full-time employment is the crucial variable in explaining the increase in unemployment and involuntary underemployment. Graph 12 shows the relationship between the full-time employment rate (as a proportion of the urban population) and the GDP, as an index with base=1 in the second semester of 1990. As can be seen, in the eighties and until the second semester of 1990 the full-time employment rate and the product evolve on the same trend. However, these trends have opposite signs in the nineties.

GRAPH 12: Rate of full-time employment/GDP ratio. Index=1 in 1990:2

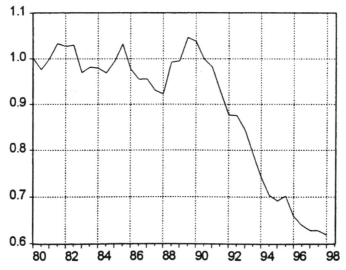

Data from Greater Buenos Aires

Figure 1 presents four tables on Greater Buenos Aires in the nineties. The tables show the employment rate, the full-time employment rate (35 hours and over), the involuntary underemployment rate (TASANSUBI) and the voluntary underemployment rate (TASANSUBV), as proportions of the GBA population[12]. The employment rate of the first graph is the sum of the three other components. Two features stand out regarding the behavior of these variables. First of all, full-time employment and voluntary underemployment vary jointly in a cycle that hits a maximum around the first semester of 1992 and a minimum in the second semester of 1996. Second, involuntary underemployment varies counter-cyclically, reaching a minimum around the second semester of 1992 and a maximum in the

FIGURE 1: Proportions of GBA population (%)

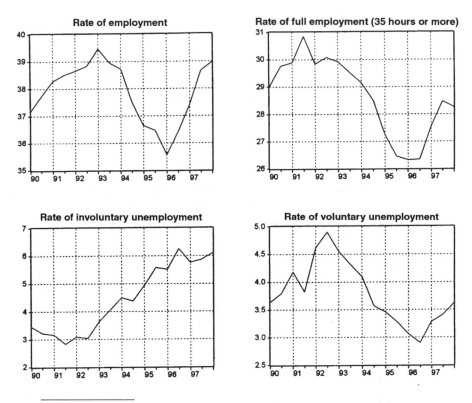

12. The activity and employment levels in GBA are higher than those at the national level, but the dynamic and the changes between the eighties and nineties are similar and we will therefore not comment on them. In the cases of equivalent series the name of the series is maintained without the initial letter N (e.g., TPEAPOB is the activity rate in GBA, equivalent to NTPEAPOB at the national level).

second semester of 1996. The dynamics of involuntary underemployment is analogous to the dynamics of unemployment. These observations suggest aggregating full-time employment and voluntary underemployment as the dependent variable in the employment model and treating involuntary underemployment as a type of unemployment.

4. The aggregate model of the labor market

From the preceding section it can clearly be seen that a structural change in labor demand occurred in the nineties. The new incentives and constraints induced a restructuring in foreign trade and domestic production, the organization and technology of production and labor demand. Let us assume that the macroeconomic dynamics analyzed in Section 1 affected the firms via changes in domestic demand and relative prices.[13] The incentives and constraints that characterized the nineties did not arise gradually. The relative prices in effect during the period had been defined practically from the very beginning as we explained in Section 1. In contrast, the restructuring of labor demand induced by the new incentives and constraints as a gradually developing process throughout the nineties can be considered. The formal treatment we give this issue follows.

We assume a labor demand equation of the form

$$log\ E = \alpha\ log\ Y + \gamma\ log\ (W/PK) + \delta$$

where E is employment, Y the product and W/PK the wage/capital goods relative price. Say $t=0$ is a point in time before the changes, i.e. the eighties, and $t=1$ is a point in time when the process of changes in the labor demand developed considerably, i.e. 1996. Thus:

$$log\ E_0 = \alpha\ log\ Y_0 + \gamma\ log\ (W_0/PK_0) + \delta_0\ \text{and}$$
$$log\ E_1 = \alpha\ log\ Y_1 + \gamma\ log\ (W_1/PK_1) + \delta_1$$

The difference between both observations being:

$$\Delta\ log\ E = \alpha\ \Delta\ log\ Y + (B_1 - B_0)\ \text{with}\ B_0 = \gamma\ log\ (W_0/PK_0) + \delta_0\ \text{and}$$
$$B_1 = \gamma\ log\ (W_1/PK_1) + \delta_1$$

Given that the relative price W_1/PK_1 was defined for the entire convertibility period with a jump from the beginning of the period, let us suppose that $B_1 - B_0$ follows a gradual adjustment with a constant path throughout the period:

$$d(B_1 - B_0) = \beta, \text{and so}\ \smallint \beta = B_1 - B_0$$

---

13. There are other important changes, such as domestic and international credit availability that favored the restructuring and capital goods imports, or changes in the labor market regulations, but the constraint of degrees of freedom calls for a simple model that is compatible with the available employment series.

The employment equation can then be formulated as:

$dlog(E)=\alpha\ dlog\ Y + \beta$ with $\alpha > 0;\ \beta < 0$

where β represents the gradual contractionary adjustment of employment to the conditions of the nineties.

The estimations on this equation are made with series for the periods 1980–1998 and 1991–1998. The equations for the first period take the form:

$dlog(NTASANPLE)=\alpha\ dlog\ Y+\beta\ DUM90S+h\ DUM97+k$ at the national aggregate level and

$dlog(TASANPLENO)=\alpha\ dlog\ Y+\beta\ DUM90S+h\ DUM97+k$ in Greater Buenos Aires.

With $DUM90S=0$ between 1980:1 and 1990:2, and $DUM90S=1$ for 1991:1 onwards. $DUM97=1$ in both semesters 1997 and $DUM97=0$ for the rest of the period. This last one is a dummy that captures the additional growth in full employment in 1997. The significance of the β coefficient in these estimations provides a test for structural change of the employment equation in the nineties.

The estimations on the series 1991–98 take the form:

$dlog(NTASANPLE)=\alpha\ dlog\ Y+\beta+h\ DUM97$ at the national aggregate level and $dlog(TASANPLENO)=\alpha\ dlog\ Y+\beta+h\ DUM97$ in Greater Buenos Aires.

The following table summarizes the estimations of the coefficients.[14]

	PERIOD 1980–98		PERIOD 1991–98	
	National Agg.	Buenos Aires	National Agg.	Buenos Aires
α	0.275	0.277	0.336	0.287
β	−0.014	−0.016	−0.018	−0.018
η	0.039	0.047	0.038	0.047

The estimations vary slightly. Let us consider period 1991–98. The α coefficient shows a significant short-run effect of around 0.3. The significance of β does not reject the hypothesis of a structural change from 1991 on and the value of β implies a contractionary trend in the full employment rate of 1.8 percent per semester, equivalent to 3.6 percent per year and 24 percent[15] in 1991–96. On the other hand, the estimator for h shows that the full employment rate in the two semesters of 1997 increased on average 3.8 percent (National Agg.) or 4.7 percent (Buenos Aires) above the rate estimated by the employment equation. Alternatively, the constant term for both 1997 semesters $(\beta+h)$ is positive and equal to 2 percent (National. Agg.) or 2.9 percent (Buenos Aires) per semester.

---

14. All of the coefficients are statistically significant at 5%. In these estimations for the complete period the constant (which is not shown in the table) is not significant.

15. This is the trend of the employment rate. To obtain the trend for the number of jobs add the growth rate of the urban population: $-dlog(E/P)=-dlog(E)+dlog(P)$. INDEC utilizes an annual 2% growth rate of the urban population.

Additional information suggests that the significance of h reflects a transitory situation that can be explained by circumstantial factors in 1997. In the first place, the (GBA, 1991–98) equation that includes the estimated β, projects full employment for the first semester of 1998 with a residual smaller than one standard error of estimation. This suggests that the 1997 effects were mainly transitory. On the other hand, the analysis of full-time employment composition shows that growth in 1997 can be explained by the increases in employment in the manufacturing industry and in the "other services" sector. In this last case, women in the health and education activities explain this rise which is probably the consequence of state subsidized employment programs that intensified in 1997, as well as the education reform. Although these programs remained at the same level, the effect on the full-time employment growth rate observed in 1997 is transitory.

The case of the manufacturing industry is more interesting. For this, we have complementary data on employment from INDEC's Industrial Survey. Information on the number of workers employed and hours worked is available. The econometric analysis of employed workers (an analogous equation to those estimated above with the industrial production replacing GDP), shows a significant negative β coefficient and a similar behavior in 1997 to that of the full employment rate in the Household Survey. The 1997 dummy is significant and positive and its absolute value is similar to the β coefficient. Yet, this does not occur in the case of hours worked, where the 1997 dummy is not significant.

This indicates that in 1997 the number of employed workers grew, while hours worked per unit of production continued to evolve on the same path as in the preceding years. In 1997 the ratio hours/workers declined significantly. This can be explained by the more intensive use of short-term contracts with a lower cost of labor (actually observed in 1997). This form of hiring seems to have replaced the personnel's overtime that the sharp increase in production required in 1997. These hiring procedures were eliminated by a labor legislative reform in 1998. In brief, the contractionary trend of the labor/production ratio, measured by the number of hours worked, shows no significant change in 1997. The change in the dynamics of the number of workers would result from the substitution (transitory) of overtime of factory personnel for workers on short-term contracts.[16]

To examine the behavior of involuntary underemployment we estimate at the national aggregate level and for GBA, an equation that relates the rate of growth of the involuntary underemployment rate with the rate of growth of the full employment rate. From the results of these estimations we can see that for one percentage point of increase (fall) in the full-time employment rate, the involuntary underemployment drops (increases) by about 1.6 percent. Part of the contraction in full-time employment is not reflected in an increase in unemployment but rather in an increment in involuntary underemployment. Conversely, when full-time employment grows, part of that increase originates in the

---

16. For a more detailed analysis, see the complete report of this paper.

reduction of the involuntary underemployment, cushioning the effect of the increase in full employment on total employment (and unemployment) rates.

The model is completed with the identities that define total employment and unemployment.[17]

5. Anatomy of the contraction in employment

Figure 2 presents the individual employment rates by gender and position in the household. A comparison with the graphs in Figure 1 shows that employment rates of both men and heads of households reproduce the dynamic of full-time employment rates (35 hours and more). The information in Figures 1 and 2 suggests a breakdown by periods to define the phases of the employment cycle. The following quantifies the variations experienced in the phases and analyzes its composition by activity sector, type of employment, gender and position in the household.

Table 1 presents the increases during the expansionary phase 1990:1–1992:2; in the contractionary years 1992:2–1996:2; in the whole period 1990:1–1996:2 and lastly, in the year 1996:2–1997:2. The decompositions by sector of the rises in each type of employment are expressed as a percentage of the change in the corresponding column. The decompositions by gender and position in the household are expressed in the rows as a percentage of the total of the cells in the column containing the aggregate by sector.

During the expansionary phase 1990:1–1992:2 total employment grew by 1.66 population percentage points (pp.). Both voluntary underemployment and full-time employment expanded the latter by more than 1 pp. while involuntary underemployment contracted counter-cyclically. Most of the expansion is explained by increased employment in commerce, followed by construction and the manufacturing sectors. It should be noted that employment of heads of household showed practically no growth during this phase.

In the contractionary phase, 1992:2–1996:2, total employment dropped by 2.43 pp. The fall in total employment is cushioned by the increase in involuntary underemployment. Full-time employment fell by 3.75 pp., and voluntary underemployment by 2 pp., while involuntary underemployment rises by 3.21 pp.

---

17. This formulation follows INDEC's convention in presenting data on the labor market. The involuntary underemployment is treated as a type of employment, aggregating data on total employment to it. However, as we can see, the variables that articulate the goods market with the labor market are both employment of 35 hours and more per week and voluntary underemployment, while involuntary underemployment has the counter-cyclical behavior that characterizes unemployment. One alternative model is to aggregate involuntary underemployment and unemployment rates and describe the dynamic of this variable based on the full-time employment rate. In this way the activity rate becomes endogenous. At the national level in the period 1991–98, the elasticity of the aggregate with respect to the full-time employment rate is –3.36. The estimation is different from 0 at the 5% significance level.

FIGURE 2: Rates of employment as proportions of GBA population (%)

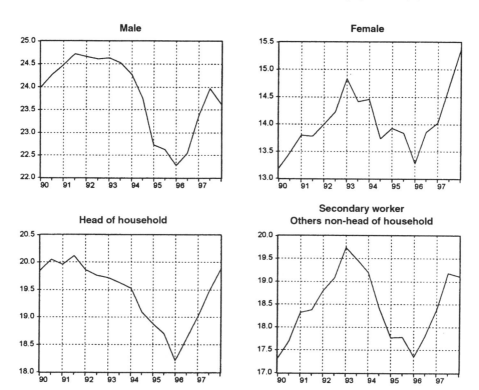

Two-thirds of the contraction in full-time employment correspond to jobs in the manufacturing sector held by males and heads of household. This is followed by contractions in commerce and construction, with the above-mentioned characteristics regarding gender and position in the household. Contractions also occur in employment in "other services," mainly for secondary workers. On the other hand, there is an increase of over 1 pp. in full-time employment in transport and communications, as well as financial services. The most significant stylized features of the fall in full employment are: two-thirds correspond to manufacturing; two-thirds are male; and, over one half are heads of household.

The reduction in voluntary underemployment is made up mostly of women and secondary workers. The contraction affects all sectors, but over one half is concentrated in "Other Services," mainly women and secondary workers.

The aggregate full-time employment and voluntary underemployment contraction totals 5.74 pp. Half of that originates in the manufacturing sector and reaches two-thirds of the contraction by adding the fall in commerce and construction. The drop in these sectors corresponds principally to males and heads of household.

TABLE 1

	INCREMENT 1990:1–1992:2				
	Total	Male	Female	Head of H.	Sec. worker
TOTAL EMPLOYMENT	1.66	37%	63%	–6%	106%
FULL EMPLOYMENT	1.08	47%	53%	–19%	119%
Manufacturing	34%	70%	30%	45%	55%
Electricity, Gas and Water	–5%	96%	4%	107%	–7%
Construction	37%	91%	9%	67%	33%
Commerce	59%	20%	80%	–8%	108%
Transport and Communications	–26%	85%	15%	122%	–22%
Financial Services	20%	40%	60%	33%	67%
Other Services	–13%	–23%	123%	143%	–43%
VOLUNTARY UNDEREMPLOYMENT	1.26	40%	60%	28%	72%
Manufacturing	23%	53%	47%	42%	58%
Electricity, Gas and Water	0%	—	—	—	—
Construction	6%	65%	35%	20%	80%
Commerce	26%	35%	65%	9%	91%
Transport and Communications	2%	110%	–10%	33%	67%
Financial Services	18%	72%	28%	35%	65%
Other Services	25%	6%	94%	41%	59%
FULL EMPLOYMENT PLUS VU	2.34	43%	57%	6%	94%
Manufacturing	28%	63%	37%	44%	56%
Electricity, Gas and Water	–2%	96%	4%	107%	–7%
Construction	20%	87%	13%	59%	41%
Commerce	41%	25%	75%	–2%	102%
Transport and Communications	–11%	82%	18%	130%	–30%
Financial Services	19%	56%	44%	34%	66%
Other Services	7%	30%	70%	–42%	142%
INVOLUNTARY UNDEREMPLOYMENT	–0.41	44%	56%	23%	77%
Manufacturing	24%	–17%	117%	–46%	146%
Electricity, Gas and Water	2%	100%	0%	0%	100%
Construction	27%	82%	18%	78%	22%
Commerce	71%	61%	39%	60%	40%
Transport and Communications	–16%	58%	42%	77%	23%
Financial Services	–33%	61%	39%	40%	60%
Other Services	24%	41%	59%	–6%	106%

TABLE 1(continued)

	INCREMENT 1992:2–1996:2				
	Total	Male	Female	Head of H.	Sec. worker
TOTAL EMPLOYMENT	−2.43	85%	15%	47%	53%
FULL EMPLOYMENT	−3.75	72%	28%	51%	49%
Manufacturing	64%	72%	28%	55%	45%
Electricity, Gas and Water	−0%	—	—	—	—
Construction	13%	94%	6%	68%	32%
Commerce	25%	72%	28%	68%	32%
Transport and Communications	−13%	98%	2%	70%	30%
Financial Services	−19%	39%	61%	61%	39%
Other Services	30%	51%	49%	34%	66%
VOLUNTARY UNDEREMPLOYMENT	−2.00	36%	64%	30%	70%
Manufacturing	15%	78%	22%	55%	45%
Electricity, Gas and Water	−0%	—	—	—	—
Construction	5%	73%	27%	28%	72%
Commerce	17%	28%	72%	18%	82%
Transport and Communications	1%	171%	−71%	46%	54%
Financial Services	10%	91%	9%	46%	54%
Other Services	54%	14%	86%	29%	71%
FULL EMPLOYMENT PLUS VU	−5.74	60%	40%	44%	56%
Manufacturing	47%	73%	27%	55%	45%
Electricity, Gas and Water	0%	—	—	—	—
Construction	10%	90%	10%	61%	39%
Commerce	22%	61%	39%	55%	45%
Transport and Communications	−8%	95%	5%	71%	29%
Financial Services	−9%	18%	82%	68%	32%
Other Services	38%	33%	67%	31%	69%
INVOLUNTARY UNDEREMPLOYMENT	3.21	41%	59%	42%	58%
Manufacturing	13%	41%	59%	29%	71%
Electricity, Gas and Water	0%	0%	100%	0%	—
Construction	14%	98%	2%	79%	21%
Commerce	17%	66%	34%	44%	56%
Transport and Communications	1%	57%	43%	18%	82%
Financial Services	6%	41%	59%	38%	62%
Other Services	50%	17%	83%	36%	64%

TABLE 1(continued)

	INCREMENT 1990:1–1996:2				
	Total	Male	Female	Head of H.	Sec. worker
TOTAL EMPLOYMENT	−0.77	188%	−88%	162%	−62%
FULL EMPLOYMENT	−2.67	82%	18%	79%	21%
Manufacturing	76%	72%	28%	57%	43%
Electricity, Gas and Water	1%	90%	10%	31%	69%
Construction	3%	106%	−6%	73%	27%
Commerce	12%	176%	−76%	218%	−118%
Transport and Communications	−8%	117%	−17%	−2%	102%
Financial Services	−34%	39%	61%	55%	45%
Other Services	48%	43%	57%	46%	54%
VOLUNTARY UNDEREMPLOYMENT	−0.74	30%	70%	35%	65%
Manufacturing	0%	—	—	—	—
Electricity, Gas and Water	−1%	100%	0%	100%	0%
Construction	3%	100%	0%	54%	46%
Commerce	0%	—	—	—	—
Transport and Communications	0%	—	—	—	—
Financial Services	−2%	−140%	240%	−91%	191%
Other Services	103%	18%	82%	23%	77%
FULL EMPLOYMENT PLUS VU	−3.40	71%	29%	70%	30%
Manufacturing	59%	76%	24%	59%	41%
Electricity, Gas and Water	1%	87%	13%	11%	89%
Construction	3%	105%	−5%	68%	32%
Commerce	9%	167%	−67%	226%	−126%
Transport and Communications	−6%	110%	−10%	−4%	104%
Financial Services	−28%	35%	65%	52%	48%
Other Services	60%	33%	67%	38%	62%
INVOLUNTARY UNDEREMPLOYMENT	2.80	40%	60%	45%	55%
Manufacturing	12%	59%	41%	51%	49%
Electricity, Gas and Water	−0%	—	—	—	—
Construction	12%	104%	−4%	79%	21%
Commerce	9%	73%	27%	25%	75%
Transport and Communications	3%	58%	42%	65%	35%
Financial Services	12%	49%	51%	39%	61%
Other Services	54%	15%	85%	38%	62%

TABLE 1(continued)

	INCREMENT 1996:2–1997:2				
	Total	Male	Female	Head of H.	Sec. worker
Total Employment	2.25	63%	37%	39%	61%
Full Employment	2.13	46%	54%	34%	66%
Manufacturing	28%	57%	4%	44%	20%
Electricity, Gas and Water	–2%	—	—	—	—
Construction	–2%	–2%	–2%	–11%	3%
Commerce	4%	–11%	16%	26%	–8%
Transport and Communications	–0%	–8%	6%	–14%	7%
Financial Services	19%	37%	3%	8%	24%
Other Services	43%	11%	71%	35%	48%
Voluntary Underemployment	0.50	73%	27%	49%	51%
Manufacturing	–19%	–7%	–52%	–11%	–27%
Electricity, Gas and Water	0%	—	—	—	—
Construction	17%	24%	0%	25%	10%
Commerce	5%	19%	–32%	29%	–17%
Transport and Communications	21%	21%	19%	7%	34%
Financial Services	9%	26%	–39%	4%	13%
Other Services	60%	14%	184%	54%	67%
Full Employment plus VU	2.64	51%	49%	37%	63%
Manufacturing	19%	40%	–2%	30%	13%
Electricity, Gas and Water	0%	—	—	—	—
Construction	2%	5%	–3%	–2%	4%
Commerce	4%	–3%	11%	27%	–9%
Transport and Communications	4%	0%	7%	–8%	11%
Financial Services	17%	34%	–2%	7%	22%
Other Services	47%	12%	83%	40%	51%
Involuntary Underemployment	–0.38	–29%	129%	43%	57%
Manufacturing	70%	–105%	31%	49%	85%
Electricity, Gas and Water	0%	—	—	—	—
Construction	–18%	71%	2%	17%	–44%
Commerce	65%	–201%	5%	92%	45%
Transport and Communications	–16%	64%	2%	–11%	–20%
Financial Services	19%	–24%	9%	–5%	37%
Other Services	–19%	295%	51%	–53%	6%

Let us complete the analysis with an examination of the rise in involuntary underemployment. Half of the observed increase is concentrated in "Other Services," most of which is women and secondary workers. The other half is distributed among the other activity sectors.

The features of the contraction in employment in the period 1990:1–1996:2 are similar to those in the contractionary phase. In brief, the conclusions of this analysis highlight the importance that the employment contraction in the manufacturing sector has had in the evolution of the global employment rate. To a lesser degree, employment in commerce and construction also fell. This reduction principally affected males and heads of household. On the other hand, employment levels in transport and communications, financial services and electricity, gas and water increase. As a result, the reduction in urban employment appears to have been mainly the consequence of the restructuring process and the concentration in the production and distribution activities in the nineties, particularly in the manufacturing (tradable) sector.

In the year 1996:2–1997:2 full-time employment shows an increase, as was already mentioned. Half of this corresponds to the "other services" sector and is represented almost entirely of women. Less than a third corresponds to the manufacturing sector.

6. Employment, productivity and trade opening in the manufacturing industry[18]

This section analyzes the mechanisms through which the conditions in the nineties affected the behavior of employment, production and productivity in the industrial sector.[19]

Let us suppose that the variation in industrial employment in the nineties was the outcome of the combined effect of three factors. First, the growth in production: greater demand induced increased production which, in turn, led to higher demand for labor. The second factor is the displacement effect of imports: the expansion in demand with the concurrent change in relative prices produced a more than proportional increase in imports. These replaced domestic production in the aggregate supply of manufactures, with a direct displacement effect with a negative sign on the rise in labor demand resulting from the increase in internal demand. The third factor is an autonomous reduction process in labor per unit of production resulting from changes in the basket of products, in technology, and in the organization of firms.

---

18. This section draws on Frenkel y González Rozada (1999).

19. Data used here were taken from INDEC's Monthly Industrial Survey compiled since 1990. The sample has national coverage and corresponds to some 1300 firms with 10 or more employees. The series beginning before 1990 puts together the previous industrial series with that beginning in 1990.

Leaving aside the above second effect, the other two can alternatively be expressed as the decomposition of the rise in productivity for a given amount of production. If the sensitivity of short-run employment to the variations in production is non-zero, the observed rise in productivity can be decomposed into two: the increment attributed to the growth in production and the rise in productivity resulting from the changes in the production structure, in technology and in the organization by firms to gain competitiveness in the new context. The first issue analyzed in this section is the individualization and estimation of the above effects.

Cyclical effects and employment and productivity trends

To isolate the effects of the cycle and the trend in employment's dynamic we estimate the following equation:[20]

$$dlog(E) = \alpha \; dlog \; Y - \beta \quad (1)$$

Where E represents employed workers and Y represents the gross value of production. α is the short-run labor-production elasticity and β is the constant in the period that represents the trend in the increase in productivity independent of the cycle.

We estimate equation (1) with quarterly data from 1991:2. The result of the estimation can be seen in the following table.

$dlog(E)=0.210 \; dlog \; Y-0.009 \qquad R^2=0.25 \qquad Sample: 1991:2–1996:2$
  $(2.23) \qquad (2.64)$

Both estimators α and β are significant at the 5 percent level. The partial labor-production elasticity is 0.21 and the estimation of β gives a quarterly rate of –0.93 percent, equivalent to an annual rate of –3.8 percent.

In the following we use the results obtained to decompose the increase in productivity (as a rate) between 1990 and 1996, one component attributed to the increase in production and the other to the autonomous component. Given that β is the estimator of the quarterly autonomous productivity increase, we calculate $BETA=(1+\beta)^{24}-1$ as an estimator of the increase rate of the autonomous productivity for the period 1990–96 as a whole (24 quarters). With this estimator we can calculate the component attributed to production growth by difference. The results are:

$$\Delta Q/Q = \Delta QC/Q + BETA$$
$$47\% = 22\% \; + 25\%$$

As can be seen, less than half of the increase in productivity for the period $\Delta Q/Q=47\%$ is attributed to the growth in production.[21]

---

20. The foundation is similar to that in Section IV. Let us suppose a gradual adjustment at a constant rate to the conditions of relative prices existing from 1991.

21. If the estimation of α obtained is used, then: $(1-\alpha)=0.79; \Delta Y/Y-22.5\%$, from where the productivity increase attributed to production growth is 18%.

We follow a similar procedure to decompose the contraction in employment between 1990 and 1996 into a negative component, determined by the decreasing trend in the labor force per unit of production, and a positive component attributed to the expansion in production:

$$\Delta E/E = \Delta EC/E - BETA$$
$$-17\% = \quad 8\% \quad - 25\%$$

The employment reduction with constant production level would have implied a contraction of 25% for the period. However, the increment in production induced by the expansion in demand had a positive effect of 8%, cushioning the fall to 17%.

The employment effects of variations in imports and exports

We now estimate the displacement effects of imports (and the expansionary effect of exports) on production and employment on industrial production for the period 1990–96. We will use the following identity:

$$\Delta Y/Y = \Delta CA/Y + \Delta X/Y - \Delta M/Y$$
$$35\% = 57.6\% + 10.2\% - 32.8\%$$

where CA is domestic consumption of manufactures, X represents exports and M imports, all valued at the 1986 constant price level.[22]

Between 1990 and 1996 the increase in domestic demand for industrial goods was 57.6% of 1990 production. The increase in exports during this period added 10.2% to total demand. In the same period, the expansion in imports of industrial goods accounted for 32.8% of 1990 production. Therefore, the increment in imports represented practically half of the increase in domestic demand. The variations in the demand components and the aggregate supply of industrial goods determine the respective effects on the rising employment trend induced by increased production:

$$\Delta EC/E = EFCA + EFX - EFM$$
$$8\% = 13.3\% + 2.3\% - 7.6\%$$

The 8% increment in industrial employment, induced by the increase in production, is the result of two effects: a positive effect of 15.6%, stemming from the rise in domestic demand and exports, and a negative one of 7.6%

---

22. Domestic apparent consumption is estimated by residuals from the data on production, exports and imports. The data used correspond to National Accounts at constant 1986 prices that differ from the data on production in the Industrial Survey. In several industrial sectors data in the National Accounts replicate those in the Industrial Survey. In others, these data are complemented with additional information, which explains the differences. In the calculations presented here we use exclusively data from the Industrial Survey for the estimations on employments and productivity. In constant, as was mentioned above, we use the data on production from the National Accounts to decompose the final demand.

owing to the a larger participation of imports in aggregate supply of manufactures. The direct displacement of employment by imports represents more than half of the expansionary effect that can be attributed to increased domestic demand. In the following equation we summarize the decomposition of all of the effects on the employment variations observed between 1990 and 1996.

$$\Delta E/E = -BETA + \alpha \Delta Y/Y = -BETA + EFCA + EFX - EFM$$
$$-17\% = -25\% + 8\% = -25\% + 13.3\% + 2.3\% - 7.6\%$$

7. Income and wages[23]

The per capita income of the working and active population and the unemployment effect

Graph 13 shows the per capita income of the employed and active population. The data are monthly, expressed in constant May 1998 pesos.[24] Income followed a cyclical pattern that was correlated with the GDP cycle. In the first expansionary phase the increase reached a maximum in the first semester of

GRAPH 13: Per capita income of employed and active population
(monthly, in constant May 1998 pesos)

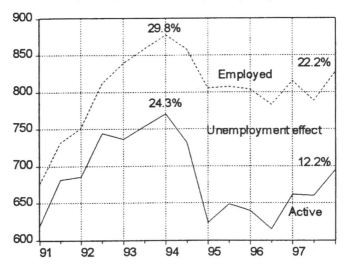

---

23. For the sake of consistency, all the calculations in the section are based on cases with income response. The employment rate calculated this way is approximately 2 pp. of the active population lower throughout the period. The variations in the employment rates are not significantly affected.

24. We have calculated employed population income from jobs and ownership of assets. This does not include social security transfers. Data are based on EPH of INDEC in Greater Buenos Aires.

1994. The later contraction hit a relative minimum in the second semester of 1996. Obviously, the contraction was deeper in the average income of the active population owing to the strong increase in unemployment. The graph registers the increases of initial per capita income at its maximum and at the end of the period. In 1998 the employed population income level is 22.2 percent greater than in 1991 and is 5.8 percent lower than its 1994 maximum. For the average income of the active population, the increment for the period as a whole is 12.2 percent and the fall with respect to the 1994 maximum is 9.8 percent.

The effect of the rise in unemployment can be estimated by expressing the income rate of the active population as a function of the rate of the per capita income of employed population and the unemployment variation. Defining: A: size of active population; D: the unemployed; YE: per capita income of the employed population; YA: per capita income of the active population. Thus, it can be seen that:

$$\Delta YA/YA \cong \Delta YE/YE - \Delta(D/A)(YE/YA) \quad (3)$$
$$12.2\% \cong 22.2\% - 8.2\%$$

The rates on the lower line correspond to variations between the ends of the period. If the unemployment rate had not grown, then the average income in the active population would have risen by 22 percent. Instead, it went up 12.2 percent. The 10 percentage point difference, can be attributed to the rise in unemployment. On the other hand, if the per capita income of the employed had remained constant, the effect of the increase in unemployment would have implied an 8.2 percent contraction in the average income of the active population. (The difference between –10 percent and –8.2 percent corresponds to crossed effects).

Men's and women's incomes show an analogous evolution with the aggregate income cycle. In the contractionary phase, employed women's income drops by 6.7 percent while that of men's falls 5.9 percent. Between 1991 and 1998 women's unemployment incremented by 9.4 pp. of the active female population and that of men's was 6.4 pp. of the active male population. For this reason, the average income of active women grew by 14.7 percent at its peak in 1994, and 8.2 percent at the end of the period compared with 1991.

However, it is important to note that the unemployment effect on per capita income of the total active population cannot be explained by the higher unemployment level of the active female population. In effect, in the period as a whole, the unemployment effect on the average income of active males is similar in size to the unemployment effect on the average income of the total active population.

Income of the employed population

Graph 14 shows the evolution of the per capita of income of employed population in three job categories: full-time wage earners, full-time non-wage earners and involuntary underemployed. Per capita income in the three categories demonstrates a cyclical pattern with a relative maximum in the first semester of 1994. The graph includes the variations with respect to the first semester in 1991, at the maximum in 1994 and at the end of the period. In 1998, the involuntary underemployed income practically matches that of 1991, having contracted by 18.9 percent with respect to the maximum. In the case of the wage earners, the increment for the period as a whole is 22.3 percent and the drop compared to the maximum is 4.9 percent. The non-wage earners showed an increase of 49.2 percent and grew 8.5 percent with respect to the 1994 income level.

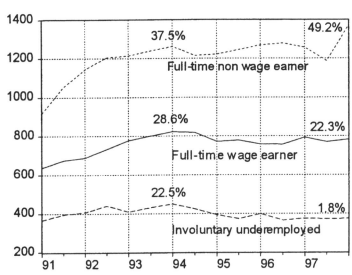

GRAPH 14: Per capita income by occupation category
(monthly, in constant May 1998 pesos)

The following table shows the decomposition of the rate of increase of the per capita income of each category between the ends of the period.

	Income Contribution	Employment Contribution	Total Contribution
Wage earners	14.9%	−4.7%	10.2%
Non-wage earners	14.5%	−3.9%	10.9%
Involuntary underemployment	0%	4.2%	4.2%
Total	29.4%	−4.4%	25.0% ≅ 22.2%

Each cell in the table can be read as the rate of variation employees' average income would have registered if only the corresponding variable had varied. For example, the drop in wage earners employment would have implied, ceteris paribus, a contraction of 4.7 percent. With the 1991 employment structure the increase in per capita income would have implied a rise of 29.4 percent. The restructuring of employment effect was negative: the contraction in the proportion of full-time wage earners and non-wage earners would have meant an 8.6 percent fall. The total effect of the change in the employment structure, then, is –4.4 percent.

We can now show the rate of increase of the per capita income of the active population as a function of the rise in per capita income plus the negative effects of employment restructuring plus the increase in unemployment:

$$\Delta YA/YA \cong Income\ effect + Employment\ restructuring\ effect + Unemployment\ effect$$
$$12.2\% \cong 29.4\% \qquad\qquad -4.4\% \qquad\qquad\qquad -10\%$$

This summary highlights the importance of quantity effects. If the proportions of full-time employment, involuntary underemployment and unemployment (as proportions of the active population) had remained the same as those in 1991, then, the per capita income of the active population would have gone up 29.5 percent. The quantity effects of the decline in full-time employment, together with the increase in unemployment and involuntary underemployment, explain over half of this rise.

Per capita income by schooling

Graph 15 shows the evolution of per capita income by schooling (primary, secondary and tertiary education, complete or incomplete in all cases). The per capita income at each of the educational levels follows a similar cycle to the average income—an initial expansionary phase followed by a stagnant or contractionary one. However, the maximums in the period were reached at different moments. The graph includes the rate of growth between April 1991 and the corresponding peak, as well as the rate of growth for the total period. Income for the employed with primary schooling hit a maximum in the second semester of 1992 with an increase for the period as a whole of 9.0 percent. There was a 15 percent contraction between this maximum and the end of the period. In the case of those with secondary schooling, the maximum income was attained in the first semester of 1993 and the total increase in the period is 10.7 percent, showing a 14.1 percent contraction with respect to the maximum. Finally, income at the higher education level peaked in the first semester of 1994 and its increase for the entire period registers 14.5 percent, representing a fall of 5.6 percent compared to the maximum. In the first semester of 1998 the higher education/secondary level income ratio is 1.8 and the higher education/primary level income ratio is 2.6. The importance of the composition effect on the increase in the average income must be stressed. The per capita income at each of the levels of schooling went up at significantly lower rates than the average income. The greatest rise corresponds to jobs at the higher education level, 14.5 percent, while the average income of workers grew by 22.2 percent for the entire period owing to the composition effect.

GRAPH 15: Per capita income by education level
(monthly, in constant May 1998 pesos)

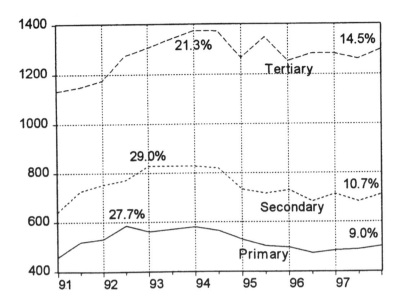

The evolution of the educational structure of the active population was mainly the reflection of the educational structure of the total population between the ages of 15 and 65, not only in the period as a whole, but also in the defined sub-periods. On the other hand, unemployment rates showed an increase in the period across all levels of schooling. In addition, all employment rates tended to fluctuate with the cycle of the aggregate employment rate. Compared with the total employment rate, the reduction is stronger during the contractionary phase and the increase in the following one is lower at the primary and secondary school levels.

Unemployment and income by schooling

We can now see the effects of the increase in unemployment on the average income of the active population at each level of education. We do so expressing the rate of variation in the average income of the active population as a function of the average income rate of the employed population and the increase in the unemployment rate at each level of schooling. The table below presents the results.

**Decomposition of the rate of income of the active population
by level of education (in % for the period 1991:1–1998:1)**

	Rate of income of active pop.	Rate of income of employed pop.	Total unemploy. effect	Partial unemploy. effect
Primary	−1.2	+9.0	−10.2	−8.7
Secondary	0.0	+10.7	−10.7	−9.7
Tertiary	+8.4	+14.5	−6.1	−5.4

The total unemployment effect is simply the difference between the average income rate of the active population and the average income rate of the employed population. The partial unemployment effect is the variation rate that the average income of the active population would have experienced had workers' income remained constant from 1991:1. Note that at all levels of schooling the average income rate of the active population is lower than the rate of increase of the average income of the total active population. This reached 12.2 percent as a result of the change in the educational structure of the active population. At the same time, the per capita income of the primary level active population fell by 1.2 percent , showed no variation in the case of the secondary level active population and gained 8.4 percent in the case of the active population with a higher education level. Among the active population with primary and secondary levels, the absolute value of the unemployment effect is greater or the same as the respective rate of increase in the income of employed population. At the higher education level, the unemployment effect reduced the effect of the increase in the average income of employed population by less than half.

Income distribution

In closing this analysis on per capita income, we would like to present the evolution of income distribution in the employed and active population. In the latter, we attribute zero income to the unemployed. Income distribution in the working population can be seen in the following table.

Income distribution in the employed population

Deciles of the employed pop.	Percentage of total accumulated income		
	1991:1	1994:1	1998:1
1	2.10	2.06	1.71
2	5.90	5.82	5.09
3	10.60	10.60	9.56
4	16.15	16.27	14.91
5	22.79	22.88	21.28
6	30.24	30.62	28.87
7	39.57	39.99	38.13
8	51.16	51.48	49.49
9	66.77	66.96	65.08
10	100.00	100.00	100.00
Gini coefficient	0.423	0.420	0.456

Between 1991 and 1994 income distribution in the employed population remained stable. Forty percent of the lower-income group in this population received 16.2 percent of total income in 1991 while 16.3 percent did so in 1994. Ten percent of the higher-income group absorbed 33.2 percent of total income in 1991, and 33.0 percent in 1994. The Gini coefficient is practically the same at both moments. Distribution showed a deterioration in the sub-period 1994–98. In 1998, 40 percent of the lower-income group reduce their share 14.9 percent and 10 percent of the higher-income group improved theirs 34.9 percent. The Gini coefficient increments to 0.456.

Distribution changes are stronger if income distribution in the active population is computed in order to consider the rise in unemployment. Distribution in the active population follows.

Income distribution in the active population

Deciles of the active pop.	Percentage of total accumulated income		
	1991:1	1994:1	1998:1
1	0.14	0.00	0.00
2	3.02	1.73	0.56
3	7.58	5.97	3.88
4	12.98	11.44	8.89
5	19.56	18.20	15.24
6	27.30	26.21	23.11
7	36.86	35.84	32.67
8	48.85	48.03	44.79
9	65.07	64.37	61.54
10	100.00	100.00	100.00
Gini coefficient	0.471	0.490	0.534

Income distribution in the active population tends to deteriorate throughout the whole period. Forty percent of the lower-income groups reduce their share from 13.0 percent in 1991 to 11.4 percent in 1994, and to 8.9 percent in 1998. Ten percent of the higher-income group raise their share from 34.9 percent in 1991 to 35.6 percent in 1994, and to 38.5 percent in 1998. The Gini coefficient rises from 0.471 in 1991 to 0.534 in 1998.

Comparing the Gini coefficients in the above tables, it can easily be seen that until 1994 the deterioration in income distribution in the active population was the result exclusively of the rise in unemployment during the first phase. Afterwards, between 1994 and 1998, the greatest deterioration took place because of the joint effect of the growth in unemployment and deeper inequality in the income distribution of employed population.

Inequality of wages by schooling

This point considers hourly wages of full-time wage earners. Graph 16 presents the hourly wage quotients at the higher and secondary education level with respect to the primary school level. The secondary/primary level ratio shows a stable trend. In contrast, the higher education/primary level ratio tends to rise (and, consequently, so does the higher education/secondary level ratio). Taking this into account, we define an inequality index (II) as the quotient between the hourly remuneration at the higher education level and that at the primary school level.

The index shows a significant positive trend (at 5 percent) of 1.56 percent per semester. The fluctuations around the trend are associated with the significant elasticity of the primary level hourly wages with respect to unemployment, as will be seen below. The index has a 2.25 value in 1991:1, 2.53 in 1994:1 and 2.57 in 1998:1. Between 1991 and 1998 there is a 14.2 percent increment.

The following table shows the factors of the rise in the inequality index between 1991 and 1998.[25]

Decomposition of the rate of increase of the inequality index between 1991 and 1998

Sector	(In % of the rate of increase index)			Rate of the index of the sector (%)	Trend of the index (%)
	Composition ef.	Inequality ef.	Total		
2	+48.0	−62.8	−14.8	−23.7	−0.50
5	+4.7	+16.6	+17.1	+39.3	0.15
6	−55.6	+22.3	−33.2	+59.3	1.53
7	+4.1	+39.4	+40.0	+7.2	0.32
8	+14.6	+77.4	+92.0	+20.3	3.41(*)
Total	−7.1	+92.9	100.0	+14.2	1.57(*)

(*) significant at 5%.

It can be seen that the inequality index in Sector 2 (Manufacturing) contracted by 23.7 percent, unlike all of the service sectors 5 to 8 (Commerce, Transport and Communication, Financial Services, Other Services) which show an increase in the index. The 14.2 percent rise in the aggregate index was the exclusive result of the increase in inequality in services. In effect, the total composition effect is negative though small. The total effect of the growth in sectoral inequality explains 92.9 percent of the rise in the aggregate index. The fall in inequality in Manufacturing was more than offset by the increase in inequality in the services. Altogether, the services sectors contribute 115 percent of the aggregate index rate. In particular, the contribution of the sector "Other services" is 92.0 percent. This is the only sector to show an increasing inequality trend (3.41 percent per semester) that is significant (at 5 percent). Given the weight of this sector, the increasing aggregate inequality index trend (1.5 percent per semester) is also significant (at 5 percent). We will present an interpretation for the rise in the increase in wage inequality further on, but first let us analyze the sensitivity of salaries to the conditions of the labor market.

---

25. The decomposition can be obtained by differentiating the inequality index.

**GRAPH 16: Hourly wages ratios by education level
Inequality index (II)**

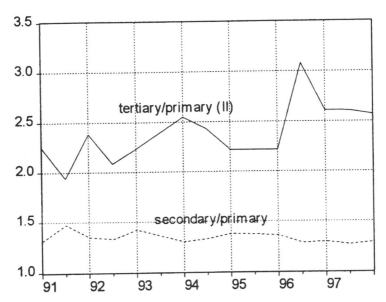

Hourly remuneration and unemployment

We can see in Graph 17 the average hourly wage of full-time wage earners and the seasonally adjusted GDP, as deviations with their respective log trends. It seems clear that the short-run dynamic of wages has been pro-cyclical. If this wage is included as variable in the full-time-employment equations in the preceding sections, the estimation shows a positive employment-wage elasticity, although it is not significant.

Both the employment and wage rates tend to fluctuate in the same direction in the short run along longer-run paths that are discussed in this and preceding sections. Wage flexibility does not appear to have cushioned the jump in unemployment. On the other hand, its negative effect on the lower wages seems to be significant, especially in the later phase after 1994. However, as a stylized fact it should be underlined that this negative redistribution effect takes second place to the increase in unemployment effect, as was demonstrated above.

This point analyzes the sensitivity of hourly remuneration to labor market conditions. The equations we estimate take the form of:

$dlog(s_i)=\varepsilon\ d(U_i)+b\ dlog(GDPD)+c$ and
$dlog(s_i)=\varepsilon\ d(U_i)+c$

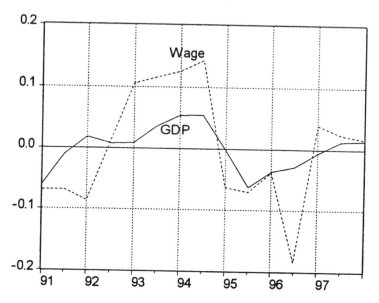

GRAPH 17: Average hourly wage of full-time workers and GDP
deviations around log-trends

where U_t is the sum of the unemployment and involuntary underemployment rates (as proportions of the active population); s_t are the real per hour remuneration of different categories of employed population and GDPD is the seasonally adjusted product. In each job category, both equations produce estimations of the elasticity ε of similar magnitude and of similar significance. The coefficients of the GDPD rate are not significant. For this reason, we present the results of the estimations with the second equation in the following table.

Hourly remuneration-unemployment elasticity

Category	Elasticity	Statistic	R^2
FULL TIME WAGE EARNER	−2.01	−2.07(**)	0.34
Primary	−2.43	−2.85(*)	0.40
Secondary	−2.26	−2.16(*)	0.28
Tertiary	−1.08	−0.63	0.07
FULL-TIME NON WAGE EARNER	−2.61	−2.68(*)	0.25
Primary	−5.15	−2.47(*)	0.29
Secondary	−3.40	−2.40(*)	0.29
Tertiary	0.71	0.43	0.02
INVOLUNTARY UNDEREMPLOYMENT	−1.16	−2.99(*)	0.26
Primary	−1.61	−2.18(*)	0.20
Secondary	1.05	0.74	0.04
Tertiary	−2.36	−2.14(*)	0.24

(*) significant at 5%. (**) significant at 10%.

The elasticity of the average wage of full-time wage earners is –2 (the wage tends to fall 2 percent for every percentage point of increase of U) and significant at 10 percent. The magnitude and significance of the elasticity of the aggregate in the category is determined by the behavior of the primary and secondary schooling levels, whose elasticity is of greater absolute value and significant at 5 percent. Instead, the elasticity of the hourly wage of wage earners at the higher education level is not significantly different from zero. It should be added that the elasticity of the wages at the primary school level in Manufacturing is negative (–1.25) but is not significant. (The wage at this level in Manufacturing is relatively more "rigid" than the average). In the case of non-wage earners, the average income per hour shows an elasticity of –2.6. The size and significance of the average in the category is determined by the elasticity at the primary and secondary levels of education, –5.2 and –3.4, respectively, while the elasticity at the higher education level is positive and is not significantly different from zero. The average hourly income for the involuntary underemployed also shows a negative and significant elasticity. This employment category presents a higher education level elasticity of –2.4 that is significant at 5 percent.

Some final considerations on the increase of inequality among full-time wage earners

The jump in inequality has been observed in a number of trade-opening experiences, as well as in the United States since the seventies. The more conventional interpretation claims that the trend in relative wages corresponds to the change in equilibrium wages in the qualified and non-qualified segments of the labor market. This, in turn, is derived from the change in the labor demand structure before a supply structure that is modified at a relatively slower pace.

The principal problem with this explanation in the experience we analyze here is the conception of wages as equilibrium prices in the labor-market segments. In our case, this vision is ostensibly inadequate. Far from constituting a change between two equilibria in the labor market, there was a strong jump in unemployment and involuntary underemployment at all levels of schooling. So, it would be incorrect to ascribe this to the differential effects of excess demand in market segments.

What is true, though, is a trend in the employment structure toward a growing proportion of more qualified levels. As we have pointed out, this change reflects mainly a modification in the educational structures of the aged 15–65 population and of the active population. However, the data also suggest indirectly that the labor-demand structure evolved in the same direction. In effect, if there had not been a change in the labor-demand structure, we would have witnessed a somewhat uniform decline in the employment rates by level of schooling. The argument is reinforced if one takes into account the fact that the more highly qualified workers receive higher wages. Consequently, there is a greater incentive to reduce this segment as a way to lowering labor costs. Therefore, given the observed changes in the educational structure of the active population, unemployment at the higher education level would have shown a larger than average increase, and this was not the case.

Some literature has emphasized that the jump in inequality found in several trade-opening experiences contradicts the predictions in the Stolper-Samuelson theorem about the effects trade opening has on countries with a relatively greater proportion of low-skilled labor. One explanation for the observed rise in inequality combines the vision of the labor-market equilibrium with two additional hypotheses. One is the bias in the labor-demand structure derived from the adoption of new technologies. The other is the assumption that the requirements for more skilled work are complementary to the equipment in which in these new technologies are incorporated. According to these hypotheses, the greater inequality appears to be associated with trade opening as it establishes incentives and pressures to raise productivity in the tradable sector of the economy, which lead to the adoption of new technologies and tend to modify relative prices in the labor-market segments.

This explanation focuses on the tradable sector of the economy and for this reason could not account for the experience we have analyzed. In this experience, the inequality in wages in the more tradable sector, the manufacturing industry (Sector 2), not only did not grow but fell. In effect, the EPH does not allow for a fine disaggregation of activities so as to be able to distinguish the tradable-goods sector with precision. Nonetheless, although Sector 2 includes activities that are clearly non-tradable (e.g., bakeries), it is indisputable that the sector does embrace the large share of tradable activity. The changes that occurred in Manufacturing do not explain the increment in the inequality index of wage earners.

Manufacturing shows a generalized decline in employment rates at all levels of schooling, although the contraction in employment at the primary education level was by far greater. Likewise, the trend in the labor-demand structure in this sector is consistent with the effects of trade opening on the tradable sector by the aforementioned hypothesis. And yet, demand at the higher education level in Manufacturing also declined.

The behavior of wages at the primary school level in Manufacturing (the relative trend and reduced flexibility in the face of unemployment) could be explained by considerations of wage efficiency of the workers who stayed on at their jobs in the context of rising productivity and the increase in the equipment/worker ratio. In general, the efficient wage argument is applied to explain the smaller relative flexibility in wages in the Manufacturing sector. Therefore, it is rather paradoxical but no surprising, that low wage flexibility is found precisely in the tradable sector during the trade opening process.

The anticipated effects of the trade (and financial) opening are not limited solely to the tradable sector. Here are found the results of new incentives and competitive pressures. In the non-tradable sector, these pressures are less important, but incentives are not. The conjunction of trade opening and the appreciation of the exchange rate reduces the relative price of equipment, as well as inducing the adoption of new technologies and organizational strategies in the non-tradable sector. The complementary assumption between skilled labor, new equipment and organizational structures may explain the change in the composition of labor demand that can be seen in services. It is in these sectors where higher education level wages rose after 1994, together with wage inequality. And these are the sectors that account for the increment in inequality across the entirety of salaried workers.

Finally, we must consider an important and specific point that imparts a nuance into the preceding discussion. Even if the above behavior of employment and higher education level salaries in the services activities are characteristic of all those sectors, the data in Sector 8 (Other Services) determine that this is the one that contributes the main sectoral effect in the higher education wage variation and in the growth in the aggregate inequality index. The greater share of higher education level employment is found in this sector and it is this sector that counts with a significantly larger proportion of higher education jobs than the other sectors. Jobs in this heterogeneous sector encompass the whole of public employment. Therefore, one should incorporate into the preceding explanations, with considerable weight, the salary policies for the city, provincial and national public sectors.

REFERENCES

Damill, M. and S. Keifman (1993) "Trade Liberalization in a High-Inflation Economy: Argentina, 1989–91," in Agosín, M. and D. Tussie (eds.), *Trade and Growth: New Dilemmas in Trade Policy,* New York: St. Martin Press.
Fanelli, J. M. and R. Frenkel (1999) "The Argentine Experience with Stabilization and Structural Reform," in Lance Taylor (ed.), *After Neoliberalism: What Next for Latin America?,* Ann Arbor: Michigan University Press.
Frenkel, R., J. M. Fanelli and C. Bonvecchi (1998) "Capital Flows and Investment Performance in Argentina," in R. Ffrench-Davis and H. Reisen (eds.), *Capital Flows and Investment Performance. Lessons from Latin America,* UN ECLAC-OECD Development Centre, Paris.
Frenkel, R. and M. González Rozada (1999) "Apertura comercial, productividad y empleo en Argentina," in Tokman, V. E. y Martínez, D. (eds.), *Productividad y empleo en la apertura económica,* Lima: OIT (Oficina Internacional del Trabajo).
Frenkel, R. and M. González Rozada (1999a) "Liberalización del balance de pagos. Efectos sobre el crecimiento, el empleo y los ingresos en Argentina," *Serie de Documentos de Economía No. 11,* Centro de Investigaciones en Economía, Universidad de Palermo–CEDES, Buenos Aires.

4

Colombia:
Structural Adjustment,
Macroeconomics and Equity

JOSÉ ANTONIO OCAMPO *and* CAMILO TOVAR*

Colombia, like most other Latin American countries, has been immersed in the 1990s in a rapid process of structural reforms. Contrary to regional patterns, however, this process has involved both a liberalization of the economy and an attempt to increase social sector spending to address the sizable equity gaps accumulated in the country. This has been part of a major political reform, the major manifestation of which was the replacement of the century-old 1886 Constitution by a new political charter in 1991. As we will see, the attempt to mix a more liberal economy with an active social policy has been no easy task. Difficulties have been reflected in rising fiscal strains. At the same time, the economy continued to grow at moderate rates up to early 1998, with two troublesome features: more instability than in the past, particularly in aggregate domestic demand growth, and a weakening of tradable sectors. International shocks, the strongly contractionary monetary policy used to manage them, and uncertainties associated with rising violence led to the strongest recession in several decades in 1998–1999.

The social reflections of these policies have been mixed. On the positive side, several indicators of living conditions and coverage of social services have improved at a faster rate than in the past. Also, though at a moderate pace and a pro-cyclical pattern, urban poverty has continued its slow, long-term decline. On the negative side, employment has been negatively affected and unemployment has experienced a recent, sharp increase. Income distribution and rural

*Executive Secretary, Economic Commission for Latin America and the Caribbean, CEPAL/ECLAC and Advisor to the Executive Secretary, respectively.

poverty have shown a mixed record. There is evidence that structural reforms have had adverse effects on urban income distribution and a significant anti-rural bias. In the countryside, however, reforms strongly hit rural rents and, thus, income distribution actually improved in a generally adverse scenario. Thus, the major gains were those experienced by the top decile of urban income distribution while the major losses were those of the top decile of the rural distribution. These distributive changes have largely netted out, generating only small variations in the overall income distribution.

This paper analyzes the link between structural adjustment, macroeconomic performance and social indicators in Colombia. The first two sections briefly overview structural reforms, the evolution of macroeconomic policy, and their outcomes. The third takes a look at the labor market. The fourth considers the evolution of social policy and major indicators of living conditions. The fifth analyzes in greater detail the evolution of poverty and income distribution. Finally, the sixth draws some conclusions.

1. Structural Reforms

The liberalization of external economic relations

The liberalization that took place in Colombia in the early 1990s is generally known in the country by the term *apertura* or opening up of the economy. This term was used by the Gaviria Administration[1] in a broad way, to include the liberalization of external economic relations and domestic markets, and the redefinition of the role of the State, including central bank independence.[2] According to this definition, it included policies to increase domestic competition, particularly among financial intermediaries, a moderate liberalization of the labor market and a more ambitious reform of the social security system. However, we will concentrate our analysis on the two basic components of structural reforms: the liberalization of external economic relations and the redefinition of the role of the State. As we will see, the term *apertura* or "liberalization" is certainly inadequate to describe the latter process.

Trade liberalization, the reform of the foreign exchange regime and the elimination of virtually all regulations on foreign direct investment are the three components of the liberalization of external relations which took place from 1990 to 1993. Trade liberalization was launched at the end of the Barco Administration, in February 1990. Both this program, as the more ambitious one put in place by the Gaviria Administration a few months later, focused on

---

1. This paper covers basically two Administrations, those of César Gaviria (August 1990–August 1994) and Ernesto Samper (August 1994–August 1998). However, some references are also made to that of Virgilio Barco, which ended in August 1990, and of Andrés Pastrana, which started in August 1998.

2. See DNP (1991), Hommes et al. (1994), and Ocampo (1999).

a rapid dismantling of quantitative import restrictions, a more gradual reduction of tariffs (over five and three years, respectively), and the substitution of tariff and non-tariff protection by a more competitive exchange rate. However, as part of a macroeconomic adjustment program (see Section 2), in August 1991 the tariff schedule due for 1994 was adopted. Thus, the elimination of import controls took place in nine months, and tariffs were reduced in 18 months from an average of 43.7 to 14.3%. In March 1992, when a virtual common Colombian-Venezuelan tariff was adopted, the average tariff was further reduced, to 11.7%. To stabilize the effects of volatile international prices, a system of variable levies was designed for agriculture. Simultaneously, from 1990 to 1992 exports subsidies were cut, from an average of 15 to 6%. Finally, the real devaluation, which was initially expected to compensate falling protection and export subsidies, did not take place. Rather, for macroeconomic reasons, real appreciation was the rule from mid-1991 to mid-1997 (Table 1).

Integration efforts accelerated in a parallel fashion. In December 1989, the Presidents of the Andean Group countries launched an initiative to negotiate a customs union in the region. By early 1992 Colombian-Venezuelan trade had been fully liberalized. With a lag, a similar process took place with other Andean countries, with the exception of Peru. A virtual common Colombian-Venezuelan tariff was designed in March 1992; this was the basis for the Andean common tariff, which was adopted (with some exception) in December 1994. A free trade treaty was signed with Chile in 1993, and the Group of Three Treaty (Colombia-Mexico-Venezuela), which will generate a free trade zone with Mexico after a transition of ten years, was signed in 1994. In more recent years, integration negotiations have concentrated on the strengthening of the Andean Community, including the (still incomplete) incorporation of Peru into that scheme, and in the trade negotiations between the Andean Community and Mercosur.

The liberalization of foreign exchange controls was more limited in scope. The major innovation introduced in 1991 was decentralization of foreign exchange transactions: financial intermediaries were allowed to manage such transactions without prior controls by the central bank (*Banco de la República*). However, most transactions continued to be highly regulated, including the obligation to channel them through intermediaries legally allowed to operate in the market. Strong regulations on the final use of external lending and some sectoral discrimination were also maintained. An important innovation was introduced in February 1992, which allowed firms, for the first time, to contract credits abroad for working capital.

An additional liberalization of foreign exchange controls was adopted in September 1993. Domestic financial intermediaries were then allowed to lend to foreigners in international currencies and to invest abroad in liquid assets. More importantly, the traditional system of regulation of capital flows based on their *final use* was replaced by a price-based system based on their *maturity*. Debts of less than certain maturity were forced to keep a deposit or reserve requirement in the central bank or to pay its opportunity costs to the bank. In

TABLE 1: Policy and Policy Induced Variables

	1975 - 79	1980 - 85	1986 - 90	1991-98
REAL EXCHANGE RATE (1994 = 100)	81.0	73.0	103.0	102.5
REAL INTEREST RATE				
DEPOSIT RATE (90 DAYS)		10.3	6.4	5.9
AVERAGE LENDING RATE			14.1	14.4
GROWTH OF REAL DOMESTIC SUPPLY				
M1	4.1	0.2	2.7	0.3
M3		10.3	4.0	63.7
GROWTH OF REAL DOMESTIC CREDIT		11.7	7.7	7.8
TOTAL GOVERMENT EXPENDITURE (% OF GDP)				
DANE (ACCRUALS)	20.3	28.1	30.1	
BANCO DE LA REPUBLICA (CASH PAYMENTS NET OF TRANSFERS)				
MINISTRY OF FINANCE				
OVERALL FISCAL SURPLUS OR DEFICIT, NET OF PRIVATIZATIONS (% of GDP)	-1.5	-5.3	-1.5	-1.1
CENTRAL GOVERMENT	-0.2	-3.3	-0.9	-2.0
REST OF PUBLIC SECTOR	-1.3	-2.0	-0.6	0.9
PRIVATIZATIONS				
GDP GROWTH	5.0	2.6	4.6	3.6
VALUE ADDED TRADABLES	4.9	1.8	5.7	1.7
VALUE ADDED NON TRADABLES	5.1	3.2	3.7	4.3
AGGREGATE DOMESTIC DEMAND GROWTH	4.8	2.4	3.4	5.7
URBAN EMPLOYMENT (% OF WORKING AGE POPULATION)	45.8	48.2	50.9	53.8
URBAN UNEMPLOYMENT (% OF LABOR FORCE)	9.4	11.1	11.4	10.7
INFLATION (CPI END YEAR)	23.9	26.7	26.3	21.6
EXPORTS (% OF GDP AT 1975 PRICES)	15.0	14.4	18.5	25.1
EXTERNAL ACCCOUNT BALANCES				
(% OF GDP AT 1994 PARITY EXCHANGE RATE)				
TRADE ACCOUNT	3.5	-3.1	3.9	-1.2
CURRENT ACCOUNT	1.5	-6.8	0.3	-3.3
FOREIGN DIRECT INVESTMENT (% OF GDP AT 1994 PARITY EXCHANGE RATE)	0.3	1.7	1.1	2.5
EXTERNAL DEBT (% OF EXPORTS OF GOODS AND SERVICES)	155.0	235.0	250.4	202.1
GROSS FIXED CAPITAL FORMATION (% OF GDP AT 1975 PRICES)	15.6	17.1	15.5	18.2

Sources: Banco de la República, DANE (National Statistical Department), DNP (National Planning Department) and Ministry of Finance

May 1997, the maturity-based system was replaced with a flat forced deposit on all capital inflows.[3] Both systems have been actively used to either discourage or encourage capital inflows, as well as to maintain a good debt profile.[4] These restrictions have been combined with specific rules on import payments and export prefinancing, controls on net foreign exchange assets of financial

---

3. Explicit taxes on capital inflows were decreed by the government in January 1997 but were ruled unconstitutional by the Constitutional Court in March, due to the procedure used to decree them.

4. For a history of capital controls in recent years and estimation of their effects, see Cárdenas and Barrera (1997) and Ocampo and Tovar (1997 and 1999). Both agree that they have improved the debt profile but disagree on their effect on the magnitude of capital flows.

TABLE 1 (continued)

1990	1991	1992	1993	1994	1995	1996	1997	1998
114.8	113.0	106.7	107.5	100.0	102.1	98.9	93.3	98.5
4.9	4.8	-0.5	2.5	5.4	9.5	8.6	4.7	11.6
12.6	12.8	8.1	10.9	14.3	18.1	17.6	13.3	19.4
-15.4	-1.2	9.9	8.5	6.7	-11.2	-1.7	5.1	-19.1
1.1	-2.0	11.3	13.3	15.2	10.9	0.7	6.9	2.0
8.0	-6.9	11.0	24.4	17.6	14.7	2.0	8.1	-4.2
30.1	29.7	30.7	32.0	34.3	35.4			
30.4	31.8	31.0	31.3	31.4	34.0			
				30.3	32.0	35.8	37.2	36.0
-0.5	0.0	-0.1	0.1	0.1	-0.4	-1.9	-3.1	-3.3
-0.7	0.4	0.2	-0.3	-1.4	-2.4	-3.7	-4.0	-4.5
0.2	-0.4	-0.3	0.4	1.5	2.0	1.8	0.9	1.2
				2.6	0.3	0.9	3.6	0.5
4.3	2.0	4.0	5.4	5.8	5.8	2.0	2.8	0.6
5.1	2.2	0.8	2.1	1.3	4.7	-0.4	1.3	1.5
3.2	2.0	5.4	5.3	7.8	6.2	4.3	3.4	0.1
2.3	0.1	10.0	12.1	12.0	4.8	1.9	4.5	0.0
52.2	53.5	54.6	55.0	54.6	54.6	52.9	52.6	52.6
10.5	10.2	10.2	8.6	8.9	8.8	11.2	12.4	15.3
32.4	26.8	25.1	22.6	22.6	19.5	21.6	17.7	16.7
20.7	22.7	23.1	23.3	22.0	23.8	27.6	28.5	30.1
4.3	6.2	2.3	-2.8	-3.3	-3.3	-2.9	-3.1	-2.8
1.2	4.9	1.7	-3.7	-5.2	-5.6	-5.6	-6.6	-5.8
1.0	0.9	1.3	1.2	2.1	1.2	3.6	6.2	3.2
207.8	190.6	188.4	194.8	192.1	192.3	211.8	211.6	235.0
14.0	12.9	13.9	18.0	20.7	21.7	20.6	20.8	17.3

intermediaries and complementary regulations of foreign investment funds and service transactions.

Finally, foreign direct investment was also liberalized in 1990 and 1991. This process had started in 1987, when the autonomy to manage it—restricted up to then by Decision 24 of 1970 of the Andean Group—was given back to Andean countries. Based on this autonomy, the Barco Administration eliminated most sectoral restrictions on FDI and increased the caps to profit remittances. In 1990 and 1991, FDI was freed from all sectoral restrictions, except national defense and toxic waste disposal. All capital and profit remittance caps were abolished. Prior authorizations were also eliminated, except for investment funds, financial intermediation and public utilities. In 1991, the

Andean Group granted all foreign firms access to intra-regional free trade rules. Investment abroad by Colombian firms was simultaneously freed.

Growth and reform of the public sector

The political reform implemented in Colombia in parallel to the above more traditional structural reforms generated significant effects on the size and the structure of the State. This particular mix of economic liberalization and increasing public sector expenditure is certainly peculiar in the Latin American context and, as we pointed out, largely reflects an attempt to complement liberalization with a more active social policy. Trends in the structure of the State have followed a more normal pattern.

Consolidated public sector expenditures, net of intragovernmental transfers, increased from 30% of GDP in 1990 to 36–38% in recent years (Table 1).[5] The most important decisions that led to this expansion were those adopted by the 1991 Constitutional Assembly to significantly increase transfers to departments and municipalities to finance social spending, to extend the coverage of the social security system and to reform the judicial system. It has been estimated that the expenditure dynamics decreed by the 1991 Constitution and the Laws that implemented it had permanent costs equivalent to over 4% of GDP.[6] On the less structural side, both the Gaviria and the Samper Administrations increased expenditures in specific areas (defense and justice, in the first case; social spending and infrastructure, in the second).

The expansion has, nonetheless, been accompanied by a parallel increase in public sector revenues, particularly central government taxes and social security contributions. For this purpose, five tax reforms have been adopted throughout the decade (in 1990, 1992, 1995, 1997 and 1998). As a result of them, the basic VAT rate increased from 10 to 16% (it is expected to decrease to 15% in November 1999), its coverage was significantly expanded, the maximum income tax rate increased from 30 to 35%, and several new mechanisms were introduced to improve controls. Simultaneously, basic social security contributions were raised from 13.5% of the wage bill in 1990 to 25.5% in 1996.[7] Given higher revenues, increased expenditures were consistent with balanced overall public sector finances up to 1995. In recent years, the signs of fiscal deterioration have become evident, particularly in central government finances. However, due to the net surpluses in the rest of the public sector, the peak consolidated public

---

5. For a detailed analysis of trends in public sector finances in recent years, see Comisión de Racionalización del Gasto y de las Finanzas Públicas (1997), Hernández and Gómez (1998), Ocampo (1997) and Sánchez et al. (1995) See also Cordi (1998) for estimates of the size of the public sector.

6. See Ocampo (1997).

7. These rates include contributions for pensions, health and professional risks, paid by the employer as well as the employee.

sector deficit—between 3% and 4% of GDP in 1997–1999—remained significantly below the imbalances of the early 1980s, which exceeded 7% of GDP in
1982 and 1983.

The growth of the State has been accompanied since the early 1990s by
significant changes in its structure, which include, in particular, central bank
independence, decentralization and access of the private sector to areas traditionally reserved to the State. Central bank independence in monetary and foreign exchange management was decreed in the 1991 Constitution. As was
indicated, there has been a decentralization in social spending, matched by
rapid growth of transfers from the national to the regional and local governments, from less than 30% of central government tax revenues in 1990 to 40%
in 1998. This is expected to further increase in the next few years. The decentralization model that has evolved over this process is a hybrid between the prin-
cipal/agent and the local choice models. This hybrid model has been difficult
to manage, as it has turned out to be hard to define the precise responsibilities
of different levels of government and to coordinate financing sources.

Privatization and the opening up of traditional areas of State action to the
private sector has covered mining, financial services, social security and infrastructure. Manufacturing has played a secondary role, as the State was never a
major investor in this sector in Colombia. Nonetheless, the presence of state
investments and firms in all these areas continued to be important. Several
mechanisms of association with or concessions to private investors in infrastructure have also been designed. In 1994, the old public utilities tariff commission was substituted by three regulating Commissions—for Energy and Gas,
Telecommunications, and Water and Sanitation. The implicit model that has
evolved is thus a mixed one, in which private and (national and municipal)
public sector firms were expected to coexist, in competition, in those sectors
where that was possible, or under several forms of association.

2. Macroeconomic Policy and Performance

Policy

Macroeconomic policy was subject to sharp stop-go cycles during the period.
Because of rising inflation, a harsh stabilization package was adopted in December 1990/January 1991, which included drastic monetary contraction, revaluation, the acceleration of the trade liberalization program and a moderate fiscal
restraint (Table 1). However, the massive open market operations of the central
bank, which characterized this policy, were subject to significant criticism. Thus,
beginning in September 1991, the newly independent central bank accelerated
exchange rate appreciation, but made a U-turn in monetary policy. Since late
1991, it focused on reducing domestic interest rates to slow down the accumulation of international reserves associated with interest arbitrage operations and
to reduce the quasi-fiscal costs of open market operations. As a result of the

policy shift, all monetary and credit aggregates boomed. Simultaneously, the rapid increase in government revenues, enhanced by the 1992 tax reform, was translated into one of the most rapid expansions of public sector expenditure in Colombian economic history. Overall fiscal balances remained, nonetheless, under control. The 1991 "stop" was, thus, followed, by a striking "go" in 1992 and 1993.

By late 1993, the central bank became increasingly concerned with the rapid increase in aggregate demand. This set the stage for a return to a more restrictive monetary stance in 1994. As fiscal policy continued to be expansionary, the combined actions of the central bank and the government meant that the economy effectively moved into an expansionary fiscal-contractionary monetary policy mix. The initial preoccupation of the central bank in moving into a more restrictive policy was how to regain monetary control under the conditions of a more open economy. This led to the decision, in January 1994, to establish a foreign exchange rate band. Flexibility within the band was seen as essential to regaining monetary control.[8] Aside from this flexibility, the new exchange rate system had two major features: it was dirty floating, as the central bank intervened in the market within the band, and it *preannounced exchange rate policy* for the first time in contemporary Colombian economic history. A new wave of appreciation followed, accompanied by rising interest rates and a reduction in the rate of growth of monetary and credit aggregates— though at a very slow pace. The explicit 7% revaluation of the exchange-rate band in December 1994 was largely a ratification of the revaluation that had been experienced throughout the year. Price-based capital controls were strengthened in August 1994; a more moderate move in that direction in March 1994 had been clearly insufficient to stop the private debt boom, which had followed the partial liberalization of the capital account in September 1993 (see Section 1). [9]

A rapid increase in interest rates during the second semester of 1994 led to heated macroeconomic debates in 1995–1996, a reflection of significant differences between the Government and the central bank on how restrictive monetary policy should be to guarantee the reduction in aggregate demand growth and inflation, objectives which both clearly shared.[10] Negotiations between the Administration and *Banco de la República* led in mid-1995 to a more balanced fiscal-monetary policy mix: interest rates were subject to temporary controls in June–August 1995, some reserve requirements were reduced and fiscal policy was marginally tightened. However, the renewed rapid increase of interest rates in late 1995 led to a new wave of controversies in the early part of 1996.

---

8. See Urrutia (1995).

9. A basic reason for that was the acceleration of inflows due to expectations by private agents that controls would be strengthened. See Banco de la República (1995).

10. The government views of the fiscal-monetary policy mix were summarized in mid-1996 in Ministerio de Hacienda y Crédito Público (1996).

The controversies were further complicated by discussions on the effects of the domestic political crisis on economic activity. New agreements between the government and the central bank led, in February and March of 1996, to some liberalization of foreign borrowing. These measures were accompanied by a move to a more expansionary monetary stance, which allowed interest rates to fall starting in the second quarter of 1996. Reserve requirements were generally reduced to facilitate this process.

However, the reduction of interest rates was not rapid enough to avoid both a building up of capital inflows during the second semester of 1996, a new revaluation wave and an important slowdown of economic activity. Stronger capital controls were adopted during the first semester of 1997 to induce exchange-rate depreciation. The accumulated reduction in interest rates and the policy-induced exchange-rate depreciation, in the context of a moderate fiscal restraint, facilitated a recovery of economic activity through 1997.

However, this recovery was short-lived. During 1998, macroeconomic developments were dominated by exchange rate speculation, associated particularly to international shocks in the capital and commodity (particularly oil) markets. The run on reserves was particularly severe in January–February, May–June, and August, largely coinciding with similar processes in regional or emerging markets worldwide. To defend the exchange rate band's ceiling, the central bank used domestic interest rates as the adjustment variable, with particular severity during the second run. Domestic interest rates increased dramatically, particularly in May–June, rapidly exceeding in real terms even the previous records in late 1995 and early 1996. The normalization of emerging markets, a 9% devaluation of the exchange rate band in September, and the reduction of reserve requirements and central bank interest rates decreed since late 1998, facilitated a strong reduction in interest rates since then. However, by mid-1999, economic conditions remained complex: the economy faced a credit crunch and a strong recession, and rising violence was generating considerable uncertainties. To avoid increasing interest rates in the face of a new speculative attack, the exchange rate band was devalued again and widened in June 1999. Soon thereafter, the government announced that it would negotiate an IMF loan for the first time since the late 1960s.

Macroeconomic performance

Effects of the 1991 stabilization package were reflected in a slowdown in GDP growth, to 2%, and a stagnation in domestic demand. The expansionary monetary and fiscal policies that followed led to a spectacular boom in aggregate domestic demand, which increased in real terms by 10.0% in 1992 and 12.1% in 1993. As Figure 1 indicates, the major source was a large boom in private demand, which replaced the external sources of demand expansion that had

FIGURE 1: Aggregate Demand Sources of Growth, 1985–1998

A. Domestic Demand vs. GDP

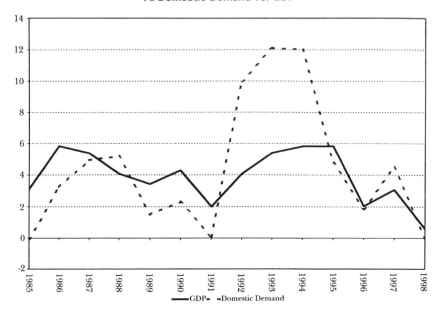

B. Aggregate Demand Growth Decomposition

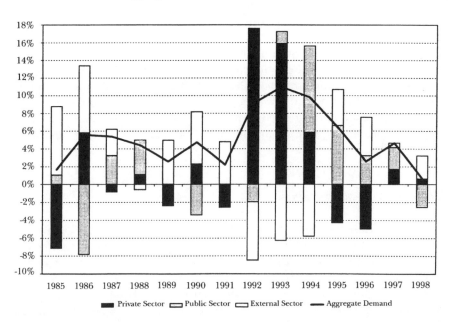

Source: DANE

predominated during the 1980s.[11] Economic growth picked up, reaching 5.4% in the latter year. The new policy mix, which characterized 1994 and 1995, led to a substitution of the private by a strong public sector demand stimulus. GDP growth accelerated, to 5.8% in 1994 and 1995. The recovery of economic growth in 1992-1995 was strongly dependent on non-tradables (Table 1). Many tradable sectors, particularly agriculture and some light manufactures experienced, indeed, deep crises during the period (see below).

The difference between the growth of aggregate domestic demand and GDP indicates that, in the very open trade regime in place since 1990, increased domestic demand was transmitted largely into an import boom. Simultaneously, as a result of a strong exchange rate appreciation, and despite the positive effects of integration agreements on interregional sales, the export boom, which had started in the mid-1980s, came to an end in mid-1991. Both factors induced a negative contribution of the external sector to aggregate demand and a sharp deterioration in the current account of the balance of payments. The deficit was basically financed by long-term capital flows, particularly by growing foreign direct investment. On the other hand, the 1991 stabilization package had been successful in breaking the rise in inflation. However, since 1992, the continuation, at a slower pace, of the downward trend in inflation, in the midst of a very rapid growth of domestic demand and monetary aggregates, was clearly associated with real exchange rate appreciation and the absorption of the demand boom by a deterioration of the current account of the balance of payments. A tripartite social pact (incomes policy), signed in December 1994, also facilitated this process in 1995.

The evolution of savings and investment also experienced an abrupt turn associated with the demand boom. After reaching, relative to GDP, a three-decade minimum in 1991 the real investment rate increased sharply, reaching by 1995 a three-decade peak (Table 1). This cycle was sharper for private investment, and particularly for real rather than nominal investment, indicating strong fluctuations in the relative price of capital goods. Indeed, the nominal private investment rate was *not* particularly high in 1995 and not very different from those reached in the late 1970s. This indicates that the high real private investment ratio was basically a reflection of the reduction in the relative price of capital goods or, what is equivalent, of a massive transfer of resources towards private capital accumulation associated with the real appreciation of the peso and lower import tariffs. The increase in private investment coincided with a collapse of private savings. As a result, whereas the private sector ran consistent surpluses since the mid-1970s, peaking at 4% of GDP in 1991, these surpluses fell dramatically in 1994, generating a record

---

11. Figure 1 follows Taylor (1998). Changes in demand associated to private investment and variations in the savings rate are included in the private sector. Those due to public sector consumption and investment, as well as those due to variations in the tax rate, are included in the public sector. Finally, the external sector includes the effects of export growth and variations in the propensity to import.

deficit of over 6% of GDP. There is no comparable deterioration of the private sector balance in Colombian economic history. The deterioration of private balances was, thus, the major domestic counterpart of the deterioration of the balance of payments.[12]

High interest rates were finally reflected in economic activity in 1996. GDP grew modestly, 2.0%, reflecting a demand pattern which was established in 1995: a contraction in private demand, a positive but weakening fiscal stimulus and a return of export growth, led by the boom in oil and mining. Despite slow domestic demand growth, inflation rose, reflecting supply shocks from indexed services (education and public utilities). Nonetheless, the rapid growth of domestic demand, which had characterized the 1992–1994 boom, was finally brought under control. This was reflected in an improvement of the trade balance for the first time since 1992.

The moderate easing of monetary policy through 1996 set the stage for economic recovery, which took place beginning in the second quarter of 1997. By the last quarter of that year and the first quarter of 1998, it was in full swing, with annual rates of growth exceeding 5%. On the demand side, the expansionary effects of fiscal policy declined considerably and were substituted by a recovery of private demand. However, recovery was brief. The contractionary monetary policy adopted to face the speculative attacks on the peso, combined with an austere fiscal policy, oriented to correct the structural fiscal imbalance, manifested into an outright recession during the second semester. Annual GDP growth slowed down to 0.6% in 1998; a negative figure is expected for 1999. The slowdown coincided with historically high investment rates up to 1997 (20.7% of GDP in 1996–1997), but a strong contraction ensued since 1998. From the perspective of a strong inertia, the reduction in inflation is also a relative success, particularly as the historical "floor" of domestic inflation over the past quarter century (20%) was broken in 1997 and one digit inflation levels have been the rule through most of 1999.

Overall, economic growth has maintained a moderate long-term path. GDP growth fell from 4.0% in 1985–1991 to 3.6% in 1991–1998, but the latter figure does not include the full effects of the 1998–1999 recession. The expectation that structural reforms would, by themselves, generate faster economic growth has thus been frustrated so far. Labor productivity growth has been dynamic, though at the cost of rising unemployment (see below), and has been compensated by rising capital-intensity in the economy as a whole, at least partly a result of relative price incentives generated by the structural reforms. Thus, the major objective of liberalization policies, the growth of total factor productivity, experienced a slowdown in the 1990s with respect to the patterns typical before the debt crisis: 1.2% vs. 2.4% in 1950–1980, according to ECLAC estimates. Moreover, economic and, particularly, aggregate demand growth has been more unstable than in the past, reflecting the sharp stop-go cycles in monetary policy. Thus, the standard deviation of GDP growth increased from 1.3 in 1985–1991

---

12. See Ocampo and Tovar (1997).

to 2.0 in 1991–1998. Greater volatility is largely explained by the pattern followed by aggregate demand: the standard deviation of its growth rate increased from 2.1 to 5.1 between these two periods. Central bank independence has been reflected, paradoxically, in a more pro-cyclical monetary management than was typical in Colombia in the past. As we have seen, the increase in public sector expenditure also fueled the demand boom up to 1995 and the slowdown of demand growth in recent years.

As we have seen, the joint effects of real exchange rate appreciation and trade liberalization was a sharp deterioration of the current account of the balance of payments, which has been difficult to reverse in recent years. As Table 1 indicates, although the trend of the trade account was moderately positive in 1996–1998, increasing interest payments and, particularly, profit remittances, were reflected in a further deterioration of the current account. On the domestic side, this reflected the inability to reverse the adverse trends in domestic savings. On the external side, this took place despite a renewed upward trend in the ratio of exports to GDP and, particularly, regardless of the dynamism of real oil exports. Thus, the lack of a clear positive trend in the trade balance was associated both with the evolution in key commodity prices— particularly oil—and with the evolution of the real exchange rate. Rising oil prices and domestic recession will generate, however, a significant improvement of external balances in 1999.

Heated domestic debates surround the analysis of the determinants of the real appreciation. The dominant view by the central bank and most academic observers was that overvaluation largely reflected fiscal pressures. Some authors also emphasized the effects of the rapid growth of private spending in the early part of the decade.[13] Alternative views underscore the effects of capital inflows and the fact that, in the context of strong indexation, the nominal exchange rate has real effects of a permanent or (at least) prolonged character.[14] Although, as we have seen, up until the Russian crisis, the central bank board was sympathetic to price-based capital account regulations, it manifested a revaluation bias when fixing the nominal exchange rate.[15]

It should be emphasized that, despite the high current account deficits, the magnitude and structure of external financing remained quite favorable. In particular, foreign direct investment became the major source of financing,

---

13. See the papers collected in Montenegro (1997) and Carrasquilla (1999).

14. Ocampo and Gómez (1997). However, the strongest criticism to the orthodox idea, according to which revaluation was associated to fiscal conditions came from the most influential entrepreneurial analyst, Javier Fernández. See *Prospectiva Económica y Financiera*, several issues.

15. This preference was "revealed" in two ways. First, two explicit decisions were adopted by the bank which resulted in nominal appreciation (the change in the system of exchange rate certificates in October 1990 and the revaluation of the exchange rate band in December 1994), despite strong pressures on the ceiling of the band on several occasions since 1995. Second, the exchange rate bands were always fixed on the basis of *expected* inflation; since the inflation targets were not met prior to 1997, this generated a real appreciation, as there was no ex-post corrections in the band to adjust for this fact.

increasing from less than 1% of GDP in the early part of the decade, to an average of 4.3% of GDP in 1996–1998. Growth was faster in non-oil activities, particularly in service sectors that were subject to restrictions prior to 1990. Thus, external accounts have been consistent with external debt ratios below those typical in the 1980s and an excellent debt profile.

Structural changes

During the second half of the 1980s growth and diversification of Colombian exports had emerged as the most notorious characteristic of the renewed dynamism of the economy. The export ratio (exports as percentage of GDP) increased from 15.6% in 1985 to 22.7% in 1991. This dynamic performance took place in a policy environment characterized by non-neutral high protection and export subsidies, combined with an active devaluation policy. Throughout this period, exports diversified rapidly: coffee fell from half to a fifth of exports of goods, as the share of non-traditional exports increased from less than a third to half of total exports; minerals, mainly oil and coal, also increased their export share.[16]

Despite the boom of intrarregional exports, the real appreciation of the exchange rate led to a slowdown of export growth and a stagnation of export diversification after 1991. Non-traditional exports experienced a strong slowdown, particularly light manufactures and agricultural goods, whereas the better performance of more sophisticated manufactures was facilitated by the growth of regional markets, to which they are mainly exported. Also, revaluation led to an import boom, mainly of consumer and capital goods.

At a more global level, the policy environment of the 1990s resulted in a strong bias against tradable sectors, mainly manufacturing and agriculture, while benefiting non-tradable activities (Table 2). On the tradable side, agricultural production experienced a sharp slowdown since the early 1990s, strongly affecting coffee, among exportables, and cereals, cotton and oilseeds, among importable crops. Some exportables (bananas, flowers, palm oil and sugar) and non-tradable agricultural and pecuary production expanded, but this was insufficient to counteract the contraction of the affected crops. As we will see below, the agricultural crisis generated significant distributive effects, and generated the strongest lobby against trade liberalization. This led to the return to selective protection and a more active agricultural policies since 1993, which were, nonetheless, unable to reverse the slow growth and structural changes in agricultural production.[17]

With respect to manufacturing, labor-intensive activities, especially those with a high export coefficient (apparel and leather, in particular) were hurt in the early 1990s by exchange rate appreciation, as were capital-intensive sectors

---

16. Ocampo (1999).
17. Balcázar et al. (1998), Jaramillo (1998), and Ocampo and Perry (1995).

TABLE 2: Sectoral Composition of GDP and Employment

Economic Sector	GDP				Employment		
	1985	1991	1995	1998	1991	1995	1997
Agriculture	21.9%	21.8%	19.3%	18.3%	26.7%	22.2%	22.9%
Mining	2.3%	4.6%	4.3%	5.0%	1.2%	0.8%	0.7%
Manufacturing	21.2%	21.4%	19.0%	17.8%	15.0%	15.7%	13.2%
Electricity, water and gas	1.0%	1.1%	1.1%	1.1%	0.6%	0.5%	0.9%
Construction	4.4%	3.0%	3.7%	3.0%	4.5%	6.1%	5.3%
Commerce	12.1%	11.5%	11.9%	11.6%	20.7%	21.7%	21.9%
Transport	9.4%	8.6%	8.7%	9.4%	5.0%	5.5%	5.5%
Financial Services	14.2%	14.6%	16.3%	16.2%	3.6%	4.6%	5.0%
Other services	13.2%	13.2%	12.9%	14.1%	22.6%	22.8%	24.7%
TOTAL	100.0%	100.0%	100.0%	100.0%	100.0%	100.0%	100.0%
Tradables	45.4%	47.8%	42.6%	41.1%	43.0%	38.7%	36.8%
Urban					14.2%	14.1%	12.5%
Rural					28.8%	24.7%	24.3%
Non-tradables	54.3%	52.0%	54.7%	55.4%	57.0%	61.3%	63.2%
Urban					43.9%	47.0%	49.4%
Rural					13.1%	14.3%	13.8%

Source: National Household Surveys and National Accounts

which faced strong import competition (e.g., paper and rubber). However, rapid domestic demand growth benefited the production of construction materials and transport equipment, though the latter was also subject to selective protection. Some sectors continued the persistent boom experienced since the mid-1980s (chemicals) and benefitted from the boom in intra-regional trade. Demand contraction in 1996 and 1998–1999 strongly affected most manufacturing activities.[18] Although the contractionary effects of trade liberalization were stronger in manufacturing than its expansionary effects, the perception that liberalization had adverse effects on manufacturing development was not as forceful as that of agriculture. The industrial lobby against trade liberalization was, thus, weak and fragmented. A major reason for this result was the massive transfer of resources towards fixed capital investment which took place over the period (see above), which largely benefited manufacturing firms. Mining performance has been the exception to slowdown on the tradable side. Due to the major oil discoveries of the late 1980s and early 1990s, and to a parallel boom of coal and gas production, this sector has experienced rapid growth over the decade.

The slow growth of agriculture and manufacturing in the post-liberalization period was initially compensated by a boom in construction and services. Among the latter, those which grew fastest were financial, government and telecommunication services. Reliance of growth in the post-liberalization period on non-tradable sectors indicates that demand expansion was the major driver of growth in the first half of the 1990s. Up to 1995, this factor prevailed over the contractionary demand effects of trade liberalization. The competition-productivity-growth link used to defend liberalization played no role in the process. As we have seen, the

---

18. For a detailed analysis of manufacturing during liberalization, see Garay *et al.* (1998).

demand engine was exhausted by the rapid turnaround of the balance of payments, leading to contractionary policies and a GDP slowdown, which has hit non-tradable activities since 1996, with particular severity in the case of construction activities.

Overall, structural changes in the 1990s indicate, contrary to simplistic analyses of the link between trade policy and export dynamics, that the real exchange rate has certainly been more important than the "bias" or the "neutrality" of the trade regime as a determinant of Colombian exports. Also, contrary to the links emphasized in the literature, the elimination of the "bias against agriculture" implicit in the protectionist trade regime which prevailed up to 1989, was accompanied by a slowdown of agricultural growth. Finally, dependence on non-tradable sectors has also made GDP growth more dependent on demand management, which has at the same time become more pro-cyclical than in the past. Thus, the new policy mix has determined a structure of economic growth that is more volatile and more sectorally disperse than in the past.

3. The Labor Market

Global trends

As Figure 2 indicates, the 1980s were a time of very rapid growth in labor force participation, largely as a result of the rapid incorporation of women into the labor force. However, the first half of the decade was characterized by slow

FIGURE 2: Labor Market Indicators, National and Major Urban Areas

A. Unemployment Rates

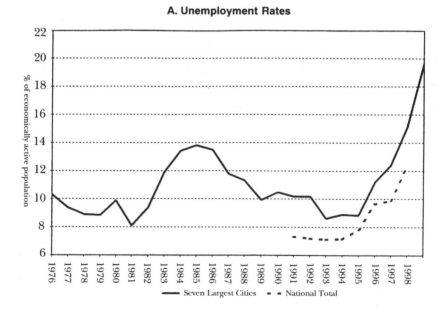

B. Employment Rates

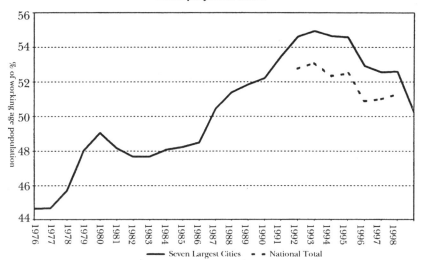

C. Participation Rates

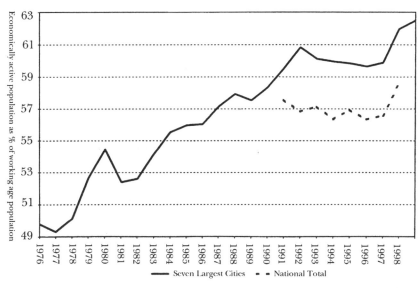

Source: DANE

economic growth and employment generation; urban unemployment thus increased rapidly, peaking at 14.7% of the labor force in June 1986. The return to stable, moderate growth in the second half of the decade led, on the contrary, to a rapid growth in employment and a reduction in unemployment. These trends continued until 1992 in large urban centers.

Despite the demand boom and rapid economic growth, employment generation in the large urban areas slowed down considerably after 1992. The employment rate in large urban areas stagnated at 1992 levels until 1995. A temporary reversal in the upward trend in labor force participation was thus crucial for the additional reduction in unemployment, which reached an average of 8.8% in 1993–1995, the lowest level since the early 1980s. These trends are also evident in the national surveys, although in this case the turning points seem to have been reached with a one-year lead.

The deterioration of the urban labor market has been significant given the reduction of employment and, since 1998, the renewed increase in labor participation rates. Unemployment rapidly increased since 1996, reaching after 1998 the highest levels in recorded history. The same trends can be seen in the national household rate, with a one year's lead. Whereas the lack of employment dynamism in 1992–1995 can hardly be attributable to weak domestic demand and activity, and must thus be found in more structural factors, slow GDP and demand growth have certainly played a crucial role in weak employment generation since 1996.

A more detailed analysis of national surveys offers a closer look at labor market dynamics in the 1990s. As a first step, Table 3 breaks down changes in the labor market into those caused by changes in the labor supply and those deriving from changes on the demand side. Those originating on the supply side are broken down, in turn, into those associated with demographic factors and those having to do with variations in labor participation. Changes on the demand side are broken down into employment in tradable and non-tradable sectors, and in unemployment. All variables are measured as proportions of total population.

Labor supply increased at a slow rate, relative to population, when the economy was expanding. This was the net effect of two opposing patterns: an upward trend in the relative size of working-age population and a downward trend in labor participation, with a sharp break in the latter case with respect to trends in the 1980s. In 1995–1997, the demographic factors ceased to exert an upward pressure on labor supply but, as we have seen, labor participation started to do so in 1998.

On the demand side, two features stand out in the 1990s: weak job creation throughout the decade and a sharp rise in unemployment in recent years. The low rate of job creation is evident in a decrease of 2.2 percentage points (of total population) in the employment rate between 1991 and 1997. It is interesting to note that sluggish rate of job creation is a feature not only of the recent adjustment phase, but also of economic expansion in the first half of the decade. Indeed, employment as a proportion of total population, grew modestly between 1991 and 1995. The fall in labor participation was thus crucial to counteract the modest rate of job creation in this period. This favorable mix of trends in labor supply and employment underwent a drastic change since 1996. The collapse of job creation translated then into a significant rise in unemployment, which climbed, relative to total population, by 2.9 percentage points between 1995 and 1997.

TABLE 3: Decomposition of Global Changes in the Labor Market
(% of changes of rates, defined in relation to total population)

		1991-1995	1995-1997	1991-1997
CHANGES IN LABOR SUPPLY	Total * /	1.2%	-0.6%	0.5%
	Demographic	2.2%	-0.1%	2.2%
	Participation	-1.0%	-0.6%	-1.6%
CHANGES IN LABOR DEMAND	**Employment * /**	0.7%	-2.9%	-2.2%
	Tradables	-3.9%	-3.0%	-7.0%
	Non-tradables	4.7%	0.1%	4.8%
	Unemployment	0.5%	2.1%	2.6%

*/ The decomposition excludes the combined effects of the changes in both components.
Note: For definitions see text.
Source: National Household Surveys. Data processed by the authors.

Composition and sources of job creation

The overall analysis of job creation can be extended to the single-digit level for different categories of economic activity. In particular, changes in employment can be translated into weighted changes in the differential between the growth of per capita output and of labor productivity in each sector (Table 4). The results of this exercise show that in the course of the decade there has been a general decline in tradable sectors, particularly agriculture and manufacturing. Specifically, these sectors have experienced a decrease in per capita output along with increases in labor productivity, with the result being a sharp decline in the employment rate, equivalent to 7.0 percentage points of the total population between 1991 and 1997. On the other hand, non-tradable sectors (construction and services) experienced an increase in per capita output that has outpaced the growth of labor productivity. Consequently, non-tradable sectors have been steady contributors to the job creation process. However, this process has been strongly pro-cyclical, as it concentrated in 1991–1995. The slowdown in job creation by non-tradable sectors since 1996 and the long-term decline of employment in tradable sectors has led to a sharp decrease in total employment in the economy as a whole.

These general sectoral trends have some particular sector-specific features. On the one hand, the downturn in employment in the agricultural sector between 1991 and 1995 was extremely pronounced. This was particularly true in rural areas, where the share of total employment represented by tradable sectors (basically agriculture) fell sharply (Table 2). On the other hand, the decrease in total employment in tradable sectors experienced between 1995

TABLE 4: Sectoral Decomposition of Labor Productivity,
per Capita Output and Employment Changes

	1991-1995	1995-1997	1991-1997
Labor productivity growth			
Agriculture	18.7%	-4.1%	13.8%
Mining	65.6%	22.7%	103.2%
Manufacturing	-2.8%	18.4%	15.2%
Electricity, water and gas	34.1%	-38.6%	-17.6%
Construction	7.2%	14.1%	22.3%
Commerce	13.2%	1.1%	14.5%
Transport	2.5%	10.6%	13.3%
Financial services	-3.0%	0.1%	-2.9%
Other services	11.7%	4.4%	16.6%
TOTAL	**10.4%**	**4.2%**	**15.0%**
Tradables	12.0%	5.6%	18.3%
Non-tradables	10.8%	4.0%	15.2%
Per capita output growth			
Agriculture	-0.7%	-3.9%	-4.6%
Mining	9.0%	8.5%	18.3%
Manufacturing	2.7%	-3.7%	-1.1%
Electricity, water and gas	11.7%	2.6%	14.6%
Construction	46.9%	-4.1%	40.8%
Commerce	19.8%	-0.9%	18.7%
Transport	13.6%	6.1%	20.4%
Financial services	24.4%	4.4%	29.9%
Other services	13.4%	9.9%	24.6%
TOTAL	**11.2%**	**1.2%**	**12.5%**
Tradables	1.7%	-2.6%	-0.9%
Non-tradables	19.8%	4.2%	24.8%
Change in the employment rate (relative to total population)			
Agriculture	-4.4%	0.0%	-4.3%
Mining	-0.4%	-0.1%	-0.5%
Manufacturing	0.8%	-2.9%	-2.1%
Electricity, water and gas	-0.1%	0.3%	0.2%
Construction	1.7%	-1.0%	0.7%
Commerce	1.2%	-0.4%	0.8%
Transport	0.5%	-0.2%	0.3%
Financial services	1.0%	0.2%	1.2%
Other services	0.3%	1.2%	1.5%
TOTAL	**0.7%**	**-2.9%**	**-2.2%**
Tradables	-3.9%	-3.0%	-7.0%
Non-tradables	4.7%	0.1%	4.8%

Source: National Household Surveys. Data processed by the authors.

and 1997 was primarily attributable to manufacturing and was fundamentally an urban phenomenon.

The non-tradable sectors, for their part, have experienced a significant upswing in the course of the decade, with their share of total employment rising from 57.0% in 1991 to 63.2% in 1997. However, as noticed, job creation in non-tradables was particularly rapid during the economic expansion in the first half of the decade, but gave way to a slowdown in job creation during the subsequent adjustment. Among the non-tradable sectors, the pro-cyclical performance of employment in construction stands out.

These trends indicate that the contribution of tradables to the growth of the economy's labor productivity is basically the joint effect of slow growth in output and a negative trend in job creation. This was particularly true of the agricultural sector in 1991–1995, and of manufacturing in 1995–1997. More rapid output growth in non-tradables facilitated a positive contribution to both employment generation and productivity growth, particularly during the expansionary phase. Additional decomposition exercises (not shown) indicate that the effects of the reallocation of output and labor across sectors on overall labor productivity have been minimal.

The analysis of employment growth can be extended by matching the employment dynamics in each sector according to educational attainment, occupational position and gender. Two main patterns are defined when sectoral employment is matched with educational attainment: skilled employment creation has been concentrated in the non-tradable sector, while job destruction in the tradable sector has hit the less educated most severely (Table 5).

The destruction of low skilled jobs (workers with primary and incomplete secondary education, i.e., up to 10 years of schooling), between 1991 and 1995 was led by the agricultural sector, but shifted to the manufacturing sector in 1995–1997. In the case of non-tradables, the demand for low-skilled labor had a clear cyclical pattern, largely related to the construction sector. During the boom phase this sector was very dynamic in the generation of low-skill employment, but its crisis in recent years has been an additional blow to less educated workers. On the other hand, the sectoral dynamics of the demand for intermediate skills (complete secondary education, 11 years) and for workers with incomplete and complete university studies (12–15, and 16 years or more, respectively) has been concentrated in non-tradables, with some biases for the former in commerce and transport, and for the latter in financial and other services.

The evolution of employment rates by occupational categories and gender shows three distinctive patterns (Table 5). The first is a sharp cyclical pattern of wage earners in the private sector. Indeed, during the boom phase, this type of employment was the most dynamic. However, between 1995 and 1997 employment losses have concentrated in this occupational category. Second, self-employment shows an important dynamism throughout the decade. Together with a reduction in wage employment since 1996, it suggests an important informalization process in recent years. Finally, female employment

TABLE 5: Changes in the Employment Rates

Average years of education	1991-1995	1995-1997	1991-1997
A.- By educational attainment			
0-5 Years	**-3.0%**	**-2.5%**	**-5.6%**
Tradables	-3.7%	-1.4%	-5.1%
Non-tradables	0.6%	-1.1%	-0.5%
6-10 Years	**0.3%**	**-3.0%**	**-2.7%**
Tradables	-0.5%	-1.4%	-2.0%
Non-tradables	0.8%	-1.6%	-0.7%
11 Years	**3.2%**	**0.3%**	**3.5%**
Tradables	0.6%	-0.3%	0.3%
Non-tradables	2.6%	0.6%	3.2%
12 - 15 years	**0.0%**	**0.6%**	**0.7%**
Tradables	-0.1%	-0.1%	-0.2%
Non-tradables	0.1%	0.7%	0.8%
16 and more	**0.2%**	**1.7%**	**2.0%**
Tradables	-0.3%	0.3%	0.0%
Non-tradables	0.5%	1.5%	2.0%
Total	**0.7%**	**-2.9%**	**-2.2%**
Tradables	-3.9%	-3.0%	-7.0%
Non-tradables	4.7%	0.1%	4.8%
B.- By occupational category			
Private sector wage earner	3.7%	-3.4%	0.3%
Public sector wage earner	-1.9%	-0.3%	-2.2%
Employers	-0.3%	-0.5%	-0.9%
Workers in household activities	-0.2%	-0.2%	-0.4%
Self-employed	2.2%	1.8%	4.0%
Family workers without payment	-2.8%	-0.2%	-3.0%
C.- By gender			
Male	-0.8%	-1.8%	-2.6%
Female	1.5%	-1.1%	0.4%
TOTAL	**0.7%**	**-2.9%**	**-2.2%**

Note: Sectoral contribution of each sector to the employment ratio referred to total population.
Source: National Household Surveys. Data processed by the authors.

rates have increased in relative terms, although there is a slowdown in this dynamic in recent years.

4. Social Policy and Basic Needs

During the seventies and eighties, social spending fluctuated within 7 and 10% of GDP, with a slight increasing trend and two cycles. If pension payments are excluded, the first of them was a decreasing phase between early seventies and 1977, followed by an increase in the latter year and 1984. The second had a decreasing phase during the years of macroeconomic adjustment in the mid-1980s and a recovery in the rest of the decade (Figure 3).

An impressive increase of social spending took place in the 1990s. In 1994 it had reached 12.2% and peaked at 15.4% of GDP in 1996–1997. Half of the increase has been associated with the expansion of the social security system. The other half has been associated with transfers to departments and municipalities for social spending—particularly education and health—and with direct expansion of central government social outlays. At a sectoral level, social security expenditures explain an important part of the increase, but education and health

FIGURE 3: Social Spending

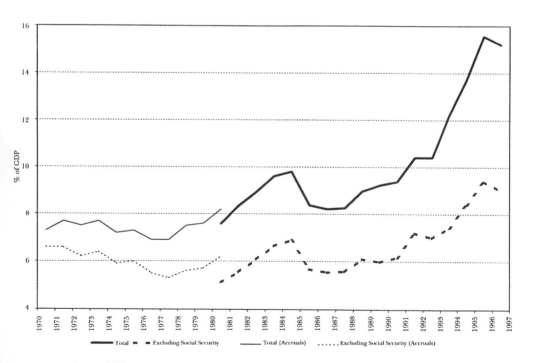

Source: DNP

have also shown an important dynamism. As a result, whereas Colombia was regarded until very recently as a country that underinvested in social sectors, this has largely ceased to be true.[19]

Long-term efforts in social policy have resulted in a sustained and substantial improvement in indicators of basic needs and the coverage of social services. Indeed, indicators of health and educational attainment, the characteristics of dwelling or the availability of public utilities show a steady improvement over the past few decades. As a result, poverty measured by unsatisfied basic needs declined from 70.2% in 1973 to 45.6% in 1985 and to 37.2% in 1993, according to census data (Table 6). The gap between rural and urban areas has also declined, but remained large. Also, gender discrimination fell and in some cases (such as life expectancy and education) women's achievements overcame those of men.[20]

This positive trend experienced a slowdown in the 1980s[21] but has speeded up in recent years. Increased expenditure was reflected in a significant expansion of social services in 1993–1997 (Table 6). The most rapid expansion was that experienced by the health coverage of the social security system, which increased from 24% to 57% over this period. School attendance rates also increased, particularly for secondary education. The coverage of water and sewage also increased rapidly. Increased coverage benefited, in particular, poor people and rural areas.[22] As a result of this fact and the increased coverage of other public utilities, poverty, as measured by unsatisfied basic needs, declined: from 33 to 27% in 1993-1997, according to household surveys, faster than the rate at which this index improved in 1985–1993. Moreover, the improvement was particularly rapid in rural areas.

5. Income Distribution and Poverty

General trends

Contrary to the positive trends in indicators of basic needs, poverty, measured by the proportion of population below the poverty line, and income distribution exhibited an adverse trend up to the late 1960s or early 1970s, but improved considerably in the latter decade.[23] The significant reduction in rural surplus labor and the lagged effects of the educational policies adopted since the 1950s, which were reflected in significant increases in human capital since the mid-1960s,

---

19. See the relevant regional comparisons in ECLAC (1999).
20. DNP (1998).
21. Londoño (1997).
22. Sánchez and Núñez (1999).
23. See Carrizosa (1987), Londoño (1995), Misión de Empleo (1986), Ocampo (1992 and 1999), Reyes (1987) and Urrutia (1984).

TABLE 6: Indicators of Social Progress

	CENSUS DATA		QUALITY OF LIFE SURVEY	
	1985	1993	1993	1997
A.-UNSATISFIED BASIC NEEDS				
NATIONAL				
Poor (%)	45.6	32.2	32.7	26.9
Extremely poor (%)	22.8	13.5	13.5	9.0
URBAN				
Poor (%)	32.3	20.6	20.6	17.5
Extremely poor (%)	12.6	6.1	4.0	3.3
RURAL				
Poor (%)	72.6	58.9	60.9	49.6
Extremely poor (%)	44.4	30.8	35.5	22.8
B. COVERAGE RATES				
SCHOOL ATTENDANCE (NET)				
Primary	61.5		75.2	83.4
Secondary	37.7		47.8	59.7
SOCIAL SECURITY HEALTH				
% of total population			23.7	57.2
PUBLIC UTILITIES				
Energy	78.5		86.0	93.8
Water	73.1		80.0	85.6
Sewage	59.4		63.3	70.8
C.QUALITY OF HOUSING				
Inadequate materials	13.8	7.3	7.3	7.6
Overcrowding	19.4	12.8	12.8	11.0
Lack of access to basic utilities	21.8	10.4	10.4	5.7

Source: DNP

were the two major factors behind this lagged but strong improvement in these social indicators in the 1970s. The Colombian economy thus reached the 1980s in the midst of a rapid improvement in income distribution and poverty. Macroeconomic events in the 1980s and structural adjustment in the 1990s would determine major shifts in these trends.

Changes in national income distribution from 1978 on are summarized in Table 7. Table 8 provides more detailed information on income distribution for the four years on which our analysis of national household surveys will focus (1978, 1991, 1995 and 1998). The available information for the country's largest cities makes it possible to estimate consistent quarterly income distribution

TABLE 7: Income Distribution and Poverty

	year	GINI Household per capita income	NATIONAL POVERTY LINE				INTERNATIONAL POVERTY LINE			
			Incidence	Intensity	Poverty gap	Foster-Greer Thorbecke	Incidence	Intensity	Poverty gap	Foster-Greer Thorbecke
TOTAL NATIONAL	1978	0.5039	56.5	45.3	25.6	14.7	20.2	32.6	6.6	3.2
	1991	0.5284	60.5	47.3	28.6	17.2	23.2	38.4	8.9	4.9
	1992	0.5258	59.4	45.2	26.8	15.5	20.1	35.5	7.1	3.7
	1993	0.5219	57.3	45.0	25.8	15.0	18.5	36.5	6.7	3.6
	1994	0.5278	55.4	44.3	24.5	14.0	17.9	35.0	6.3	3.3
	1995	0.5314	53.9	43.9	23.7	13.5	16.8	35.8	6.0	3.1
	1996	0.5334	53.0	43.0	22.8	12.8	15.4	35.4	5.5	2.9
	1997	0.5427	54.7	45.8	25.1	15.0	18.4	40.6	7.5	4.6
	1998	0.5378	55.0	46.6	25.6	15.6	19.3	41.4	8.0	4.9
URBAN AREA	1978	0.5030	53.4	43.7	23.3	12.9	13.8	28.0	3.9	1.7
	1991	0.4842	48.0	40.1	19.2	10.2	8.1	27.7	2.2	1.0
	1992	0.5030	51.6	41.2	21.3	11.3	11.0	27.8	3.1	1.3
	1993	0.4935	50.8	41.5	21.1	11.5	10.5	29.1	3.1	1.4
	1994	0.5124	46.1	39.5	18.2	9.6	8.2	28.3	2.3	1.0
	1995	0.5252	44.8	39.6	17.7	9.3	7.6	29.8	2.3	1.0
	1996	0.5132	43.6	38.7	16.9	8.8	7.1	29.1	2.1	1.0
	1997	0.5228	46.7	40.8	19.0	10.2	9.6	29.5	2.8	1.3
	1998	0.5246	45.7	41.4	18.9	10.2	9.5	30.2	2.9	1.3
RURAL AREA	1978	0.4767	60.6	47.1	28.5	17.0	28.5	35.5	10.1	5.2
	1988	0.5572	71.1	51.4	36.6	23.2	36.0	40.5	14.6	8.2
	1991	0.5624	69.6	49.0	34.1	21.0	32.0	39.0	12.5	6.9
	1992	0.5189	66.6	48.9	32.5	20.1	29.8	40.2	12.0	6.8
	1993	0.4995	67.7	48.5	32.9	19.9	30.7	37.4	11.5	6.2
	1994	0.4754	66.0	47.8	31.6	19.2	28.9	37.9	11.0	5.9
	1995	0.4373	65.6	46.8	30.7	18.2	26.6	37.6	10.0	5.4
	1996	0.5033	67.3	51.3	34.5	22.4	32.2	45.8	14.7	9.6
	1997	0.4810	69.6	52.1	36.3	23.9	34.6	46.3	16.0	10.5
	1998	0.4977	66.1	49.8	32.9	20.8	30.3	41.8	12.7	7.6

Note: Data correspond to Septembers, except 1976, June, and 1991, December.
Source: National Household Surveys. Data processed by the authors.

figures since 1984, and wage differentials since 1976. These series appear in Figure 4 and 5.[24]

Throughout the period analyzed, income distribution in Colombia has remained highly skewed. Looking at figures for the country as a whole, in 1978 the wealthiest decile of the population received 42.2% of total income, while the poorest half of the population received 17.1%. In 1998, the former figure had risen to 44.5% while the latter had fallen to 15.0%; the middle income groups (deciles 6–8) also experienced a reduction in their shares in total income (Table 8). Overall, the Gini coefficient experienced an increase of 3.4 percentage points (Table 7). It is interesting to note that, as a reflection of the greater demographic dependence characteristic of the poorest households, income distribution among the working-age population is somewhat less skewed. The less uneven distribution patterns correspond to wages and independent-labor income, whereas the distribution of capital revenues, investment income and pensions are highly skewed (not shown).

The variations that have occurred since 1978 reflect major positive and negative distributive shocks. These shocks have tended to offset each other, however, since they have generally affected urban and rural households in opposite directions. For this reason, their effects on national income-distribution indicators have been moderate. It is also interesting to note that trends in the large cities are not always of the same magnitude as trends in urban areas in general, although they usually move in the same direction. This indicates that the patterns observed in large cities differ from those displayed by small and medium-sized ones.

During the period 1978–1991, income distribution worsened notably in rural areas and improved in urban areas. The deterioration in rural areas outweighed improvements in urban areas, producing a moderate increase in the Gini coefficient. In the case of major cities, the available quarterly information indicates that improvements during the second half of the 1970s were interrupted at the beginning of the 1980s, throughout which the distributive situation was essentially trendless (Figure 4). Looked at in terms of changes in relative wage broken down by educational attainments, the available data for

---

24. For the purposes of the analysis, the income-distribution deciles were grouped into five income brackets: deciles 1 and 2, where the nation's extremely poor are concentrated; deciles 3, 4, and 5, where most of the rest of the poor are found; deciles 6, 7, and 8, which correspond to middle-income groups; the two top deciles are considered separately. The information was adjusted to correct for traditional sorts of problems and to align it with national accounts data. This includes, in Colombia, the problems associated to censoring of high incomes in some surveys, due to the limited number of digits allowed in the questionnaires to report incomes. For a detailed analysis of the problem and the solutions used to solve it, see Pérez et al. (1996) and Núñez and Jiménez (1998). In Figure 5, educational levels have been grouped in three categories: (1) university attainment, which includes only persons with complete university education; (2) secondary attainment, those with complete secondary and incomplete university education; (3) primary attainment, the rest, including an increasing small group of persons with no education. For groups 2 and 3, Paasche wage indicators were estimated.

TABLE 8: Income Distribution, Household and Labor Market Characteristics

Deciles	1978						1991				
	TOTAL	1-2	3-5	6-8	9	10	TOTAL	1-2	3-5	6-8	9	10
PER CAPITA INCOME DISTRIBUTION (1978 constant pesos)												
National total	100.0	4.0	13.1	25.7	15.0	42.2	100.0	3.6	12.3	24.3	14.7	45.1
Urban area	100.0	4.2	13.0	25.5	15.3	42.1	100.0	4.4	13.8	26.2	15.5	40.2
Rural area	100.0	4.2	14.2	27.3	15.2	39.1	100.0	3.3	11.5	21.6	12.6	51.0
7 largest cities	100.0	4.2	13.2	26.2	16.0	40.4	100.0	4.3	13.3	25.8	15.5	41.0
INCOME DISTRIBUTION OF THE WORKING AGE POPULATION												
National total	100.0	4.0	13.1	25.6	15.0	42.3	100.0	3.6	12.4	24.3	14.7	45.1
Urban area	100.0	4.2	13.0	25.4	15.3	42.0	100.0	4.4	13.8	26.1	15.4	40.2
Rural area	100.0	4.2	14.3	27.3	15.2	39.0	100.0	3.3	11.6	21.7	12.7	50.7
7 largest cities	100.0	4.3	13.2	26.1	16.0	40.4	100.0	4.3	13.3	25.8	15.5	41.1
HOUSEHOLD SIZE												
National total	5.6	6.8	6.2	5.5	4.9	4.2	4.7	5.6	5.1	4.5	4.0	3.5
Urban area	5.5	6.6	5.9	5.3	4.9	4.3	4.5	5.3	4.8	4.4	3.9	3.4
Rural area	5.8	6.8	6.5	5.8	5.2	4.0	4.9	5.6	5.4	4.9	4.2	3.8
7 largest cities	5.4	6.5	5.8	5.3	4.9	4.4	4.3	5.1	4.8	4.2	3.7	3.3
AVERAGE YEARS OF SCHOOL ATTENDANCE (POPULATION OF 18 AND OLDER)												
National total	4.5	2.7	3.5	4.3	5.6	7.6	6.3	3.8	5.0	6.5	8.2	9.6
Urban area	5.8	3.9	4.7	5.7	7.3	8.9	7.8	5.3	6.6	7.9	9.3	11.0
Rural area	2.6	2.1	2.3	2.6	2.6	3.6	4.2	3.1	3.7	4.3	4.9	5.6
7 largest cities	6.3	4.1	4.9	6.2	7.9	9.6	8.3	6.0	7.0	8.5	10.2	11.6
% OF WORKING AGE POPULATION												
National total	72.8	62.6	68.0	76.5	82.0	85.5	74.4	65.6	69.8	77.9	83.9	85.2
Urban area	75.8	64.3	72.9	79.8	83.1	86.5	74.3	60.7	70.4	79.1	84.6	86.7
Rural area	68.8	62.5	62.9	71.1	78.1	82.6	74.6	68.4	70.5	76.9	83.1	83.7
7 largest cities	77.1	65.8	73.4	81.9	84.8	86.8	75.6	61.9	71.7	81.0	85.2	87.2
EMPLOYMENT RATE: EMPLOYEES/WORKING AGE POPULATION												
National total	44.9	35.4	39.7	48.1	53.0	54.1	53.6	46.8	50.2	56.2	56.9	61.5
Urban area	43.1	29.8	38.8	47.5	49.7	53.2	52.9	42.8	50.9	55.3	56.3	61.5
Rural area	47.6	40.2	41.6	49.0	55.4	61.2	54.5	49.8	50.1	56.1	61.0	61.9
7 largest cities	43.9	31.1	40.0	48.3	49.6	53.5	54.0	42.0	51.3	56.8	59.5	63.2
UNEMPLOYMENT RATE: UNEMPLOYED/ECONOMICALLY ACTIVE POPULATION												
National total	5.1	6.3	6.2	4.8	4.8	3.3	7.1	8.2	7.9	7.3	6.8	4.1
Urban area	7.4	12.4	8.9	6.7	6.7	3.0	9.3	14.6	10.5	8.7	7.7	4.2
Rural area	2.0	2.0	2.7	2.0	1.3	1.4	4.2	5.6	4.9	3.9	2.6	3.2
7 largest cities	8.0	14.1	10.3	6.5	6.1	3.7	9.2	15.8	11.0	8.4	5.8	3.9
DEPENDENCY RATE: INACTIVE AND UNEMPLOYED/EMPLOYED												
National total	205.9	351.6	270.1	171.7	130.1	116.1	150.8	225.6	185.7	128.4	109.6	91.0
Urban area	206.4	421.6	253.7	163.6	142.1	117.4	154.5	284.8	179.2	128.9	109.9	87.6
Rural area	205.2	298.1	281.9	187.0	131.1	97.8	146.0	193.8	183.1	131.8	97.3	93.1
7 largest cities	195.4	388.4	240.3	152.7	138.0	115.1	145.1	284.5	171.6	117.2	97.3	81.3
FORMALITY RATE: FORMAL EMPLOYMENT/TOTAL EMPLOYMENT												
National total	60.4	43.0	60.6	64.4	66.8	61.1	59.6	33.9	56.6	67.2	72.2	64.5
Urban area	67.0	61.6	66.5	71.0	69.5	61.1	64.9	45.0	63.1	70.8	70.8	67.4
Rural area	51.9	33.1	49.9	57.9	58.5	55.8	53.0	24.8	49.3	61.5	67.1	61.6
7 largest cities	68.7	63.8	68.3	73.2	72.1	59.9	68.7	52.3	68.1	74.6	73.4	66.3

Source: National Household Surveys. Data processed by the authors.

large cities indicate a sharp narrowing of differentials between 1976 and 1981 or 1982, depending on the series, followed by a stagnation in relative wages in 1983–1991 (Figure 5).

The period 1991–1995 experienced large distributive shocks, which were, in many ways, the opposite to those of the previous phase. While levels of inequality rose notably in the cities (six percentage points in the Gini coefficient for large cities and four points in urban areas as a whole), they fell even more steeply in rural areas (13 percentage points). These strong distributive

TABLE 8 (continued)

	1995						1998				
TOTAL	1-2	3-5	6-8	9	10	TOTAL	1-2	3-5	6-8	9	10
100.0	3.6	12.2	24.2	14.6	45.4	100.0	3.2	11.8	24.6	15.8	44.5
100.0	3.9	12.4	23.8	14.3	45.6	100.0	3.6	12.1	25.0	16.1	43.2
100.0	4.7	15.9	29.0	16.1	34.3	100.0	3.5	13.8	26.7	15.4	40.6
100.0	3.9	12.2	23.4	14.1	46.4	100.0	3.4	11.6	25.1	16.7	43.2
100.0	3.6	12.2	24.2	14.6	45.5	100.0	3.2	11.8	24.6	15.9	44.5
100.0	3.9	12.5	23.8	14.3	45.6	100.0	3.6	12.1	25.0	16.1	43.1
100.0	4.7	15.9	29.0	15.9	34.5	100.0	3.5	13.9	26.8	15.4	40.5
100.0	3.9	12.2	23.4	14.1	46.3	100.0	3.4	11.5	25.3	16.7	43.1
4.4	5.3	4.8	4.2	3.8	3.5	4.3	5.3	4.7	4.1	3.6	3.3
4.3	5.0	4.7	4.1	3.7	3.5	4.2	5.1	4.5	4.0	3.6	3.2
4.6	5.3	5.2	4.5	3.9	3.3	4.5	5.4	5.1	4.4	3.9	3.1
4.2	4.9	4.5	4.0	3.6	3.3	4.0	4.9	4.4	3.8	3.6	3.1
6.7	4.2	5.3	6.8	8.5	10.7	7.0	4.4	5.5	7.0	9.2	11.4
8.2	5.9	7.0	8.2	10.0	11.7	8.5	6.0	7.0	8.5	10.5	12.4
4.5	3.7	3.9	4.4	5.1	6.0	4.4	3.3	3.7	4.4	5.2	6.7
8.4	6.0	7.1	8.4	10.1	12.0	9.0	6.4	7.3	9.2	11.3	13.0
76.1	66.5	72.3	79.6	84.8	86.9	75.9	66.8	71.4	80.0	84.3	86.1
76.6	64.4	73.0	81.4	85.3	87.5	76.7	65.2	73.1	81.3	86.1	86.5
75.5	67.8	70.7	78.9	83.4	86.7	74.6	67.0	70.7	77.4	84.4	83.0
76.9	64.0	73.1	82.3	85.4	88.4	77.7	65.4	74.6	83.0	85.5	87.4
52.7	42.7	47.9	56.0	60.1	62.7	51.9	43.4	48.1	54.8	57.3	61.1
53.2	40.1	49.9	56.7	60.8	62.8	51.3	39.8	48.0	54.8	56.0	61.5
51.9	43.6	47.5	52.1	61.0	65.7	53.1	45.7	48.6	54.7	59.8	64.9
54.4	40.4	50.8	58.8	61.2	64.2	52.3	40.0	49.7	55.3	58.7	61.9
7.4	10.4	9.3	6.8	5.3	3.9	11.8	17.0	14.5	11.0	8.7	5.2
9.1	17.9	11.1	7.6	4.9	3.7	14.5	26.1	17.9	12.2	8.7	4.7
4.9	7.1	6.0	5.1	2.6	2.2	7.2	9.5	9.0	7.2	3.9	3.9
8.4	17.6	10.2	6.7	4.6	3.4	14.4	27.7	17.4	12.1	6.8	4.6
149.4	252.1	188.8	124.4	96.2	83.4	153.7	244.8	191.3	128.1	107.3	90.1
145.4	287.3	174.8	116.6	92.7	81.9	154.3	285.6	185.3	124.5	107.4	88.0
155.1	238.4	197.4	143.4	96.6	75.5	152.6	227.0	191.1	136.2	98.0	85.7
138.9	286.8	169.2	106.9	91.2	76.0	145.9	282.2	169.8	118.1	99.4	84.7
60.4	35.3	57.9	66.7	69.3	67.0	55.8	26.9	51.1	62.3	68.4	68.0
64.7	47.8	62.2	70.0	69.8	66.9	60.2	33.1	55.0	66.6	70.6	70.5
54.5	27.1	51.1	61.7	63.3	64.8	48.7	20.4	46.0	56.2	60.1	57.4
66.2	50.4	66.1	70.4	70.6	66.2	64.2	41.6	59.0	71.1	72.8	70.2

shocks in urban and rural areas tended to offset each other, with the result that income distribution in 1995 was very similar to that in 1991. These trends were accompanied by a sharp increase in the rural-urban income gap (see below). These trends were virtually continuous, although there was a temporary turnaround in the urban Gini coefficient in 1993. The increased skewness of the distribution of wage income in large cities when broken down by educational attainment was reflected in rising incomes for workers with university degrees relative to other wage earners, but not in the wages of workers

FIGURE 4: Income Distribution and Poverty in Seven Largest Cities (4 quarters moving average)

A. Households per Capita Gini Coefficients

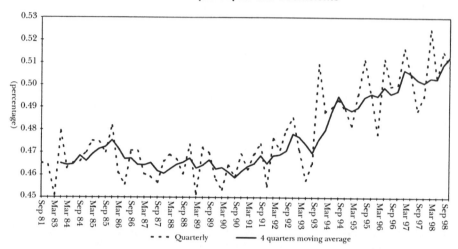

B. Poverty (National Poverty Line)

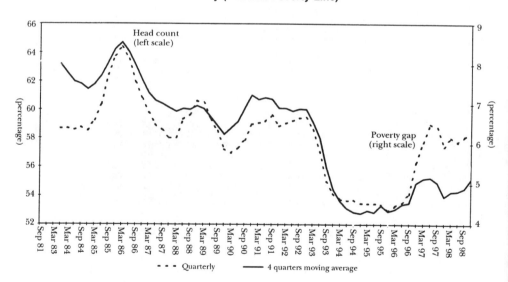

FIGURE 5: Relative Wages by Educational Attainment, Largest Cities
(Index, December 1988=100)

A. University vs. Primary Attainment

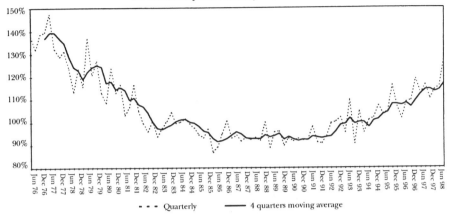

--- Quarterly ——— 4 quarters moving average

B. University vs. Secondary Attainment

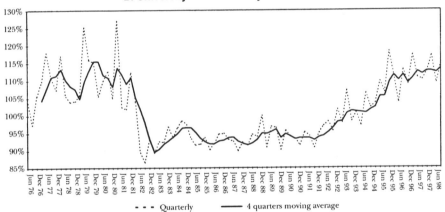

--- Quarterly ——— 4 quarters moving average

C. Secondary vs. Primary Attainment

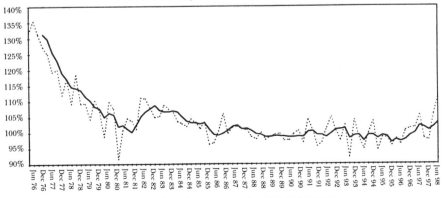

--- Quarterly ——— 4 quarters moving average

with a secondary education relative to those having only primary education. Adverse trends in urban distribution generally continued in 1995–1998. In rural areas, there was a reversal of the favorable distributive trends characteristic of 1991–1995, though the estimated Gini coefficients remained below those in the early part of the decade and experienced a somewhat erratic pattern.[25]

These trends are borne out by other recent studies, including Reyes et al. (1996), Berry and Tenjo (1998) and Cárdenas et. al. (1998) for large cities, Leibovich (1998) for rural areas, and DNP (1998) for the country as a whole. They are also consistent with analyses by Robbins (1998) and Núñez and Sánchez (1998) on changing wage differentials. The moderate deterioration in distribution over the last two decades is inconsistent, however, with the moderate improvement shown in Londoño (1997) for the period 1978–1993. The deterioration in rural distribution in recent years is not consistent, either, with other estimates, which rather indicate that it continued to improve up to 1997.[26]

Londoño (1997) also estimated that there was an improvement in secondary income distribution equivalent to three percentage points of the Gini coefficient in 1978–1993. These estimates are consistent with the detailed calculation of the redistributive effects of social spending by Vélez (1996) and May et al. (1996). Sánchez and Núñez (1999) estimated an additional improvement in secondary income distribution equivalent to three percentage points of the Gini coefficient in 1993–1997, which reflects both a rapid increase in social spending (see Section 4) and better targeting. These improvements would offset the deterioration in primary income distribution shown in Table 7. For this reason, it may be concluded that the notable improvement in income distribution during the 1970s was followed by two decades of a moderate deterioration in primary income distribution. However, the redistributive effects of increased social spending and better targeting led to a significant improvement in secondary income distribution, which exceeded by two percentage points of the Gini coefficient the deterioration in the primary distribution, thus generating a moderate long-run improvement in the global (primary + secondary) income distribution.

A more detailed look at the socio-demographic and economic determinants of primary income distribution

These trends reflect a combination of socio-demographic and economic factors that have an impact on the primary distribution of income. Three socio-demographic changes are reflected in Table 8: (1) a reduction in the demographic dependency rate in the rural sector, as reflected in the relative increase of

---

25. A few outliers explain this fact. Also, correction factors for 1995 rather than annual-specific ones are used to adjust the data for 1996–1998.

26. Sánchez and Núñez (1999) estimate that the rural Gini fell from 0.49 to 0.44 in 1993–1997. ECLAC (1999) estimates that it fell from 0.49 to 0.40 in 1994–1997.

population in working age (in the cities, the transition occurred prior to the period we are analyzing); (2) a reduction in the size of households; and (3) an increase in average levels of schooling. A fourth phenomenon of a strictly economic nature, which affected the second of the aforementioned factors, was the increase of job opportunities, especially for women. A joint effect of demographic and labor-market effects has been the sharp drop in the economic dependency rate, defined as the ratio of the economically dependent population (inactive and unemployed) to the employed population.

All of these trends were much more pronounced in 1978–1991 and then slowed down sharply or broke off altogether. The most notable cases were the reduction in employment rates and the deceleration in the rate of increase in the average level of schooling among the adult population. The first of these trends has already been analyzed in Section 3. The second of these phenomena may be related to the tightening of social spending in the 1980s. Indeed, the sharp rise in social spending in more recent years has been reflected in further increases in the rates of school attendance (Section 4), which will have a lagged effect on the level of schooling among the adult population.

These trends occurred within a context of striking socio-demographic disparities, both between households in different income brackets and between rural and urban households. Thus, poor households continued to exhibit a smaller proportion of members of working age, more numerous households, lower educational levels, fewer job opportunities and, as a consequence of these conditions, higher rates of economic dependency. Between urban and rural areas, the most notable difference throughout the period analyzed has been in the area of educational opportunities. At the beginning of the period, demographic dependency in rural areas was also notably greater, but this differential has narrowed in the past two decades.

Improvements in the area of job opportunities in 1978–1991 were clearly progressive, both in rural and urban areas. Its reversal in the 1990s was, in contrast, regressive, particularly during the boom years, 1991–1995. These trends were reflected in an improvement—also of a progressive nature—in economic dependency rates in 1978–1991, but also a deterioration in the 1990s. The improvement in the distribution of educational opportunities also followed a progressive pattern in the cities throughout the two decades. Improvements in this variable in rural areas proceeded at a very fast pace, but were relatively even across income brackets. The main adverse trends had to do with differences between urban and rural areas: although educational opportunities and the demographic dependency rate improved more in rural areas, slower job creation translated into a less favorable trend in economic dependency rates in the countryside, particularly in 1991–1995.

With the exception of the phenomena of a strictly economic nature associated with job creation, we should *not* expect the foregoing variables to explain the changes in distribution that occurred during the period under analysis. Indeed, the above-mentioned factors would have generated, by themselves, a gradual *improvement* in income distribution. This is particularly true in the case of the improved distribution of educational opportunities, which is the most important factor in cross-sectional analyses of income determinants. The only relevant case in which a better distribution of educational opportunities coincided with improved income distribution was in urban areas during the second half of the 1970s and the early 1980s. However, as we shall see below, even in this case it is not clear that the improved distribution of educational opportunities was the main factor at work. This so, the explanation for these changes must be sought in those economic factors that affected job creation and opportunities throughout the period in question.[27]

The analysis of the relation between macroeconomic events and income distribution must take into account the fact that there may be significant differences between changes in real household income and in gross domestic product,[28] and between changes in *per capita* income and *per worker* income. The latter relationship can be expressed as: $Y = W E A$, where Y is per capita income, W per worker income, E the employment rate and A the proportion of working age population.

From the point of view of income patterns, the 1978–1991 period saw a very moderate increase in per capita household income, which increased at an annual rate of only 0.7% (see Table 9). This rate is below that of per capita GDP, which expanded also at a moderate annual rate (1.4%). The slower increase in household income in relation to GDP growth was basically due to the sharp decline in the proportion of total income received by households owing to a relative increase in corporate profits that were not transferred to households (from 12.7% to 21.2% of total gross income). This moderate increase in per capita income occurred within the context of a decline in per worker income in both rural and urban areas. Thus, changes in the other determinants of per capita income played a decisive role in generating the modest improvement experienced in real household income.

Expanding job opportunities, which made it possible for the labor market to absorb the increasing number of women participating in the labor market, had a very favorable effect on per capita income, especially in the cities. This factor, which had a disproportionately favorable effect on poor households, was clearly the key factor behind the improvement in income distribution in the cities, since trends in income per employed person were regressive de-

---

27. Two recent studies come to similar conclusions. Leibovich (1998) shows that sociodemographic factors tended to improve rural income distribution through the 1988–1995 period. For this reason, the major changes observed in this variable during the period—a turn for the worse in 1988–1991, and an improvement thereafter—are associated with changes in the rate of return of the various determinants of income. Similarly, Cárdenas et al. (1998) find that, although the improvement in income distribution in the large cities in 1976–1982 is largely explained by the improvement in the distribution of educational opportunities, the deterioration observed in the 1990s is accounted for by factors unrelated to this variable.

28. These variations are associated to changes in the terms of trade, in net transfers from the rest of the world, in households' share in income and in the prices of the consumer baskets relative to overall producer prices.

spite the improved distribution of educational opportunities. This indicates that the sharp reduction in education-based wage differentials was *not* the main reason for the improvement in urban income distribution during these years. In rural areas, the greater proportion of working age population also helped to counteract the effects of the reduction in per worker income, which had a strong adverse effect on poor workers. Indeed, only the top income decile escaped the general decrease in wage and non-wage income registered in Colombia's rural areas during this period. Overall, the deterioration in rural income distribution proved to be a stronger force than the improvement in the urban distribution. It is interesting to note that this occurred despite the reduction of the urban/rural income differential: rural per capita income was equivalent to 61% of the level of urban per capita income in 1978, but had risen to 64% in 1991.

The annual growth rate of per capita household income in 1991–1995 was quite high: 4.4%, slightly above to that for per capita GDP (3.9% annual). This increase was wholly concentrated in urban areas. In fact, while the income per capita of urban households rose at an annual rate of 9%, that of rural households actually *declined* at a rate of 5.2% (Table 9). This huge rural-urban distributive shock was manifested in a rapid widening of the income gap between cities and rural areas, as the per capita income of rural households fell from 64% of that of urban households in 1991 to only 42% in 1995. Unlike what had occurred in the preceding years, these trends were chiefly the reflection of changes in the levels of income per employed person, which were compounded by a reduction in employment rates in rural areas.

The downturn in rural incomes was attributable to the severe agricultural crisis that Colombia experienced in the early 1990s. This not only resulted in fewer job opportunities for low- and medium-income households, but also drove down non-wage rural income sharply, a fact that had a very strong impact on the highest rural income decile. For reasons probably associated with migration to the cities,[29] total wages and income per employed person improved for the poorest rural households, however. These factors, along with the decimation of agricultural profits and rents, which dealt a hard blow to the highest decile, translated into a strong improvement in rural income distribution.

In urban areas, the combined impact of the increased supply of unskilled workers, due to rural migration, and the skilled labor demand bias induced by the sectoral reallocation of labor towards non-tradables (see Section 3) and the biases in technical change, was to raise the wages and the employment opportunities of the highly educated workers—and hence the relative income of households in the highest deciles—much more rapidly. Just as importantly, urban non-wage incomes registered an unprecedented upswing, which was quite possibly associated with the domestic demand boom rather than economic liberalization as such. This also was particularly beneficial to the most

---

29. An additional factor may have been non-agricultural employment opportunities in rural areas. See, on this, Jaramillo (1998).

TABLE 9: Decomposition of the Per Capita Income Growth

	1978 - 1991						1991 - 1995					
	TOTAL	1 - 2	3 - 5	6 - 8	9	10	TOTAL	1 - 2	3 - 5	6 - 8	9	10
EMPLOYED POPULATION AVERAGE INCOME												
National total	-0.80	-2.18	-1.54	-1.00	-0.20	0.33	4.26	6.57	4.35	3.74	2.27	3.41
Urban area	-0.88	-1.37	-0.89	-0.43	-0.54	-0.70	7.76	5.09	5.14	4.11	3.65	12.66
Rural area	-0.57	-2.53	-2.28	-1.98	-1.36	3.32	-4.39	8.70	4.22	3.59	0.23	-13.58
7 largest cities	-0.16	-0.54	-0.44	-0.06	-0.31	0.38	5.27	3.12	3.12	1.77	2.25	9.47
EMPLOYED RATE: EMPLOYEES/WORKING AGE POPULATION												
National total	1.43	2.40	1.95	1.24	0.54	1.00	-0.46	-2.34	-1.23	-0.11	1.52	0.54
Urban area	1.70	3.22	2.31	1.20	0.98	1.16	0.15	-1.70	-0.52	0.69	2.14	0.56
Rural area	1.07	1.76	1.51	1.08	0.75	0.08	-1.25	-3.32	-1.36	-1.91	-0.01	1.65
7 largest cities	1.70	2.59	2.09	1.30	1.48	1.34	0.22	-1.04	-0.26	0.90	0.79	0.42
% OF WORKING AGE POPULATION												
National total	0.17	0.35	0.19	0.14	0.17	-0.02	0.62	0.36	0.98	0.58	0.29	0.54
Urban area	-0.15	-0.41	-0.26	-0.07	0.14	0.02	0.84	1.63	0.97	0.80	0.22	0.26
Rural area	0.62	0.70	0.89	0.60	0.47	0.10	0.32	-0.22	0.08	0.69	0.10	0.96
7 largest cities	-0.14	-0.44	-0.17	-0.08	0.04	0.03	0.46	0.91	0.50	0.41	0.06	0.37
PER CAPITA INCOME												
National total	0.65	-0.16	0.19	0.22	0.50	1.35	4.42	4.06	4.01	4.28	4.26	4.64
Urban area	0.45	0.77	0.86	0.63	0.52	0.37	9.04	4.88	5.64	5.86	6.36	13.88
Rural area	1.08	-0.79	-0.49	-0.69	-0.33	3.58	-5.18	4.03	2.73	2.15	0.32	-12.27
7 largest cities	1.32	1.32	1.32	1.14	1.15	1.84	6.10	2.93	3.39	3.19	3.18	10.55

Note: For methodology see text.
Source: National Household Surveys. Data processed by the authors.

wealthy urban households. The deterioration in urban income distribution was the net outcome of all these forces.

Thus, the relative steadiness of overall distribution indicators in 1991–1995 disguises major distributional changes, many of which were associated with the structural reforms under way. The big winners in this process were the richest urban households, and the big losers were the richest rural households. As a whole, the reforms also had an extremely strong urban bias, as reflected in the sharp increase in the rural/urban income gap. The interruption of the upward trend in employment and the skewing of labor demand toward higher skills levels were the factors that had the strongest adverse impact on poor households, but these households did benefit from higher levels of income per employed person both in the city and in rural areas.

Economic adjustment since 1996 adversely hit household incomes, with two exceptions. First of all, labor incomes of the more educated workers performed better, due to the structural trends in labor demand. Secondly, rural rents experienced a recovery, benefiting the highest rural deciles. These two factors, rather than reduced employment opportunities explain the deterioration in income distribution experienced in 1995–1998. Indeed, compared with the years of economic expansion, 1991–1995, during which employment opportunities were distributed in a regressive fashion, falling employment after 1995 hit all households in a similar way in urban areas and in a progressive fashion in rural areas.

Poverty: its extent and severity

Trends in poverty indicators give a more positive picture of social progress in recent decades than do changes in income distribution. Improvements in in-

TABLE 9 (continued)

TOTAL	1995-1998					TOTAL	1978-1998				
	1 - 2	3 - 5	6 - 8	9	10		1 - 2	3 - 5	6 - 8	9	10
-0.21	-4.73	-1.62	0.29	4.22	0.05	0.14	-1.21	-0.61	-0.02	0.93	0.89
-2.07	-5.73	-2.91	-0.48	3.54	-3.65	0.33	-0.97	-0.20	0.36	0.82	0.94
2.87	-7.49	-2.29	-0.68	2.40	13.47	-0.80	-1.59	-1.25	-0.92	-0.58	-0.01
0.88	-4.61	-1.83	4.39	7.66	-0.93	1.00	-0.53	-0.03	0.97	1.37	1.91
-0.45	0.54	0.13	-0.68	-1.58	-0.83	0.77	1.12	1.04	0.69	0.40	0.64
-1.21	-0.26	-1.27	-1.10	-2.65	-0.70	0.94	1.64	1.17	0.76	0.62	0.77
0.75	1.60	0.75	1.71	-0.64	-0.42	0.57	0.67	0.83	0.58	0.39	0.30
-1.30	-0.31	-0.73	-1.99	-1.40	-1.20	0.94	1.41	1.20	0.71	0.91	0.78
-0.11	0.16	-0.41	0.14	-0.21	-0.33	0.21	0.33	0.25	0.22	0.14	0.03
0.04	0.41	0.05	-0.07	0.31	-0.38	0.06	0.08	0.01	0.09	0.18	0.00
-0.43	-0.42	-0.02	-0.65	0.42	-1.43	0.41	0.36	0.61	0.43	0.40	0.02
0.36	0.72	0.67	0.29	0.02	-0.38	0.04	-0.03	0.08	0.07	0.04	0.03
-0.76	-4.12	-1.89	-0.25	2.21	-1.12	1.18	-0.06	0.56	0.92	1.58	1.68
-3.17	-5.60	-4.02	-1.62	0.93	-4.60	1.41	0.43	0.93	1.28	1.79	1.86
3.22	-6.59	-1.62	0.32	2.15	10.90	0.06	-0.87	-0.10	-0.05	0.15	0.31
-0.09	-4.27	-1.89	2.45	5.97	-2.45	2.19	0.69	1.25	1.91	2.59	3.03

dicators for unsatisfied basic needs and coverage of social services (Section 4) have been coupled with a reduction in the extent of poverty as measured by income. These findings are consistent with those of parallel studies, particularly May et al. (1996) and DNP (1998). Improvements in poverty indicators are less pronounced, however, than those of unsatisfied basic needs. In addition, they concentrated in large cities, a fact that has led to a growing concentration of poverty and, in particular, extreme poverty, in rural areas.

Table 7 and Figure 4 summarize the changes that have occurred in the extent and severity of poverty as measured on the basis of two alternative sets of income (poverty-line) criteria. The first approach is based on the national poverty line, but unlike traditional estimates, the line is adjusted on the basis of the trend in the low-income CPI rather than on changes in food prices. This methodological difference eliminates the fluctuations associated with variations in relative food prices. The second criterion is the international poverty line (US$60/month, estimated at parity exchange rates).

As comparative studies indicate, Colombian poverty lines are considerably higher than those used to define poverty in comparative international studies. In fact, estimates using the international poverty line of US$60 per month are more favorable than those that use Colombia's extreme poverty lines.[30] Measurements based on the Colombian lines also exceed ECLAC estimates for 1994 and 1997 by six and ten percentage points, respectively.[31]

The above-mentioned table and figure indicate that poverty has diminished at a slow rate in Colombia over the past two decades. The overall reduction in

---

30. See Ocampo et al. (1998) and May et al. (1996).
31. See ECLAC (1999).

TABLE 10: Estimated Effects of Economic Growth and Income Distribution on Poverty

	1978 - 1991				1991 - 1995			
	GROWTH	DISTRIBUTION	RESIDUAL	TOTAL	GROWTH	DISTRIBUTION	RESIDUAL	TOTAL
NATIONAL TOTAL								
National poverty line	-2.9	5.5	0.3	2.9	-7.2	1.0	-0.3	-6.4
International poverty line	-2.1	1.9	0.1	-0.1	-4.6	0.7	-0.8	-4.7
URBAN AREA								
National poverty line	-1.9	0.2	0.0	-1.8	-14.7	7.0	-0.3	-8.0
International poverty line	-1.0	-1.8	0.0	-2.8	-5.6	2.9	-1.2	-3.9
RURAL AREA								
National poverty line	-4.5	12.6	0.9	9.0	8.1	-14.6	2.6	-4.0
International poverty line	-4.7	8.7	-0.6	3.5	11.2	-13.1	-3.4	-5.4

Source: National Household Surveys. Data processed by the authors.

poverty amounts to 1.5 and 0.9 percentage points. Poverty gaps have declined somewhat in urban areas, but have increased in the countryside. Indeed, over the long term, rural poverty has increased by 5.5 and 1.8 percentage points, respectively. Furthermore, the downward trend in poverty levels has not been uniform over time.

Table 10 shows changes in the extent of poverty according to the customary breakdown into the effects of growth and income distribution. This brings together the analysis pursued in the preceding sections with an examination of poverty trends. Urban poverty decreased between 1978 and 1991, and during the first half of the 1990s, but increased in 1995–1998. This pattern has been shaped chiefly by growth in urban income. The distributive effects were moderately positive until 1991 (but only with estimates using the international poverty line), extremely adverse in 1991–1995 and moderately adverse during the recent adjustment. For the period under examination as a whole, reductions in urban poverty have been associated with significant increases in real incomes.

Rural poverty trends were opposite to those exhibited by urban poverty in 1978–1991, but similar in the 1990s. However, distributive effects have been much stronger. In 1978–1991, the main factor behind the increase in rural poverty were adverse distributive trends, since incomes trended upward. In 1991–1995, the decline in rural income alone would have increased poverty by between 8 and 11 percentage points, but this adverse effect was counteracted by a very favorable distributive shock. For the period as a whole, the weak performance of rural vis-à-vis urban incomes has been the major factor behind the increase in rural poverty.

Statistical analyses of the determinants of poverty[32] indicate that the risk of a family being poor diminishes as the educational level of the head of household (and, to a lesser extent, of the spouse) and the age of the head of household rise. It increases, on the other hand, with the number of dependents, especially children under 10 years old, and when the head of household is a

---

32. See May et al. (1996) and Ocampo et al. (1998).

TABLE 10 (continued)

	1995 - 1998				1978 - 1998		
GROWTH	DISTRIBUTION	RESIDUAL	TOTAL	GROWTH	DISTRIBUTION	RESIDUAL	TOTAL
1.2	0.9	-0.1	2.0	-8.7	6.7	0.5	-1.5
1.0	1.7	0.2	2.9	-6.7	4.7	0.2	-1.8
5.2	0.1	-0.8	4.5	-10.0	4.9	-0.1	-5.2
2.3	1.6	0.0	3.9	-6.0	3.7	-0.5	-2.8
-4.7	4.6	0.6	0.5	0.5	4.5	0.4	5.5
-3.5	7.1	0.0	3.7	0.7	0.7	0.5	1.8

woman. These analyses also indicate that there has been an increasing bias against rural households. Finally, as expected, the probability of being poor is lower when the head of household is employed in a formal position (wage earner, business owner and retiree, in particular). Self-employment has become an increasingly adverse factor in relation to poverty over the past two decades.

Formal analyses of the links between macroeconomics, liberalization policies and equity

Ocampo et al. (1998) used multiple regression analysis to determine the effects of different macroeconomic variables on the Gini coefficient and the poverty headcounts ratios in large urban areas in 1981–1995. The strongest and most consistent effects found were those of protection on income distribution. According to the estimated coefficients, a 10% increase in protection improves the Gini coefficient by about one percentage point. As average tariff and non-tariff protection fell from 46% in 1987 to 8% since 1992, its estimated effects of income distribution was an increase of some four percentage points of the urban Gini coefficient. Faster economic growth also has an adverse effect on income distribution. There is also some support for the positive effects of exchange rate devaluation on income distribution, but this result is somewhat less consistent. Other variables, including fixed capital formation, social expenditure, minimum wages, unemployment and inflation, seem to exercise no influence on income distribution. It is interesting to point out that similar exercises using data up to 1998 tend to confirm the effect of trade liberalization on the urban Gini coefficient, but not that of GDP growth.

On the other hand, according to the same study, more rapid economic growth reduces poverty. An increase in economic growth by 1% reduces poverty by about 1.5 percentage points. There is also some evidence that reduced unemployment, protection and revaluation may increase poverty, but these results are statistically weaker. Similar exercises, using data up to 1998 give an important role to minimum wages as a determinant of poverty. Indeed, this variable seems to be the only consistent determinant of reductions of extreme poverty since the mid-1980s.

Existing analyses of returns to education indicate that they have experienced significant changes over the period of analysis. Three major changes have been identified by Núñez and Sánchez (1998): a moderate reduction in the return per year of education in the 1970s and 1980s (from 8.0% in 1976 to 5.8% in 1990); a significant reduction in the "premium" associated with completing secondary education, which was very sharp and turned negative in 1976–1982, and improved somewhat since the mid-1980s; and a significant increase in the premium of completing university education over the past few decades.

Both Robbins (1998) and Núñez and Sánchez (1998) associate relative wage shifts to major changes in the demand for labor. Robbins identified a major shift in the relative demand for labor with higher educational levels in the mid-1980s (specifically between 1983 and 1985, depending on the city), i.e., during the years of macroeconomic adjustment. Whereas the supply of more educated labor tended to outpace its demand up until then, the opposite was true since the second half of the 1980s. His regression analysis indicated that these effects could be associated with trade and exchange rate policies. Trade liberalization biased the demand for labor towards higher education and, thus, increased wage differentials; devaluation had a similar effect. The first of these effects is similar but the second opposite to those found by Ocampo et al. (1998). Thus, the change in the skill bias was associated, according to Robbins, to large devaluation in the mid-1980s. The continuation in the skill biases in the demand for labor in the 1990s was associated with trade liberalization, with revaluation having some mitigating effects.

Econometric results by Ocampo et al. (1998) also indicated that trade liberalization widened wage differentials, particularly those between workers with university education and the rest, and thus increased the labor Gini coefficient. They also showed that faster economic growth had a similar effect (although its effects on the Gini coefficient were statistically weak), and that fixed capital formation widened wage differentials, particularly between workers with university education and the rest, and thus worsened the distribution of wage income. Other results indicated that human capital formation had a positive effect on wage differentials and equity. In particular, it tended to reduce the wage dispersion between workers with primary education and the rest. Finally, according to this study, minimum wages have a favorable effect on wages for workers with primary education, but no overall effect on income distribution.

6. Conclusion

This paper has analyzed the effects of structural reforms in Colombia in the 1990s. It concludes that the attempt to combine economic liberalization with a more active social policy was no easy task, as reflected in rising fiscal stains. Also, the economic authorities experienced large difficulties in dealing with a more open economy. These difficulties gave rise to sharp stop-go cycles in monetary policy and exchange-rate appreciation up to 1997, which were reflected, in turn, in a more volatile GDP and aggregate demand growth than in the past. From the point of view of the sources of aggregate demand growth, the export-led growth characteristic of late 1980s was interrupted in the early 1990s. Rising domestic demand was thus the basis of rapid GDP growth in 1992–1995, led first by private demand and later by public sector spending. The demand stimulus became eventually unsustainable due to rising external deficits and was thus followed by a series of adjustments since 1996, the most severe of which was during the recent international financial crisis. Rising oil and mining production led to renewed export growth since 1995. Sectoral growth became more dispersed with the tradable sectors experiencing a sharp deterioration, particularly in agriculture and manufacturing.

This structural transformation had large effects on the labor market, the most important of which was the weak capacity of the economy to create new jobs. This phenomenon is evident since the 1992–1995 boom, but was then counteracted by favorable labor supply trends. By sectors, weak performance of employment in tradable sectors since the boom years was compensated by the positive response of non-tradable sectors, but this factor ceased to operate as the domestic demand-led expansion was exhausted.

Less-skilled workers have been the most affected by the reduction in labor demand. Sectoral shifts are partly responsible for the skill bias: the reduction of employment in tradables was a hard blow to the less educated, as rising demand for labor in non-tradables during the boom years concentrated in more educated labor. Beyond that, it is evident that the economy experienced labor-saving technical change, affecting workers of all educational levels, but more severely those with less skills.

The strong expansion in social spending was reflected in an improvement of living condition and in the coverage of social services, and a significant improvement in secondary income distribution. On the contrary, primary income distribution remained highly skewed and deteriorated further in the 1990s. This was the result of strong distributive shocks that partially netted out. The rural-urban income gap increased sharply in the first half of the 1990s, reflecting the urban bias of the trade liberalization process. However, between 1991 and 1995, rural distribution improved as a result of the destruction of rural rents, but this was followed by adverse trends in more recent years. On the urban side, distribution worsened considerably in the 1990s, basically due to the skill bias generated by structural and technological change.

Both urban and rural poverty improved in the first half of the 1990s but deteriorated during the recent adjustment period. Over the long term, urban poverty has decreased and rural poverty has increased. This has been basically determined by real income growth in urban and rural areas, respectively, but over shorter periods variations in income distribution have had important effects on rural poverty.

REFERENCES

Balcázar, Alvaro, Andrés Vargas and Martha Lucía Orozco (1998) *Del proteccionismo a la apertura. ¿El camino de la modernización agropecuaria?*, Bogotá: Misión Rural-IICA-Tercer Mundo.

Banco de la República (1995) "Endeudamiento externo privado," *Revista del Banco de la República*, May.

Berry, Albert and Jaime Tenjo (1998) "Guessing the Income Distribution Effects of Trade Liberalization and Labour Reform in Colombia," in Albert Berry (ed.), *Poverty, Economic Reforms, and Income Distribution in Latin America*, Boulder: Lynne Rienner, Chapter 8.

Cárdenas, Mauricio and Felipe Barrera (1997) "On the Effectiveness of Capital Controls: The Experience of Colombia during the 1990s," *Journal of Development Economics*, Vol. 54, No. 1, special, October.

———, Fabio Sánchez, Raquel Bernal and Jairo Núñez (1998) "El desempeño de la macroeconomía y la desigualdad," in Fabio Sánchez (ed.), *La distribución del ingreso en Colombia: tendencias recientes y retos de la política pública*, Bogotá: TM Editores-DNP.

Carrasquilla, Alberto (1999) *Estabilidad y gradualismo: Ensayos sobre economía colombiana*, Bogotá: Tercer Mundo Editores-Banco de la República.

Carrizosa, Mauricio (1987) "Evolución y determinantes de la pobreza en Colombia," in José Antonio Ocampo and Manuel Ramírez (eds.), *El problema laboral colombiano: Informes especiales de la Misión de Empleo*, Bogotá: Contraloría General de la República-Departamento Nacional de Planeación-SENA.

Comisión de Racionalización del Gasto y de las Finanzas Públicas (1997) *El saneamiento fiscal, un compromiso de la sociedad—Informe Final*, Bogota: Ministerio de Hacienda.

Cordi, Angela (1998) "El tamaño del Estado colombiano. Indicadores y tendencias," *Planeación y Desarrollo*, vol. 29, N° 3, Bogotá: Departamento Nacional de Planeación, July–September.

Departmento Nacional de Planeación (DNP) (1991) *La Revolución Pacífica*, Bogotá.

——— (1998) *Informe de desarrollo humano para Colombia 1998*, Bogotá: TM Editores-DNP.

ECLAC (1999) *Social Panorama of Latin America, 1998*, (LC/G.2050–P), Santiago, April.

Garay, Luis Jorge, Luis Felipe Quintero, Jesús Alberto Villamil, Jorge Tovar, Abdul Fatat, Sandra Gómez, Eliana Restrepo and Beatriz Yemail (1998) *Colombia: estructura industrial e internacionalización, 1967–1996*, Tomo I, Bogotá: Departamento Nacional de Planeación, July.

Hernández, Antonio and Carolina Gómez (1998) "Ajuste fiscal: de la retórica a los acuerdos," mimeo, Banco de la República.

Hommes, Rudolf, Armando Montenegro and Pablo Roda (1994) *Una apertura hacia el futuro*, Bogotá, Ministerio de Hacienda-Departamento Nacional de Planeación.

Jaramillo, Carlos Felipe (1998) *Liberalization, Crises and Change in Colombian Agriculture*, Boulder: Westview Press.

Leibovich, José (1998) «Análisis de los cambios en la distribución del ingreso rural (1988–1995),» mimeo, CEDE-Universidad de los Andes and Misión Social-Departamento Nacional de Planeación.

Londoño, Juan Luis (1995) *Distribución del ingreso y desarrollo económico: Colombia en el siglo XX*, Bogotá: Tercer Mundo-Banco de la República-Fedesarrollo.

——— (1997) "Social rifts in Colombia," *CEPAL Review* N° 61, Santiago, April.

May, Ernesto et al. (1996) *La pobreza en Colombia: Un estudio del Banco Mundial*, Bogotá, Tercer Mundo-Banco Mundial.

Ministerio de Hacienda y Crédito Público (1996) *La coyuntura y la política económica*, July.

Misión de Empleo (1986) *El problema laboral colombiano: Diagnóstico, perspectivas y políticas*, in *Economía Colombiana*, Separata No. 10, August–September.

Montenegro, Santiago (ed.) (1997) *Los determinantes de la tasa de cambio real en Colombia*, Bogotá: Universidad de los Andes-Facultad de Economía-CEDE, Debates No. 1.

Núñez, Jairo and Jaime Jiménez (1998) "Correcciones a las encuestas de hogares y distribución del ingreso urbano," in Sánchez (1998).

———— and Fabio Sánchez (1998) "Educación y salarios relativos 1976–1995: Determinantes, evolución e implicaciones para la distribución del ingreso," in Sánchez (1998).

Ocampo, José Antonio (1992) "Reforma del estado y desarrollo económico y social en Colombia," *Análisis Político*, No. 17, September–December.

———— (1997) "Evaluación de la situación fiscal colombiana," *Coyuntura Económica*, June.

———— (1999) "An Ongoing Structural Transformation: The Colombian Economy, 1986–1996," in Lance Taylor (ed.), *After Neoliberalism, What Next for Latin America?*, Ann Arbor: The University of Michigan Press.

———— and Santiago Perry (1995) *El giro de la política agropecuaria*, Bogotá: Tercer Mundo-FONDE-DNP.

———— and Javier Gómez (1997) "Los efectos de la devaluación nominal sobre la tasa de cambio real en Colombia," in Montenegro (1997).

———— and Camilo Tovar (1997) "Capital Flows, Savings and Investment in Colombia, 1990–1996," in Ricardo Ffrench-Davis and Helmut Reisen (eds.), *Capital Flows and Investment Performance: Lessons from Latin America*, ECLAC-OECD Development Centre, Paris.

———— and ———— (1999) "Price-based Controls on Capital Inflows: Colombia's Experience in the 1990s," mimeo, ECLAC.

———— et al. (1998) "Macroeconomía, ajuste estructural y equidad en Colombia: 1978–1996," in Enrique Ganuza, Lance Taylor and Samuel Morley (eds.), *Política macroeconómica y pobreza en América Latina y el Caribe*, BID/CEPAL/PNUD, Madrid: Ediciones Mundi-Prensa; in *Coyuntura Social* No. 18, Bogotá, May; and in Sánchez (1998).

Pérez, María José, Francisco Lasso, Juan Carlos Parra and Guillermo Rivas (1996) "Evolución de la pobreza y la distribución del ingreso, 1978–1995: Aspectos metodológicos," mimeo, Bogotá: Departamento Nacional de Planeación.

Reyes, Alvaro (1987) "Tendencias del empleo y la distribución del ingreso," in José Antonio Ocampo and Manuel Ramírez (eds.), *El problema laboral colombiano: informes especiales de la Misión de Empleo*, Bogotá: Contraloría General de la República-Departamento Nacional de Planeación-SENA.

————, Stefano Farné, Jesús Perdomo and Luis Angel Rodríguez (1996) "Distribución de los ingresos urbanos en Colombia en la década del noventa," mimeo, Bogotá: Universidad Externado de Colombia.

Robbins, Donald (1998) "Liberación comercial y salarios: 1976–1994," in Sánchez (1998).

Sánchez, Fabio (ed.) (1998) *La distribución del ingreso en Colombia: Tendencias recientes y retos de la política pública*, Bogotá: TM Editores-DNP, July.

————— and Núñez (1999) "Descentralización, pobreza y acceso a los servicios sociales. ¿Quién se benefició del gasto público en los noventa?," *Documento CEDE* 99–04, Bogotá: Universidad de los Andes, Facultad de Economía, Centro de Estudios de Desarrollo Económico, April.

—————, Mauricio Olivera and Manuel Fernando Castro (1995) "Evolución del Sector Público 1981–1994," *Planeación y Desarrollo*, July–September.

Taylor, Lance (1998) "Balance of Payments Liberalization: Effects on Employment, Distribution, Poverty and Growth," Terms of Reference paper for the Project Balance of Payments Liberalization: Effects on Employment, Distribution and Growth, UNDP/ECLAC/IDB.

Urrutia, Miguel (1984) *Los de arriba y los de abajo*, Bogotá: Fedesarrollo-CEREC.

————— (1995) "La Estrategia de Estabilización de la Junta del Banco de la República 1991-1994," *Revista del Banco de la República*, March.

Vélez, Carlos Eduardo (1996) *Gasto social y desigualdad: logros y extravíos*, Bogotá: Departamento Nacional de Planeación.

5

Cuba: External Opening, Labor Market and Inequality of Labor Incomes

ANGELA FERRIOL MURUAGA
National Institute for Economic Research

Introduction

The external opening that took place in the Cuban economy in the nineties has unique characteristics that differentiate it from the experience of other countries. In the first place, the Cuban opening was accompanied by a severe external adjustment of magnitude much greater than that experienced recently by other economies of the region. Also this opening has been part of a wider process of modification of the economic model. There has been a transformation from a highly centralized system based on balancing the distribution of material resources, to a system based mainly on financial mechanisms as well as a greater degree of managerial autonomy.

Although it is a well-known fact, it is important to keep in mind that Cuba is the only socialist economy in the Western Hemisphere. After thirty years of existence, its economy was greatly affected by the political changes that took place in Eastern Europe. In spite of the economic trauma that this represented, the social and political objectives of the socialist model remained in full force. The nineties is significant because of the existing tension between the purpose of adapting the economy to the new environment and the desire to preserve—among other things—the achievements in equity obtained previously. This process of economic transformation and external opening presents characteristics which are quite different from those of others countries, because of the way economic variables react to one another, and also because of the priorities and objectives given. In particular, social concerns, not just economic considerations, were considered. Emphasis has also been given to the gradual implementation of changes, to achieving political consensus, and to the active participation of the State in the management of the economy.

On the other hand, the transformations occurring in Cuba have had a greater impact on its economic system than the process of external opening taking place in other countries. They have required important modifications to institutions, the legal framework, and managerial culture. However, the final objectives are much more limited with respect to the prevalence of the market in determining socioeconomic relations.

Once said, it becomes necessary to explain what Cuba's external opening has consisted of. Briefly it has consisted of the opening to foreign capital by way of direct investments. It has also included the decentralization of external trade and the reduction of tariffs. Also, an internal market in foreign exchange had been created, in which national enterprises compete with products offered by international firms. Free trade zones have also been created. There are some investment funds, although further development of portfolio investments is not foreseen. On the other hand, it should be pointed out, that no restrictions have been placed on the repatriation of profits to joint businesses.

A notable feature of Cuba's reinsertion into the international market, has been the formation of a *dual* economy. Activities linked to the external sector, in general, carry out all their operations in foreign exchange, while the remaining activities are conducted in the national currency. This alternative has permitted the avoidance of a devaluation, under conditions of strong monetary imbalance, and given the lack of financial and price mechanisms.

The division of the economy into two sectors explains in part why the official exchange rate has remained unchanged, at its traditional level of one peso to one dollar. The only important function of the official rate is its role in determining internal prices in national currency, since convertibility does not exist. The alleged advantage of maintaining this fixed rate is the maintenance of stable internal prices under conditions of structural disequilibrium. A modification in the rate of exchange of the magnitude required under these conditions, would have resulted in a high increase in the cost of living, with a strong regressive effect on income distribution.

To understand the purpose of this dual exchange rate system, it is necessary to explain the form in which foreign exchange circulates and how economic activity is regulated. Enterprises generating revenues in foreign exchange cover their expenditures with their own revenues and give part of their earnings to the central budget. In turn, foreign exchange is centrally allocated to activities related to the internal market that do not have revenues in foreign exchange. It was possible in this way to assign and distribute foreign exchange according to economic and social priorities, particularly when the available total foreign exchange decreased 75 percent.

For example, in the public health sector, strong restrictions on imported medicines were imposed, yet patient care remained a priority. This would not have happened if a general budgetary restriction had been applied. In this manner, with the strengthening of preventive medicine attended to by the doctors, a certain substitution effect was achieved, thus preserving the main achievements attained in this area.

The fact that the GDP decreased by over a third, while imports decreased by three fourths can be explained to a great extent by this peculiar adjustment mechanism, implemented to face the external shock. It is evident that in the long run, segmentation of the economy and the lack of a system of prices based on a more representative exchange rate can limit a more effective readjustment of the economy. But at present, the mechanisms previously described govern the links between the internal and the external economy.

Enterprises that carry out their operations in foreign exchange, as well as those entities that receive a central allocation in foreign exchange, have the possibility to acquire their inputs by way of imports or by financing a national producer. In this manner an internal market in foreign exchange has been created, to which producers have been progressively incorporated. This, in fact, has become one of the main mechanisms to stimulate the economy. Tourism, transport and telephone services, traditional exports like sugar, nickel, fishing, tobacco and others, have become the locomotive pulling the remaining sectors. New jobs are generated through these links, and they are generally better paid than already available jobs.

A significant amount of dollarization has also taken place, influencing the process of external opening. The holding of foreign exchange by the population was legalized, facilitating the reception of remittances from abroad. Together with this, a network of state stores was created with the purpose of collecting this foreign exchange. In this way, the internal market in foreign exchange was enlarged, and the incorporation of additional producers of consumer goods was made possible. This paper analyzes the effects of the dollarization process on the distribution of revenues and also on poverty.

Like other centrally planned economies, the Cuban economy in 1989 was basically restricted on the supply side. The introduction of these reforms has meant a progressive incorporation of market elements in the determination of economic activity. Yet these changes do not prevent the economy from being planned in a centralized way, although the focus and methodological instruments have been modified.

Activities that carry out their operations in foreign exchange, have their activity level conditioned by the demand of the market and its competitiveness; while internal market activities, that receive foreign exchange through a central allocation, have their production restricted on the supply side. In the critical years in which the external adjustment took place, the main form of regulation was through the conformation to the import plan and the allocation of foreign exchange. Later on, as systems of self-management in foreign exchange have expanded, demand elements have attained a growing importance.

Another significant aspect to be considered while interpreting the causal relationships that govern economic processes in Cuba, is the existence of strongly segmented markets and spheres. Besides the differences between enterprises that operate in foreign exchange and in national currency, there is also a division between the monetary circulation that takes place in the population and that of the business sphere. Until recently, the savings of the population remained practically inactive; now they are being employed for bank lending, but still at a relatively modest scale.

In the general population, there is a market rationed at low prices; a state market at supply and demand prices; a non-state market also at unregulated prices; and a state and non-state market based on foreign exchange. In general, there has been a shift, from the market rationed at low prices, toward other segments governed by demand with non-regulated prices. However the role of the rationed market and the distribution of foods through social channels still carry an important weight.

Exchange firms have been created to allow the population to purchase and sell foreign exchange, according to a non-official exchange rate. But currency exchange operations are not foreseen in the immediate future for enterprises.

In recent years, enterprise deposits in foreign exchange have been mobilized for bank lending, which has already reached significant volumes. The interest rate employed is linked to the rates obtained in the international market, and is relatively high, at around 12 percent. However, most financing is composed of external trade credits, determined by conditions prevailing in the financial market, with an increase in rates reflecting the difficulty Cuba faces in obtaining international credit.

In summary, it can be stated that Cuba's external opening has had a strong impact on all social and economic structures. It has become an important stimulating factor helping to reinsert the Cuban economy into the international economy. This is so, despite the difference in approach of Cuba's insertion with those of other economies, in conformity with the purpose of carrying out economic changes in a gradual way and within the limits of a model that restricts the influence of the market.

In what follows, there is an exposition of the main characteristics of the economic reform, with emphasis on the external opening, changes in the labor market, and social policy measures. Subsequently, three aspects are analyzed: macroeconomic performance, mesoeconomic dynamics, and changes in the labor market, including workers remuneration. All those cases that reflect a direct relationship between the opening of the economy and labor revenues obtained by the population, are also examined. Lastly, we analyze the relationship between the labor revenues of households and their economic situation. The study ends with some general conclusions.

1. Reforms, Opening and the Labor Market

Since 1989 the government has adopted measures aimed at increasing foreign exchange revenues while at the same time, minimizing the social consequences of such external adjustment. Development programs were implemented such as tourism and biotechnology. Food production was also encouraged with the intention of replacing imports. The opening to foreign capital was promoted mainly through the creation of joint ventures. At the start of this period, state workers were guaranteed employment and wages. Priority was also accorded to social programs like health and education, within the limits of available resources.

In 1992 the Constitution of the country underwent changes to take into account new ownership forms. The state monopoly on external trade was eliminated and planning was given a more flexible role. In 1994, as monetary imbalances worsened, including a high budget deficit, measures were adopted to face this situation. Since 1992 important organizational and institutional measures have been implemented to achieve permanent changes in the working of the economy, with the intent of increasing the effectiveness of resource use. Along with what has been mentioned, measures were also adopted to achieve a larger decentralization of enterprise management. Table 1 in the Annex (page 171) shows measures classified by spheres, with their chronology and main impact from the macroeconomic, social, and microeconomic points of view.[1]

With respect to the external opening, it should be pointed out that foreign capital investing directly in Cuba typically enjoys greater guarantees than those found in other countries. This includes the unrestricted repatriation of their profits and capital. The approval of associations with foreign capital is done on a case-by-case basis, with decisions based on three fundamental criteria: that they contribute technology, market or capital. Total liberalization linked to privatization, prevailing in the external opening of other countries, has not been present in Cuba. Concerning capital flows, it is important to point out that since 1964, Cuba has had no access to financing from the International Monetary Fund (IMF), the Inter-American Development Bank (IDB) or the World Bank. The effect of the United States economic blockade,[2] worsened under the Helms-Burton law, has been to increase significantly the cost of credits obtained.[3] This situation has forced the government to take important steps to mobilize available commercial credit and face the external gap.

Cuba's trade opening has brought about three main changes: (1) the emergence of an extensive entrepreneurial network dedicated to external trade activities, transforming the state monopoly;[4] (2) the creation of internal markets

---

1. The classification of the reform is based on González, A. See for example *Economía y Sociedad. Los retos del modelo económico*. Revista Temas No.11, 1997.

2. Although the United States rejects the term *blockade* and prefers the word *embargo*, it is impossible to ignore the different measures implemented with the intention of involving third-party countries in the sanctions.

3. Other consequences of the blockade are: excessive freight expenses, lower prices of Cuban exports compared with prices in the world market, losses due to changes in currency exchanges as compared with the dollar, and others.

4. Between 1989 and 1995 external trade among Cuban enterprises increased six fold. Moreover, external trade has also been carried out by foreign trade representations and associations with foreign capital, who outnumber the Cuban enterprises three-fold.

in foreign exchange; and (3) the reduction of tariffs. In 1990 the average rate for the Most Favored Nation was 17.7 percent. With the reductions, this was lowered to an average of 10.7 percent in 1996.

Social measures began in 1990 with the decision to keep state workers in their jobs and to preserve their nominal incomes, despite the abrupt contraction of the economy that was taking place. Also, almost all consumption goods available were transferred to the rationing system. Additionally, there was an expressed will to preserve as much as possible of the health and education programs. Later on, new measures were incorporated that showed an incipient trend in achieving more efficiency in social policy.

The macroeconomic measures adopted in 1994 were very significant. They embraced an increase in prices for products not considered essential goods, the eradication of certain gratuities, an increase in user rates (such as in electricity consumption), and tax reform. Also, specific actions were carried out to decrease losses faced by state enterprises, as well as other measures to reduce the budget deficit.

Another component of reform was the expansion of the area corresponding to non-state activities. Besides the opening to foreign investors, the State gave rent-free a large share of state agricultural land to newly created cooperatives[5] and also gave greater scope to self-employment activities.

An additional change has been the creation of distinct markets based on unregulated prices, both in foreign exchange and national currency. The State conceived these markets in a stratified or segmented manner,[6] for the sphere of consumer goods and services. Nevertheless, the different market segments influence each other; and the non-official exchange rate also links purchasing capacity in both currencies.

Before the reforms, the labor market was highly structured and regulated.[7] Direct recruiting by enterprises excluded a number of jobs. For example, it included neither the labor force in the capital, nor university graduates undertaking social service.[8]

---

5. In 1989, 78 percent of the land was in the hands of the State. By the end of 1997 that proportion was 33 percent (*Cuba en Cifras, 1997*, Oficina Nacional de Estadísticas).

6. A segmented market is one that possesses strata with different access defined for both buyers and sellers. There are different rules concerning the general formation of prices (due to the use of trade rates, margins, tariffs and taxes), the use of different currencies, and in general, mechanisms to catch surpluses formed in the different strata. They can be found in the agricultural market and in the industrial and handmade goods market. It includes state sales at fixed and unregulated prices, stores in national currency, stores in foreign currency, the sale and purchase of dollars, and earnings from self-employed services.

7. The labor policy pretended to achieve full employment, to eradicate unemployment as a social problem, to guarantee equal payment for equal work, and to maintain wage differences within an appropriate range. It also managed to negotiate the formation of a necessary qualified labor force that automatically places graduates. To execute these ambitious objectives, centralized labor legislation was conceived and was uniformly employed in the whole country. It was negotiated with certain decentralization in Municipal Labor Offices, but always with the direct supervision of the corresponding Ministry.

Non-official Exchange Rate

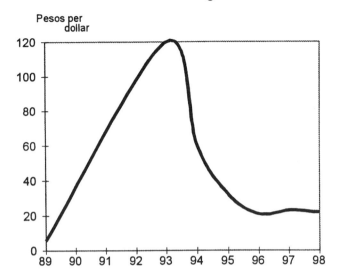

Additionally, all economic enterprises had to set aside a percentage of their jobs to employ workers assigned in a centralized way. A wage scale was centrally established—with a very narrow range—together with nation-wide rates, based on work complexity and required skills.[9]

The reforms in the labor sphere adopted some new measures but still maintained a great deal of what was previously legislated. The most important changes besides greater flexibility of self-employed activity, have been:

· Increase the protection given to surplus workers as a result of the managerial resizing processes, especially regarding wage guarantees.

· Establish new job opportunities for university graduates, when there are no possibilities for permanent contracts, including a specific wage treatment.

· Implement wage-incentive schemes, as a complement to the existing wage system. These can be either in foreign exchange, national currency, or in kind. They are applied mainly to activities generating foreign exchange.[10]

---

8. The Law of the Social Service No.1254 of 1973 states that university graduates upon completion of their studies will work for three years at an enterprise assigned to them. There, they will receive training to complete their formation and they will put the acquired knowledge (gratuitously) to the service of society.

9. The salary scale sets a minimum wage of 100 pesos and a difference of 4.5 times between the highest and lowest wages.

10. The remuneration in foreign exchange can be directly in foreign exchange or through access to purchase in stores that sell in that currency. In some cases it consists of the delivery of consumption goods. Remuneration modalities in foreign exchange in all their forms encompassed in 1997 the 37 percent of the labor force employed by the State or that works in agriculture cooperatives (Basic Cooperative Production Units). Taken from Rodríguez, J.L., *Resultados económicos en 1997 y el plan económico para 1998*. Informe a la Asamblea Nacional, Diciembre 1997.

· Design municipal employment programs; condition resizing of enterprises to the creation of new employment.

· Create a mechanism that intermediates with foreign investors, with respect to recruiting workers, wages and social security.

In summary, the labor reforms have been very moderate with respect to liberalization, and have attained wide scope only with regard to worker protection under the new environment.

Reforms of a more structural character started in 1993 and have had their sequence and development. Although it can be said that the period of reforms started mainly in 1993,[11] it should be noted that some of these processes can last several years.

2. Macroeconomic Performance

When the collapse of the socialist countries took place at the end of the eighties, Cuba lost its main trade links—in 1990, 85 percent of Cuban trade was with them. At first sight the most significant element of the large external shock was the abrupt reduction of imports. The rate of imports decreased from almost 29 percent in 1989 (with respect to the aggregate supply) to barely 15 percent in 1993–1994.

GDP (at 1989 prices) fell 30 percent between 1989 and 1993. After that, a moderate recovery process began, with only 1996 standing out, with growth of around 8 percent. In the other years between 1994 and 1998 the dynamics of the internal product did not surpass 2.5 percent in any one year. Thus, though the reform and economic opening have contributed in reversing the contraction of GDP, the dynamism has been limited.

The external imbalance that gave rise to the adjustment had as an important component, an initial trade deficit in 1989 equivalent to 12 percent of GDP.

The rate of imports (m in graph 1) contracted dramatically, not as a result of a devaluation process, but due to the government's decision to contract supply. Because of this, activities not directly linked to imports were not at first effected. Later on the rate of imports recuperated to 62 percent of its 1989 level.

The rate of net taxes (t), which was already low in 1989 due to the high proportion of intergovernmental credits received from socialist countries, fell as a result of the policies to subsidize the population and enterprises against the ill effects of adjustment. Since 1993 the fiscal gap was almost eradicated, and as will be shown below, this was due partly to the growth shown by transfers from population and enterprises to the government; and partly—although in smaller measure—to the contraction of government expenditures.

The growth experienced in the rate of private savings up to 1994, reflects mainly the increase in circumstantial savings of the population, due to the

---

11. The opening to foreign capital and the external trade decentralization began before 1993, but have only begun to have an important share in the economy since 1999.

GRAPH 1: Imports, Private Saving and Tax Rates

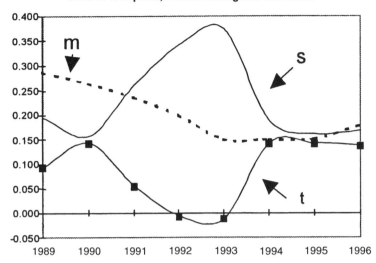

GRAPH 2: Government Expenditures

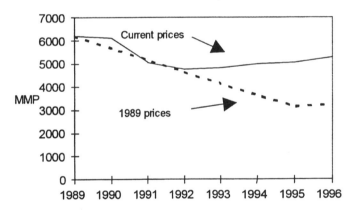

lack of consumer goods and services available.[12] The decrease later on of the saving rate is a result of the package of financial measures implemented, aimed at decreasing the monetary supply and stimulating the depressed household consumption.

The magnitude and nature of the changes is evident in the analysis of the flow of financial transfers between the government on one hand, and the managerial sector and population on the other.

12. It should be remembered that for Cuba there is a certain financial independence between the population and the enterprise spheres. For this reason, savings is not directly applicable to investment.

GRAPH 3: Net Transfers Government-Private Sector

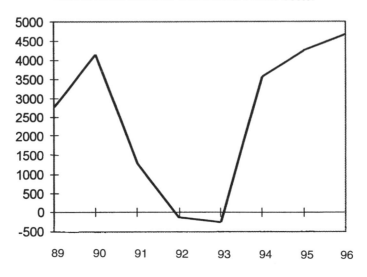

GRAPH 4: Transfers Government-Private Sector

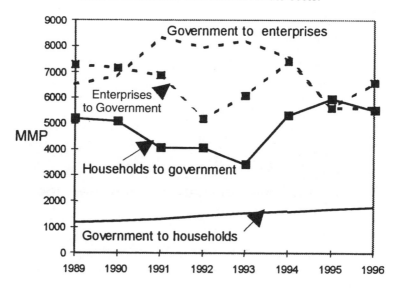

As can be observed, it was decided that social security and welfare transfers would be preserved and increased during the whole period, both during the initial years of GDP contraction, up to 1993, and during the economic recovery. Transfers from households to the government (composed almost entirely up until 1989 by consumption taxes) were reduced up to 1993, because the supply of household consumption goods decreased. Later on these transfers grew, due

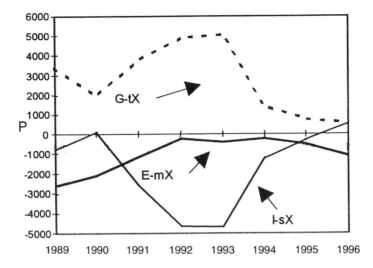

GRAPH 5: Financial Gaps (current prices)

to the recomposition and positive dynamics of the consumer goods market (with the creation of new market segments at supply and demand prices), but also as a result of the implementation of the new tax system. During the period covered, the consumer price index increased, with a conservative estimate given at 81 percent between 1989 and 1993. This inflation was concentrated in the informal economy, where prices multiplied 10 times in those years, while subsidy prices for the rationed market remained constant. Later on, prices fell around 5 percent per year between 1994 and 1996.

With regard to relations between the government and enterprises, from 1989 to 1993, they reflect the drop in economic activity, on the one hand, and on the other, the growth of state subsidies to maintain managerial capacities, without labor discharges or salary decreases. After 1993, the effect of the reform is to bring about a reversal of the previous tendencies.

The dynamics of financial imbalances can be appreciated in graph 5.[13]

The improvement observed in the trade deficit up to 1992 stems from the severe slowing of economic activity caused by the above-mentioned lack of inputs. Scarce available resources were concentrated on export activities. In the phase of external opening, the trade deficit remained under control, partly due to decisions to restrict imports. Also significant were the positive export dynamics, which increased 70 percent between 1993 and 1996 (at current prices). Another important structural change was the increase in the share of

13. In the graph, the notation is the following: deficit or commercial surplus: E-mX; deficit or fiscal surplus: G-tX; deficit or surplus of private saving: I–sX. In the first one the minus sign indicates deficit. In the others, the minus sign indicates surplus.

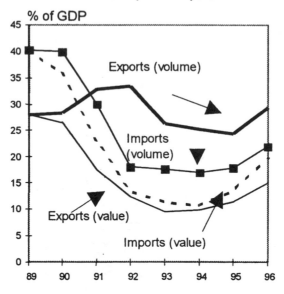

GRAPH 6: Exports & Imports

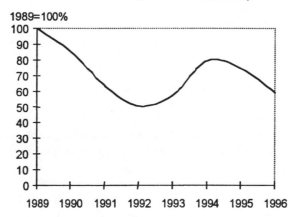

GRAPH 7: Exchange Prices Relationship

services (mainly tourism, air transport, and communications) in the value of total exports. This share grew from 11 percent in 1989, to 50 percent of the export revenue share.

The export bias of the economic reform and the corresponding structural changes can be better understood, when seen at constant prices. Maintaining the official exchange rate of 1 peso per dollar, the trade imbalance disappears. The share of exports in GDP at 1989 prices (see Graph 6) surmounts that of imports. This takes place under conditions of economic recovery after 1995. In that graph, it can also be observed that the structural change is modest in terms of value. An exchange rate that reflects more objectively the relationship of the Cuban peso with other currencies would show higher levels of external aperture for the Cuban economy than those observed in Graph 6.

The terms of trades have been adverse for the country; especially the prices for sugar and nickel—decisive items in the case of Cuba—, which have shown very depressed levels since 1994.

The greater share of export goods (at constant prices), coincided with the appreciation of the national currency in transactions for the population (where the non-official exchange rate operates). But as enterprise finances are separated from those of the population, this did not imply a loss of national competitiveness. The main consequence of the appreciation of the currency was a process of redistribution that took place in household incomes, shifting purchasing power from those that possessed foreign exchange, to those that did not have it; thus bringing about a decrease in income inequality.

In the following breakdown of aggregate demand and its components (at constant prices), the particular interpretation of the Cuban case must be borne in mind; as changes are not entirely demand-driven, but reflect to a large extent government decisions in the distribution of resources.[14]

Up until 1993, investment experienced the largest contraction (excluding household consumption). Exports, followed by government expenditures, had priority. Later on, the relative importance of investment recovers, mainly at the expense of government expenditures. In the final years—when the most dynamic activities start to operate based on demand—aggregate demand and its components seem to be reflecting, to a certain extent, the multiplying effect of the increase in exports. The important role of investment as a factor in economic growth also becomes evident.

It is convenient to analyze what were the effects to the above-mentioned financial imbalances (fiscal, external, and private saving), of interest on external debt and external current transfers (by way of remittances and donations, mainly).

The table on the following page reflects a change of a certain importance. Before the opening, and at current prices, the net balance of debt payment and transfers from donations and remittances, meant for the country a worsening of the trade imbalance, even under non-payment of the existing debt since 1986.[15] After 1993, although the interest payments increased slightly, the dynamics of the remaining net average transfers increased gradually. This already had a positive effect of a certain magnitude in 1996. The money trans-

---

14. The decomposition of the aggregate demand is as follows:

$X=((s/(s+t+m))(I/S)+(t/(s+t+m))(G/t)+((m/(s+t+m))(E/m)$ where X is the aggregate supply (GDP plus imports), s is the private saving rate, t is the net taxes rate, m is the imports rate, I is investment, G is government expenditure and E is exports.

15. The external debt of Cuba in foreign exchange amounted at the end of 1997 to 46 percent of GDP (estimate). Of this, 58 percent corresponds to official bilateral debt, 25 percent are obligations contracted with financial institutions and the remaining 12 percent corresponds to commercial firms.

PROPORTION COMPARED TO GDP

	Before transfers			After transfers		
	Ip-spX	G-tX	E-mX	Ip-spX-iDg+ ei*Fp	G-tX+iDg+ ei*Fg	E-mX- ei*F
	Current prices					
1989	-3.7	15.9	-12.2	-2.7	16.7	-14.0
1990	0.5	8.7	-9.3	1.6	9.8	-11.4
1991	-12.9	18.5	-5.6	-12.2	19.3	-7.1
1992	-22.8	23.9	-1.1	-22.4	24.5	-2.1
1993	-22.2	24.1	-1.8	-23.1	24.8	-1.8
1994	-5.4	6.3	-0.9	-6.1	7.3	-1.2
1995	-1.1	3.2	-2.1	-2.1	4.3	-2.2
1996	2.3	2.5	-4.8	-3.2	3.9	-0.7
	Ip-spX	G-tX	E-mX	Ip-spX-iDg+ ei*Fp	G-tX+iDg+ ei*Fg	E-mX- ei*F
	Constant prices					
1989	-3.7	15.9	-12.2	-2.7	16.7	-14.0
1990	-0.9	9.2	-8.3	0.2	10.2	-10.4
1991	-17.5	21.1	-3.6	-16.8	21.9	-5.1
1992	-30.6	28.7	1.9	-30.2	29.3	1.0
1993	-37.5	28.9	8.6	-38.3	29.7	8.7
1994	-14.3	6.7	7.6	-15.0	7.6	7.3
1995	-9.5	3.0	6.5	-10.6	4.1	6.4
1996	-9.5	2.0	7.4	-14.9	3.4	11.5

Source: Calculations by the author, based on data from the Anuario Estadístico de Cuba, ONE, 1996, and the book La Economía Cubana, CEPAL, 1997.[16]

fers favored the enterprise and household sectors, causing the fiscal deficit to increase after making those transfers.

Incorporating an analysis of external savings gives a more complete picture. Before the external opening, the position of the capital account reflected the negative impact of the disappearance of the links with the former socialist countries. In the later period, the opening has not yet translated into growing capital flows. The net effect on the capital account since 1993 —excluding 1995—has not exceeded 10 percent of the 1989 balance.[17]

Short-term credits have had an important role in the capital flows. In practice, a situation of chronic liquidity deficit has resulted, thus hindering the performance of the economy.

In synthesis, the reform implemented, with its external opening component and restrictive monetary and fiscal policies, resulted in a reduction of the current account and fiscal deficits, with a decrease in the forced savings of the population. At constant prices the external balance presented a surplus, which reflects the structural change implemented in the exports/imports re-

---

16. Additional notation: Dg is the internal government debt; ei*F is the interest payment on the external debt; ei*Fg is the interest payment of the government external debt and ei*Fp is the interest payment of the private external debt.

17. Between 1959 and 1989, 66 percent of Cuban external credits were obtained from Socialist countries, with favorable financial conditions.

GRAPH 8: Capital Account Balance

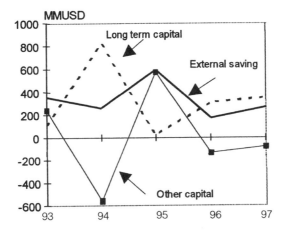

lationship. The fiscal deficit was diminished significantly, due both to the contraction of expenditures and to a decrease of net transfers to the private sector. As can be appreciated, external and internal balances improved at the same time. It must be noted that changes in the pattern of operation of the economy happened during this period. This in fact was an economic opening that tended to compensate for the contractionary policies implemented.

What share of the changes was the result of effects from external opening? It is not a simple task to delineate the different components of the reform in the analysis. In principle, in the conception of the reform itself and due to the external shock that gave rise to it, a necessary condition for any economic activity to be able to recover, is the contribution to the external balance. On the other hand, the positive effect of current net transfers coming from abroad, seems a direct consequence of the opening. Next, we will try to determine the relationship between the external opening and economic performance, through a mesoeconomic approach.

3. Sectoral Performance and Changes in Productivity

The composition of GDP by sectors does not reflect great changes. Traded production,[18] which represented 34 percent of total GDP in 1989, decreased to 29 percent in 1993, though its participation later recovered. With respect to 1989, more important contraction and recovery processes are observed.

---

18. Traded production includes agriculture, forest and fishing; mines and quarries; and manufacturing industry. All services were considered in the non-traded sector. This classification does not permit to appreciate in all its magnitude the impact of tourism.

158 Ferriol Muruaga

Growth of Traded and Non-Traded Production, 1990–1996 (1989=1)

Growth index (1989=1)	1990	1991	1992	1993	1994	1995	1996
Traded	0.961	0.825	0.710	0.605	0.630	0.676	0.745
Non-traded	0.989	0.918	0.851	0.747	0.739	0.742	0.790

The opening has not brought about a diversification of export goods. Exports are concentrated in four product groups: foods (mainly sugar, fish and shellfish), non-edible raw materials (mainly nickel); beverages and tobacco; and chemical products (mainly pharmaceutical products).

Exportable productions of nickel, fishing, and tobacco, in that order, have recovered to pre-crisis levels, and even to higher ones in the case of nickel.[19] The export of traditional and biotechnological pharmaceutical products has been increased, although with limited growth when compared with existing potential.[20] The sugar industry, the main source of external revenues, still performed poorly despite improvements in efficiency parameters in the 1989–1999 crop. It has not yet recovered to its previous level.

Tourism has become the main activity generating foreign exchange revenues.[21] International transport and communications have also contributed

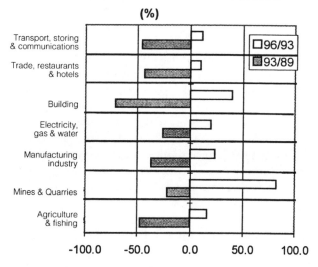

GRAPH 9: Product Sectoral Dynamics

19. With respect to nickel, it can be said that the formation of joint companies with foreign capital and the application of pay-incentive systems in foreign exchange have been relevant to the results achieved. What were significant in fishing and tobacco were the organizational changes, the new managerial methods, and the application of labor incentives in foreign exchange.

20. Marketing problems and lack of access to markets with an oligopoly structure have affected the results.

21. An element influencing its development has been the opening to foreign investments. Also, relevant is the reorganization of management as well as contracts for hotel administration with foreign firms.

to the increase in internal product, but the increase has not yet been able to compensate for the contraction of production that occurred between 1989 and 1993. This is shown in Graph 9.

The experience of the manufacturing industry highlights the strategy implemented by the economic reform and the external opening. When the external shock took place there were no massive industry closings, causing sub-utilization of industrial capacities, underemployment of the labor force, and progressive de-capitalization.[22] A gradual economic revival was conceived by creating joint ventures and linking industrial enterprises to activities generating foreign exchange. This was combined with managerial resizing. After four years, three groups of products can be distinguished in industrial production. The first one with positive dynamics, composed of those industries that have established markets in foreign exchange abroad, or that are needed by tourism, or construction linked to that sector. Products that show no significant signs of recovery compose the second group, embracing activities requiring agricultural inputs. The third group is composed of products that have almost stopped being manufactured due to lack of competitiveness as a result of technological inadequacies, in which foreign partners have not arisen to assist technological re-conversion.[23]

Until 1993, sectoral productivity reflects the policy of maintaining workers in their jobs and subsidizing underemployment during the period of adjustment. After the opening, productivity increased an average of 4 percent per year, an increase that was due mainly to the group of traded products whose productivity increased at an average rate of 11 percent per year. Within this group, mining showed exceptional growth. This sector received foreign financing, underwent technological re-conversion, was guaranteed a sure market, as well as pay incentives in foreign exchange. These factors explain the productivity increase observed. In the manufacturing industry, productivity increased during 1993 and 1996 at an average of 9.5 percent per year, after experiencing a contraction of similar magnitude between 1989 and 1993. This sector has benefited from the growing demand for Cuban products brought about by tourism and from the stores that sell in foreign exchange in the country.[24] In non-traded sectors, productivity increased after 1993 mostly in construction (15 percent annually), but starting from very depressed levels.

---

22. In 1989 the industrial network faced high coefficients of energy and material consumption, and excess capacity. Several studies have been carried out on the Cuban manufacturing sector. See, for example, Colectivo de autores, "Elementos para una reorganización del sistema empresial cubano," *Revista Cuba: Investigación Económica* No.1, 1995.

23. The dynamics of the physical volume was analyzed by products, with a selection of 197 products according to the UN International Uniform Industrial Classification, valued at 1995 constant prices.

24. The share of Cuban products as supplies for tourism and in stores selling in foreign exchange was 35 percent in 1996 and 41 percent in 1997 (*Report on the Economic Results from 1997 and the Economic and Social Plan for 1998*, speech by the Minister of Economy in the National Assembly, December, 1997).

GRAPH 10: Annual Productivity

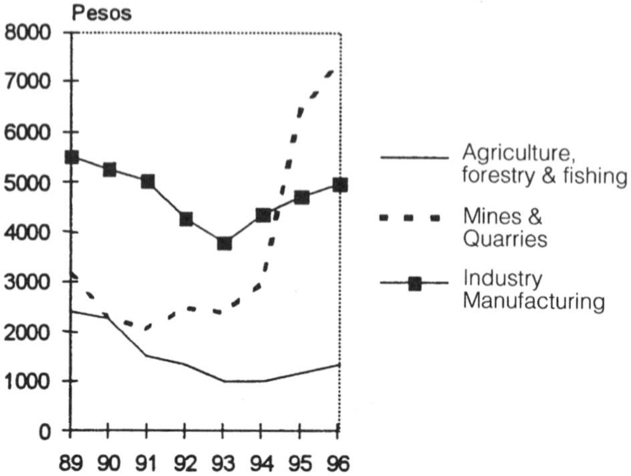

Investments in building works were to a large extent devoted to activities generating external revenues. Construction completed in recent years has mainly been for tourism and housing.

The breakdown in growth of total productivity (see table 4 in the Annex) demonstrates that productivity increases are not due to changes in the structure of production or worker reallocations, but rather that the decisive factor for this growth has been increases in the productivity of specific sectors. The biggest contribution has come from the manufacturing industry, and trade, restaurants and hotels. Agriculture and fishing also appear as important contributing sectors, particularly after 1993. However, in this case the increase was not due to a rise in efficiency, but to a decrease in its share in production and employment.

4. Labor Market and Labor Compensation

During most of 1989–1997, the share of the economically active population with respect to the working age population decreased. Employment—in correspondence with the government protection policy—was fairly stable, with decreases of only 0.2 percent per year between 1989 and 1993 (when the abrupt contraction of economic activity was taking place), and of 0.5 percent per year during the period corresponding to the external opening. Unemployment, however, experienced more marked decreases in the years of economic contraction (a drop of 6.5 percent per year), and increases of 2.9 percent per year during the recovery. This points to a certain lack of motivation for the population to search for formal employment, which is consistent with the peak reached by the submerged economy up to 1993. With respect to the labor force, potential underemployment amounted to 12 percent of the total in 1993, a share that decreased to 6 percent in 1996.[25]

The stage of external opening meant a decrease in the share of the working age population employed, to which all economic sectors contributed (excluding that of social and personal services), but particularly the traded sector.[26] This occurred because the expansion of per capita production was smaller than the increase in labor productivity, hence giving rise to a trade-off between productivity and employment. Moreover, reorganization and resizing processes are still pending. They had been postponed during the adjustment, but were restarted in 1995.

The external opening also coincided with a decrease in the contribution of state activity in employment and with an increase in the share of employment from activities in private enterprises (national and joint enterprises with foreign capital), in cooperatives, self-employment and the informal sector.[27]

On the other hand, the increase in skilled employment[28] took place during the whole period and was not linked only to the opening of the economy. This is consistent with the policies for educational development and labor guarantees applied to qualified personnel. In 1996 there were around 13 university graduates per one hundred employees, while 37 of the 100 were at least high school graduates.

It is regrettable that no general information exists regarding the educational level of those employed, broken down by economic sector. Nevertheless, individual surveys seem to point out that the attraction exerted by the sector linked to foreign capital and within other similar activities with special systems of labor retribution, caused a migration of highly qualified workers, although their new tasks might have not required all of their qualifications. Looking at other available data sources, such as change in job structure broken down by occupational categories (executives, technicians, administrative, workers and service staff),[29] it was found that only the service staff increased while the remaining categories decreased. This seems to support the above-mentioned hypothesis that foreign sector-linked jobs were more lucrative.

---

25. Potential underemployment measures the magnitude of workers in formal employment that could be done without, using the previous year's productivity as a reference. This magnitude is also adjusted according to capital/work relationships by sectors. The underemployed population had as a distinctive characteristic in Cuba in the fact that the nominal wage remained unchanged. (See Ferriol, A., "El empleo en Cuba 1980–1995," *Revista Cuba: Investigación Económica*, No.1, 1996, INIE).

26. The Annex shows a calculation of the decomposition of changes in the occupation rate by economic sectors, by ownership forms, and by qualification of the labor force.

27. The decomposition exercise carried out does not reflect the entire impact of agricultural cooperativization, since the decomposition was for the years 1994-1996 and most cooperatives were created in 1993.

28. Skilled personnel is defined as persons with 12 or more years of education.

29. The occupational category constitutes a way to classify manpower by work characteristics and nature. It includes: Workers, those who facilitate the operation of production means or change the work product; Technicians, those who apply knowledge and scientific methods; Administrative personnel, those who develop under supervision the administration of state enterprises; Service workers, those who satisfy personal and social demands; and Leading personnel, those who plan, direct, organize and coordinate the work.

Labor incomes are another topic of interest.[30] During the economic contraction, total wage revenues decreased together with a slight reduction in state jobs. However, overall income for some workers increased from earnings in the submerged economy. Since 1993, several changes are observed: on one hand, special systems of wage incentives, in national currency and in foreign exchange were applied in a growing extent. On the other hand, other labor revenues (from workers that sell their products in markets at unregulated prices) decreased due to a fall in prices. Between 1993 and 1996, prices dropped at an average of 5.3 percent per year. As a result, nominal revenues diminished by an average of 9 percent per year.

Average Annual Increase in Incomes(percent)

	1993/1989	1996/1993 Official Exch. Rate	Non-official Exch. Rate
Wage Income	−8.0	3.8	7.2
Other Income	208.9	−23.7	28.8
Total Income	37.0	−9.0	17.3

An additional element in the analysis of labor compensation is the existence of an operating non-official exchange rate within the population. Its impact has two apparent outcomes. In the first place, it increases considerably the nominal revenues (expressed in national currency) of those workers that participate in special pay-incentive systems in foreign exchange, or whose labor incomes are perceived in relation to the foreign exchange market. In the above table it can be observed that, based on the non-official exchange rate, there is a 17 percent increase per year in revenues for workers during 1993-1996, with a larger effect on other labor revenues.[31] The other effect results from changes in the non-official exchange rate. With the appreciation of the national currency, wages in this currency increase their share in total revenues and consequently improved real revenues for salary earners without a change in wages. Thus, an important objective of monetary policy since 1997 has been to appreciate the Cuban peso.

In a detailed analysis of tendencies related to labor compensation, it was observed that until 1993 wages lost their share in the value added (at factor cost), with a more marked decrease in non-traded sectors. The remaining labor revenues, from work linked to unregulated markets, favored well. Enter-

---

30. Revenues related to work have been grouped by wages and other labor revenues. The last includes revenues of agricultural cooperativists, of individual peasants, of self-employed workers and of informal workers. The cost in foreign exchange of the non-monetary special systems of remuneration was added to wages.

31. A smaller exchange rate that better reflects the purchasing power of the national currency in the entire market of consumer goods and services, offers more moderate dynamics of the effect of labor revenues in foreign exchange, but without allowing it to lose its importance. In this respect, studies of sensibility have been made.

prise income (from the capital), with low participation, experienced an abrupt fall in its share of the product. This result coincided with the above explained policy for the protection of state workers (See graph 11).

Along the recovery, and in correspondence with the reform and opening, revenues from other labor incomes falls in share while wages gains share, although slightly.[32] The improvement of the wage share in total revenues was two points greater in traded than non-traded sectors. Within the traded sector, the share of industrial wages grows, while the largest increase in the non-traded sector is in electricity, gas and water. As can be appreciated in graph 11, the most marked increase in GDP corresponded to enterprise incomes, thus strengthening the thesis of a link among enterprise incomes and external opening. As was commented previously, activities that have recovered are those that can be reinserted into the foreign exchange market (either externally or internally).

GRAPH 11: Share of Labor Incomes in the GDP

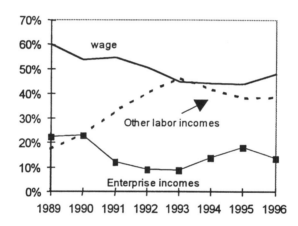

The growth of average work revenues shows inequality with regard to labor revenues, due to the development of the submerged economy. Graph 12 supports this assertion, although the difference up to 1993 may be exaggerated, as there was a learning curve with respect to estimates of informal worker earnings.[33] After 1993 the gap between wages and revenues for workers linked to markets, is reduced significantly. Salaries increase mainly in the traded sector, amplifying the difference in labor earnings within salary earners. On the other hand, the reduction in the difference between average wages in traded

32. The conversion of labor revenues in foreign exchange to national currency for graph 11, was carried out at the official exchange rate.

33. Previous studies by this author indicate that available estimates of informal occupation are undervalued up to 1993, but that later on this undervaluation decreases as the methodologies applied improve.

GRAPH 12: Average Labor

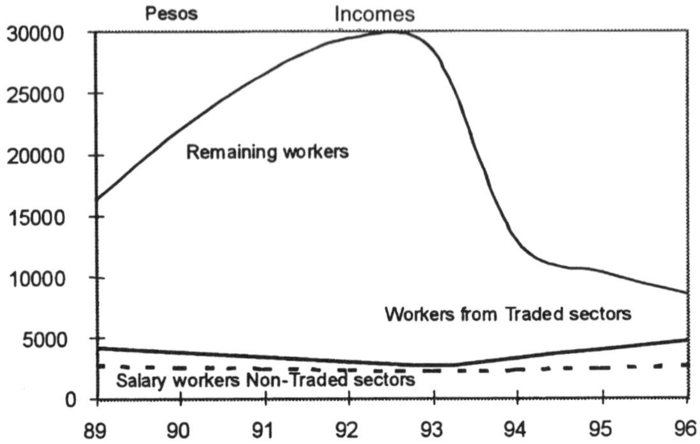

sectors with respect to other revenues explains the increase in the economically active population and unemployment at the end of the period, as formal
jobs start offering attractive salaries again.[34]

The effect of the non-official exchange rate, for example in 1996, was to
counteract to a certain extent the rise in earnings dispersion by increasing the
difference between wages and other labor revenues. This compensated, in
some measure, the relatively larger inequality between revenues of workers
from traded and non-traded sectors.[35]

The decrease in productivity between 1989 and 1993 corresponded to an
even greater decrease in real wages (except in the building sector where the
decline in employment facilitated a slight increase in productivity). Sectors
where this greater decrease in real wages occurred extensively included transport and communications, trade, restaurants and hotels, and the manufacturing industry. The drop in real wages became a factor for labor disincentive,
with repercussions in terms of bigger productivity decreases.

During the period of external opening, real wages increased more than
productivity, mainly in the manufacturing industry and in sectors such as elec-

---

34. In 1996, the average annual wage of salary earners in traded sectors was 1.8 times higher
than the average wage of workers in non-traded sectors. The average annual income of the
remaining workers was 3.3 times higher than the average wage in non-trade sectors. These estimates are based on the official exchange rate.

35. Changes are of little magnitude because of the special systems for labor remuneration
in place. These consist not only of monetary retributions, but also of payments in kind, that have
a predominant weight. According to preliminary information, almost 58 percent of that remuneration is applied to non-traded sectors, and the rest to traded ones. It should be kept in mind
that tourism, international communications and air transport are classified as non-traded sectors, although they are important sources of foreign exchange.

tricity, gas and water. The limited information available could not offer conclusions about trends in the capital/product relationship by sectors and their rate of profit, to evaluate if there was a decrease of capital endowment or a decrease of its yield.

Although since 1993 the increase of the real average wage has exceeded the increase of productivity, only in the sectors of agriculture, fishing, mining and quarry does the average real wage for 1996 exceed that of 1989. This could still be exerting a labor disincentive effect, deterring a larger productivity growth.

GRAPH 13: Increase in Real Salary and Productivity Proportion

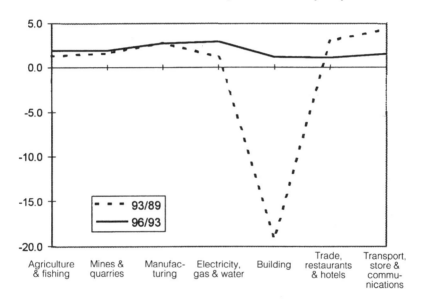

To conclude the analysis of the labor market and its compensation, it is convenient to synthesize the main conclusions from this study:

· During the time period under study, there was a peak in informal occupation, which diminished with the creation of a larger legal area for the non-state economic activity. For this reason, the sector of workers linked directly to the operation of markets gains a presence alongside wage earners. Informal occupation coexists as a complementary labor activity due to the high average earnings it offers.

· The external opening increasingly transfers the supply of manpower to traded sectors and tourism; which correlates with the increase in average wages in those activities.

· During the opening a trade-off took place between productivity and employment. This was influenced by the fact that, in correspondence with the policies applied, this period was made to coincide with measures for labor reorganization that had been postponed during the economic contraction.

· The educational level of the labor force followed its increasing trend, but symptoms were observed concerning a certain insufficient return to education.

· Wages have lost share in value added.

· The economic crisis brought about greater inequality in average labor revenues among formal and informal sectors, in favor of the latter. The reform and the opening have decreased that range, although important differences remain between the average earnings of salary earners and those of the remaining workers.[36] With respect to salaried workers, the opening has increased inequality among the wages of workers in the traded and non-traded sectors. However, a smaller difference is observed among workers in these two sectors whose labor revenues are linked to the market.

· The effect of the non-official exchange rate has been to deepen the difference between the average revenues of salary earners and the remaining workers, while shrinking the difference in average wages between the traded and non-traded sectors.

5. Opening, Inequality and Poverty: Reflections

In the case of Cuba, in correspondence with the results of a recently concluded investigation,[37] the concept of *population at risk* will be employed instead of poverty. Population at risk are those members of the population with insufficient revenues for the acquisition of a basic basket of foods and non-food products, but that at the same time enjoy benefits and social protection that surpasses what is received internationally by poor families through social policies. According to the socioeconomic system of the country, Cubans have universal and gratuitous access to things such as university studies as well as to specialized high technology medical services. They are also able to own their houses through a system of advantageous payment, among other benefits.

The percentage of population at risk increased between 1988 and 1996, more than two-fold in the urban area of the country. The information available showed that this risk situation was sharper between 1990 and 1995,[38] and since that latter year the incidence of risk has descended in the urban population.

On the other hand, in 1996 the unemployed and the non-economically active population were the groups with higher risk percentage. Among em-

---

36. This inequality is qualified as relative, because it is high compared with the situation exiting in 1989, but is very moderate when compared internationally.

37. "Efecto de las políticas macroeconómicas y sociales sobre los niveles de pobreza; el caso de Cuba en los años noventa," Capítulo 9, *Política Macroeconómica y Pobreza en América Latina y el Caribe*, PNUD. Ediciones Mundi-Prensa. 1998.

38. For example, in the capital of the country the percentage of population at risk almost quintupled between 1988 and 1995, and everything indicates that the situation in 1993 was more critical.

ployed workers, the incidence was larger for salary earners. There is no previous survey that allows a comparison with the 1996 data on the incidence of risk according to employment situation. The above analysis of the labor market gives a basis to the hypothesis that non-active persons and salary earners, in that order, probably had higher risk indexes than in 1996.

An interesting fact is that changes in the index of population at risk resulted from changes in income distribution, and had very little influence from variations of average revenues. In the eighties, different studies made on income distribution in Cuba concluded that were very small income spreads in Cuban society. The Gini coefficient obtained was 0.22 to 0.25.

Since then, sources of income have diversified causing shifts in relative importance. The present paper shows that revenues of workers linked to markets, particularly those that work in foreign exchange, have earned revenues that accentuate the difference with average labor revenues. Nevertheless, the trend seems to point toward a stabilization—or slight decrease—of these differences, with a relative improvement in the salary earnings from traded sectors. The Gini coefficient calculated for 1996 to 1998 has the inconvenience that it does not incorporate all labor earnings, because it only computes directly special pay-incentive systems in foreign exchange or in national currency, and not those that are materialized through funds for the purchase in stores or in kind. With this important limitation, a Gini coefficient of 0.37 to 0.39 was obtained.

It is important to note that in the case of Cuba, the government decision to preserve social policies during the period of adjustment and economic reforms was an important factor in compensating the inequality in monetary revenues. Estimates carried out for the Gini coefficient which take into account public expenditures in health and education, as well as for housing ownership, are around 0.30 for 1996 to 1998.

Between 1988 and 1995, the increase in the percentage of the population at risk was accompanied by a widening of the income distribution, under conditions in which the growth of average revenues contributed in decreasing the risk. Between 1995 and 1996, the opposite took effect; average revenues fell and inequality decreased, resulting in a reduction in the incidence of risk.

It is not easy to establish a relationship between the external opening and its impact on labor revenues, income distribution, and the incidence of the population at risk. In short, the situation of risk and the position attained in the distribution of incomes do not only depend on labor revenues, but also on two important additional factors that must be taken into account. On one hand, the population also has revenues not related to work (for example remittances). On the other hand, the socio-demographic and socio-occupational composition of the family can be decisive.

The characteristics of the population classified according to per capita household income were analyzed based on the household survey for 1996. A comparison is shown between the population with the lowest and highest income.

**Distribution of Economic Classification between
Higher and Lower-Income Groups, 1996**

PERCENTAGE	POPULATION AND EMPLOYMENT STATUS	
	Lower incomes	Higher incomes
Total household members	100	100
State workers	14.5	47.3
Non state workers	3.5	8.2
Unemployed	8.4	2.6
Pensioned	10.4	10.5
Others Non active	33.2	16.5
0-14 years old people	30.0	14.8

Source: INIE, based on the 1996 household survey.

As can be seen in the table above, the demographic dependency has a decisive influence in the economic situation of the household. The 73 percent of the population whose household is classified as having the lowest incomes is composed on children or other non-active people. This proportion diminishes to 41 percent for those in the high end of the income scale. On the other hand, changes in average labor revenues of all occupation categories influence all the strata of household incomes.[39]

This paper has shown some aspects of the reform and the opening that must be influencing the dynamics of the population at risk, although without being able to quantify their impact. They are: the shift of workers toward non-state activities, traded sectors and tourism; the greater spread of labor incomes; changes in the relative share of wages in total revenues from work; and the workings of the non-official exchange rate, with its differentiated effect based on the share of foreign exchange revenues, for the different worker categories.

6. Conclusion

The external opening in Cuba has taken place under conditions quite different from those of other Latin American countries. The analysis carried out shows some similarities but also significant differences. The main factors that give place to such differences are:

a) A socialist economy with a predominant state sector.

b) A large scale economic reform including the external opening as well as a significant external adjustment.

c) An economic blockade, which places obstacles to the opening; and non-access to financing from international financial organizations.

---

39. With these facts, we are not pointing to a kind of demographic fatalism of households with smaller revenues. It is considered that an interrelation exists in both directions, among life conditions reached, especially regarding education, health and employment, with social status and household behavior in the demographic, economic and social spheres.

Because of Cuba's unique history, its external opening was carried out with different premises, often times contrary premises to those of other countries in the region. This includes the importance given to social issues over economic ones, active participation of the State in economic activity, and a planned economy that restricts the influence of the market.

The essential components of the external opening have been the promotion of direct foreign investment, the decentralization of external trade, the reduction of tariffs, the creation of an internal market in foreign exchange, and the establishment of free trade areas. Additionally, important changes have been implemented in the institutional, legal and managerial workings of the economic model.

Together with the external opening, measures were applied to rectify fiscal and monetary imbalances. Labor reform mainly took the form of a restructuring of jobs by ownership sectors, and also by measures designed for the protection of workers. Proposals in social policy were also implemented with the purpose of offering additional protection to families and achieving a greater political consensus with respect to the changes.

It is not possible to separate the impact of the external opening from the effect of the rest of the reform, especially from the effect of the economic decentralization. In practice, enterprises generating foreign exchange or substituting imports, were incorporated at the same time to both processes. Nevertheless, the following economic facts linked to the external opening of the economy were observed in this study:

· The contraction of the GDP was reverted, and a process of recovery started, which has become increasingly consolidated.

· The export strategy achieved a certain amount of results. Exports of goods and services increased at a rate greater than GDP. There was also a structural change in the participation of services in total exports. However, export products were not diversified.

· The trade deficit at comparable prices was eliminated. Nevertheless, the unfavorable terms of trade determined that at current prices the trade deficit persisted, although at controlled levels.

· Net current transfers from abroad began to impact positively on decreasing the financial imbalance of the country.

· The fiscal deficit decreased to acceptable levels, as a result of the combined effect of the contraction of expenditures and the decrease of net transfers to enterprises and the population.

· Capital flow increases have not been achieved. A large proportion of the capital that enters the country is short-term credit. This, combined with the difficulty in obtaining credit, has caused a chronic situation of scarce liquidity that hinders the performance of the economy.

· Labor productivity was increased, especially in traded sectors. This increase responded to real growths of sector productivity.

· Labor supply shifted towards non-state activity, traded sectors and tourism; which corresponds with the increase in the average wage in those activities.

· Although the range of average labor revenues is wider than in 1989, it decreased with respect to 1993. There is a tendency to diminish the difference between the average salary of workers from traded sectors, with respect to the higher revenues of workers that, like self-employed and informal ones, obtain their income from direct sales in the market of goods and consumer services.

· Real wages were increased more than productivity, but they continue to be lower than in 1989.

· The educational level of the labor force followed the growing trend it showed before the opening. Yet there were symptoms that returns to education were insufficient in relation to non-state workers' incomes.

There is a sector of the population, which has been termed population at risk, that has insufficient revenues to buy a basket of foods and basic non-food products, but that at the same time enjoys benefits and social protection above those received by poor families in other countries. The population at risk was estimated at 15 percent for the urban area of the country in 1996. This can be described as a moderate incidence if compared with the levels of poverty in Latin America. The reform and opening have diminished the proportion of population at risk, with respect to the initial levels brought about from the economic adjustment.

The inequality of monetary incomes has increased with respect to the eighties, although Cuba is still among the countries having lower income inequality in the region. Wide inequalities at the beginning of the period, associated with the external adjustment, reached their highest level in 1993 and 1994. Later on these inequalities were caused by the larger role of the market in generating household revenues and also from the external opening, due to the wider range introduced into labor revenues, as well as from other sources. It should be noted that social policies compensated to a significant extent inequalities of monetary revenues, bringing the Gini coefficient estimate down to 0.30 in 1998.

Summarizing, it can be said that the external opening in Cuba has had a significant impact on all economic and social structures. It constitutes a decisive factor in reanimating and reinserting the Cuban economy into the international economy. This process has had its social costs, but at a smaller scale than what has been observed in other countries. In the Cuban case, neoliberal prescriptions recommended by international organizations were not followed. However, conditions derived from the pattern of neoliberal globalization, have proven a very complex barrier to overcome. This is exemplified by the deterioration of the terms of trade for primary products, which hinders many underdeveloped countries, so that their search for new ways to participate in the international economy brings few results. Cuba is still involved in such a process. Another important consideration, derived from the Cuban experience, is the role that should be played by social policy in order to diminish the adjustment and reform impacts. This strengthens the criteria for the need of an active government social policy, especially to avoid exclusion and poverty.

TABLE 1: Classification and Chronology of Measures from the Cuban Reform

	Start Date	Macro economic	Micro economic	Social
RECTIFICATION OF THE EXTERNAL IMBALANCE				
1. Development of tourism and other activities generating foreign exchange	1989	X		
2. Stimulate the opening to foreign capital, mainly through the creation of joint ventures	1990	X		
3. Creation of a sector that operates directly in foreign exchange	1992		X	
4. Eradication of the state monopoly on external trade	1991		X	
5. Higher use of commercial credits; renegotiation of foreign debt with some countries	1990	X		
6. Creation of markets and internal sales in foreign exchange	1993	X	X	
7. Reduction of tariffs	1996		X	
8. Creation of free trade areas and authorization for state business	1996	X	X	
9. Opening of offices of foreign banks	1995	X		
10. Special systems for remuneration in foreign exchange	1993		X	
11. Authorization of remittances and legal holding of foreign exchange	1993	X		
12. Creation of exchange houses and saving accounts in foreign exchange for the population	1995	X		
13. Creation of new mechanisms for the control, circulation and assignment of foreign exchange	1990	X		
SOCIAL				
14. Employment and salary guarantees for workers and gradual restructuring of state jobs	1990			X
15. Invigoration of social security and creation of a net of public feeding services at subsidized prices for low-income people	1996			X
16. Maintenance of social security coverage and benefits	1990			X
17. Prioritize health and education services based on currency restrictions, changes to achieve more effectiveness	1990			X
INTERNAL FINANCES				
18. Rise in prices and rates for non-essential products and services	1994	X		
19. Eradication of some gratuities	1994	X		
20. Measures to decrease losses from state enterprises	1994	X		
21. Creation of a tax system	1994	X	X	
22. New tax law for enterprises	1994		X	

	Start Date	Macro economic	Micro economic	Social
23. Creation of a national auditing office	1994		X	
24. Larger decentralization of budget incomes and expenditures	1995		X	
25. Updating of the accounting system	1994		X	
26. Restructuring of the bank system	1997		X	
AGRICULTURAL SECTOR				
27. Transformation of state companies into cooperatives	1993		X	
28. Delivery of free land to families	1994		X	X
29. Delivery of land to organizations for self-supply purposes	1992		X	
30. Development of urban orchards and organoponics	1993		X	
31. Development of acuiculture	1990		X	
32. Creation of agricultural markets to sell surpluses at free prices.	1994		X	
33. New scheme of integral financing in foreign currency for the agricultural sector	1996		X	
INDUSTRY AND SERVICES				
34. More possibilities for self-employment	1993		X	
35. Creation of a market of industrial and handmade articles	1994		X	
36. Rearrangement of the managerial system	1992		X	
37. Resizing of available capacities	1994		X	
38. Change of the enterprise management system	1998		X	
LABOR				
39. Decrease in state jobs and their transfer to the non-state sector	1993		X	
40. Increase in the protection given to spare workers	1992			X
41. Wage increases in activities generating foreign exchange as well as in health, education and interior order	1992		X	
42. Upgrading of the payment system to improve relationships between retributions and productive results	1992		X	
43. Employment programs for Easter provinces	1995			X
OTHERS				
44. Decrease in the number of ministries and other national entities. Decentralization of economic decision-making for enterprises	1994		X	
45. Use of new planning approaches and tools	1995		X	

TABLE 2: Macroeconomic Indicators

		1989	1990	1991	1992	1993	1994	1995	1996	1997*
TRADE LIBERALIZATION										
Average rate		17.7						10.7		
% Change								−39.5		
Exports (current prices)	MMP	5993	5940	3563	2522	1992	2197	2687	3380	
Exports /GDP		0.280	0.265	0.175	0.124	0.095	0.098	0.114	0.150	
Imports (current prices)	MMP	8608	8017	4702	2737	2373	2408	3187	4462	
Imports/GDP		0.402	0.358	0.231	0.134	0.113	0.107	0.135	0.198	
GDP (current prices)	MMP	21418	22394	20378	20399	20993	22411	23616	22491	
Exports (1989 prices)	MMP	5993	5480	4967	4453	3940	3893	3846	5019	
Exports/GDP		0.280	0.277	0.273	0.268	0.263	0.253	0.244	0.294	
Imports (1989 prices)	MMP	8608	7117	5626	4135	2644	2731	2818	3748	
Imports/GDP		0.402	0.359	0.309	0.249	0.176	0.178	0.179	0.220	
GDP (1989 prices)	MMP	21418	19811	18204	16597	14990	15376	15761	17061	
LIBERALIZATION CAPITAL ACCOUNT										
Portfolio invest./GDP		0	0	0	0	0	0	0	0	
Direct investment	MMP					54	563.4	4.7	82.1	442
DI/GDP						0.003	0.025	0.000	0.004	
Other capitals	MMP					302.1	−301	591.5	91.8	−171.8
Other capitals/GDP						0.014	−0.013	0.025	0.004	
Total	MMP	3122	2469	1487	421	356.1	262.4	596.2	174.4	270.2
Total/GDP		0.146	0.110	0.073	0.021	0.017	0.012	0.025	0.008	
DEBT										
Total external debt	MMP					8785	9082.8	10504	10465	10146
Total external debt/GDP						0.418	0.405	0.445	0.465	
Total internal debt						0.418	0.405	0.445	0.465	
Total internal debt/GDP										
REAL EXCHANGE RATE										
% Exchange		1	0.856	0.6636	0.506	0.575	0.797	0.746	0.591	
Fiscal policy										
Public expenditure	MMP	6185	6111	5053	4746	4814	4997	5033	5263	
Public expen./GDP		0.289	0.273	0.248	0.233	0.229	0.223	0.213	0.234	
Transfers and taxes	MMP	2781	4153	1288	−123	−236	3576	4268	4695	
Transfers and taxes/GDP		0.130	0.185	0.063	−0.006	−0.011	0.160	0.181	0.209	
GDP growth	%		−7.5	−8.1	−8.8	−9.7	2.6	2.6	8.2	
Population growth	%	7.9	7.3	7.7	6.1	6.2	6.7	7.9	6.8	
Population (in thousands)		10577	10694	10793	10869	10940	10960	10999	11028	
LABOR MARKET										
Rate of unemployment	%	7.9	7.3	7.7	6.1	6.2	6.7	7.9	6.8	
Avg. real wages (1989=100)		100	77.0	61.7	50.3	41.9	51.4	58.4	69.6	
Min. real wage (1989=100)		100	83.1	71.1	62.1	55.2	56.3	57.5	65.0	

* Available figures for 1997 are still preliminary and not complete.
Source: Calculations from the *Anuario Estadístico de Cuba 1996* and *La Economía Cubana*, CEPAL, 1997.

TABLE 3: Changes in the Rate of Economic Share, Labor, and Unemployment Rates

	P	E	L	U	Employed TE.TO	Unemployed TD1.TD	Share (1−TD1).−TP*
1989	6210	4728	4356	372			
1990	6399	4742	4394	348	−0.020	−0.005	−0.025
1991	6490	4737	4374	363	−0.017	0.003	0.014
1992	6549	4635	4352	283	−0.013	−0.012	0.028
1993	6645	4597	4313	285	−0.022	0.001	0.021
1994	6659	4496	4195	301	−0.027	0.006	0.022
1995	6677	4484	4131	353	−0.016	0.014	0.005
1996	6695	4550	4240	310	0.022	−0.009	−0.011

Notation: P: population in working age; E: economically active population; L: working; U: unemployed. TP: share rate; TD: unemployment rate; TE: employment rate; TO: rate of employment.
Source: Author's calculations based on data from the *Anuario Estadístico de Cuba de 1996*, ONE and *La Economía Cubana 1997*, CEPAL.

TABLE 4: Analysis of Productivity Changes

1989–1993	(Xi/X)pi*	((Xi/X)−(Li/L)Li*
Agriculture, hunting, forestry and fishing	−6.0	−2.6
Mining and Quarries	−0.2	0.0
Manufacturing Industry	−7.2	−0.2
Electricity, gas and water	−1.1	0.6
Construction	−3.5	1.2
Trade, restaurants and hotels	−9.8	0.5
Transport, storing and trade	−2.3	0.0
Financial establishments, Real estate and services enterprises	2.4	−1.4
Social, community and personal services	1.3	0.2
Total	−29.4	0.0
Traded	−15.1	−0.7
Non-traded	−12.4	−0.6

1993–1996	(Xi/X)pi	((Xi/X)−
Agriculture, hunting, forestry and fishing	2.5	2.1
Mining and Quarries	1.7	0.1
Manufacturing Industry	6.5	−0.1
Electricity, gas and water	0.7	−0.1
Construction	1.3	0.4
Trade, restaurants and hotels	3.9	−0.6
Transport, storage and trade	0.6	0.0
Financial establishments, real estate and service enterprises	2.8	−1.9
Social, community and personal services	−4.8	0.9
Total	12.7	0.0
Traded	10.9	1.6
Non-traded	0.2	0.9

Notation: Xi: product of the i sector; X: GDP; LI: sector i employment; pi*: productivity growth.
Source: Author's calculations based on data from the *Anuario Estadístico de Cuba de 1996*, ONE and *La Economía Cubana 1997*, CEPAL.

TABLE 5: Analysis of Changes in the Employment Rate

1989–1993	Toi(xi*–pi*)
Agriculture, hunting, forestry and fishing	1.05
Mining and Quarries	–0.02
Manufacturing Industry	–1.30
Electricity, gas and water	0.10
Construction	–1.10
Trade, restaurants and hotels	–0.11
Transport, storage and trade	–0.66
Financial establishments, real estate and service enterprises	–0.59
Social, community and personal services	–1.88
Total	–4.51
Traded	–0.32
Non traded	–4.73

1993–1996	Toi(xi*–pi*)
Agriculture, hunting, forestry and fishing	–2.76
Mining and Quarries	–0.97
Manufacturing Industry	–1.05
Electricity, gas and water	–0.66
Construction	–1.01
Trade, restaurants and hotels	–0.06
Transport, storage and trade	–0.28
Financial establishments, real estate and service enterprises	2.74
Social, community and personal services	–4.12
Total	–4.39
Traded	1.64
Non traded	0.2

Notation: Toi: rate of employment in the i sector; xi* increase in the productivity of sector i (in reference to the population in labor age);pi*: increase in the productivity of the sector.

Source: Author's calculations based on data from the *Anuario Estadístico de Cuba de 1996*, ONE and *La Economía Cubana 1997*, CEPAL.

TABLE 6: Employment Skill Level

1986–93	Si/L(Si/P)*
Primary or lower	–0.06
Medium	–0.07
High School	0.07
University	0.03
SUBTOTAL	–0.04
Not classified	–0.02
Total	–0.05
Skill	0.10
Remaining ones	–0.15

Notation: Si: employed with i qualification; L total of employed people; P population in working age.

TABLE 7: Employment by Ownership Forms

1994–96	Si/L(Si/P)*
State	–0.079
Cooperative	0.005
Joint enterprises and mercantile societies	0.007
National private enterprises	0.011
Self–employment	0.000
Informal	0.038
Others	0.001
Subtotal	–0.017
Not classified	0.027
Total	0.005

Notation: Si: Employed by ownership sector i; L: total employed; P: population of working age.
Source: Author's calculations based on data from the *Anuario Estadístico de Cuba de 1996*, ONE and *La Economía Cubana 1997*, CEPAL.

REFERENCES

Acevedo, R. (1998) "Entrevista al Presidente del Instituto de Aeronáutica Civil de Cuba," *Semanario Opciones*, Diciembre.

Aguilar, A. (1988) *Globalización y extraterritorialidad*, INIE.

Aguilar, A. (1996) *Afectaciones a la Economía Cubana ocasionadas por el Bloqueo Económico a Cuba por los EEUU*, INIE.

Alvarez, E. (1995) "Impacto de la inversión extranjera en la sociedad cubana," *Revista Cuba: Investigación Económica* No.4.

Alvarez, E. (1996) "La apertura externa cubana," *Boletín CIEM*, No. 26 y 27.

American Association for World Health (1997) *The Impact of the U.S. Embargo on Health and Nutrition in Cuba.*

Banco Central de Cuba (1997) *Informe Económico.*

Banco Central de Cuba (1998) *El Sistema Bancario en Cuba.*

CEPAL (1997) *La Economía Cubana. Reformas estructurales y desempeño en los noventa.*

CETSS (1985) *Código del Trabajo, Comité Estatal del Trabajo y Seguridad Social*, Ciudad de La Habana.

Colectivo de autores (1996) *Las UBPC y su necesario perfeccionamiento*, INIE.

Colectivo de autores (1995) "Mercado Agropecuario: apertura o limitación," *Revista Cuba: Investigación Económica* No. 4.

Colectivo de autores (1995) "Elementos para una reorganización del sistema empresarial cubano," *Revista Cuba: Investigación Económica* No.1.

Ferradaz, I. (1998) "Entrevista al Ministro para la inversión extranjera y la Colaboración Económica," *El Economista*, junio-julio.

Ferriol, A., Quintana, D. y Pérez, V. (1998) "Política social en el ajuste y su adecuación a las nuevas condiciones," Proyecto de investigación PCTN Economía Cubana, INIE.

Ferriol, A. (1996) "El Empleo en Cuba 1980–1995," *Revista Cuba: Investigación Económica*, No.1.

Ferriol, A, et al. (1997) *Efecto de Políticas Macroeconómicas y Sociales sobre los niveles de Pobreza: el caso de Cuba en los años noventa,* Proyecto PNUD RLA/92/009, PNUD.

Figueras, M.A. (1997) "Intervención del asesor del Ministro para la Inversión Extranjera y la Colaboración," Congreso de Economistas de América Latina y el Caribe, *El Economista,* Septiembre.

García, A. (1997) "Mercado Agropecuario: Evolución actual y perspectiva," *Revista Cuba: Investigación Económica* No.3–4, INIE.

González, A. (1995) "Modelos Económicos Socialistas: Escenarios para Cuba en los años noventa," *Revista Cuba: Investigación Económica* No.3.

González, A. (1997) "Economía y Sociedad. Los retos al modelo económico," *Revista Temas* No.11.

González, A. (1995) "La Economía Sumergida en Cuba," *Revista Cuba: Investigación Económica* No.2, INIE.

Lage, C. (1998) "Intervención del Vicepresidente del Consejo de Estado y Secretario del Comité Ejecutivo del Consejo de Ministros en la Asamblea Nacional del Poder Popular," *Periódico Granma,* 23 de diciembre.

Los Derechos Laborales y la disciplina ante el trabajo (1984) Ediciones Jurídicas, Editorial Ciencias Sociales, La Habana.

Mañalich, I. (1996) "Cuba y las zonas económicas especiales en el mundo," *Revista Cuba: Investigación Económica* No.2, INIE.

Martínez, O. (1995) Seminario Internacional, "La Pequeña Empresa en el desarrollo Económico y Social," La Habana.

Nova, A. (1996) *La reactivación económica del sector agropecuario cubano,* INIE.

ONE (1996) Anuario Estadístico de Cuba.

Opciones (1996).

Periódico Granma (1998) 27 de octubre.

Pico, N. (1995) "El sistema empresarial del comercio exterior en Cuba: una caracterización general," *Revista Cuba: Investigación Económica* No.4.

Quintero, J. (1998) "La ALADI en la inserción de la economía cubana," *Boletín Economía Cubana* No.35.

Quintana, D. (1997) "El sector informal urbano en Cuba, " *Revista Cuba: Investigación Económica* No.2, INIE.

Reunión de Jefes de Estado y de Gobierno sobre Comercio, Turismo y Transporte (1995) "Informe," Trinidad y Tobago, agosto.

Rodríguez, J.L.(various years) "La Deuda Externa Cubana: Una evaluación actual," *Boletín Economía Cubana* No. 10, 11, 12, CIEM.

Rodríguez, J.L. (1996) *Perspectivas económicas de Cuba 1996,* World Economic Forum, Davos, 1–6 de febrero, Ministerio de Economía y Planificación.

Rodríguez, J.L. (1997) "Resultados económicos de 1997 y el Plan económico y social para 1998," Informe a la Asamblea Nacional, Diciembre.

Rodríguez, J.L. (1999) "Resultados económicos de 1998 y el Plan económico y social para 1999," Informe a la Asamblea Nacional del Poder Popular.

Taylor, L. (1992) *Estabilización y crecimiento en los países en desarrollo: un enfoque estructuralista,* México: Fondo de Cultura Económica, Primera edición en español.

Valdés, S. (1998) "Entrevista concedida por el Ministro de Trabajo y Seguridad Social," *Periódico Granma,* agosto.

6

India: Globalization and its Social Discontents

AMITAVA KRISHNA DUTT *and* J. MOHAN RAO

Introduction

Since mid-1991, India has been embarked on economic reforms which aim—in the words of its government—to liberalize and globalize the economy. Not unlike many other developing and transitional economies, the main reform initiatives were undertaken after a fiscal and foreign exchange crisis which brought India to the verge of default on its foreign loans. Besides a stabilization program, both internal and international economic activity have been sought to be de-regulated and liberalized. Internal liberalization included the dismantling of a complex industrial licensing system, opening up of a number of sectors previously reserved for the public sector to private investment, some divestment of stock in the state sector, and decontrol of administered prices. External liberalization measures included removal of non-tariff barriers to imports, reduction in import tariffs, removal of restrictions on—and active encouragement of—foreign investment, some freeing up of technology imports, and attempts to increase portfolio inflows.

As might be expected, the reform program has evoked a variety of responses. They range from euphoria about freeing a caged tiger from *dirigiste* shackles to ride the crest of free markets, to dogged mistrust about free markets among those supportive of autarkic, government-directed development.

*The authors would like to thank CEPA Conference participants, especially John Langmore, Ute Pieper, Servaas Storm, and Lance Taylor for their many useful comments. If the paper has not drawn full benefit from their reactions, the responsibility lies with the authors alone.

Others hold guardedly optimistic expectations for certain aspects of the reforms. Among many, a major concern about globalization and liberalization is with their "social" impact which encompasses effects on employment, poverty, income inequality, and the quality of life for the majority of people. Table 1 places diverse views about the reforms along two axes of their potential longer-term impact: economic growth and social outcomes.

Reform-minded governments and economists such as Bhagwati and Srinivasan (1993) view globalization as not only quickening growth but also promoting mass well-being. Compared with India's *dirigiste* and autarkic policies, foreign competition and foreign direct investment are expected to improve allocative and technical efficiency. Trade liberalization, it is argued, will increase the demand for semi-skilled and unskilled workers, increase their wages, and thereby reduce poverty and improve income distribution. Higher growth will also augment fiscal resources for health, education and other social needs. The further argument is made that the reforms can release any foreign exchange or aggregate demand constraints on economic growth.

TABLE 1. Alternative Views on the Effects of Economic Reforms

		Social Outcomes		
		POSITIVE	NEUTRAL	NEGATIVE
Growth Impact	POSITIVE	Official view Bhagwati & Srinivasan (1993) Bhagwati (1994) Joshi and Little (1996) World Bank (1998)	Dreze and Sen (1995)	
	NEUTRAL			
	NEGATIVE			Patnaik (1997)

An alternative view has it that the reforms, while desirable for promoting growth, may be largely orthogonal to the trajectory of social outcomes. Dreze and Sen (1995), for example, argue that reforms which increase growth will not automatically expand opportunities to lead a normal span of life, to live in good health, to read and write, and not to go hungry. Rather, their social impact depends on whether reform benefits are channeled to improving the conditions of the poorest, to breaking down caste and gender hierarchies, and in generating employment. They therefore argue that the "removal of counterproductive government controls may indeed expand social opportunities for many people. However, to change the circumstances (such as illiteracy and ill health) that severely constrain the actual social opportunities of a large part of the population, these permissive reforms have to be supplemented by a radical shift in public policy in education and health" (Dreze and Sen, 1995, p. 16).

A third view, articulated by some economists and social activists, is that even if they have a positive growth effect, economic reforms will have an adverse impact in social terms. A primary concern here is that globalization will intensify the technological treadmill in Ricardian fashion: while increasing technological change and perhaps output growth, they will slow employment growth especially for unskilled labor, and thereby increase income disparities. Even the sectoral changes that are supposed to ensue from the reforms are likely to cause employment losses for the many who are ill equipped to find employment in the sectors which will expand. Second, a shift in employment towards unprotected and low-paid informal, casual, labor is feared as employers try to respond to the reforms by seeking greater flexibility in terms of labor costs. Third, if reforms shift the terms of trade towards agriculture, the rise in the price of the principal wage good will reduce the real income of the poor. Lastly, cuts in social spending which accompany liberalization and globalization will also reduce the disposable income of the poor and government services available to them.

A final view (see, for instance, Patnaik, 1997) is that the reforms are likely to have a negative effect on both growth and mass well-being. The distribution of income, as noted in the previous paragraph, will shift away from the poor and towards the rich, depressing domestic demand. Import liberalization will increase imports but not significantly affect exports, thereby reducing aggregate demand further. All this will depress industrial growth. Cuts in government spending, especially on infrastructural investment, will further reduce industrial demand, and also have adverse effects on industrial and agricultural growth from the supply side. Agricultural growth will not respond to price incentives, especially in the absence of land reforms which are not on the reformist agenda. The liberalization of foreign capital inflows is unlikely to increase direct foreign investment inflows significantly, given the low level of development, the low educational levels of unskilled workers and political uncertainty, while portfolio flows, if they increase, are likely to increase economic uncertainty and lead to intermittent foreign exchange crises.

This paper examines the record with a view to assessing these diverse views about India's reforms. In the following section, we briefly examine the content of reforms undertaken and describe how we will explore the effects of globalization in the following sections. Section 3 looks at some macroeconomic dimensions of performance including the realized effects of openness on external transactions, on economic growth, and on trends in the rural sector which remains the mainstay of employment. Section 4 summarizes trends in employment and unemployment, and the changing commodity composition of employment and its distribution across the formal/informal divide. Section 5 delves into some controversies surrounding the assessment of changes in income distribution and poverty under the impact of reforms. Section 6 turns to government policy toward social safety nets. Section 7 concludes.

2. The Reforms, Openness and Globalization

This section provides a summary description of the reform policies, clarifies the meaning and significance of the term "globalization," and discusses the method we use to examine its consequences on the economy.

Reform Planks

India's post-colonial governments pursued determinedly interventionist and autarkic policies. Apart from high walls of tariffs and quotas, the accumulation regime rested on the twin pillars of state-led investment and state-led coordination of economic activity. The public sector grew from small beginnings to acquire a GDP share of one quarter and an investment share of one half in the late 1980s. Significant parts of the private, especially formal, sector were controlled through an industrial licensing system, financial and credit controls, price and distribution controls, and labor laws. In addition to extensive quantitative restrictions on foreign trade, foreign direct investment was heavily restricted as to both sectors and the equity share of participation.

After the crisis of June 1991, the self-professed policy of the government has been liberalization and globalization. However, this policy change was not an altogether abrupt one: throughout the 1980s, there were attempts at reducing state control and autarky. Apart from a modicum of liberalization under the Janata government which removed Indira Gandhi from power in 1977, policies turned rightwards towards further liberalization when Mrs. Gandhi returned to power in 1980. A further fillip in that direction was given by the elections of December 1984 which brought Rajiv Gandhi to power.

In July 1991, immediately following the general elections, the balance of payments crisis, and the imposition of IMF conditions, the new government of P. V. Narasimha Rao announced a radical policy overhaul in its Industrial Policy Statement.[1] The changes included the removal of most non-tariff restrictions on imports of capital and intermediate goods, the broadening and simplification of export incentives, and the elimination of state trading monopolies. A negative list of restricted imports was drawn up to include items of national sensitivity (chiefly defense and health-care), and some capital goods and most consumer goods (the number of which has subsequently been reduced) for protectionist reasons. Imports of all other goods were allowed except those still reserved for import through the government's canalizing agencies.

The percentage of products covered by non-tariff barriers, using the harmonized system of trade classification, came down from 90% in the pre-reform period to 44% by 1995 (Mehta, 1997). As for tariffs, the unweighted average

---

1. See Government of India (1993) for further details.

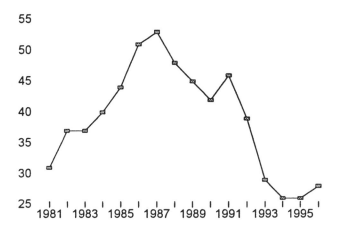

FIGURE 1: Import Duties as a Percentage of Imports

nominal tariff was 125% in 1990–91, the highest rate being 355%. In 1993–94 these figures fell to 71% and 85% respectively, and have been reduced steadily thereafter. According to one estimate, the average economy-wide effective rate of protection declined from 87% in 1989–90 to 62% in 1993–94 and further to about 30% in 1995–96 (Mehta, 1997). The ratio of import duties to the total value of imports, fell from a peak of 53% in 1987 to 28% in 1996 (see Figure 1). Notwithstanding the reduction in tariffs being sharpest in respect of the highly protected capital goods sector, the dispersion in import tariffs remains high (Mehta, 1997).

The rupee was devalued by 20% against the US dollar in July 1991 and further in February 1992 when an official dual exchange market was created. Since the inflation rate was about 14% in 1991–92, the depreciation of the real exchange rate was only by 7.89% Subsequently, a unified, floating exchange rate regime was adopted with the rupee becoming fully convertible on the current account.

Restrictions on foreign capital inflows have also been considerably reduced. Foreign equity holding of up to 51% was allowed in 34 high priority industries requiring large investments and advanced technology, departing from the earlier restriction of 40%.[2] With a view to encouraging technology transfers from abroad, the government announced that it would provide automatic approval for technology agreements related to high priority industries within specified parameters. There has also been a deregulation of portfolio capital flows: nonresident Indians and foreign institutional investors (FIIs) were allowed to own stock in the corporate sector and larger Indian firms were allowed to obtain long-term low cost financing from the international capital markets.

---

2. Also, trading companies engaged mainly in exporting activities were allowed up to 51% foreign equity while 100% foreign ownership has been allowed in the power generation sector.

Sweeping measures of internal deregulation—the virtual dismantling of the licensing system, for instance—have also been implemented. Moreover, a program of economic stabilization has accompanied the above measures: in particular, the fiscal deficit was reduced by over a third. The government has also announced intentions to bring down import tariffs to international levels, replace quantitative controls with price signals, and to make the rupee fully convertible.

Globalization and openness

Much of the literature, and common parlance in India even more, uses openness and globalization synonymously. In this paper, however, we reserve the term *openness* to refer to policies which aim to bring about economic integration with international markets, and take *globalization* to be some measure of increased external integration actually achieved.[3] The reason for distinguishing between the two terms, despite the close relation between them, openness may not go hand-in-hand with globalization, as defined here.[4]

The importance of openness and globalization in India's economic reforms is obvious. The official case for the reforms relies on both positive and negative arguments. The key positive arguments are: (1) that trade liberalization will improve allocative efficiency by shifting resources from capital-intensive to labor-intensive sectors; (2) that reduced protection will raise technical efficiency by exposing Indian firms to foreign competition; (3) that lowered barriers to foreign capital inflows will speed up capital accumulation and raise productivity levels through technology upgradation and spillovers. The official case also takes aggregate demand and foreign exchange constraints on growth to be the consequences of an autarkic policy orientation, the remedy for which lies in openness and globalization; this constitutes the negative case for the reforms. Each of these arguments makes external integration—or globalization—the engine of economic growth, and openness the centerpiece of policy. As described above, the reforms also involve internal de-regulation and liberalization, and the adoption of other elements of domestic policy orthodoxy. However, these are viewed as *economic pre-requisites*, or at least facilitators, for pursuing a successful policy of openness for increasing globalization and, in turn, the likely *political consequences* of a policy of openness. Therefore, open-

---

3. See Rao (1998c) for further discussion and a cross-country empirical attempt to separate openness from globalization as related to trade.

4. To illustrate, openness with respect to FDI implies policies which reduce restrictions and controls on foreign direct investment, while globalization may be measured by increases in the FDI/GDP ratio. On the one hand, openness may not increase globalization, as the experience of a number of LDCs—including Bangladesh—shows, due to the problems of low growth, low levels of education of the labor force and labor unrest; on the other hand, countries which have been quite restrictive in their policies towards TNCs, including Taiwan and Malaysia, have been able to increase FDI inflows, because of their high rates of growth (Dutt, 1998).

ness does indeed constitute the focal point, and globalization the touchstone, of the new regime as it is perceived by its architects.

Since our purpose is to examine the consequences of globalization, we will focus mostly on import liberalization, removal of restrictions to capital flows and on technology imports—which are the main elements of greater openness. However, we will also take into account domestic policy changes— internal liberalization as well as those involving general macroeconomic policy—given that these reforms are inextricably linked to, and flow from, the logic of globalization.

Methodological remarks

In assessing the growth and social impacts of globalization, our method will be to compare trends before and after the onset of the reforms in 1991. It is important to be forewarned of the problems of this method.

The "before/after" method is problematic because the year 1991 witnessed a harvest failure and a severe payments crisis which obliged government to undertake stabilization measures which are not necessarily part of the structural reforms. Moreover, as we have seen, the government not only embarked on external liberalization but also on reforms liberalizing domestic activities. Given that the post-1991 outcomes are likely to be affected by all of these changes, it would seem impossible to attribute the "before/after" differences solely to policy changes affecting external economic relations. We will guard against this problem by causal mechanisms linking aspects of the reform to economic performance in addition to general trends relating to growth and the social sector.

It may be thought preferable to examine the effects of "globalizing" reforms by means of a suitable computable general equilibrium model of the Indian economy and to solely consider the effects of reforms in the foreign sector. Although this could isolate the effects of external policy changes, this method has the difficulty that it ignores the close relationship between external and domestic policy changes discussed above—not only because the requirements of consistency might force domestic policy changes to conform with external policy changes but also because elements of avowedly "domestic" policy might raise or reduce an economy's level of "globalization." For instance, devaluation can be thought of as a way of stabilizing the economy, but it may also make the economy more open to foreign trade. Conversely, the dismantling of the licensing apparatus, usually thought of as an internal liberalization measure, may make exports more competitive and the economy more attractive to foreign investors.

A second issue is whether 1991 is an appropriate date for our before/ after comparison. It is generally accepted in the Indian discussion that the most important policy discontinuity occurred in 1991. However, some have argued that since liberalization started in the 1980s and even earlier, it is not appropriate to compare the period before and after 1991 as showing the effects of reforms. But the weight of opinion rejects this view. Not only was the liberalization of the 1980s halting and partial (indeed, some evidence indicates greater protectionism in this period than in the 1970s) but most observers attribute the higher growth of that period, especially in the industrial sector, to expansionary fiscal policies. We share this view and therefore take 1991 as the crucial divide.

A third issue concerning the before/after method is that the beneficial effects of external integration take time to be felt and too few years have passed (and fewer still for which the evidence is complete) since 1991 to judge these longer-term effects. While there is some merit in this argument, too much should not be made of it. We propose to examine both what happened immediately after 1991 and what happened thereafter and expect that this can shed some light on the short- and long-term distinction.

3. Openness and Economic Growth

In this section we examine whether opening up the economy has had any identifiable effect on economic growth and related macroeconomic indicators as compared with trends prior to 1991. We first discuss the extent to which the Indian economy has become more globalized under the new regime using alternative indicators, and examine mechanisms by which these changes affected the economy. We then turn to the overall trends in growth and other macroeconomic indicators and finally turn to the agricultural sector which is home to over three-fifths of the labor force and an even higher fraction of the poor.

Increased Openness and Globalization

(1) *Trade Flows* India's foreign trade has increased substantially in the post-reform period. Foreign trade as a fraction of GDP has grown from around 15% in the 1980s to over 27% in 1995 and 1996 (see Figure 2). Whereas India's share of world exports fell consistently from about 2% in the 1950s to about 0.6% in the 1970s, and then stayed at around 0.5% from 1973 onwards through the 1980s, the share has now risen smartly to 0.8% in the post-reform period. In growth terms, the dollar value of India's exports increased annually at 12% between 1990–91 and 1995–96, which is significantly higher than the 7.5% growth rate for world trade. By any standard, this must be reckoned rapid globalization. But the aggregate trend in exports and imports conceals other elements suggesting continuity.

(i) The import-GDP ratio has risen even faster after 1991 than the export-GDP ratio, peaking in 1995 with a one-percent drop in the following year (see Figure 3). This means that the trade deficit has worsened due to the increase in imports and despite the rise in exports, both presumably due to liberalization.

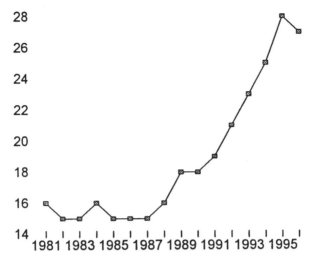

FIGURE 2: Foreign Trade as Percentage of GDP

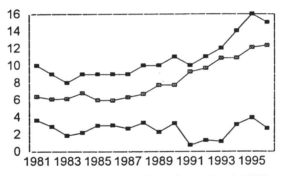

—■— Imports of goods and services (% of GDP)

—■— Exports of goods and services (% of GDP)

—■— Trade Deficit (% of GDP)

FIGURE 3: Imports, Exports and Trade Deficit (% of GDP)

(ii) Based on a measure of structural change, it has been shown that while there was a shift in the composition of imports between 1980–81 to 1990–91, no further shift can be detected during the post-reform period (Mehta, 1997). This is surprising considering the large changes in the structure of protection. It suggests that changing trade policy measures on the relative competitiveness of import-competing sectors may have been neutralized by other policy shifts.

(iii) Econometric evidence does not support the conventional conjecture that changes in competitiveness have increased India's exports; nor do the reforms appear to have had an appreciable effect (Mehta, 1997). As with imports,

Mehta (1997) finds that the composition of India's exports has not changed significantly in the 1990s, while it did so between 1980–81 and 1990–91. India's export growth acceleration appears to have been a shift in export composition toward the Asian markets, which experienced higher rates of trade growth than the world as a whole.

(2) *FDI Flows* After a long period of stagnation in the 1970s, the inflow of FDI has speeded up in recent years, as shown in Figure 4. After the slow liberalization in the 1980s the FDI stock nearly tripled in that decade. Following the new policies of 1991, although approvals of FDI inflows increased spectacularly—compared to $200 million in 1991, about $17 billion worth of FDI proposals was approved in 1997—actual inflows have been considerably smaller. In 1993–94 FDI was at $586 million, which increased to $1314 million in 1994–95, to $2133 million in 1995–96 and to $3.2 billion in 1997.

Over the period when policies were restrictive, the sectoral composition of FDI stock moved in favor of manufacturing, its share rising from 40.5% in 1964 to 86.9% in 1990 (Kumar, 1995). After the slow liberalization of the 1980s, the composition changed to favor services and infrastructure rather than manufacturing, and lower-technology rather than higher-technology sectors. Though the number of foreign collaboration approvals has been highest in core sectors such as telecommunications (25%) and energy development (21%), the actual flows by industry follow the 1980s pattern.

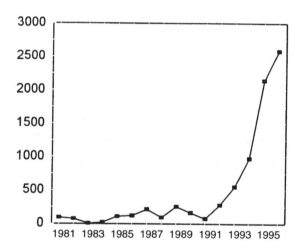

FIGURE 4: Net Foreign Direct Capital Inflow (current US$ million)

While FDI is supposed to contribute to economic growth in part by raising the rate of capital formation, the volume of FDI has remained very low relative to both GDI and GDP (see Figure 5). In fact, the state has remained the principal financier of local enterprises, in both public and private sectors, through the financial institutions that it controls. The share of foreign firms in fixed asset formation in the corporate sector remained unchanged at about

10% in the 1990s. Moreover, as compared to Indian firms, foreign firms used a smaller fraction of their investable resources in physical investment; during the five years since 1991–92, the ratio of gross fixed assets to total uses of funds for the foreign private sector was lower than that for the indigenous private sector by about 13% (Nagraj, 1997, citing CMIE data). Nagraj (1997) surmises that a large proportion of FDI thus represents acquisition of managerial control of existing firms, and does not represent new capital formation.

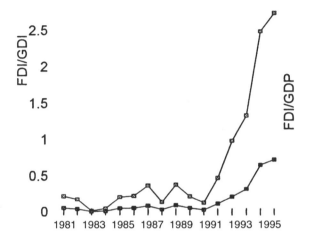

FIGURE 5: FDI as % of GDI and GDP

According to one view, India's restrictive attitude towards TNCs during the 1970s and 1980s was a factor in her technology lag (Encarnation, 1989). A widely-held expectation is that the new liberalization of FDI will help upgrade India's technology, enhance product innovation and transfer management skills. But the evidence provides little support in favor of this expectation. The growth rate of productivity for industries in which the inflow of advanced foreign technology is relatively high is not significantly greater than that for industries in which the inflow of foreign technology is low (Goldar, 1993). Moreover, the sectoral composition of FDI flows noted above does not auger well for technological change.

Finally, there is scepticism about the claim that the increase in FDI that has occurred since 1991 is due to the liberalization policy. Kumar (1998) has drawn attention to the fact that this increase occurred at a time when global flows of FDI, including that to developing countries, expanded dramatically. True, since infrastructural sectors from which India previously barred FDI accounted for nearly half of total FDI approvals in the post-liberalization period, one may conclude that at least a part of the increase is liberalization-driven. However, an examination of India's share as a host of FDI flows from Germany, France and the US do not show any significant change, suggesting that FDI liberalization has not had a major impact.

(3) *Portfolio Investment and Foreign Currency Bank Deposits* The opening up of the stock market to international capital flows produced a boom in stock prices in India. Total foreign portfolio investment in India expanded rapidly, from $6 million in 1990–91 to over $3 billion in 1996–97. Foreign currency deposits in banks have also increased rapidly.

Despite these trends, the expected growth effects of portfolio inflows have not been fulfilled. It is clear that the volatility of stock prices has increased, partly due to the growing influence of the Foreign Institutional Investors (FIIs), a direct consequence of deregulation. This rising influence also makes the markets increasingly sensitive to political uncertainty which has also risen during the 1990s. While market enthusiasts hoped that stock market stimulation from foreign inflows would help bump up the saving rate, no such connection has materialized. While the volume of household savings held in the form of shares and debentures and in units of the Unit Trust of India (a public sector mutual fund) has risen 35-fold since 1980–81, the overwhelming part of this reflects a shift from bank deposits to stocks. After the sharp falls in stock prices mentioned above, the share of stocks has gone down again in favor of bank deposits (Pal, 1998). Moreover, a large proportion of these inflows did not contribute to fixed capital formation in manufacturing since the ratio of Gross Fixed Capital Formation to the supply of long term funds available to that sector fell significantly during 1992–96 (Nagraj, 1997). Nagraj argues that the resources were more important for intercorporate investment, financing mergers and takeovers, and to fuel the real estate boom.

The volatility of these hot money flows seen elsewhere in the world is also reflected in Indian experience since 1991. The fact that the rupee is not convertible on the capital account has shielded India from the crises which has affected East and South East Asia. Nevertheless, the volatility of these flows puts upward pressures on the rupee when inflows are high, which may erode the competitiveness of Indian products abroad, and lead to pressures on the balance of payments when outflows occur, requiring import compression and restrictive government policies which reduce the growth of the economy. Given the political uncertainty (with a minority government which is doing poorly in opinion polls and state elections), the possibility of sudden outflows cannot be ruled out, making these inflows a fickle financier of growth.

Economic Growth and Other Macroeconomic Indicators

Figure 6 shows the behavior of the annual rate of growth of the economy. Leaving out the high-growth year of 1988 and the crisis year of 1991, real GDP growth has fluctuated between 3.5% and 7.5%. Given the fluctuation, it is difficult to come to any clear conclusions about trends before and after 1991. On the one hand, the highest rate of growth of any single year occurred before the 1991 reforms. On the other hand, between 1994 and 1996 the economy

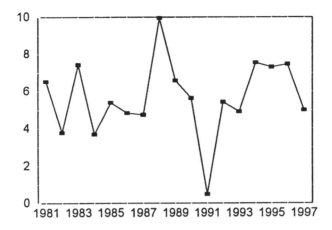

FIGURE 6: Real GDP Growth, 1981–1997

grew consistently above the 7% level, a feat not achieved in the pre-reform years. This high rate of growth, however, has not been maintained in 1997–98, when it has fallen to about 5%.

Average and trend growths are more revealing. The average GDP growth was 5.3% for the post-reform period 1992–96 as compared to 5.7% for 1981–85 and 5.9% in 1986–91 (see Table 2). Thus the rate of growth for the post-reform period (even leaving out the low-growth year of 1997) is lower than the previous decade. Even on a disaggregated view, one finds that the primary, secondary and tertiary sectors all grew at a lower rate in the post-reform period than in the five years immediately preceding the reforms, and only the tertiary sector grew faster than in the 1981–85 period. Using a dummy variable for the post-1991 years in log-linear trend regressions, Nagraj (1997) finds no statistically significant break in 1991 for total GDP, and for the primary and tertiary sectors, and a modest fall for the secondary sector of 0.4 % since 1991.

The fiscal deficit of the Central and State governments (measured by the excess of total expenditure, including loans net of recovery, over revenue receipts and external grants and non-debt capital receipts) averaged 9.5% of GDP during 1985–90, reaching 10.1% in 1990 just before the reforms, fell to 8.0% in 1991–92 and 7.7% in 1992–3 after the fiscal correction, and rose again

TABLE 2. GDP and Sectoral Growth Rates, 1981–96

	Primary	Secondary	Tertiary	GDP
1981–85	5.8	6.1	5.4	5.6
1986–91	3.7	7.4	7.1	5.9
1992–96	2.5	6.3	6.8	5.3
1981–96	4.0	6.6	6.5	5.7

Source: Nagaraj (1997), from *National Accounts Statistics*, various issues.

to 9.0% in 1993–94 and 8.3% in 1994–95, and 7.9% in 1995–96 (Patnaik, 1997). There has been an increase in the deficit during the last year and the present, due mainly to the revenue or current account deficit which for the Central and State governments averaged 2.8% in 1985–90, increased to 4.5% in 1990–91, fell to 3.6% and 3.4% during the next two years, and climbed up again to 4.6% during 1993–94 and to 4.0% and 3.9% in the next two years (Patnaik, 1997). The interest burden on the central budget has continued to rise throughout the 1990s, its share in current expenditure increasing from 21.6% in 1990 to 27.7% in 1996. While this is the primary source of the fiscal squeeze, another source of revenue squeeze, especially noticeable during the last 2 years, is import tariff revenue. Customs revenue as a ratio of total Central Government revenues fell from above 33% in 1991 to below 30% in 1998; in 1995 it reached about 23%. The effect of this on the government budget deficit can be seen by comparing the actual Central Government deficit to GDP ratio to what it would have been had the 1991 ratio of customs to total revenue been maintained, as shown in Figure 7.

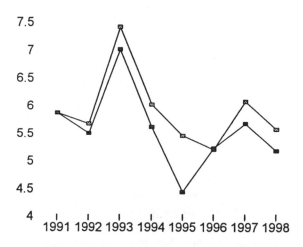

FIGURE 7: Central Government Deficit to GDP

One predictable consequence of this fiscal squeeze is that public capital formation has slowed down during the 1990s. It is widely acknowledged that one of the major explanations of India's strong growth performance in the 1980s is the increase in infrastructure investment, especially in railways and power generation (Ahluwalia, 1991: 85–87). Such investment not only has a positive supply-side effect, but there is also evidence that there is a positive demand-side effect as government investment "crowds in" by private investment, both in the industrial and agricultural sectors. There is a consensus now that between the declining fiscal capacity of the state and the unresolved regulatory complexities surrounding privatization, the infrastructure sectors loom increasingly large as a constraint on economic growth, especially given India's low level of infrastructure development (World Bank, 1996).

Figure 8 shows trends in domestic saving and investment rates. Savings in the post-reforms period rose from 22 per cent of GDP in 1992–93 to 26.2 per cent in 1996–97, and aggregate investments went up from 24 per cent to 27.8 per cent. Household savings averaged 19.4 per cent, with investments in financial assets showing a marked growth. While this may be counted as a positive payoff to the financial (internal and external) liberalizations of the reform program, it has not resulted in higher growth, so that the added accumulation seems to have contributed to increased capital intensity in the economy rather than to income growth as such. Data on actual capital-output ratios confirms this: the net fixed capital to output ratio for the economy, after falling from 2.63 in 1980 to 2.38 in 1990, increased in the 1990s it increased to 2.46 in 1994. The increase has been particularly striking in the manufacturing sector, where it increased from 2.13 in 1990 to 2.57 in 1994 (EPW, 1997).

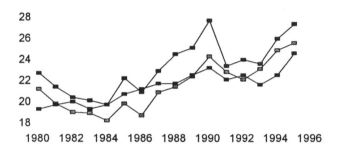

-□- Gross Domestic Saving
-■- Gross domestic capital formation
-■- Gross fixed capital formation

FIGURE 8: Saving and Investment Rates, 1980–95

Figures 9 and 10 show trends in price indices and in bank interest rates. The sharp spurt in prices in 1991 is the combined effect of the drought, monetary restriction associated with the stabilization program, increases in administered prices and in the issue prices of government-subsidized foodgrains, and subsequently, the extraction of an export surplus from the economy. Bank rates were jacked up to curb inflation, to entice capital inflows and as part of a program of financial liberalization. While lending rates rose abruptly, the cooling of inflation helped bring them down again. Indeed, they have fallen 2 to 3 points below where they had been prior to liberalization reflecting the massive growth of the primary issues market after 1994 and recessionary conditions in industry during the last two years.

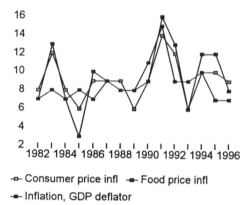

-□- Consumer price infl   -■- Food price infl
-■- Inflation, GDP deflator

FIGURE 9: Inflation Rates

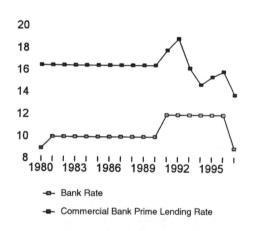

-□- Bank Rate
-■- Commercial Bank Prime Lending Rate

FIGURE 10: Interest Rates, 1980–97

We conclude this subsection by examining the contribution made to growth by different components of demand and by total factor productivity growth (*TFPG*), using two alternative approaches to growth accounting reflecting different constrains on growth.[5]

---

5. Another potential constraint on growth is the balance of payments. If the economy's rate of growth is constrained by the availability of foreign exchange, or if the economy is exchange constrained in the sense of being subject to period shocks due to foreign exchange shortages, the rate of growth of the economy on average will be determined by its balance of payments position. Following stabilization and reforms, there is little evidence of this constraint being effectively binding although a return to exchange shortage can by no means be ruled out.

Although the concern with the role of aggregate demand as a determinant of growth has been lately drowned by the focus on supply-side cures implicit in the reforming agenda, we believe that aggregate demand issues remain highly relevant especially for non-agricultural sector, in stimulating investment, raising utilization in the oligopolistic industrial and service sectors of the formal economy, and thereby output and savings (see Dutt, 1996). The role of different components of aggregate demand—private investment, government spending and export—in stimulating growth is analyzed in Figure 11, where X is total supply (GDP plus total imports), I is private investment, G is total government expenditure (including government investment), E is exports, and s, t and m are the ratios of private saving, taxes, and imports to total supply. X, I, G and E have been deflated by the GDP deflator and expressed in real terms.

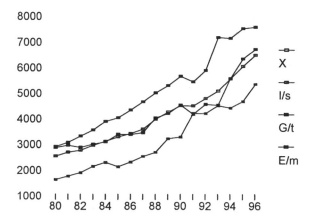

FIGURE 11: Contributions of Investment, Goverment Spending and Exports to GDP

Following Godley and McCarthy (1997), we can take I/s, G/t, and E/m to be the contributions of investment, government spending and exports to GDP (since they show the real levels of these components multiplied by the respective "own" multipliers); X is therefore a weighted average of these three contributions. We find that government spending has, since the 1980s, always been the major expansionary component of demand, since G/t consistently lies above the X line. The domestic private sector has more or less played a neutral role, since I/s has been close to X, while exports has consistently played a depressive role, since E/m is consistently below X. This pattern, strongest during the 1980s, confirms the importance of government fiscal policy in generating growth in the 1980s. The contraction of fiscal spending during the crisis of 1991 is reflected in the data, as is the contraction in the private domestic sector and the expansion in the role of exports. However, soon thereafter we find the fiscal factor recovering its role, though leveling off in recent years as the role of the private domestic sector and exports has grown. Despite these changes, however, the basic pattern remains that of fiscal policy being the major expansionary component of aggregate demand even after the reforms. With the development of recessionary tendencies over the last 2 years, this analysis finds further confirmation in the growing clamor for fiscal boosts to the sagging growth of industry.

Turning to the supply-based approach, we use the simple and popular method of calculating *TFPG* using Solow's residual, despite the well-known problems it has in measuring technological change. Our estimates of the residual, using the equation

$$TFPG = g(Y/L) - \alpha_K \, g(K/L),$$

where g (i) refers to the rate of growth of i, Y is real output, L is total employment, K is real net fixed capital stock and α_K is the share of capital in output,[6] are shown in Figure 12. As expected, *TFPG* is negative in the crisis year of 1991. Leaving aside 1991 (when *TFPG* is negative), the average *TFPG* is 3.4 for the period 1980–90 and 2.5 for the period 1991–95, suggesting that there has been a decline in *TFPG* after the 1991 reforms compared to the 1980s.

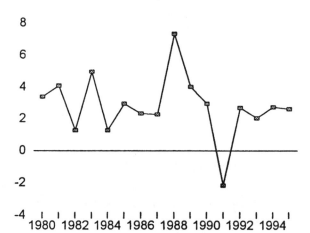

FIGURE 12: Total Factor Productivity Growth

---

6. Employment and real output data is taken from World Bank data, and net real fixed capital and the share of operating surplus in NDP from EPW (1997). Two adjustments were made for the operating surplus share. First, India has a large share of income (around 50%) which falls in the category of mixed income of the self employed. We used the assumption that the capital share for that income is the same as the share for the rest of the economy to find the share of capital stock (operating surplus) for the economy as a whole. Second, data on income shares was available for the years 1980–81 to 1993–94; we computed the figures for the next two years using ordinary least squares on a time trend.

Agriculture under the Reforms

Critics of the liberal program since 1991 have tended to maintain that it neglects agriculture. They fear that structural adjustment policies of the 1990s together with the falling trend in public investment in agriculture dating from the 1980s are undermining the basis for labor-absorbing and equitable growth. Defenders of the program argue that agriculture is a prime if indirect beneficiary due to reduced protection for industry and the (partial) removal of restrictions on agricultural exports. Further movement on this reform path, including especially freeing up the food and agricultural markets, can only further these benefits as India will then emerge as a major exporter in this sector.

But experience for the seven years since reforms began to bear out the critics. Despite the highly unusual succession of ten normal monsoons that has included that seven-year period, foodgrains output growth has decelerated from 3.5 per cent in the 1980s to a mere 1.7 per cent in the 1990s the latter implying a declining trend in per capita supply. The GDP share of agriculture at 1980–81 prices has fallen from 29.96 per cent in 1991–92 to just 24.38 per cent in 1997–98.[7] While one might argue that this decline reflects a healthy process of structural change, this seems distinctly implausible not merely because trade reforms, in the liberal reckoning, greatly reduced "urban bias" but also because poverty increased at least during the early years and food consumption fell. How could it be that as a "pro-agriculture" policy took root, the share of agriculture fell off so significantly? Perhaps, the liberal diagnosis and prescription for agricultural development are flawed.

At the same time, however, the notion that there is an overwhelming discontinuity in agricultural and food policies cannot be taken at face value. On the production side, recent governments have tried to step up outlays for public investment in agriculture while on the food consumption side, after the early years when issue prices in the Public Distribution System (PDS) had been raised sharply, those price increases have been sharply slowed or reversed. These moves are rather in keeping with the long-established understandings of the determinants of agricultural production, food consumption and poverty in India.

Moreover, the effectiveness of partly restored fiscal allocations for agriculture and its infrastructure will remain low if inertial elements in policy are not overcome. These elements include: (1) a continuing reliance on a high-input and high-capital intensity strategy that is evident in the heavy subsidisation of inputs, the failure to mobilise surplus labor on farm or for infrastructure building off the farm; (2) capital-intensive and environment-unfriendly programs to augment the effective supply of land; (3) the assumption of the immutability of the particular combination of agrarian inequalities and market

---

7. Economic Survey 1997–98 cited in Devarajan (1998).

failures together with government policies themselves that alone can account for the low rate of labor-absorption in Indian agriculture.[8]

External liberalization, whereby the agricultural sector is sought to be integrated with the global market, will not only raise the key wage goods prices and fuel inflation but also holds the potential to effect a contraction in aggregate demand and employment. As Nayyar and Sen (1994) have argued, if the trade reforms are not supplemented by a supportive agricultural policy, emphasizing public irrigation investment and institutional changes, medium-term stagflation may result. Empirical support for this argument is provided by the dynamic general equilibrium estimates of the effects of agricultural trade liberalization, reported in Storm (1997), which also indicate that the reforms on their own will be distributionally regressive. The main factors underlying these results are, first, the lack of adequate rural infrastructure and second, the prevailing agrarian structure. These factors, rather than the lack of price incentives, are the dominant constraints on private investment and the use of 'modern' inputs (see Rao, 1998b).

4. Changes in the Employment Structure

Employment and wages are probably the most important potential channels through which the social impact of increased openness and globalization are felt. In this section, besides presenting the evidence on overall employment and unemployment trends, we examine trends in formal sector employment and in informalization, and in the sectoral composition of the labor force.[9] The reader is cautioned at the outset that in an economy characterized by the preponderance of household and tiny enterprises, high rates of underemployment, a very high incidence of casual, frequently part-time, work, and widespread seasonal and gender gaps in employment opportunities in spatially dispersed, often localized, labor markets, employment statistics should be taken with a dose of scepticism.

Shrinking Formal Employment

Figure 13 shows the changes in employment levels in the "organized" sector which includes all public sector employment (mostly in industry and services),

---

8. The New Agricultural Strategy's relative success in achieving food self-sufficiency in the three decades since the food crisis of the mid-1960s has masked the economic, social and environmental costs of that Strategy. Low labor absorption is perhaps the chief of these costs. For elaboration of this thesis, see Rao and Storm (1997).

9. The growth of rural non-farm employment and the role of government employment programs will be discussed separately in connection with their effects on poverty in a later section.

and employment in private sector units that employ more than 10 persons.[10] It shows that organized sector employment has grown sluggishly during the 1980s and the 1990s, and that most of this has been in the public sector while private sector employment has stagnated.

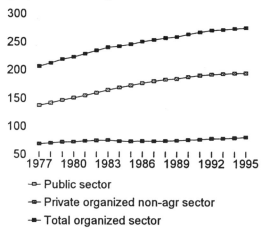

FIGURE 13: Employment in Organized Sector, 1977–95

Figure 14 shows that the growth rate of organized sector employment has fallen steadily over the entire period, a trend dominated by the decline in the rate of growth of public sector employment. Private sector employment growth, throughout the 1980s, was slower than public sector employment growth. Only as late as 1992 did it equal the latter. Thereafter, it has fluctuated at a level that has not been able to counter the decline in the growth of public sector employment, so that total organized sector employment growth has continued to fall.

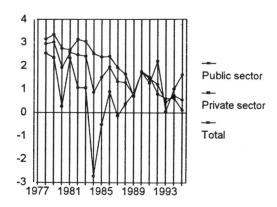

FIGURE 14: Growth Rates of Organized Sector Employment

10. The organized sector corresponds roughly with commonly accepted notions of formal employment.

While the trend in organized sector employment is suggestive, this sector accounts for only around 10% of total employment. We therefore need to examine figures for total employment, to which we now turn.

Aggregate Employment and Employment Structure

Employment figures for the economy as a whole (including the unorganized sector) are available only from the *decadal* censuses and from the periodic surveys conducted by the national sample survey (NSS) organization. Census figures available for 1981 and 1991 cannot reveal any trend changes that may have been caused by the recent reforms. NSS estimates, however, are available for 1983, 1987–88 and 1993–94. NSS figures are disaggregated for urban and rural areas and for males and females. Considering the usual status of workers in all age groups and including people from subsidiary employment as workers, for urban areas the male worker participation rate (WPR) increased marginally from 50.6% to 52.0% between 1987–88 to 1993–94, while the female WPR also increased marginally from 15.2% to 15.4%. For rural males the increase was from 53.9% to 55.3%, the figures being 32.3% and 32.8% for females. Broadly similar conclusions are obtained if we consider the daily and weekly status of workers rather than their usual status; if we exclude children rather than including them; and if we consider only people's principal employment rather than their subsidiary employment as well. The important exception is that for rural males in the 15–59 age group, for whom the daily status WPR fell from 83.5% to 80.9%.

Data on unemployment rates are also available from the NSS rounds. Comparison between the major NSS surveys of 1987–88 and 1993–94 shows that unemployment rates have gone *down* for all categories of workers, and especially so for women; the only figure which shows an increase is that for rural men by daily status, from 4.6% to 5.6%. Comparisons with 1983 also show reductions, although smaller ones in most cases (though the daily status rural male unemployment rate now shows a decline in 1993–94). However, results of additional smaller—"thin"—surveys, if taken to be roughly comparable to those of the broader surveys, show that the 1987–88 figures for unemployment are consistently *higher* than those of the next four rounds (1989–90, 1990–91, July–December 1991 and 1992) and that compared to the levels for these years, the 1993–94 unemployment rates are usually higher.

Turning next to data on the composition of employment, consider first the information on the type of employment—self-employment, regular and casual employment—shown in Table 5, which reveals several trends. One, the share of self-employed in employment has fallen for all categories from 1977–78 to 1993–94 (the trend continuing after 1987–88), with the exception of urban males, where the proportion increased marginally. Two, there is a steady fall in the share of regular employees and a rise in that of casual labor in all categories except for urban females. Three, for urban female workers there has been a steady increase in the proportion of regular workers both in terms

**TABLE 5. Composition of Usually Employed Persons
by Type of Employment, 1977–1994**

| Year | Usually Employed | | | | | |
| | Principal Status | | | All Workers | | |
	Self-Employed	Regular Employees	Casual Labor	Self-Employed	Regular Employees	Casual Labor
RURAL MALES						
1977–78	62.2	10.8	27.0	62.8	10.6	26.6
1983	59.5	10.6	29.9	60.5	10.3	29.2
1987–88	57.5	10.4	32.1	58.6	10.0	31.4
1993–94	56.9	8.5	34.6	57.9	8.3	33.8
RURAL FEMALES						
1977–78	56.3	3.7	40.0	62.1	2.8	35.1
1983	54.1	3.7	42.2	61.9	2.8	35.3
1987–88	54.9	4.9	40.2	60.8	3.7	35.5
1993–94	51.3	3.4	45.3	58.5	2.8	38.7
URBAN MALES						
1977–78	39.9	47.2	13.9	40.4	46.4	13.2
1983	40.2	44.5	15.3	40.9	43.7	15.4
1987–88	41.0	44.4	14.6	41.7	43.7	14.6
1993–94	41.1	42.7	16.2	41.7	42.1	16.2
URBAN FEMALES						
1977–78	42.2	30.8	27.0	49.5	24.9	25.6
1983	37.3	31.8	30.0	45.8	25.8	28.4
1987–88	39.3	34.2	26.5	47.1	27.5	25.4
1993–94	36.4	35.5	28.1	45.4	28.6	26.0

Source: Kundu (1997), from National Sample Survey Organization (1988, 1996).

of principal status and for all workers; as just noted, this is the opposite of the trend for all other types of workers. Four, the trend away from regular employment and towards casual labor seems to have intensified between 1987–88 and 1993–94; indeed, for rural females 1987–88 was a peak for the proportion in regular employment.

The other important dimension of employment composition concerns its sectoral distribution. It is well known that with the process of development, economies undergo a change in the structure of employment away from lower productivity agricultural sectors to industrial and service sectors. This trend out of agriculture is observed in Table 6, especially for males in both rural and urban areas. However, the table also shows that this structural shift seems to have been stalled after 1987–88 for all categories of workers other than for urban females. Since the Census figures do not show such a stalling until 1991, Kundu (1997) argues that this has occurred in the years after the reforms of 1991.

The percentage of workers in manufacturing in urban areas has decreased since 1977, a trend that has continued apace between 1987–88 and 1993–94, while two sectors that have experienced systematic increases in employment share are wholesale and retail trade and community and other services. Kundu (1997) explains the loss of manufacturing employment in terms of jobs being subcontracted out by large manufacturing units to smaller ones which are

TABLE 6. Sectoral composition of workers
(principal and subsidiary status) 1977–1994

Sector	Male				Female			
	1977–78	1983	1987–88	1993–94	1977–78	1983	1987–88	1993–94
RURAL								
Agriculture	80.5	77.8	74.6	74.0	86.8	87.8	84.8	86.1
Mining & quarrying	0.5	0.6	0.7	0.7	0.3	0.3	0.4	0.4
Manufacturing	6.5	7.0	7.4	7.0	6.1	6.4	6.9	7.1
Electricity	0.2	0.2	0.3	0.3	0.0	0.0	0.0	0.1
Construction	1.7	2.2	3.7	3.2	0.7	0.7	2.9	0.9
Trade, etc.	4.0	4.4	5.1	5.5	2.3	1.9	2.1	2.1
Transportation, storage etc.	1.2	1.7	2.0	2.2	0.1	0.1	0.1	0.1
Financial, insurance etc. services	0.2	0.3	0.4	0.4	0.0	0.0	0.0	0.1
Community, etc. services	5.2	5.8	5.8	6.6	3.7	2.8	3.0	3.3
URBAN								
Agriculture	10.2	10.3	9.1	9.0	25.1	32.0	29.4	24.7
Mining & quarrying	0.9	1.3	1.3	1.3	0.6	0.8	0.8	0.6
Manufacturing	27.7	27.0	25.7	23.5	29.4	27.1	27.0	24.1
Electricity	1.1	1.1	1.2	1.2	0.1	0.0	0.2	0.3
Construction	4.2	5.2	5.8	6.9	2.6	3.3	3.7	4.1
Trade, etc.	21.6	20.2	22.0	21.9	9.8	9.0	10.0	10.0
Transportation, storage etc.	9.9	9.9	9.7	9.7	1.2	1.6	0.9	1.3
Financial, insurance etc. services	3.0	3.5	3.5	3.8	0.7	0.4	1.2	1.9
Community, etc. services	21.5	21.4	21.7	22.6	30.4	25.8	26.6	33.1

Source: Kundu (1997), from National Sample Survey Organization (1988, 1994 and 1996).

often household units that classify themselves as service units. While such misclassification may well occur, some of it is undoubtedly real. Since the declines are too large to be accounted for by the organized or factory sector alone, they must reflect loss of employment in household and other non-factory modes of manufacturing. This loss of manufacturing employment should be seen in the light of our earlier conclusion that, for the economy as a whole, output growth has hot kept pace with investment growth, both possibly manifestations of capital deepening.[11]

There is enough grist here for the reform critics' mills. First, the decreases in participation rates for rural workers in the 15–59 age group is worrisome. It may be symptomatic of slowed employment growth in an economy long accustomed to high rates of underemployment disguised as non-participation. Second, the decline in formal employment growth (both public and private) below the

---

11. Kambhampati, Krishna and Mitra (1997) have taken annual estimates of total and manufacturing labor force and found that the reforms have had little effect on employment at a macroeconomic level. The total labor force expanded steadily from 1987 to 1993 from 298 to 341 million workers. The number of workers in manufacturing increased steadily as well, though at a faster rate. But there were no significant changes in trends after 1991. Since the annual labor force figures are presumably no more than rough estimates, it is not clear how much credence to attach to these propositions.

rate of growth of the labor force over a period of nearly a decade when formal sector output has grown at its fastest pace in history suggests a clearly unhealthy pattern of development. When this is coupled with the increasing incidence of casual labor and the decline in self-employment, it appears that a process of *informalization* seems to have become endemic in the Indian labor markets. This has potentially serious consequences for wages, job security, inflation protection, workers' basic rights, and the future of the Indian labor movement. It is undoubtedly a symptom of the further weakening of labor vis-a-vis capital. Third, the increasing feminization of the regular labor force (recall the rise in the regular-to-casual ratio among females versus a decline in the same ratio among males) may well be a further cause of concern for the working classes. At first sight, it would seem to be a trend towards greater gender equality. But as Kundu (1997) has argued, this is probably a continuation of a trend starting in the 1980s in which female regular employment has been in low-wage, low-productivity sectors; indeed, female regular wages are often no higher, even less, than casual male wages. A final cause for concern is the stalling of changes in the sectoral composition of employment, especially in rural areas. Using some of the "thin" NSS survey data, Sen (1996) found that the share of agriculture in rural employment in 1992 increased both for men and women. In conjunction with the evidence on increases in poverty rates, he interprets this to imply a decrease in non-agricultural employment opportunities in rural areas, which pushed workers back to the lower-productivity agricultural sector characterized by the underemployment of labor.

But there is also room for debate as to whether these trends have to do mainly with the reforms or are due to other factors. One point of contention is whether the year which is usually taken as the pre-reform year, 1987–88, is suitable for making comparisons. Kundu (1997) argues that the year was a year of severe drought with higher-than-normal unemployment so that any estimate of unemployment in post-reform years compared to it is likely to be understated. Deshpande and Deshpande (1998) argue that the fact that 1987–88 was a drought year implies that unemployment and underemployment will be lower than otherwise, since drought conditions can be expected to have increased government relief employment programs and increased the share of employment in non-agricultural sectors in rural areas. While the point about the composition of employment may have some merit, it is implausible that government relief programs in response to drought conditions actually reduce unemployment rates below expected levels. Even more to the point, several of the trends, with adverse social implications, that we have found do not hinge on the choice of 1987–88 as the representative pre-reform year.

Another point of contention is whether or not the reforms or rather, the bad harvest of 1991 coupled with the stabilization program following the foreign exchange crisis, were responsible for the employment problems immediately following 1991. We will return to this issue when poverty later; here it suffices to note that we have not made use of data immediately following 1991 to examine trends in employment and unemployment, but rather data for 1993–94.

5. Income Distribution and Poverty

Growing income inequality has been a nearly ubiquitous concern about globalization in both rich and poor countries. In India, absolute poverty has traditionally received overwhelming attention in both academic research and
policy debate long before the "globalizing" reforms of 1991, and this tendency
has continued after the reforms. The neglect of relative inequality may not be
entirely, perhaps even mainly, a matter of social priority; it may also be seen as
resting on the remarkable stability of the expenditure distribution over several decades. But as with employment statistics, income distribution statistics
too leave much to be desired. In what follows, we will try to tease out some
conclusions about trends in poverty and inequality from such numbers as are
available and attempt to link these with the reform process.

Income Distribution

India's income distribution as measured by the Gini coefficient of consumption expenditure (which undoubtedly understates *income* inequality) shows
little change over the years. Table 7 shows that in both rural and urban areas
this coefficient has fluctuated without a clear trend. However, it may be noted
that both rural and urban inequality increased between 1990–91 and 1991–
92, but then improved in the next year.

There is anecdotal evidence on rapid rates of increase in the incomes of
highly-skilled workers and managers in the 1990s, especially in transnational
corporations. These increases are especially among those who are graduates of
leading management and technology institutes, suggesting increases in the
skilled-unskilled wage differential. However, we know of no aggregate data con-
firming this trend.

TABLE 7. Gini Coefficient of Consumption Expenditure Distribution

Year	Rural	Urban
1960–61	0.322	0.348
1970–71	0.283	0.326
1977–78	0.339	0.345
1983–84	0.298	0.330
1987–88	0.298	0.354
1988–89	0.290	0.338
1989–90	0.278	0.350
1990–91	0.272	0.331
1991–92	0.287	0.367
1993–94	0.282	0.339

Source: Hashim (1998), estimated from NSS Consumer Expenditure Distribution, Government of
India, *A Technical Note to the Eighth Plan of India, 1992–97*, 1995.

Poverty

As defined by the Indian Planning Commission, the all-India poverty line equals a per capita monthly expenditure of Rs. 49 for rural areas and Rs. 57 for urban areas at 1973–74 all-India prices. Between 1951 and 1975, the proportion of people below the poverty line (the headcount ratio) showed sharp fluctuations but no long-run trend. Table 8 shows trends in three measures of poverty incidence from the mid 1970s using this definition. These numbers have been refined to correct for price level variations across states and survey period following the 1993 recommendations of the Planning Commission's Expert Group on Poverty Estimation (World Bank, 1998). As the Table shows, the headcount ratio fell rapidly and fairly steadily from the mid 1970s to the late 1980s, the average annual rate of decline being 2.4% (World Bank, 1998). These patterns hold for both the rural and urban areas, and the trends are also reflected in the two other widely-used measures of poverty, the poverty gap (which measures the average distance below the poverty line and thus estimates the depth of poverty) and the squared poverty gap (which raises the individual poverty gaps to a power of two and therefore is a measure of the severity of poverty). After 1986–87 the poverty measures started fluctuating again, and registered increases after 1991, the headcount ratio rising from 36% in 1990–91 to 41% in 1992. For rural India, Sen (1996) estimates that over 60 million people were added to the rolls of the poor during the first 18 months after the initiation of reforms. But note also that the head-count ratio fell back in 1993–94.

TABLE 8. Poverty in India, 1977–1994

NSS Survey Round	period	Head count index Rural	Urban	Total	Poverty gap index Rural	Urban	Total	Squared poverty gap Rural	Urban	Total
28	Oct 73–Jun 74	55.72	47.96	54.10	17.18	13.60	16.43	7.13	5.22	6.73
32	Jul 77–Jun 78	50.60	40.50	48.36	15.03	11.69	14.28	6.06	4.53	5.72
38	Jan 83–Dec 83	45.31	35.65	43.00	12.65	9.52	11.90	4.84	3.56	4.53
42	Jul 86–Jun 87	38.81	34.29	37.69	10.01	9.10	9.79	3.70	3.40	3.63
43	Jul 87–Jun 88	39.23	36.20	38.47	9.28	9.12	9.24	2.98	3.06	3.00
44	Jul 88–Jun 89	39.06	36.60	38.44	9.50	9.54	9.51	3.29	3.29	3.29
45	Jul 89–Jun 90	34.30	33.40	34.07	7.80	8.51	7.98	2.58	3.04	2.69
46	Jul 90–Jun 91	36.43	32.76	35.49	8.64	8.51	8.61	2.93	3.12	2.98
47	Jul 91–Dec 91	37.42	33.23	36.34	8.29	8.24	8.28	2.68	2.90	2.74
48	Jul 92–Dec 92	43.47	33.73	40.93	10.8	8.82	10.35	3.81	3.19	3.65
50	Jul 93–Jun 94	36.66	30.51	35.04	8.39	7.41	8.13	2.79	2.42	2.69

Note: Poverty line = Rs. 49 per capita per month at Oct 73–Jun. 74 rural prices.
All poverty measures are expressed as percentages.
Source: World Bank (1998).

The poor in India are concentrated among the landless, especially landless wage laborers, among members of scheduled castes and tribes, and households in which all members are illiterate (World Bank, 1998). These are not disjoint groupings. The vast majority—74 %—of the Indian poor make their living in the rural, still mainly agricultural, economy.

India's progress in the fields of education and health has been similarly tardy. At the last census, 1990–91, the literacy rate among women and men aged 7 and above was 39% and 64% respectively, up from 30% and 56% in 1980–81. Life expectancy at birth was 59.2 years in 1990–91 compared to 50.4% in 1980–81. Estimates for these measures after 1990–91 suggest that the upward trend is continuing. Although the improvements compared to 1950–51 (when the female and male literacy rates were 9% and 27%, and life expectancy at birth was 32.1%) are notable, India lags far behind other developing countries, including some Asian neighbors.

It is useful to examine the general determinants of trends in poverty before we turn to a consideration of the particular effects of globalizing reforms. One route to reducing poverty is agricultural growth. Using time series data on agricultural poverty which they obtain by modifying NSS data, Datt and Ravallion (1996) find that trends in poverty are explained mainly by agricultural growth. According to their estimates, overall growth in the economy accounts for most of the reduction in the headcount poverty measure—80% for the entire period and almost 100% since 1970. The evidence across states, according to Datt and Ravallion, shows that poverty reduction has occurred fastest in states that have experienced rapid rural growth with strong infrastructure development (such as Punjab and Haryana) and in those that have relied on human resource development (such as Kerala). By contrast, Sen (1996) finds that, for the period after the Green Revolution, there is a rather weak link across states between the rate of per capita agricultural growth and reduction in rural poverty.

A second route to reducing poverty is through labor-intensive industrial or non-agricultural growth in urban or in rural areas. While Datt and Ravallion find no empirical support for this view, Sen (1996) reports that increases in non-agricultural incomes tend to reduce poverty in both rural and urban areas. Of particular importance in this respect is the role of increases in non-agricultural employment in rural areas not merely because it may reduce unemployment and underemployment but also because, as a number of authors have noted, it is strongly associated with rising real wages in agriculture during the 1980s. This rise in real wages seems to discredit the view that increases in rural non-agricultural employment were due to the distress needs of those pushed out of labor-shedding agriculture. It has seemed natural to suppose instead that the association between rising wages and rising non-farm employment must reflect the pull of demand. Sen (1996) has argued that rising government expenditures in rural areas, on revenue and capital account, have provided a major impetus for the growth. This view is compatible with the further observation that non-farm employment growth is broadly unrelated to the rate of agricultural growth across states.[12]

A paradox of the 1980s experience is that the sharp decline in rural poverty and a rise in rural real wage rates occurred despite the very slow growth of urban organized sector employment and the slower growth of agricultural employment than that of the labor force. An alternative hypothesis, which departs from the assumption of full employment, and relies on an exogenous rise in rural wage rates (due perhaps to increased bargaining power of labourers) helps to explain this paradox (see Rao, 1998b). Such a wage rise can explain both the falling ratio of employment to output within agriculture as also the concomitant fall in poverty rates. A relative rise in non-farm employment can still occur provided labor demand also increases due to increased government expenditure (as argued by Sen), but also because of the rise in the wage share (Sen produces evidence that real wages increased almost twice as fast as labor productivity in agriculture), given a higher marginal propensity to consume (in general and for non-agricultural goods in particular) out of rural wages than out of non-wage income, increases the demand for non-agricultural rural products.

A third determinant of poverty which has attracted much attention is the price of food.[13] It has been argued, consistent with all available evidence, that an increase in the price of food increases poverty by reducing the real incomes of wage earners for whom wages do not keep up with food prices. The fact that this holds for rural areas as well as urban areas is not a puzzle because most of India's rural poor (and even some of the non-poor) are net purchasers of food. Ravallion (1998), however, argues that the correlation between the two variables is actually spurious. He finds that the movement in both the poverty rate and the relative price of food are the result of changes in a third variable, agricultural output: a bad harvest can be expected to increase the relative price of food and also increase rural (and total) poverty. Pooling time-series data for 1960–61 to 1993–94 across states, Sen (1996) finds, however, that a rise in the relative price of cereals increases poverty even if agricultural output per worker is included as a variable.

Ravallion's argument that a food price change affects poverty via its impact on mean rural consumption but not on the distribution of rural consumption (or income) rests on erroneous inequality measures. His measures of inequality are premised on the assumption that the cost of living index is undifferentiated for the rural poor and non-poor which, in fact, does not hold. While his conclusion that price changes have statistically zero distributional effects applies to the nominal inequality of rural incomes, the same

---

12. Sen (1996) rejects the view that agricultural growth provided an impetus to rural non-agricultural employment (as a result of an increase in the demand for non-agricultural goods), and that the evidence overwhelmingly supports the hypothesis that non-agricultural growth has occurred due to factors outside rural areas, including an expansion in government expenditure.

13. Dharm Narain made the pioneering contribution which has spawned a large literature on this (see Mellor and Desai, 1986).

data nevertheless imply a worsening of real inequality (see Rao, 1998a). This last conclusion leads us directly back to the established understanding that food price increases hurt the poor through the mechanism of (real) inequality increases. It also follows that price reforms incur the risk of both transitional and permanent reductions in real wages and corresponding increases in poverty.

Many analysts have attributed the rise in poverty in 1992 to the economic reforms but this remains a contentions issue. In absolving the reforms, Tendulkar and Jain (1995) attribute the rise in poverty to a weather-related supply shortfall which simultaneously raised open-market food prices, reduced rural employment and incomes and cut down rural foodgrain availability. Critics of the reforms have attributed it instead to the PDS issue price increases, the consequent open market price rise and the curtailment in supplies.[14] The part of food subsidies actually accruing to consumers has fallen since 1991 through a combination of price increases and quantity reductions (Swaminathan, 1996). Indeed, over the seven-year period of the reforms, both open market (wholesale) prices and about issue prices through the PDS have nearly doubled. That this has most likely had an adverse effect on poverty can be seen from Sen (1996), which adds a relative price of food term to what is essentially the Ravallion-Datt (1996) equation discussed above, and finds that this modified equation is able to explain the increase in poverty after 1991.

6. Aspects of Social Policy

Past experience suggests that government policy regarding the "social sector" has an important influence on the incidence of poverty, the distribution of income, and the social opportunities availabile to the mass of the population. Given India's low level of achievement in terms of poverty alleviation and in expanding social opportunities, and given the likely adverse socio-economic impact of the globalizing reforms discussed above, government policy has an important role in the future. In this section, we examine trends in government social spending and the robustness of existing social safety nets in the face of these reforms.

Trends in Government Expenditure

Several studies have argued that the reforms had adverse effects on government spending on the social sector (see Guhan, 1995): for instance, expenditure on rural development and social services declined by 0.4% of GDP

---

14. See Suryanarayana (1996) for a critique which shows that there were roughly symmetric declines in cereal availability in both rural and urban areas and that the reforms were responsible for the adverse effect on poverty.

between 1990–91 and 1992–93. Considering a longer span of time and including both central and state governments, Nagraj (1997) finds that government final consumption expenditure as a percentage of GDP (at factor cost) has declined from an annual average of 11% for 1986–91 to 10.1% during 1992–95. However, the expenditure on health, education, housing and social services—which include, but are not confined to, spending on items which benefit the poor—stayed the same over the two periods at 2.9% of GDP, and was in fact higher than the 2.4% level for 1981–85. Defense and economic services bore the brunt of the cuts. For the same two periods, government current expenditure as a percentage of GDP fell from 19.4 to 17.9%, and government capital expenditure fell from 7.5% to 5.7%. Here, current expenditure on health, education, housing and social services as a percentage of GDP fell slightly, from 6.1 to 6.0 per cent, but capital expenditure stayed the same; the losers again were defense and economic services.

These budgetary figures show that government social spending did not decrease as a percentage of GDP except immediately after the crisis. However, this does not imply that the benefit the poor received did not fall since this depends on the effectiveness of the programs funded by these expenditures, the extent to which the poor actually benefited, and changes in relative prices affecting the real delivery of services (this is considered below). Nor does it imply that globalizing reforms had 'no effect' if the counterfactual would have allowed increases in these expenditures from increased revenue mobilization rather than the fiscal compression that was actually pursued. The need for increased social expenditures and their potential for raising both living standards and economic growth may be judged rather from the evidently low levels of social opportunity both before and after the reforms. The tradeoff imposed by globalizing reforms arguably consists in the failure to cultivate this complementarity between growth and social opportunity.

Social safety nets

Recognizing social security as an obligation of provincial and central governments, the Indian Constitution calls upon the state, within the limits of its capacity, to make effective provision for 'public assistance in the case of unemployment, old age, sickness, and disablement, and in other cases of undeserved want' and for maternity relief. Since independence, social security legislation has been extended in several directions by acts relating to retirement funds, maternity benefits, family pension schemes, deposit-linked insurance schemes, and medical, disability and, employment injury benefits (see Guhan, 1992). Organized labor is covered under these various enactments, and public and quasi-public employees are covered by nonlegislated directed benefits. Social security expenditures are estimated to be less than 3 per cent of GNP (see Guhan, 1992).

However, social security for over 90 per cent of workers, who are in the unorganized sector or are self employed, is extremely meagre, being confined to some 'means' tested old-age pension, and accident, group life and health insurance schemes for specific groups. Moreover, the legislation suffers from shortcomings which thwart the effectiveness of the programs, allowing evasion by employers in providing contributions. Areas in which benefits are provided by state governments show enormous differences in coverage. No western-style unemployment relief is offered in India, which is a severe problem for self-employed and unorganized sector workers for whom no employment security exists. Some relief from unemployment, particularly in drought-affected regions, is offered in rural areas through schemes of employment creation to which we now turn.

Employment Generation Schemes

The highly successful Maharashtra Employment Guarantee Scheme, which was established to provide relief during severe droughts in rural Maharashtra in 1970–73, has become a country-wide model. The scheme had a wide coverage (its daily attendance reaching a seventh of the total rural population at its peak, was well targeted (since the very cash wage allowed the program to self-select the poorest), and it had the clear objective of providing (Joshi and Little, 1996, p. 235). Given its success in reducing widespread misery, starvation and death, the scheme continued beyond the droughts, but with the wage increasing steadily and with reduced funding, it became progressively less successful, and the amount of employment it generated declined.

All-India public employment generation schemes are similar to the Maharashtra. The biggest of these schemes, the Jawahar Rozgar Yojna (JRY), was established in 1989 by merging two previous programs. Its main aim was to create additional employment for the unemployed or underemployed below the poverty line who lived in rural areas, but its additional aim was to create rural assets, especially those which would benefit scheduled castes and tribes. Among the program's stimulations was that the wage could not be below prevailing legal minimum wage rates. Portions of the JRY are confined to backward areas. The JRY and its various components take up as much as 60% of the central government's budget on rural development and social expenditures.

The JRY provides an average monthly employment of five person-days per beneficiary family. However, the employment provided in the larger poorest states was much lower. Moreover, its ability to reach the poor within states is also limited. In 1992, 57% of participants were from families above the family poverty line and only 18% fell in the category of the very poor or worse (partly because the higher wage removed the self-selection advantage enjoyed by the Maharashtra program). The net transfer to the poor, taking into account the fact that other work is reduced, has been estimated at only about 14% of expenditure (Joshi and Little, 1996, p. 238).

Education policy

Despite the stated objective of providing free and compulsory education up to the age of 14 (one of the directive principles of the Constitution urged the state to provide such education by 1960!), compulsory education has not been implemented anywhere in India. As noted above, literacy rates are low, lower than in China, lower than in many east and south-east Asian countries more than thirty years ago, lower than in the average for low-income countries other than China and India, and no higher than in sub-Saharan Africa. There are great disparities in literacy rates by regions and by sex. The student teacher ratio for the 6–10 age group is 58, drop out rates are extremely high, and public expenditure on education remains low by international standards with a strong bias against primary education. Some improvements in the 1980s seems to have gone to higher emoluments, not to increasing the number of teachers. Structural adjustment measures in the 1990s slowed down education expenditure growth and even caused a decline in the number of primary and upper-primary school teachers between 1991–92 and 1992–93 (Dreze and Sen, 1995, 111–23). These trends, however, have subsequently been partially reversed.

Public Distribution System (PDS) for Foodgrains

This is a public safety-net program which buys agricultural products from farmers to protect them against excessive losses in periods of surplus production and sells them to consumers to protect them from high prices during years of shortage. The PDS distributes rice, wheat, edible oil, kerosene and sugar at subsidized prices through a network of 400,000 shops in urban and rural areas all over the country. The implicit subsidy under the PDS has been stable at around 0.5 per cent of GDP. Retail prices are fixed by each state government taking into account local distribution costs and retailer margins, besides the issue price fixed by the Food Corporation of India, and some states provide additional subsidies.

The ability of the PDS to provide effective protection and help to the poor has been questioned. It has been found that States making the greatest use of the PDS are not necessarily the poorer ones. The poor are not more likely to consume basic foodgrains distributed through the PDS than are the non-poor. It has been estimated that only about 40% of the total quantity of wheat and 47% of rice supplied through the PDS are consumed by the poorest 40% of the population (World Bank, 1998, Joshi and Little, 1996, p. 233). Moreover, the costs of administering the program are high for a number of reasons, including pilferage and inefficiency.

After 1991 the issue price of food has been increased and the spread between purchase price and sale price has been reduced (Sen, 1996). In December 1991, the issue price of rice was raised by 30% and that of wheat by 21%, and procurement prices were also increased in 1991 by 12.% for rice and

212 Dutt and Rao

22.2% for wheat, and raised again (in part to contain the effects of a cut in fertilizer subsidies). Other changes include making available additional amounts of cereals at a reduced issue price for 1,775 blocks in backward areas.

It has long been implicitly understood in India that the stabilisation of cereal price dynamics is the most important form of 'social safety net' available. It is also the closest thing to an 'incomes policy' that a poor country can wield. While orthodox stabilization concerns itself with lowering the rate of inflation, orthodox structural adjustment in relation to agriculture and food consists in market liberalization which, many believe, will lead to a rise in the relative price of food. Had actual liberalization of agricultural prices taken place, the increase in the relative price of food would have been even higher. If wholesale agricultural trade liberalization and other aspects of a "getting agricultural prices right" program, presently on policy-makers' anvil, are carried through in full, the adverse impact on poverty can be expected to be high. Even if there is a net efficiency gain from such reforms (a more than doubtful proposition given the weak supply efficacy of prices and the continuing importance of infrastructure investment), it is hard to see how a compensation of the (poor) losers can be arranged without confronting the deficiencies of the existing PDS, let alone jettisoning the PDS altogether. And if genuinely equitable agricultural growth and rapid rural poverty alleviation are to be achieved, this will require a substantial step-up in public investment in rural infrastructure and thorough-going reforms in land relations and credit delivery. There is little room to believe, however, that such a program can be pursued without producing major contradictions within the existing fiscal, economic and, ultimately, political priorities of the reform regime presently in place.

7. Conclusion

The aim of this paper has been to assess the effects of the economic reforms undertaken in India since the crisis of 1991. The assessment pays particular attention to the impact of reforms, both directly and via economic growth, on mass well-being. We have argued that openness, in the sense of policies which aim at increased economic integration with international markets, has been the focal point of the reforms whilst globalization, which we take to mean the increased external integration actually achieved, has been the touchstone of the new policy regime as perceived by its architects. Our main conclusion can be summarized as follows.

1. There has been an increase in globalization in respect of both international trade and capital transactions. But while the rate of increase in trade has been remarkably high, the increase in capital inflows—especially foreign direct investment—has been small by international standards. Moreover, the trade deficit has worsened due to the increase in imports and despite the rise in exports, both presumably due to liberalization. The composition of imports as well as of exports reveal no noticeable changes as compared to the

pre-reform period.

2. Although economic growth has maintained its momentum, increased openness has not led to higher rates of GDP growth. For the economy as a whole, output growth has not kept pace with investment growth, reflecting an increase in the capital-output ratio. The conventional index of total factor productivity growth shows a definite decline between 1980–90 and 1991–95 contrary to the liberal expectation of increased resource use efficiency from globalization.

3. Agricultural growth has slowed down markedly and the GDP share of agriculture has declined sharply despite the liberal claim that the reforms favor agriculture by removing price biases against it. Rather than the lack of price incentives, this deceleration is due to the lack of rural infrastructure and the distortions produced by the prevailing agrarian structure. At the same time, liberalizing reforms have not produced sharp discontinuities in agricultural policies.

4. The labor force has experience increased rates of casualization and informalization. This has potentially serious consequences for wages, job security, inflation protection, workers' basic rights, and the future of the Indian labor movement. The loss of urban manufacturing employment, which may be partly due to the process of informalization disguised as employment growth in services, suggests loss of employment in household and other non-factory modes of manufacturing.

5. Immediately following the reforms, there was an increase in both poverty and inequality reflecting policy-directed increases in food prices and cutbacks in public expenditure. These developments were reversed subsequently as policy responded to the political reaction that followed. It is clear that globalization has not served to reduce poverty and inequality but, to the contrary, seems to have slowed the declining trends of the 1980s. If the reforms go through in full force, there may be further adverse consequences on income distribution and poverty. In particular, the failure to carry agricultural price liberalization to its logical conclusion has limited the damage so far.

6. The Indian economy continues to be severely constrained on the fiscal account. While significant fiscal compression was carried through during the first five years after 1991, there have been significant reversals thereafter. The continuing rise in the interest burden and the decline in trade tax revenues, both related to globalizing reforms, have been major factors behind the high levels of the revenue account deficit. It is acknowledged now on all hands that between the declining fiscal capacity of the state and the unresolved regulatory complexities surrounding one or another form of privatization, the infrastructure sectors loom increasingly large as a constraint on economic growth. This also seems to be the chief factor behind the agricultural slowdown, the rise in economy-wide capital intensity and the deceleration in productivity growth.

7. Public expenditures on social safety nets have not suffered a decline despite the fiscal cutbacks following reforms. This does not mean, however,

that policies to improve social opportunity for the masses can be pursued independently of economic reforms aimed at globalization. One aspect of the tradeoff between the two is apparent in the adverse consequences in terms of employment, food prices and poverty noted above. Nor does it imply that globalizing reforms had 'no effect' on social expenditures if the political-economic counterfactual would have allowed increases in these expenditures from increased revenue mobilization rather than the fiscal compression that was actually pursued. The need for increased social expenditures and their potential for raising both living standards and economic growth may be judged rather from the evidently low levels of social opportunity both before and after the reforms. Policymakers preoccupied with the mantras of openness and globalization, and the political and fiscal constraints that these impose, are liable to neglect important changes which can improve income distribution and living standards for the majority—through land reform, improvements in education and health, and infrastructural investment. The social-economic tradeoff imposed by globalizing reforms consists chiefly in the political failure to cultivate the complementarity between economic growth and social opportunity.

REFERENCES

Ahluwalia, Isher J. (1991) *Productivity and Growth in Indian Manufacturing*, Delhi: Oxford University Press.
Bhagwati, Jagdish (1994) *India in Transition. Freeing the Economy*, Delhi: Oxford University Press.
Bhagwati, Jagdish and Srinivasan, T. N. (1993) *Indian Economic Reforms*, New Delhi: Ministry of Finance, Government of India.
Deshpande, Sudha and Deshpande, Lalit (1998) "Impact of Liberalisation on the Labour Market in India. What Do Facts from the NSSO's 50th Round Show?" *Economic and Political Weekly*, May 30, L31–L39.
Devarajan, P. (1998) "Economic Data—What the Survey Does Not Say," *Business Line*. June 1.
Dreze, Jean and Sen, Amartya (1995) *India. Economic Development and Social Opportunity*, Delhi: Oxford University Press.
Dutt, Amitava K. (1996) "The role of Keynesian policies in Semi-industrialized economies: Theory and Evidence from India," *International Review of Applied Economics*, 10(1), January, 127–40.
Dutt, Amitava K. (1998) "Globalization, Foreign Direct Investment and Southern growth: Evidence from Selected Asian Countries," J. R. Chen, ed., *Economic Effects of Globalization*, Avebury, 1998, p. 45–96.
Economic and Political Weekly Research Foundation (1997) *National Accounts Statistics of India, 1950–51 to 1995–96*, Mumbai: EPW Research Foundation.
Godley, Wynne and McCarthy, George (1997) "Fiscal policy will matter," unpublished, Jerome Levy Institute, Bard College, New York.

Goldar, B. N. (1993) "Impact of Technology and Productivity Growth in Indian industry," *Productivity*, 34(1), April–June, pp. 87–90.

Guhan, S. (1992) "Social Security in India: Looking one step ahead" in B. Harriss, S. Guhan and R. H. Cassen, eds., *Poverty in India. Research and Policy*, Bombay, Oxford University Press.

Guhan, S. (1995) "Social Expenditures in the Union Budget: 1991–96," *Economic and Political Weekly*, May 6.

Joshi, Vijay and Little, I. M. D. (1996) *India's Economic Reforms, 1991–2001*, Oxford: Oxford University Press.

Kambhampati, Uma; Krishna, Pravin; and Mitra, Devashish (1997) "The effect of trade policy reforms on labor markets: evidence from India," *Journal of International Trade and Economic Development*, 6(2), 287–97.

Kumar, Nagesh (1998) "Liberalisation and Changing Patterns of Foreign Direct Investments. Has India's Relative Attractiveness as a Host of FDI Improved?" *Economic and Political Weekly*, May 30, 1321–29.

Kundu, Amitabh (1997) "Trends and Structure of Employment in the 1990s. Implications for Urban Growth," *Economic and Political Weekly*, June 14, 1399–1405.

Mehta, Rajesh (1997) "Trade Policy Reforms, 1991–92 to 1995–96. Their Impact on External Trade," *Economic and Political Weekly*, April 12, 779–84.

Mellor, John W. and Desai, Gunvant M. (1986). *Agricultural Change and Rural Poverty: Variations on a Theme by Dharm Narain*, Oxford: Oxford University Press.

Nagaraj, R. (1997) "What Has Happened since 1991? Assessment of India's Economic Reforms," *Economic and Political Weekly*, Nov. 8, 2869–79.

National Sample Survey Organization (1996) *Key Results on Employment and Unemployment, 50th Round*, Department of Statistics, New Delhi.

Nayyar, Deepak and Abhijit Sen (1994) "International Trade and the Agricultural Sector in India," in G.S. Bhalla (ed.) *Economic Liberalisation and Indian Agriculture*, New Delhi: Institute for Studies in Industrial Development.

Pal, Parthapratim (1998) "Foreign Portfolio Investment in Indian Equity Markets. Has the Economy Benefited?" *Economic and Political Weekly*, March 14, 589–98.

Patnaik, Prabhat (1997) "The context and consequences of economic liberalization in India," *Journal of International Trade and Economic Development*, 6(2), 165–78.

Rao, J. Mohan (1998a) "Food Prices and Rural Poverty: Liberalisation without Pain?" *Economic and Political Weekly*, 33:799–800.

Rao, J. Mohan (1998b) "Food, Agriculture and Reforms: Change and Continuity," *Economic and Political Weekly*, 33:1955–1960.

Rao, J. Mohan (1998c) *Openness, Inequality and Poverty*. Background Paper prepared for the Human Development Report (1999). New York: UNDP.

Rao, J. Mohan and Servaas Storm (1997) "Distribution and Growth in Indian Agriculture," in T. J. Byres (Ed.), *The Indian Economy: Major Debates Since Independence*, Delhi: Oxford University Press.

Rao, V. M. (1998) "Economic Reforms and the Poor: Emerging Scenario," *Economic and Political Weekly*, July 18, 1949–54.

Ravallion, Martin (1998) "Reform, Food Prices and Poverty in India," *Economic and Political Weekly*, January 10, 29–36.

Sen, Abhijit (1996) "Economic Reforms, Employment and Poverty. Trends and Options," *Economic and Political Weekly*, Sept., 2459–77.

Storm, Servaas (1997) "Agriculture Under Trade Policy Reform: A Quantitative Assessment for India," *World Development*, 25:425–436.

Suryanarayana, M. H. (1996)"Economic Reforms, Nature and Poverty," *Economic and Political Weekly*, 31:617–624.

Swaminathan, Madhura (1996) "Structural Adjustment, Food Security and System of Public Distribution of Food," *Economic and Political Weekly* , 31:1665–1672.

Tendulkar, Suresh D. and L. R.Jain (1995)."Economic Reforms and Poverty," *Economic and Political Weekly*, 30:1373–1376.

World Bank (1996) *India. Five Years of Stabilization and Reform and the Challenges Ahea*d, Washington D. C.: The World Bank.

World Bank (1998) *India. Achievements and Challenges in Reducing Poverty*, Washington D. C.: The World Bank.

7

Mexico: Trade and Financial Liberalization with Volatile Capital Inflows:
Macroeconomic Consequences and Social Impacts during the 1990s

JAIME ROS *and* NORA LUSTIG

By the mid 1980s, the Mexican economy was still suffering the consequences of the 1982 debt crisis and these were compounded by the difficulties created by the collapse of oil prices in early 1986. Three years later, a turnaround had taken place. Following a successful heterodox stabilization program which began in late 1987, a sharp reduction in domestic and external public debt, facilitated by a Brady agreement in mid 1989 and financed with large privatization revenues, Mexico returned to the international capital markets and its economy appeared finally to be on its way to recover economic growth and price stability after almost a decade of economic decline and high inflation. In fact, many observers at the time believed that Mexico, a model reformer and successful emerging market, was going to turn into a Latin American economic miracle. When the North American Free Trade Agreement (NAFTA) was approved in 1993, optimistic expectations became even more rampant. The optimistic view was also reinforced by the fact that, besides wide-ranging economic reforms, the Mexican government had engaged in an anti-poverty program geared to reduce the gap in health and education infrastructure. To many, thus, Mexico appeared to be on a firm path towards economic and social modernization.

At the end of 1994, scarcely a year after NAFTA's approval, the Mexican economy was in a financial crisis and entering its worst recession since the

Paper prepared for the CEPA's conference on Globalization and Social Policy, New York, January 1999. The authors are grateful to Maiju Perala for research assistance and to Bill Gibson, Jorge Katz and Lance Taylor for comments on an earlier version of the paper. The usual caveat applies.

Great Depression of the 1930s. Moreover, the country had been experiencing political turmoil and violence throughout 1994: the armed uprising by the Zapatistas in January (on the day NAFTA came into effect), the assassinations of the presidential candidate (in March) and of the Secretary General of the ruling party in September, and the resignation in November of the Assistant Attorney General who had been in charge of investigating the assassination of his brother (the PRI's Secretary General). Following the December devaluation of the peso, and in the midst of surging fears of default, the Mexican government was unable to roll over its debt, and an unprecedented international rescue package was required to stop panic selling of Mexican debt in early 1995.

What explains how the country which was supposed to enter a period of sustained prosperity, and one of the most successful emerging markets, found itself in the mid 1990s immersed in the worst economic crisis in the last seventy years? How could it be that four years after the first Brady agreement and a substantial reduction of external and domestic government debt, the Mexican government found itself on the brink of default? How are these developments related to the balance of payments liberalization measures undertaken during the late 1980s? These are the questions addressed by this paper. In section 1, the paper briefly reviews the balance of payments liberalization measures that preceded the episode of massive capital inflows of the early 1990s and discusses its macroeconomic consequences. Section 2 then examines how these macroeconomic developments were reflected in the labor market. Section 3 turns to the evolution of income distribution and poverty since the mid 1980s. A concluding section draws lessons from the Mexican experience and discusses the prospects of the economy after the crisis.

1. Balance of Payments Liberalization and Macroeconomic Developments

The main balance of payments liberalization measures are adopted in the second half of the 1980s and early 1990s. Table 1 summarizes the main policy changes in this area together with some relevant events during the period (for a more detailed discussion of policy reforms, see Lustig and Ros, 1998, and Lustig, 1998). These changes culminate with the North American Free Trade Agreement (NAFTA) which comes into effect in January 1994. Since then, the NAFTA constitutes Mexico's basic institutional framework for trade and capital movements, including a regime of free trade and capital mobility with the U.S., its main trading partner and source of foreign investment.

Trade liberalization was followed by a rapid expansion of foreign trade after 1988. As shown in table 2, the trade to GDP ratio (exports plus imports as percent of GDP) soars from 25.6% in 1988 to 39.5% in 1994. This expansion, however, is highly unbalanced: of the 14 percentage points increase in the trade ratio, nearly 11 points are accounted for by a boom in imports while the export ratio raises only by a little more than 3 percentage points. Simi-

TABLE 1: Main Stabilization and Balance of
Payments Liberalization Measures 1985–94

1985: First phase of the trade liberalization program (July). Import licenses for capital and intermediate goods are eliminated and the number of tariff rates reduced.

1987: The stabilization program (Pacto de Solidaridad Económica) begins in December. Second phase of the trade liberalization program (December). Import licenses for consumer goods are eliminated. The average tariff and dispersion of tariff rates are reduced.

1988: Beginning of financial liberalization. Elimination of credit quotas (to high priority sectors) and liberalization of reserve requirements. Some controls on interest rates are also abolished (October/November).

1989: Controls on interest rates are abolished (April). Reform of foreign investment regulations (May). Liberalization of the neutral investment regime which opens the domestic stock market to foreign investors. Agreement in principle on the debt relief program with creditor banks (July).

1990: The debt relief agreement with the creditor banks is signed in February.
The domestic bonds market is opened to foreign investment with the elimination of restrictions to portfolio investment in government bonds (December). Some restrictions, on investments in Bondes, Ajustabonos and Tesobonos, but not on CETES (Treasury bills) had been eliminated in July 1989. "Regulation S" and "Rule 144A" of the US SEC (April) NAFTA negotiations begin.

1991: The US SEC recognizes Mexico's stock market as an "offshore designated securities market" (February). Privatization of the State Telecommunications company (TELMEX) (which began in December 1990) and main privatizations in the banking system.

1992: Conclusion of NAFTA negotiations (October) and signature of the agreement by the Executives of the three countries (December).

1993: New Foreign Investment Law (December) which replaces the 1973 Law which had established a maximum share of 49% to the foreign investment in companies as a general rule.

1994: NAFTA comes into effect in January.

---

larly, the opening of the domestic bond and stock markets to foreign investors in 1989 and 1990 is followed by veritable surge in capital inflows which rise from insignificant numbers in 1988–89 to represent 12.6 percentage points of GDP at their peak in 1993 (see table 2). Fuelled by favorable external circumstances—a continuous reduction (up to early 1994) of foreign interest rates, a US recession in the early 1990s, and regulatory changes introduced by the US Securities Exchange Commission which facilitated portfolio investments abroad[1]—the composition of these inflows is strongly biased towards highly

---

1. See on the subject Ffrench-Davis and Reisen (1998), CEPAL (1998).

TABLE 2: Macroeconomic Performance Indicators Since 1988

	1988	1989	1990	1991	1992	1993	1994	1995	1996	1997	1998
(percentages)											
GDP Growth	1.2	4.2	5.1	4.2	3.6	2.0	4.4	−6.2	5.2	6.7	4.8
Inflation	51.7	19.7	29.9	18.8	11.9	8.0	7.1	52.0	27.7	15.7	18.6
Real Exchange Rate	100.0	94.6	89.9	82.0	75.0	70.8	73.6	106.6	96.7	85.5	86.4
Private Savings Rate [1]	17.5	14.8	13.2	10.6	10.5	11.6	11.4	15.8	16.7		
Domestic Savings Rate [1]							19.8	19.3	22.5	24.1	20.5
Trade *(percentages of GDP)*											
Exports	13.9	14.0	14.1	14.2	14.4	15.2	17.2	23.9	26.8	27.9	29.2
Imports	11.7	13.2	15.0	16.6	19.2	19.2	22.3	20.2	23.5	27.1	29.5
Capital Account *(percentages of GDP)*											
Direct Investment	1.6	1.5	1.1	1.8	1.6	1.5	3.5	3.1	2.9	3.7	2.9
Portfolio Inflows	0.5	0.2	1.4	4.9	6.6	10.1	2.6	−3.2	4.2	1.5	0.4
Loans	-1.8	0.4	4.7	3.1	-0.6	1.0	0.4	7.5	−3.8	-2.6	1.1
Debt *(percentages of GDP)*											
Gross External	43.7	36.6	32.1	30.1	28.4	27.5	27.1	31.0	31.1	26.9	24.9
Gross Internal	22.4	23.4	20.9	16.8	11.8	10.2	10.8	9.5	6.9	7.3	8.7
Public finance *(percentages of GDP)*											
EXPENDITURE (total)	36.4	30.6	27.5	23.9	22.2	22.5	23.1	23.0	23.3	23.7	21.5
Operating Expenditure	12.5	11.2	10.5	9.9	8.8	9.1	8.9	8.2	8.1	8.3	7.2
Investment	2.9	2.4	2.7	2.9	2.7	2.5	3.0	2.5	2.9	2.5	1.8
Internal Interest Payments	12.5	9.0	6.8	3.1	2.2	1.5	1.1	2.6	2.3	2.5	1.5
External Interest Payments	3.6	3.3	2.3	1.9	1.5	1.2	1.2	2.0	2.1	1.6	1.4
Other	4.9	4.7	5.2	6.1	7.0	8.2	8.9	7.7	7.9	8.8	9.6
REVENUE (total)	27.7	25.8	25.3	23.5	23.7	23.1	22.8	22.8	23.2	23.0	20.3
Federal Government (total)	16.3	16.4	15.9	15.5	16.0	15.5	15.2	15.3	15.7	15.8	14.1
Taxes	11.4	11.1	10.7	10.7	11.3	11.4	11.3	9.3	9.0	9.8	10.4
Non-Tax Federal Revenue	5.0	5.3	5.2	4.8	4.8	4.1	3.9	6.0	6.7	6.0	3.7
Labor Market											
Urban Unemployment	3.6	3.0	2.8	2.6	2.8	3.4	3.7	6.2	5.5	3.8	3.2
Average Real Wage	100.0	105.9	107.4	114.2	122.8	130.6	136.9	118.8	109.1		
Average Real Wage in Manufacturing	100.0	109.0	112.1	119.4	129.9	139.2	144.3	124.4	111.1	110.4	112.8
Real Minimum Wage	100.0	93.9	85.2	81.5	77.7	76.6	76.6	66.7	61.6	60.9	61.1

1. As a percentage of GDP.
   Source: INEGI National Accounts, Indicadores de Competividad; Banco de México, Información Económica; OECD Economic Surveys, various years; Secretaría de Hacienda y Crédito Público, historical data; IMF, International Financial Statistics.

liquid assets: practically inexistent in 1989, portfolio investments increase to $3.4 billion in 1990 and to $28.4 billion in 1993 (85% of the gross inflows).

For a while, these large capital inflows and the stabilization and reform programs interacted in a virtuous way. The renewed access to international capital markets was an indicator of the positive response of local and foreign investors to the reform process since the mid 1980s. On the other hand, the capital flows themselves, by reversing the sign of the massive transfer of resources abroad that Mexico had been making during the previous decade, put an end to the financial difficulties that followed the 1982 debt crisis and contributed, in particular, to the success of the stabilization program of late 1987. At the same time, the liberalization process and the capital surge are followed by a number of macroeconomic developments that were to play a major role in the unfortunate conclusion of the episode of massive capital inflows at the end of 1994.

Currency overvaluation, the profit squeeze and the consumption boom: 1988–94

A first and persistent trend was the real appreciation of the peso. As shown in table 2, against the background of an exchange rate based stabilization program which had been successful in bringing inflation down, the large amounts of capital inflows put pressure towards a real appreciation of the domestic currency. Even when the exchange rate regime passed through several modifications—from a fixed to a crawling peg and, subsequently, to an adjustable band (which in time, had its boundaries widened)[2]—the appreciation continued as actual inflation remained systematically above the target. Thus, from 1988 to 1993, the peso appreciated by over 40 percent in real terms (the real exchange rate fell by 30 percent). By 1993, the real value of the peso was only around 10 percent below that of 1981, before the massive devaluations of early and mid 1982, even though the economy had in the meantime undergone a radical trade liberalization and had much less oil export revenues than in the early 1980s.

---

2. The policy based on a fixed exchange rate, designed to fight inflationary pressures, was implemented at the end of February, 1988. Beginning in 1989, the fixed exchange regime was replaced by a crawling peg. Originally, the crawl was fixed at one peso per day (equivalent to the annual depreciation rate of 16%), in 1990 this was reduced to 80 centavos daily (11% annual depreciation) and, in 1991, the crawl was fixed at 40 centavos daily (5% annual depreciation). In November 1991, the crawling peg was replaced by a band within which the exchange rate was allowed to fluctuate. The ceiling of the band was adjusted daily by 0.0002 new pesos (or 20 cents of the old pesos). This adjustment was increased in October, 1992 to 0.0004 new pesos daily while the floor was maintained at 3.0512 new pesos per dollar. On December 20, 1994 the ceiling of the band was increased by 15% while its subsequent daily increase of 0.0004 new pesos was maintained. This policy proved to be unsustainable and was abandoned two days later when the Mexican authorities were forced to adopt a floating exchange rate regime because they had run out of international reserves [Bank of Mexico (1995 and 1994)].

The capital inflows also led to the expansion of domestic banking credit, to the extent that their monetary effects were not fully sterilized. Part of this credit expansion was channeled to the finance of new investment but another, and sometimes the most significant part, ended up fueling a private consumption boom in the midst of an artificial atmosphere of bonanza. In addition, the inadequate disclosure requirements and the limitations of existing prudential regulation of a recently privatized banking system contributed to the over expansion of consumer credit. The growing indebtedness of households implied a decline in household savings (see, on the subject, Calderón, 1996, and Székely, 1998).

Combined with trade liberalization, the real appreciation of the peso meant a shift in relative prices against tradable goods which led to a profitability squeeze in the tradable goods sectors. This profit squeeze is shown in table 3: the property income share falls continuously from 1988 to 1994, with a cumulative decline of 7 percentage points. The impact of the profit squeeze is very different among sectors, with a large redistribution taking place from the traded towards the non-traded goods sectors.

The profit squeeze in the tradable goods sectors contributed in turn to a fall in business savings and had also adverse effects on *aggregate* investment, to the extent that the increased profitability in non-traded goods was less than the reduced profitability of the traded goods sectors.[3] Together with the distributive effects of the profit squeeze against incomes with relatively high savings

TABLE 3: Profit and Wage Shares, 1982–1996

	1982-87	1988	1989	1990	1991	1992	1993	1994	1995	1996
Profits and Interest[1]	53.4	56.5	56.0	54.5	52.9	51.8	50.4	49.8	54.6	55.9
Tradeable Goods Sector	33.8	25.1	21.3	19.1	17.5	16.0	14.2	13.8	17.0	19.2
NonTradeable Goods Sector	19.5	31.4	34.7	35.4	35.4	35.8	36.2	36.0	37.6	36.7
Skilled Labor Earnings[2]	8.2	9.8	11.7	12.3	14.0	15.6	17.2	18.2	16.6	15.5
Other Labor Earnings[3]	38.4	33.8	32.3	33.2	33.0	32.6	32.4	31.9	28.7	28.6

1. Operating surplus (excluding oil, agriculture, commerce and other services), less property income paid abroad plus interest on public debt.
2. Estimated using the average wage in the construction sector as the upper limit of unskilled labor earnings.
3. Unskilled labor and self-employed. Estimated as a residual.
Source: Based on INEGI, National Accounts.

---

3. And also under the reasonable assumption that the capital intensity at the margin in the traded goods sectors is higher than in non-traded goods.

rates, these adverse effects on investment explain why the rapid expansion of bank credit that accompanied the capital surge ended up fuelling a consumption boom. As shown in table 2, the large increase in the gap between private investment and savings was associated with a collapse in private savings (6 to 7 percentage points of GDP) rather than with a significant increase in investment rates.

The sharp decline in domestic savings and the effects of real appreciation and trade liberalization on the trade balance explain thus why record current account deficits emerged in the midst of sluggish growth. While in the past, current account deficits of the order of 7–8 percent were an exceptional feature in periods of very fast economic expansion (with GDP growth rates above 7 percent), in the early 1990s these large deficits appeared in a semi-stagnant economy and showed no signs of being reversed as growth decelerated from 1992 onwards (see table 2 and figure 2; for a fuller discussion, see Ros, 1994, and Lustig and Ros, 1998).

Figure 1 illustrates the sources of the combination of slow growth with high and growing current account deficits. Following Taylor (1998), the figure decomposes the evolution of GDP into the demand injections coming from the government fiscal stance (G/t), private spending (I/s) and net exports (E/m).[4] As can be seen in the figure, from 1988 to 1994 the fiscal stance

FIGURE 1: Sources of Demand Growth 1988–1997

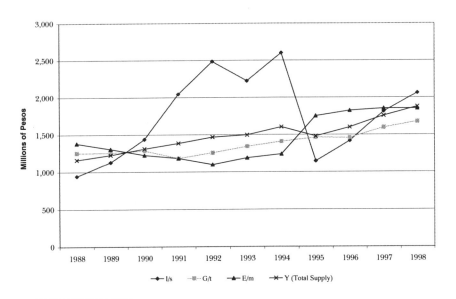

4. The exact decomposition is:

$$Y = [s/(s+t+m)] \ (I/s) + [t/(s+t+m)] \ (G/t) + [m/(s+t+m)] \ (E/m)$$

where Y, I, G and E are respectively total supply (output plus imports), investment, government spending and exports, and s, t and m are the private savings, tax and import leakages.

FIGURE 2: Trade Balance and GDP Growth, 1970–1997

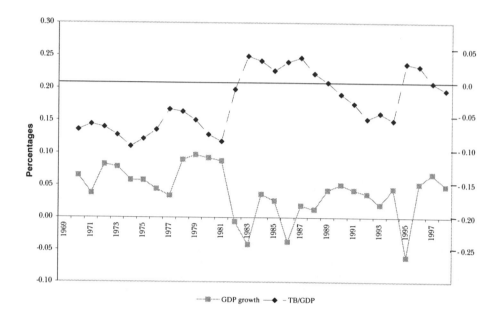

····▒···· GDP growth ——◆— – TB/GDP

was only moderately expansionary while the behavior of the trade balance provided an overall negative stimulus to aggregate demand. The growth of output during the period was then largely due to the expansionary stance of private spending. In turn, the positive and large demand injection from the private sector (the increase in I/s) was largely due, as we have seen, to the decline in the private savings rate (a fall in s) more than to an increase in private investment (I) (or, at least, more than to an increase in the private investment rate, I/Y). The negative stimulus provided by net exports followed from the sharp increase in the propensity to import (m) despite a rapid export growth: thus the downward trend in E/m. Given the combination of a rapid increase in the propensity to import and the sharp decline in the savings rate, it is not surprising that the rapid deterioration of the current account balance took place in the midst of relatively slow growth of output and productive capacity.

The contraction of capital inflows, crisis and adjustment

The implications of this path was a continuous accumulation of external liabilities. Between 1989 and 1993, the current account deficit (excluding debt service) averaged 31.7% of exports. Given an export growth rate of 8.7% per year (the average for 1989–93), Dadush et al. (1994) estimate a steady-state foreign liabilities to export ratio of 3.6.[5] This ratio is well above the 220% of exports or 80% of GDP that the World Bank Debt Tables uses to classify a country as severely indebted. It is thus unlikely that foreign investors would have been willing to finance the required factor service payments. This suggests then that well before reaching the steady state, the Mexican economy would face severe balance of payments problems.

The slowdown of capital inflows came in 1994 and, given the political shocks of that year, partly took the form of a series of speculative attacks associated to these shocks. In an effort to reverse the slow down, the government took a number of policy decisions that set the stage for the financial crisis at the end of the year[6]: 1) the dollarization of the stock of domestic government debt with the conversion of peso-dominated Treasury bills (CETES) falling due into dollar-indexed short-term bonds (Tesobonos); 2) the shortening of the average maturity of government bonds, as the dollarization of debt involved not only peso denominated Treasury bills but also peso denominated securities with longer maturities: long term Bondes and inflation-adjusted Ajustabonos. A consequence of this shortening of the average maturity of the debt is the large amount of debt coming due in 1995: in the case of Tesobonos, US$ 28.6 billion were coming due during 1995, of which 35% (9.9 billion) were due in the first quarter (see Cole and Kehoe, 1996; Ibarra, 1997).

In addition, the Central Bank decided to sterilize the effects on the money supply of the reserve losses that followed the speculative attacks (especially in March 1994 following the Colosio assassination) as well as those, more gradual, that resulted from the large current account deficit in the face of a slowdown of capital inflows. This prevented the money supply from shrinking and contributed to keep interest rates relatively low. Any other measure in this respect would probably been ineffective in avoiding the devaluation. The upshot, however, is that with a reduction of US$ 20 billion of reserves by the end of the year and nearly US$30 billion of additional short-term debt indexed to the dollar, the conditions were created for a financial panic following the devaluation of December 20, 1994. A 50 billion dollar package was necessary to calm down the markets after the financial panic but the need for adjustment was such that it could not prevent a deep recession in 1995.[7] The severe hit to the living standards of Mexicans—with real manufacturing wages falling over 20 percent in 1995—will take several years to reverse.

---

5. Ros (1993 and 1994) reaches similar conclusions. See also McLeod and Welch (1992); Oks (1992); Oks and van Wijnbergen (1992).

6. The sequence of events and policy dilemmas in 1994 leading to the December crisis in that year has been examined by the authors in Lustig and Ros (1998). For more details, see Lustig (1998), chapter 7.

7. The final package included $20 billion of loan guarantees from the U.S. government, $17.8 billion of credits from the International Monetary Fund, $10 billion in short-term loans from central banks via the Bank for International Settlements, and several billion dollars of loans from other governments in North and South America. The IMF loan amounted to over seven times Mexico's IMF quota and was unprecedented in the history of the IMF. The Mexican government declared its intention to reduce government spending by 1.3% of GDP and to cut the amount of credit granted by state development banks. A National Accord among workers,

2. The Labor Market: Employment, Productivity and Wage Inequality

The real appreciation of the peso resulted in a slow economic expansion which affected especially the tradable goods sectors. This slow expansion implied sluggish job creation, especially in manufacturing, where a poor output performance combined with an acceleration of labor productivity increases.

These trends are shown in table 4 together with the employment and productivity performance during the crisis and post-crisis period (1993–97). The first column of table 4 shows the growth of employment—for the whole economy and each sector—as the difference between output growth and productivity growth (second and third columns). The last column in the table decomposes the sources of expansion of the labor supply (in the period 1988–93) as well as the sources of employment absorption. Thus, for example, the annual growth of overall employment from 1988 to 1993, determined by socio-demographic factors, plus the increase in the labor supply due to the decline of employment in mining and manufacturing was absorbed by the employment absorbing sectors (agriculture and non-traded goods sectors). Perhaps the most striking feature of the period 1988–93 is the negative contribution of manufacturing to employment growth. As shown in the second and third columns, this is the result of a very high rate of growth of labor productivity (6.0 per cent per year) in the face of a rather slow rate of output growth (4.2 per cent per year).

Productivity and employment in manufacturing

Table 5 shows developments within manufacturing. Both of these trends, slow output growth and rapid productivity growth in manufacturing, appear to be closely related to the profit squeeze and import penetration. The reaction to the profit squeeze varies, however, across manufacturing industries depending on the extent of import penetration, the fall in profit margins and the sector's potential for intra-industry trade. In one group of industries, import penetration is inversely correlated with output and employment growth. Firms in these sectors react to the fall in profit margins with defensive increases in productivity. Where the decline in mark-ups is very large, many firms do not manage to cover variable costs and disappear. This generates a contraction of employment due to the crowding out of domestic production by imports. This is the case of a number of segments of the textile, wood and non-metallic

---

business, and government was set up to contain the inflationary pressures arising from the devaluation. The Mexican government also emphasized its commitment to market-oriented reforms and pledged to propose constitutional amendments to open previously restricted areas of the economy to private investment and to increase foreign participation in the domestic banking system. As a source of collateral the Mexican government agreed to have importers of Mexican oil products make payment through an account at the Federal Reserve Bank of New York.

**TABLE 4: Output, employment, and productivity growth
(average growth rates per year)**

Sector	Employment Growth		Output Growth		Productivity Growth		Employment Contributions	
	1988–93	1993–97	1988–93	1993–97	1988–93	1993–97	1988–93	1993–97
Total	3.1	3.2	3.7	2.4	0.6	–0.8	3.1	3.2
Mining [1]	–7.4	8.8	2.0	4.1	9.4	4.7	–0.1	0.1
Manufacturing	–1.8	4.9	4.2	4.7	6.0	–0.2	–0.3	0.8
Agriculture	5.8	0.5	1.9	1.7	–3.9	1.2	1.5	0.1
Non tradeables	3.6[3]	3.9[3]	3.1	1.8	–0.5	–2.1	2.0	2.2
Construction	4.1	–1.7	4.9	0.1	0.8	1.8	0.2	–0.1
Transport & Communication	5.0	2.7	4.1	5.0	–0.9	2.3	0.2	0.1
Commerce [2]	5.1	3.4	4.3	1.0	–0.8	–2.4	0.8	0.6
Services	3.0	5.5[4]	3.9	1.6[4]	0.9	–3.9[4]	0.8	1.7[4]
Government	0.8		0.9		0.1		0.03	

1. Includes electricity
2. Includes restaurants and hotels
3. Includes unspecified activities
4. Includes government

Note: The last column decomposes the growth of the employment rate (or of employment per capita) $(L^* - P^*)$ as:
$(L^* - P^*) = \Sigma\ (Li/L)\ (L^*i - P^*)$
where L^* and P^* refer to the growth rates of employment and population (L^*i being thus the growth rate of employment in sector i) and Li/L is the share of sector i in total employment. Each sector's contribution to the growth of the employment rate is estimated as $(Li/L)\ (L^*i - P^*)$ and, thus, the sum of these contributions adds up to the total in the first row. In turn, along each row the component L^*i is decomposed for each sector as $Q^*i - gi$, where Q^*i is the output growth rate and gi is the labor productivity growth rate. The growth rate of output $(Q^*i\ )$ is shown in the second column and the growth rate of labor productivity is shown in the third column. The growth rate of variable Y between 0 and t is estimated as: $(LogYt - LogYo)/t$, where Log refers to the natural logarithm.
Source: INEGI, National Accounts and National Survey of Employment 1997.

minerals industries (see table 5).[8] Where the decline in mark-ups is more moderate or non-existent, as in food processing and paper and printing, the slowdown in output and employment growth is also less pronounced. As shown in table 5, in all these cases initial export and import ratios are relatively low indicating an initially high degree of protection of the domestic market and export ratios that are also relatively low and suggest a lack of experience of firms in these sectors with exporting activities.

In a second group of industries, with the initially highest import and export ratios and a large potential for intra-industry trade, import penetration is correlated with export growth. This is the case of the Chemical, Basic metals,

---

8. We emphasize segments of these industries. Other segments, as would be revealed by a more disaggregated analysis, follow different patterns that fit better with the second group of industries discussed below. One example is the restructuring of the garment industry where a number of activities are successful cases of export growth. Still, even here, success became clear only after the currency devaluation of late 1994.

TABLE 5: Trade, Profit Margins and Productivity Growth in Manufacturing

	Division of Manufacturing Sector	Year	Import ratio	Export ratio	Profit margin	Productivity growth[1]
VI	Non-Metallic Mineral Products,	1988	4.4	14.3	71.2	
	except Petroleum and Coal	1994	12.0	12.5	60.5	7.2
I	Food, Beverages and Tobacco	1988	10.6	13.2	32.9	
		1994	19.8	9.7	35.2	3.5
III	Wood and Wood Products,	1988	7.3	14.3	46.2	
	Including Furniture	1994	27.8	11.0	33.8	4.2
IV	Paper and Paper Products,	1988	25.9	14.0	30.9	
	Printing and Publishing	1994	41.2	6.3	26.7	1.7
II	Textile, Wearing Apparel and	1988	11.5	16.6	36.3	
	Leather Industries	1994	35.6	19.4	26.7	3.2
V	Chemicals and Chemical, Petroleum,	1988	31.5	23.0	36.0	
	Coal, Rubber and Plastic Products	1994	51.9	29.6	28.2	5.6
VII	Basic Metal Industries	1988	44.4	41.3	35.9	
		1994	64.7	53.3	32.2	8.6
IX	Other Manufacturing Industries	1988	53.2	31.8	52.6	
		1994	76.4	43.6	34.6	0.4
VIII	Fabricated Metal Products,	1988	67.5	56.1	21.5	
	Machinery and Equipment	1994	89.0	78.8	18.3	8.1
	Total	1988	33.3	26.8	32.8	
		1994	54.7	34.1	28.5	5.4

1. Annual growth rates in percentages.
Import ratio = M/(VA+M–X)
Export ratio = X/VA
Where M, X, and VA are imports for the sector of origin, exports for the sector of origin and the total value added, respectively. All series are in constant 1993 prices.
Profit margin=OS/(W+IC), where OS, W and IC are operating surplus, wage bill and intermediate consumption, respectively.
Source: INEGI Cuentas Nacionales.

Machinery and equipment (including in particular, the automobile industry), and Other manufacturing industries. By modifying the output mix (reducing diversity) and reducing value added (complementing with imports), investing in labor saving technologies, and adopting organizational changes to reduce direct labor costs (downsizing and outsourcing), firms in these sectors manage to survive and prosper by increasing their specialization in intra-industry trade. Here import penetration leads, through specialization in intra-industry trade, to high rates of export growth and, in almost all cases, to the highest rates of output and productivity growth. In fact these four industries are those with the highest rates of both import penetration and export growth.

The slowdown of productivity growth in the whole economy

The acceleration of productivity growth in manufacturing did not lead, however, to a trend increase in productivity growth in the economy as a whole. In fact, as shown in table 6 (first column), this acceleration in manufacturing from 1988 to 1993 was, paradoxically, accompanied by a slowdown in the overall rate of productivity growth compared to the second half of the 1970s. The reasons for this behavior are illustrated by the decomposition exercise shown in the table. The second column of the table presents the unadjusted contributions of each sector to overall productivity growth (each sector's contribution being equal to the sector's productivity growth times the sector's employment share). These contributions do not add up to the overall productivity growth rate (thus the qualification "unadjusted") since part of productivity growth results from the reallocation of the labor force from low productivity to high productivity sectors. These reallocation effects are equal to the difference between the overall rate of productivity growth and the sum of the unadjusted contributions and are shown in the table's last row.

These reallocation effects were very large in the second half of the 1970s, equivalent in fact to slightly more than the overall growth of productivity (the explanation being the decline in agricultural productivity which offset the productivity gains in other sectors, leaving reallocation effects as the only source of net gains). While this reallocation effects remain positive in the 1988–93 period—indicating that on average high productivity sectors grew faster than

TABLE 6: Contributions by Sector to Productivity Growth

Sector	Labor Productivity Growth		Unadjusted Contributions		Adjusted Contributions	
	1974–79	1988–93	1974–79	1988–93	1974–79	1988–93
Agriculture	−3.0	−3.9	−1.2	−1.0	−1.3	−1.4
Mining [1]	5.1	9.4	0.1	0.1	0.2	0.1
Manufacturing	1.9	6.0	0.3	1.1	0.8	1.1
Non Tradeables	1.3	−0.5	0.5	−0.3	2.0	0.8
Total	1.6	0.6	1.6	0.6	1.6	0.6
Reallocation Effect			1.8	0.7	0.0	0.0

1. Includes electricity
2. Includes restaurants and hotels
Note: The unadjusted contribution by sector i to overall productivity growth is estimated as (Li/L) gi, where Li/L is the share of sector i in total employment and gi refers to the annual productivity growth rate. The adjusted contribution by sector i to overall productivity growth is $(Li/L)gi+ [(Yi/Y)-(Li/L)]Y*i$, where $Y*i$ is the output growth rate of sector i (annual) and Yi/Y is the output share of sector i. The growth rate of variable Y between years 0 and t is estimated sa: $(LogYt-LogY0)/t$, where Log refers to the natural logarithm.
Source: INEGI, National Accounts, National Survey of Employment 1997, and ILO Yearbook of Labour Statistics 1982.

low productivity sectors—they are much smaller than in the 1970s. In fact, the slowdown in overall productivity growth can be fully explained by the substantial reduction in the size of these reallocation effects between the two periods. Since, at the same time, the contribution to productivity growth by manufacturing increased considerably, this means that this higher contribution was counteracted by a reduction in the contribution of productivity growth in the non tradable goods sectors (the contribution of agriculture being slightly less negative in the second period).

In fact, the lower contribution to productivity growth by the non-tradable sectors is behind the decline in the size of reallocation effects. The third column of the table shows the adjusted contributions to productivity growth so that, for example, the contribution to productivity growth of a high productivity sector is attributed to the sector rather than being part of the reallocation effect. The sum of these adjusted contributions is then equal to the overall rate of productivity growth and the residual is zero. The results in the third column indicate that the higher contribution of manufacturing in the second period was indeed counteracted by the much higher reduction in the contribution of the non-traded goods sectors (with again the contribution of agriculture being of about the same size).

The fall in the (adjusted) contribution of the non-traded goods sector can in turn be attributed to two factors: the slowdown in these sectors' productivity growth (from 1.3 to 0.3%) and the fall in the relative productivity of these sectors that took place between the two periods. This fall was the result of the economic stagnation of the 1980s and contributed to reduce the contribution of these sectors (with still a higher than average productivity level) to overall productivity growth. Both of these factors—in particular, the slowdown in the productivity growth in the non-traded goods sectors—can be related to the sluggish, and later negative, rate of employment creation in manufacturing, first as a result of the recession of the 1980s and later to the acceleration of productivity growth. The result was higher rates of underemployment in services and commerce that hindered the growth of productivity in these sectors. This hypothesis finds support in the fact that after 1993 when employment creation in manufacturing becomes again positive, the productivity growth rate of the non-traded goods sectors increases relative to the 1988–93 period (see table 4).

Trade liberalization and wage inequality

All the available evidence points to a substantial increase in wage inequality since the mid 1980s. According to the income and expenditure household surveys, the Gini coefficient of wage inequality increases from 0.44 in 1984 to 0.46 in 1989, then to 0.49 in 1992 and 0.53 in 1994 (Lustig and Székely, 1997). Figure 3 shows the decline since 1988 in the relative labor earnings of the low wage sectors (agriculture, construction, commerce and services with wages below the

FIGURE 3: Relative Labor Earnings in Low Wage Sectors

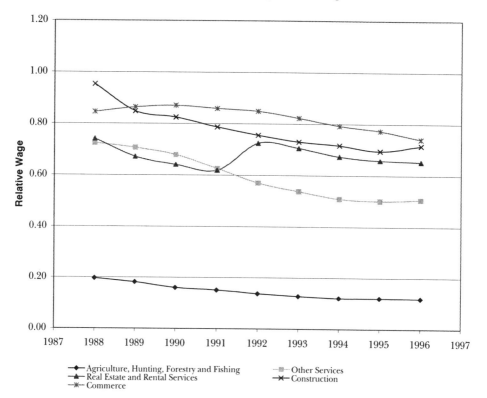

- ◆ Agriculture, Hunting, Forestry and Fishing
- ▲ Real Estate and Rental Services
- ✳ Commerce
- ▦ Other Services
- ✕ Construction

economy's average). Figure 4 illustrates the rising trend of white-collar worker earnings relative to blue-collar worker earnings in all manufacturing industries. Table 3 illustrates the redistribution between skilled and unskilled labor earnings that took place from 1988 to 1994. Other evidence reported in a number of studies similarly documents the increase in wage dispersion and shows that it largely revolves around the increase in skilled relative to unskilled labor incomes (see Hanson and Harrison, 1995; Cragg and Epelbaum, 1996; Alarcón and McKinley, 1997; Meza, 1998).

The rapid increase in the wage premium for skilled labor raises an initial question: Is it the result of a demand shift in favor of skilled labor or is it largely a supply side phenomenon resulting from either a relatively fast growth of the unskilled labor force or a higher labor supply elasticity for unskilled labor? The available studies on the subject have focused on explaining the shift in the composition of labor demand. Table 7 confirms the importance of demand factors within manufacturing. The table shows that the change in employment ratio of skilled to unskilled labor (measured very imperfectly by the ratio of white collar to blue collar employment) tends to be positively correlated across industries

FIGURE 4: Ratio of White Collar to Blue Collar Workers' Earnings in Manufacturing

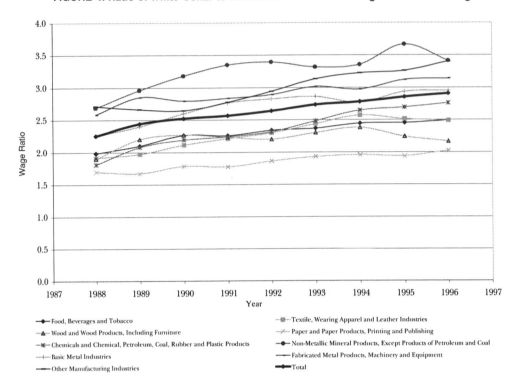

Legend:
- Food, Beverages and Tobacco
- Wood and Wood Products, Including Furniture
- Chemicals and Chemical, Petroleum, Coal, Rubber and Plastic Products
- Basic Metal Industries
- Other Manufacturing Industries
- Textile, Wearing Apparel and Leather Industries
- Paper and Paper Products, Printing and Publishing
- Non-Metallic Mineral Products, Except Products of Petroleum and Coal
- Fabricated Metal Products, Machinery and Equipment
- Total

with the change in the relative wages of skilled labor: those industries where unskilled labor falls more rapidly, relative to skilled labor, are those where the skill premium increases faster. If supply factors where responsible for the substitution of skilled for unskilled labor, we would expect to observe the contrary: a negative relationship between relative earnings and employment ratios, with the increase in the skill premium leading to a fall, rather than an increase, in the employment ratio of skilled to unskilled labor.

The attention given to the demand shift arises not only from its visible importance but also from the fact that it appears to have operated in exactly the opposite way to that expected from conventional trade theory. According to the Stolper-Samuelson theorem, the relatively abundant factor in Mexico (unskilled labor) should have gained from trade liberalization relatively to the scarce factors (including skilled labor). The mechanisms are well known: assuming similar technologies in the domestic and international economies, trade liberalization raises the relative prices of unskilled intensive goods, produced at relatively low costs by the domestic economy, given the abundance of unskilled labor. The shift in relative prices increases the demand for labor in industries intensive in unskilled labor thus causing the wages of unskilled labor to increase relative to those of skilled labor. The consequence of the increase in international trade is

TABLE 7: Earnings and Employment in the Manufacturing Sector
(percentage changes)

	Division of Manufacturing Sector	Relative Wage Ratio[1]	Employment Ratio[2]	Growth in Employment[3]	Growth in Blue Collar Employment[3]	Growth in White Collar Employment[3]
VII	Basic Metal Industries	63.1	11.0	–5.7	–5.9	1.6
II	Textile, Wearing Apparel and Leather Industries	63.0	9.8	–4.4	–4.4	1.4
VI	Non-Metallic Mineral Products, except Petroleum and Coal	61.9	7.5	–2.6	–2.9	1.1
IV	Paper and Paper Products, Printing and Publishing	60.3	2.5	–2.5	–2.6	0.4
V	Chemicals and Chemical, Petroleum, Coal, Rubber and Plastic Products	57.3	9.8	–1.8	–2.3	1.6
I	Food, Beverages and Tobacco	57.2	14.4	0.2	–0.4	2.1
III	Wood and Wood Products, Including Furniture	35.4	–8.7	–3.6	–3.4	–1.2
VIII	Fabricated Metal Products, Machinery and Equipment	16.5	–18.5	–1.7	–0.9	–2.6
IX	Other Manufacturing Industries	9.4	–18.6	1.3	2.3	–2.7

1. Ratio of White Collar to Blue Collar Earnings. Percentage change during the period.
2. Ratio of While Collar to Blue Collar Employment. Percentage change during the period.
3. Annual growth rate.
Source: INEGI Monthly Industrial Survey.

---

then a greater equality in the distribution of wage incomes, rather than the increased inequality observed in Mexico after trade liberalization.

Why didn't the mechanisms identified by standard trade theory operate? Or, if they did operate in the direction described, which factors counteracted their effects? A first hypothesis found in the recent literature is consistent with the *logic* of the Stolper-Samuelson theorem: contrary to common beliefs, trade liberalization benefited industries intensive in skilled labor through exactly the Stolper-Samuelson mechanisms (an increase in the relative prices of skilled-labor intensive goods which shifted employment towards the skill intensive sectors). This broad hypothesis is consistent with at least three logical possibilities. First, before trade liberalization, the structure of protection in Mexico may have favored industries intensive in unskilled labor (see Hanson and Harrison, 1995). Trade liberalization could then conceivably have shifted relatively prices in the 'wrong direction'. Second, even though relatively abundant in unskilled labor relative to the United States, Mexico may be relatively abundant in skilled labor with respect to the rest of the world given, in particular, the emergence in world trade over the past two decades of low wage competitors in unskilled intensive industries (see Londoño and Székely, 1997). Third, even though Mexico is relatively abundant in unskilled labor (both with respect to the United States and the rest of the world) it may not have a comparative advantage in many activities intensive in unskilled labor for reasons related to differences in production functions (technological backwardness in unskilled intensive industries) and/or factor intensity reversals. This could be the case of agriculture which is intensive in unskilled labor in Mexico and relatively capital intensive in the United States, so that the United States may have a comparative advantage in agricultural trade despite Mexico's abundance in unskilled labor (see, on the subject, Larudee, 1998).

Hanson and Harrison (1995) have discussed the first two possibilities for the period 1984–90 and Cragg and Epelbaum (1996) provide additional relevant evidence for the period 1987–93. Both papers find "industry effects" to be small, i.e., the shift in labor demand in favor of skilled workers and the increasing skill premium can be explained only to a small extent by intersectoral employment shifts from unskilled to skilled intensive industries. In Hanson and Harrison, for example, these industry effects account for 7% and 20% of the change in the white collar wage share depending on the data source (respectively the Industrial Census or a sample of medium and large plants from the Ministry of Trade and Industrial Promotion [SECOFI]). It is worth noting that the quantitative strength of inter-industry effects operating in possibly different directions is hard to assess through these accounting exercises. The fact that the net balance of these effects is small is not inconsistent with important inter-industry effects that tend to neutralize each other. Findings by Revenga (1995), cited by Hanson and Harrison, indicate that Mexico's net exports are negatively correlated with skill intensity, suggesting that Mexico has a comparative advantage in many goods produced with a relatively high intensity of unskilled labor. If this is so, the intersectoral employment shifts should have favored the demand for unskilled labor while some other unidentified, but possibly important, factors operated in the opposite direction.

In any case, the small net industry effects clearly suggest that a complete explanation of the increasing wage inequality must take into account other effects of a 'within industry' nature, i.e., a full explanation must rely on the fact that the increase in the skill premium and the relative demand for skilled labor took place within specific industries, even at the firm or plant level, more than as a result of intersectoral changes in employment and wages.

Cragg and Epelbaum (1995, 1996) suggest an explanation based on the effects of trade liberalization on the prices of imported capital goods under the assumption of complementarity between skilled labor and physical capital. To the extent that trade liberalization drove down the relative price of imported capital goods, it stimulated the adoption of more capital intensive techniques and thus a skill-biased shift in the demand for labor given the complementarity between skilled labor and physical capital. This increased demand for skilled labor caused then the increase in the skill premium.

A second hypothesis, which Cragg and Epelbaum (1996) themselves suggest without further exploring it, is that the intensified competition from imports, resulting from trade liberalization and the real overvaluation of the peso, accelerated the rate of technology adoption and reduced the demand for low skilled workers in manufacturing. This hypothesis can be elaborated in the framework of a two-sector model (tradables and non tradables) in which tradable goods are produced under imperfect competition with unskilled labor as the variable factor while skilled labor, being complementary to physical capital, is largely fixed in the short run. Trade liberalization implied greater competition in the domestic market and increased the share of imports in domestic demand. As a result of this increased competition and of the real currency appreciation associated to the capital inflows, the increased demand for non tradables and exchange rate policy, the profit mark-up over marginal costs in the importable goods sectors falls. Thus the profit squeeze in the traded goods sector documented in section 1. The lower profit mark-up means an increase in the product wages of skilled and unskilled workers. The negative effect on employment falls on unskilled workers, as this is the variable factor that firms can adjust in the short run. Thus the tendency to the substitution of skilled for unskilled labor that is observable in the industrial employment data.

Figure 5 illustrates more formally the argument. It shows the determination of the real wage and the level of employment in the importables sector at the intersection of two schedules. The NN locus is a schedule of equilibrium in the markets for non-traded goods (intensive in unskilled labor) and in the market for unskilled labor. The schedule slopes upwards: an increase in employment in the importables sector reduces the labor supply to the non-traded sector and increases the real wage. The TT locus is a schedule of equilibrium in the market for importable goods. It is downward sloping since an increase in the wage increases costs and prices in this sector and this reduces the demand for importables (at the expense of imported goods and non-traded).

FIGURE 5

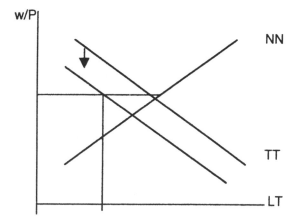

The effects of trade liberalization on the labor market operate through three channels. First, the relative price of imported goods falls and shifts the TT locus down and to the left. In the short run, demand and employment in the importables sector fall. With given nominal wages in the importables, the adjustment involves an expansion of employment in the non-tradables sector. The higher employment there reduces productivity and wages. This opens a gap between the wages of unskilled labor employed in the two sectors (observable in Mexico in the increasing wage inequality among sectors). Eventually, the downward pressure on the real wages in the importables sector tends to reduce the product wage of unskilled labor there, generating an intra-sectoral increase in the wage premium of skilled labor. At the same time, the costs and relative price reductions in the importables sector tend to reestablish the initial relative prices, shifting the TT schedule upwards. However, even if the initial relative prices are reestablished in the long run, the displacement of local production by imports may have hysteresis effects, which lead to a permanent increase of the ratio of imports to domestic production of importables. In this case, the downward shift of the TT schedule is permanent and has long lasting effects on employment and real wages in the importables and non-traded sectors.

Finally, the intensified competition in the local market leads to an increase in the price elasticity of demand facing producers of importables. The higher price elasticity reduces the firms' profit margins in the sector. This has two consequences. First, it implies a fall in the relative price of importables relative to non-tradables and imported goods, which increases demand for importables. This tends to shift the TT schedule upwards. The second effect is the fall in profitability, which tends to reduce investments in the importables sector and has negative longer run effects on employment. As we shall argue below, this second effect—together with the short run and long run effects of import penetration discussed above—appears to have clearly dominated in the Mexican experience.

The two hypotheses on how trade liberalization affected the composition of labor demand—through the fall in the relative prices of capital goods or through the fall in profit margins in the importables sectors—are both consistent with the large quantitative importance of within industry effects found by Hanson and Harrison as well as with the generalized within industry increases in the demand for skilled labor found by Cragg and Epelbaum. Yet they are inconsistent with each other in a number of other implications, the reason being that one hypothesis views the increase in the skill premium as a result of trade liberalization creating an excess demand for skilled labor while the other sees import competition as creating an excess supply of unskilled labor.[9] The empirical evi-

---

9. Note that an excess supply of unskilled labor is not inconsistent with the real wages for unskilled labor rising during the period. In the explanation suggested above, the increase in real wages was the consequence of the fall in profit margins.

dence, as we shall now see, appears to clearly support the explanation based on import competition and declining profit margins.

First, the explanation based on import competition implies that the shift in the composition in labor demand should be limited to the tradables sector and not observable in the non tradables sectors where there was no such intensified competition from imports. This is precisely what Cragg and Epelbaum find: the substitution of skilled labor for unskilled labor was much faster in the tradables sectors, specifically in manufacturing and largely limited to this sector. If the cause of the demand shift had been the fall in capital goods prices the substitution of skilled for unskilled labor should have been equally present in the non-tradable sectors. In fact, one can argue that it should have been faster in these sectors. To the extent that the composition of investment shifted in favor of these sectors, in the face of a decline in the profitability of the tradable sectors, the complementarity between physical capital and skilled labor should have induced a faster rate of unskilled-skilled labor substitution in the non tradable goods sectors.

Second, if trade liberalization affected the skill premium through the fall in profit margins we should expect that those industries where the skilled-unskilled employment ratio increased faster are those which reduced most their overall employment (since in this hypothesis the shift in the composition of labor demand reflects the changes in the variable factor, unskilled labor). This negative correlation is observable in table 7. This correlation is inconsistent with the alternative hypothesis: if the stimulus to labor substitution came from the fall in the relative prices for capital goods, the industries that benefited most from the lower prices of capital goods should be those where the capital stock and employment increased most and also those which increased faster their skilled-unskilled employment ratios. The expected correlation in this case should thus be positive rather than negative. Moreover, the fact, clearly observable in table 7, that the ratio of white to blue collar employment in manufacturing increases as a result of a decline in the employment of blue collar workers rather than an increase in the employment of white collar workers raises serious doubts about any explanation of the increased skill premium that relies on an rising demand for skilled labor.

Finally, it is worth noting that within manufacturing the rate of employment decline is positively correlated with two exceptions with the percentage decline in profit margins.[10] This suggests that, indeed, the employment reductions were a reaction to the fall in mark-ups; and since the shift in the composition of labor demand is closely related to the change in employment (table 7), these two observations link the shift in the composition of labor demand to the fall in profit margins. The two exceptions (metallurgy and

---

10. Regressing employment growth (gL) on the percentage change in profit margins (gp), excluding the two outliers, yields:

gL=–0.64 + 0.13 gpR^2(adj.)=0.75 t-statistics in parentheses
    (–1.1) (4.5)

other manufacturing) are the two industries with the fastest and the lowest rates of productivity growth during the period. Due to these characteristics, the behavior of their profit margins is consistent with our hypothesis. Indeed, in our explanation the employment reductions on the part of firms are, strictly speaking, a reaction to the ex-ante fall in profit margins, i.e., to the fall in margins before taking into account the effects that the more or less successful increases in productivity (resulting from the employment falls) had on the ex-post evolution of margins. If our hypothesis is correct, the industry with the fastest rate of productivity growth (metallurgy) can be expected to become an outlier because it managed to offset with those very large productivity gains the effects of a large ex-ante decline in margins: thus its relatively small ex-post reduction of profit margins in the context of a sharp decline in employment. The sector least successful in increasing productivity (other manufacturing) is also an outlier because its relatively small employment contraction determined a relatively large ex-post reduction in profit margins.

So far we have focused on explaining the change in the composition of labor demand. Yet, supply factors also appear to have had some role in the increase in skill premium. First, the labor demand shift in manufacturing implies a shift in the composition of labor supply growth from the perspective of other sectors in the economy. In their 1996 paper, Cragg and Epelbaum illustrate the fact that low skill occupations (such as sales persons, service and transport workers) experienced rapid employment growth and relatively small wage increases between 1987 and 1993.

Second, even if in the absence of a shift in the composition of demand, the composition of labor supply for the economy as a whole may have favored an increase in the skill premium. Alarcón and McKinley (1997) refer to evidence, based on household surveys, suggesting a relatively fast growth of the unskilled labor force: according to this evidence, between 1984 and 1992 the fraction of urban employees with tertiary education fell from 18.5% to 15.5% and the fraction of those with secondary education fell from 53.7% to 46.3%.[11]

Finally we should add the fact, already alluded to, that trade liberalization did not benefit unskilled labor intensive agriculture. The resulting slow growth of the *demand* for unskilled labor in this large economic sector—which is not inconsistent with the rapid increase in the agricultural labor force resulting from the difficulties of unskilled workers in finding employment in other sectors—drove down the supply price of unskilled labor to the urban sectors. Combined with the other factors mentioned, including the demand shift in manufacturing away from unskilled labor, the result was indeed a rapid increase in the skilled-unskilled wage gap.

---

11. Other data sources do not confirm, however, the same trends. The data from INEGI's urban employment surveys used by Cragg and Epelbaum suggests an increasing percentage of skilled workers in the urban labor force.

3. Income distribution and poverty[12]

In the previous section we saw that the wage gap between skilled and unskilled workers went up considerably, and that this increase is the result, primarily, of trade liberalization and skill-biased shift in the demand for labor. How much of the trends in overall inequality can be explained by the rising gap in returns to skill? How much is accounted for by other factors such as regional disparities? Before we address these questions, let's first look at the trends in poverty and inequality.

The crisis and adjustment of the 1980s led to sharp declines in income, and in particular, wages. Given the characteristics of Mexico's labor market (with real wages being very flexible), the adjustment primarily involved a reduction in real wages, while the increase in open unemployment was short-lived. As might be expected, the fall in wages was accompanied by an increase in the incidence of extreme and moderate poverty. Lustig and Székely (1998) estimate that the extreme poverty rose from 13.9% to 17.1 % and moderate poverty increased from 28.5% to 32.6%, 1984 and 1989 (see table 8). The depth and severity of poverty also increased considerably. Moreover, the burden of adjustment was not equitably distributed.[13] While the share of income in the upper ten percent of the population rose, it fell in the remaining ninety percent (see Székely, 1995). Income concentration as measured by the Gini coefficient increased quite sharply (and unambiguously) between 1984 and 1989 (see table 9). As the Lorenz curves present no crossings, the results are unambiguous (Figure 6).

Trends in poverty and inequality in the recent period

Tables 8 and 9 indicate that during the incipient, and frustrated, recovery of the early 1990s, moderate poverty and income inequality remained virtually unchanged, while extreme poverty declined slightly and wage inequality rose.[14]

---

12. This section draws from Lustig (1998) and Lustig and Székely (1998).

13. These estimates are calculated from Household Income and Expenditure Surveys for 1984, 1989, 1992, and 1994. Although the survey for 1996 has been completed, the results had not been released by the time of completion of the Lustig and Székely (1998) study.

14. To measure the incidence of poverty we used the extreme and moderate poverty lines for urban and rural areas developed by the Mexican National Institute of Statistics, Geography, and Informatics. Table 8 shows the poverty lines in current pesos and in dollars. The extreme poverty line was calculated as the cost of the basic food basket, reflecting the spending patterns of the poor population and the prices paid by that sector. The moderate poverty line, following Orshankys procedure, is equivalent to twice the extreme poverty line for urban areas, and 1.75 times that line for rural areas. Our calculations were made using the corresponding urban and rural poverty lines for each of the two population groups (urban and rural) and the number of individuals is added up to obtain the proportion of poor individuals for the country as a whole. The appendix discusses other methodological aspects of measuring poverty.

TABLE 8: Poverty Incidence and Poverty Lines:
Total and by selected groups

Subgroup	1984 H	1984 POP(%)*	1989 H	1989 POP(%)*	1992 H	1992 POP(%)*	1994 H	1994 POP(%)*
Total moderate poverty	28.5	100.0	32.6	100.0	31.3	100.0	31.8	100.0
Total extreme poverty	13.9	100.0	17.1	100.0	16.1	100.0	15.5	100.0
*Rural workers	37.9	86.2	48.71	71.0	53.0	75.8	51.0	73.1
*Primary sector	37.5	96.8	46.1	82.6	51.7	84.8	50.0	86.2
*Southern region	16.7	7.6	25.1	12.5	19.8	11.9	29.0	19.1
*Southeastern region	15.6	6.7	34.0	24.3	47.4	33.6	37.2	22.5
LINE IN CURRENT PESOS								
Extreme urban	4969		86400		167955		198287	
Extreme rural	4233		68810		124751		147280	
Moderate urban	9938		172800		335910		396573	
Moderate rural	7408		120418		218314		257740	
LINE IN CURRENT US DOLLARS								
Extreme urban	24		32		53		50	
Extreme rural	20		26		39		37	
Moderate urban	47		64		106		99	
Moderate rural	35		45		69		64	

Source: ENIGH Surveys. Authors' calculations.
*Percentage that the group represents in total extreme poor.
H: Headcount Ratio in %.
POP: Population Share in %.

Table 9: Gini Coefficient
(Total and by Source of Income)

	1984	1989	1992	1994
Total income	0.47	0.53	0.53	0.54
Labor Income*	0.44	0.46	0.49	0.53
Income from Property	0.57	0.72	0.67	0.57
Agricultural income	0.35	0.3	0.34	0.3
Imputed income**	0.53	0.56	0.47	0.48

Source: Calculations by the authors, ENIGH surveys, 1984, 1989, 1992, and 1994. Not all income sources are reported.
* "Labor" includes income from self-employment and some service activities.
** Refers to owner's occupied housing.

FIGURE 6: Mexican Lorenz Curves

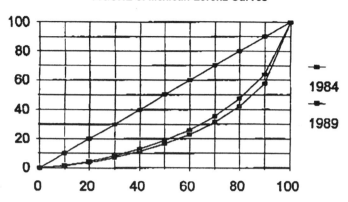

Source: ENIGH 1984 and 1989.

To test for the sensitivity of the results on poverty to the selection of poverty line, the income frequency curve was estimated from zero income up to the highest available poverty line. The results are presented in Figure 7. Visual examination shows that for the lower poverty lines, the function corresponding to 1989 is stochastically dominant with respect to the function for 1994, meaning that, for the lower poverty lines, the incidence of poverty was always lower in 1994 than in 1989. However, for higher poverty lines, no clear conclusion could be drawn as to the direction of the change. The results presented in table 8 are obtained by "adjusting" the household survey data for under-reporting. We performed several robustness tests to check for the sensitivity of our results to different methods of correction and found that in terms of trends our results are robust.

Since in this period the structure of relative wages changed significantly and wage inequality rose considerably, as we have seen in section 2, it is unlikely that these trends in poverty and inequality were fairly uniform for all population groups. If we classify households by occupation, economic activity and geographic location, we observe a differentiated pattern. Table 8 shows trends in subcategories in which the incidence of poverty followed an inverse direction from the national headcount between 1989 and 1994: poverty rates increased among rural workers, in the primary sector (agriculture, in particular), and in the Southern (Tabasco and Veracruz) and Southeastern (Chiapas, Guerrero, and Oaxaca) regions of Mexico.[15] The proportion of poor increased in occupational categories, regions, and production sectors associated with the rural areas, and in which the poverty incidence was highest in 1989. Those are also the groups or sectors where a high proportion of the total population lives in extreme poverty.

---

15. A more detailed discussion of poverty profiles is available from the authors upon request

FIGURE 7: Poverty in Mexico Using a Range of Lines

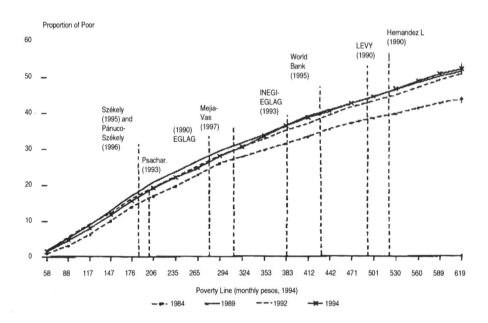

Per-capita income adjusted to National Accounts (Adjustment 2)

Given that total poverty practically remained unchanged, these trends mean that the decline in poverty in other population groups and/or migration to richer regions (or activities) were sufficiently large to offset the negative trends in the groups that didn't do well. Using the disaggregation formula applicable to additive poverty measures, we determined the contribution of each of the above categories to the total change in poverty, distinguishing the portion that should be attributed to demographic changes among categories and to changes in poverty within individual categories.[16] The results of the disaggregation corresponding to 1989 and 1994 are presented in table 10. The total contribution of the three subcategories—rural workers, household units operating in the

---

16. Morely (1995) and Ravallion and Huppi (1991) demonstrated that a change in total poverty can be expressed as the sum of changes in poverty in the corresponding subcategories and of changes in the proportion the population of this subcategory represents in the total population, plus a residual term. Algebraically, it is expressed with the following equation:

$$(1) \quad \Delta P = \sum_{k=1}^{n} P_{i,i} \Delta \beta_i + \sum_{k=1}^{n} \beta_{i,i} \Delta(P_i) + \sum_{k=1}^{n} \Delta(P_i) \Delta \beta_i$$

Where P is the change in the poverty index (in this case, the proportion of poor), β_k is the proportion of the population in subgroup I; P_k is the poverty index within group I, and the last term is a residual. The first component of the disaggregation is termed the demographic change effect, while the second is referred to as the poverty change effect.

primary sector and households living in Southeastern Mexico—to changes in total poverty is negative. This finding can be attributed to the fact that, despite the increase in poverty within the subgroups, demographic changes also occurred, offsetting the changes in poverty. In other words, there were household units that "moved out" of these subcategories. The only subgroup in which both effects were positive is for the Southern region.

What factors lie behind the observed increase in overall income inequality? Bouillon, Legovini and Lustig (1998) attempt to answer this question applying a decomposition methodology first developed by Almeida dos Reis and Paes de Barros (1991). The methodology is similar to that applied by Juhn, Murphy and Pierce (1993) in the context of earnings inequality in the U.S. but generalized to the household level in a model first proposed by Bourguignon, Fournier and Gurgand (1998). In essence, the methodology allows identifying the contribution of the changes in income distribution by source: endowments (education, experience, etc.) and the returns to those endowments.[17]

The results of this exercise revealed that the widening gap in the "returns" to education explain close to fifty percent of the observed increase in household income inequality, while the "returns" to regional location explain over 15 percent and to geographic location (urban/rural) explain another 9 percent (see table 11). Hence, most of the rising inequality in Mexico should be ascribed to increasing disparities in returns. Population effects—that is, the distribution of skills, etc.—account for about a fourth of the increase in inequality. In Mexico, thus, the widening gap in the returns to skill was not compensated by a more equal distribution of skills.

TABLE 10: Breakdown of Changes in Extreme Poverty
(1989–1994, in percent)

Subgroup	Population change effect	Poverty effect	Residual (percent)	Total Contribution (percent)*
Rural workers	−7.7	3.3	−0.4	−4.8
Primary sector	−10.5	7	−0.9	−4.4
Southern region	2.5	1.9	0.4	4.8
Southeastern region	−5.7	2.3	−0.5	−3.9

Source: Calculations by the authors, ENIGH surveys.
* Contribution to change in total extreme poverty.

---

17. Because the decomposition method is applied to a reduced form household income model, strictly speaking the estimated coefficients are not returns. They capture not only the market returns to the corresponding characteristics but also a whole range of endogenous decisions such as labor force participation and occupational choice.

TABLE 11: Decomposition of the Sources of Rising of Household Income Inequality on Per Capita Income (1984–1994, in percentage)

| | 1984 Contribution to | | | 1994 Contribution to | | | Average 84/94 Contribution to | |
	Gini	Return effects only	Actual change in the Gini	Gini	Return effects only	Actual change in the Gini	Return effects only	Actual change in the Gini
Sources								
ORIGINAL INCOME	49.1			54.9				
ESTIMATED INCOME	49.1			54.8				
SIMULATED INCOME								
Total (I+II+III+IV)			100.0			100.0		100.0
I. Return Effects r(X, ε) (a+b+c)	52.7	100.0	63.0	50.0	100.0	83.4	100.0	73.2
a. Household Characteristics	51.5	65.6	41.3	51.6	67.2	56.0	66.5	48.7
Demographics	49.2	1.6	1.0	55.4	−12.4	−10.4	−6.4	−4.7
Education	52.1	80.2	50.5	51.3	73.7	61.5	76.5	56.0
Working age	52.1	81.3	51.2	51.2	76.1	63.5	78.3	57.3
Male	52.0	73.0	46.0	52.0	61.0	51.0	66.0	48.2
Female	49.4	6.1	3.9	54.0	18.1	15.1	13.0	9.5
Older than working age	49.1	−1.0	−0.6	55.0	−2.9	−2.4	−2.1	−1.5
Male	49.0	−6.8	−4.3	55.1	−5.9	−4.9	−6.3	−4.6
Female	49.3	5.2	3.2	54.7	2.5	2.1	3.6	2.6
Assets	49.0	−3.0	−1.9	54.9	−0.2	−0.2	−1.4	−1.0
Absent Head	49.1	−1.5	−0.9	54.9	−0.9	−0.7	−1.1	−0.8
Interaction*		−11.8	−7.5		7.0	5.8	−1.1	−0.8
b. South Regional Effects	49.8	17.5	11.0	53.7	23.4	19.5	20.9	15.3
Fixed effects	49.5	9.8	6.2	54.1	15.0	12.5	12.8	9.3
Urban	49.1	0.1	0.1	54.9	−0.2	−0.2	−0.1	−0.1
Rural	49.5	9.8	6.2	54.1	15.1	12.6	12.8	9.4
Household Characteristics	49.4	7.3	4.6	54.4	9.1	7.6	8.3	6.1
c. Non-South Regional Effects	49.8	17.1	10.8	54.5	7.9	6.6	11.8	8.7
Urban	49.3	3.4	2.1	54.8	0.9	0.8	2.0	1.4
Rural	49.6	13.7	8.7	54.5	7.0	5.8	9.9	7.2
II. Error Terms Effect ε (r,X)	49.4		3.8	54.6		3.8		3.8
III. Endowment Effect** X (r′,ε′)			33.8			12.3		23.0
IV. Residual Effect ε(r′,X)−ε (r,X)			−0.5			0.5		−0.0

Note: Based on the decomposition presented in the Technical Appendix. Also, see Figure 2.

*Calculated as a difference, other interaction terms are not shown since they are small (see appendix for a complete decomposition.

**Calculated as the difference between total change and other components.

The exercise also showed that the returns for households living in the rural sectors deteriorated between 1984 and 1994, particularly in the South and Center regions. The fixed effect of the South region alone can explain 9 percent of the increase in income inequality. It is also the only region where both the urban and rural fixed effects are negative and worsening over time. This points to a divergence of the conditions in the South from those prevailing in the rest of the country. Hence, dynamics in the South may be able to explain about a fifth of the rising income inequality in Mexico attributable to changes in returns. The greatest contribution may come from the South East region, which includes Chiapas, Guerrero and Oaxaca, where poverty rates increased from 17 to 37 percent in the 1984–94 period.[18]

Causes of the worsening conditions in rural areas and the South

As indicated above, between 1989 and 1994 poverty, both extreme and moderate, increased among rural workers, in the primary sector, and in Southern and Southeastern Mexico, while during the same period it declined or remained unchanged in the rest of the country's sectors and regions.

When income is broken down by sector, we can observe the deficient performance of agriculture during the period (see table 12). As a result, households whose principal source of income was agriculture were necessarily affected. Indeed, in the case of agriculture, the shift in relative prices against tradable goods and the resulting profit squeeze meant a decline in real incomes for small and medium farmers. Moreover, the trends in relative wages against unskilled labor adversely affected rural workers.

However, we must also consider other factors in determining why poverty increased in agriculture. According to a study on the agricultural sector focused on the common land or *ejido sector,* the income collected by the common land farmers, or *ejidatarios,* was not only affected adversely by the appreciation of the peso, but also by the collapse in the real guaranteed price for the major basic crops, high interest rates, and the loss of subsidies in the sector (de Janvry, Gordillo and Sadoulet, 1997). Privatization, reduction or liquidation of many government institutions supporting the sector also occurred in connection with the modernization process. In general, this reduction in the institutionalized

---

18. Lustig and Székely (1998). Also, the inequality indicator most affected by the deterioration of the returns to Southern household variables is the mean log deviation. This is because the mean log deviation is the most sensitive to changes in the lowest deciles of the distribution among the selected indicators, and the South holds a much larger proportion of the poor than the rest of the country (as compared to a national average of 25% in 1994, the poverty count in the South central region was 41%, in the South Eastern 47% and in the South Western 24%). The fixed effect for the South alone accounts for 12 percent of the variation. The remaining 8 percent is accounted by changes in the return to household characteristics of the population living in the South (Table A.5).

TABLE 12: Wage and Nonwage Income, Agricultural and Nonagricultural Sectors

	1989	1990	1991	1992	1993	1994
		Yearly Growth Rates in %				
AGRICULTURAL SECTOR						
Wage income	−0.042	−0.088	−0.001	−0.028	0.001	0.001
Nonwage income	0.109	0.112	0.003	−0.1	−0.045	−0.044
NONAGRICULTURAL SECTOR						
Wage income	0.098	0.071	0.098	0.098	0.077	0.077
Nonwage income	0.099	0.054	0.023	0	−0.003	0.057
Real rate of change	83.6	83.2	91.2	96.9	103.2	97.2

Source: ENIGH, "Sistema de Cuentas Nacionales de México: 1988–1995," Volume I (México 1996), Table 3, pp. 40–41,
Table 65, p132 and Table 77, p.156. Exchange rates calculated based on the Bank of Mexico's CPI, "The Mexican Economy 1996", (Mexico 1996),Table 24, p.286.

support for agriculture drove up the cost of access to credit, insurance, markets, modern inputs, seed, water, and technical assistance. In this context of more flexible public controls, an unfavorable macroeconomic cycle, and institutional gaps, a process of social differentiation occurred, in which a small group of farms became successful businesses, while others were left behind, with some farmers even abandoning their properties. Those who created successful businesses were relatively wealthy, that is, they possessed larger land areas, or had greater access to credit and irrigation services. At the other end of the spectrum are the small farmers and members of indigenous communities, for whom it is difficult to modernize and diversify their activities as a result of limited access to financial resources and institutional services.

The increases in extreme poverty observed in Southern and Southeastern Mexico may also be attributed to the trends in prices of the major crops produced by the farmers in these regions. Between 1984 and 1992, the prices of coffee and cocoa declined by more than 70 percent in the international markets. It is estimated that the subsistence income for small farmers in the southern states of the Pacific coast declined an average of 15 percent (World Bank, 1996). The states of Chiapas, Veracruz, and Oaxaca are Mexico's three leading coffee producers. In the early 1990s, primarily as the result of the dismantling of the International Coffee Agreement,[19] the price of coffee on the international markets plummeted from an average of US$1.32 per pound in 1986–1988 to US$0.53 per pound in 1992.[20] Although direct calculations are not available, it seems reasonable to attribute some (if not all) of the observed

---

19. The International Coffee Agreement, the member countries of which undertook to reduce wide swings in coffee prices, was eliminated in 1989 and reinstated in March 1994. Report of the UN Secretary General (1995).

20. Food and Agricultural Organization of the United Nations (1992 and 1994).

increase in poverty in Mexico's Southeastern and Southern states to coffee price trends. In fact, indigenous producers were one of the groups most severely affected by the decline in the price of coffee, as 65 percent of all coffee producers are indigenous and produce one-third of Mexico's coffee output (World Bank, 1996).

4. Concluding comments: the medium term prospects of the economy

The liberalization of the balance of payments took place in the midst of a persistent real overvaluation of the peso and a large volatility of capital flows. The inconsistency between trade and exchange rate policies and the vulnerability generated by massive portfolio capital inflows had an unfortunate denouement in late 1994. After a deep recession in 1995, and unlike what had happened after the 1982 debt crisis, the economy has recovered a growth rate of the order of 5 to 6% per year and open unemployment has fallen to rates of the order of 3%. How viable is a scenario of sustained growth at rates higher than those observed since the early 1980s?

A number of factors lend some credibility to such a scenario. First, the international environment is more favorable today than in the aftermath of the 1982 debt crisis despite the increased volatility and probability of contagion effects such as those experienced in the aftermath of the East Asian and Russian financial crises. As compared with the early 1980s, foreign interest rates remain low and, unlike what happened then, the international rescue package appears to have successfully prevented a financial panic from degenerating into a decade long credit run in the international credit markets. In this setting, fiscal and exchange rate policies that ensure the economy is operating at full capacity and with a high real exchange rate have greater chances of success than in the 1980s.

Second, despite the fact that the adverse consequences of the 1994–95 crisis on living standards and income distribution will take years to reverse, the crisis itself may have substantially altered the long-term macroeconomic outlook in a positive direction. The huge real devaluation of the peso has abruptly eliminated the inconsistency between trade and exchange rate policies, which, as argued earlier, played a major role in the process leading to the crisis. The macroeconomic impact of the export expansion is enhanced in the context of a more open economy and greater integration with the US economy under NAFTA.[21] As shown in figure 1, net exports have had an expansionary effect

---

21. A comparison of the performance of Mexico's exports during the 1995 crisis with the 1983 recession may be illustrative of the positive side of the legacy of a more open economy. In 1995, the exchange rate increased by 86 percent (end of period). In that year, non-oil and non-maquiladora exports expanded by 37 percent, while maquiladora exports increased by 30 percent. Instead, in 1983, following a 466 percent increase in the exchange rate in 1982, maquiladora exports increased by 29 percent while non-maquiladora/non-oil exports fell by nearly 6 percent.

since 1995, contrary to what happened in the period 1988–94, the 1995 recession being explained by the collapse of private investment and a contractionary fiscal stance.

Given its large size, the real devaluation of the peso has also contributed to a reversal of the factors underlying the profit squeeze in the tradable sectors and the fall of the private savings rate (see tables 2 and 3). Through its positive effects on the profitability of the traded goods sector, the higher real exchange rate must have contributed to the increase in foreign direct investments. These investments now represent nearly 20% of total private investment and, between 1996 and 1998, around 60% of total foreign investment (including portfolio inflows). This means that the current account deficit is now being financed much less by short-term capital than in the first half of the 1990s, thus making the economy less vulnerable to new domestic or external shocks.

Private savings increased substantially in 1995, following the real devaluation, and continued to increase up to 1997. The increase was probably due not only to the real devaluation, but also to the domestic banking crisis and the associated credit crunch. As credit constraints become less acute, the upward trend of private savings may be reversed. In fact, a negative recent development is the significant decline in the domestic savings rate in 1998, much of which must have come from private savings.

REFERENCES

Almeida dos Reis, J. and R. Paes de Barros (1991) "Wage inequality and the distribution of education: A study of the evolution of regional differences in inequality in Metropolitan Brazil," *Journal of Development Economics*, vol. 36, pp. 117–43.
Banco de México (1997) *Informe Anual*. Internet address: http://www.banixco.org.mx.
_____ (1996) *The Mexican Economy, 1996: Economic and Financial Developments in 1995, Policies for 1996*, México: Banco de México.
_____ (1995) *The Mexican Economy 1995: Economic and Financial Developments in 1994, Policies for 1995*, México: Banco de México.
_____ (1992) *The Mexican Economy 1992: Economic and Financial Developments in 1991, Policies for 1992*, México: Banco de México.
Bouillon, C., A. Legovini and N. Lustig (1998) *Rising inequality in Mexico: Returns to households characteristics and the 'Chiapas effect'*, Preliminary draft, Poverty and Inequality Advisory Unit, Inter-American Development Bank.
Bourguignon, F., M. Fournier, and M. Gurgand (1998) "Labor Incomes and Labor Supply in the Course of Taiwan's Development, 1979–1994," mimeo.
Bourguignon, F., F. Ferreira and N. Lustig (1998) *The Microeconomics of Income Distribution Dynamics in East Asia and Latin America*, IDB-World Bank Research Proposal.
Cragg, M. and M. Epelbaum (1996) "Why has wage dispersion grown in Mexico? Is it the Incidence of Reforms or the Growing Demand for Skills?," *Journal of Development Economics*, Vol. 51, No. 1.

CEPAL (1998) *Políticas para mejorar la inserción en la economía mundial*, Fondo de Cultura Económica, Chile.

De Janvry, G. Gordillo and E. Sadoulet.(1997) *Mexico's Second Agrarian Reform*, San Diego: University of California, Center for U.S.-Mexican Studies.

French-Davis, R. and H. Reisen (1998) *Capital Flows and Investment Performance*, Paris: OECD Development Centre.

Hanson, G. and A. Harrison (1995) "Trade, Technology and Wage Inequality in Mexico," National Bureau of Economic Research (NBER) Working Paper No. 5110, May.

INEGI (1994) *Documento Metodológico de la Encuesta Nacional de Ingresos y Gastos de los Hogares de 1992*, Aguascalientes, México: INEGI.

_____ (1994) *Encuesta Nacional de Ingresos y Gastos de los Hogares de 1994*, Aguascalientes, México: INEGI.

_____ (1992) *Encuesta Nacional de Ingresos y Gastos de los Hogares de 1992*, Aguascalientes, México: INEGI.

_____ (1989) *Encuesta Nacional de Ingresos y Gastos de los Hogares de 1989*, Aguascalientes, México: INEGI.

_____ (1984) *Encuesta Nacional de Ingresos y Gastos de los Hogares de 1984* Aguascalientes, México: INEGI.

_____, y Comisión Económica para América Latina (1993) *Magnitud y Evolución de la Pobreza en México 1984–1992*, Aguascalientes, México: INEGI.

Juhn, C., K. Murphy and B. Pierce (1993) "Wage inequality and the rise in returns to skill," *Journal of Political Economy*, vol. 3, pp. 410–448.

Larudee, M. (1998) "Integration and income distribution under the North American Free Trade Agreement: the experience of Mexico," in D. Baker, G. Epstein and R. Pollin (eds.), *Globalization and Progressive Economic Policy*, Cambridge University Press.

Londoño J. and M.Székely (1997) "Persistent poverty and excess inequality: Latin America during 1970–1995," OCE Working Paper Series No. 358 (September).

Lustig, N. (1998) *Mexico: The Remaking of an Economy*, Second Edition, Brookings Institution.

_____ and J. Ros. (1999) "Economic Reforms, Stabilization Policies and the Mexican Disease," in L. Taylor (ed.), *After Neoliberalism*, Ann Arbor: University of Michigan Press.

_____ and M. Székely (1998) "Economic Trends, Poverty and Inequality in Mexico," mimeo, Interamerican Development Bank.

McLeod, D. y J. Welch (1992) "El libre comercio y el peso," *Economía Mexicana*, Nueva Epoca, Vol.I, No 1, (Enero).

Oks, D. (1992) *Stabilization and Growth Recovery in Mexico: Lessons and Dilemmas*, The World Bank, Latin America and the Caribbean Regional Office, January.

_____ and Van Wijnbergen. (1992) "Mexico After the Debt Crisis: Is Growth Sustainable?," *Journal of Development Economics* 47 (1) (June).

Organización de las Naciones Unidas.(1997) Informe del Secretario General de las Naciones Unidas: Actividades operativas para el desarrollo. Cooperación técnica entre los países en desarrollo: Situación de la cooperación Sur-Sur, 11 de septiembre, Homepage ONU.

Organización de las Naciones Unidas para la Alimentación y la Agricultura (1992) *Commodity Review and Outlook 1991–1992*, Roma: FAO.

_____(1994) *Commodity Review and Outlook 1993–1994*, Roma:FAO.

Ravallion M. and Huppi (1991) "Measuring Changes in Poverty: A Methodological Case Study of Indonesia During an Adjustment Period," *World Bank Economic Review*, 5.

Revenga, A. (1995) "Employment and Wage Effects of Trade Liberalization: The Case of Mexican Manufacturing," World Bank Mimeo.

Ros, J.(1994) "Mercados Financieros y Flujos de Capital en México," en Ocampo, José A, (ed.), *Los Capitales Externos en la Economías Latinoamericanas*, Fedesarrollo y BID.

Spilimbergo, A., Londoño, L., and Székely, M.(1997) "Income Distribution, Factor Endowments and Trade Openness," Working Paper No. 358, Office of the Chief Economist, Inter-American Development Bank.

_____ (1995), "Poverty in Mexico During Adjustment," *The Review of Income and Wealth*, Series 41, No. 3, September, pp. 331–348.

Taylor, L. (1998) "Project on the effects of balance of payments liberalization. Methodology for country studies," mimeo, CEPA, New School for Social Research.

United Nations Children's Fund (1996) *State of the World's Children 1996.*

_____ (1992) *State of the World's Children 1992.*

Van Wijnbergen, S. (1991) "Debt Relief and Economic Growth in Mexico," *World Bank Economic Review*, 5, no. 3.

World Bank (1996) "Mexico, Rural Poverty," Report No. 15058–ME, September 30.

_____ (1996) "Mexico: Poverty Reduction: The Unfinished Agenda," Report No.15692 ME, diciembre 9.

8

Russia: Globalization, Structural Shifts and Inequality

ALEXANDER VOROBYOV* *and* STANISLAV ZHUKOV*

Sweeping historical processes shape out what is vaguely defined as "Russia's transition." These interrelated and mutually reinforcing processes include an all-out attempt at economic liberalization combined with external opening of the national economy, disintegration of the Soviet (and Russian) empire, a demographic crisis threatening to lead to depopulation, progressive political and economic decentralization, degeneration of the inherited economic system, and deep institutional changes and restructuring of the social fabric of the society.

The outcomes include large and increasing levels of foreign debt; extreme dependence of the production process, investment, and consumption, on foreign trade and continuing inflows of foreign currency; and effective control of local markets by foreign capital. External or global factors and forces now dominate the Russian economic and political scene.

By introducing convertibility of the national currency and liberalizing both current and capital accounts of her balance of payments, Russia fully exposed herself to globalization. In this paper we ascribe to globalization a narrow functional meaning. Convertibility—with minor exceptions the exchange rate regime in force from the end of 1994 until August 1998—combined with free movements of capital and hard currency pushed local producers into global competition. For Russia, with an economy historically built upon absolute and relative prices (and production costs) totally different from prevailing world prices, entering into global competition was an enormous shock. Seen in this perspective globalization is the driving force in Russia's transition.

* Institute of World Economy and International Relations, Moscow Russian Academy of Sciences.

This paper is organized in six sections: post-Soviet social and economic chaos, external liberalization, dual economic structures, "shadowization" of economic activity, segmentation of labor markets, and conclusion.

1. Post-Soviet social and economic chaos

Depending on one's ideological inclinations and personal preferences the ongoing Russian transition can alternatively be seen as a full-fledged catastrophe or a cardinal re-shaping. Summarizing this yet unfinished drama is beyond anyone's individual capacity. Contemporary Russia is in chaos, fuelled by the disintegration of the empire, the demographic crisis, degeneration of the inherited economic system, political and economic decentralization, and rapidly rising income inequality.

Disintegration of the empire. Disintegration of the USSR led to a surge in migration flows among the former Soviet republics. Intensive inter-republican migration is rooted in the Soviet past. In the second half of the eighties 700–800 thousand people were leaving Russia annually. The reverse flow amounted to 850–950 thousand per year (see table 1). In the nineties, the number of outward migrants from Russia decreased substantially, while the opposite flow remained high and even increased. In 1992–1997 Russia was absorbing about 550 thousand migrants net (inward migrants minus outward ones) per year. Assuming that 80% of incoming migrants were settling permanently, by the beginning of 1998 recent migrants accounted for 5–6% of the total Russian population.

Most inward migrants are of working age and add to the employed labor force. Resettlement in post-Soviet economic space is expensive—migrants usually have to accept any work conditions and payment flows that they can find. Assuming that four-fifths of inward migrants in 1986–1998 are of working age and that 80% of them find jobs, they constitute no less than 10–11% of employed workers in the Russian economy. The combined share of re-settlers and illegally working temporary migrants in the total labor force can be conservatively estimated at 12–14%.[1]

Demographic crisis and depopulation: The population of Russia decreased in absolute terms after 1992. In 1993–1998 the decrease reached 750–800 thousand per annum. The reasons are a decline in the birth rate and a parallel rise in the death rate. In 1995 the death rate started to fall, but that could be the result of statistical manipulation. Until 1998 the drop in the residential population was offset by the massive inflow of migrants. Russia's population in 1989–1998 remained stable.

Demographic tendencies are extremely inertial. In the view of experts, present demographic processes are rooted in the Soviet past and just happened

---

1. Some estimates put the number of illegal workers in Russia on January 1, 1999 at more than 5 million or about 8% of the labor force (*Izvestia*, 18 June 1999, p.2).

Table 1. Demographic changes in the nineties

	1986	1987	1988	1989	1990	1991	1992	1993	1994	1995	1996	1997	1998
Population, million*	143.8	145.1	146.3	147.4	148.0	148.5	148.	148.7	148.4	148.3	148.0	147.1	146.7
–urban residents, %	73	73	74	74	74	74	73	73	73	73	73	73	73
Net migration, thousand	236	120	82	115	184	17	253	440	810	520	355	365	301
–CIS and the Baltic	238	129	103	161	287	105	356	554	914	613	440	433	362
–Far abroad	-2	-9	-21	-46	-103	-88	-103	-114	-104	-93	-85	-68	-61
=outward migration	722	774	792	739	729	675	673	483	337	347	292	233	213
–CIS and the Baltic	719	764	771	693	626	587	570	369	232	229	191	150	133
–Far abroad	3	10	21	46	103	88	103	114	104	118	101	83	80
=inward migration	957.5	894	874	855	913	692	926	923	1147	867	647	598	514
–CIS and the Baltic	957	893.5	874	855	913	692	926	923	1146	842	631	583	495
–Far abroad	0.5	0.5	0	0	0	0	0	0	1	25	16	15	19
Economically active population, million		75.4	75.5	73.9	76.0	75.2	74.0	72.6	73.0	72.6	73.0	72.5	72.2
Employment, million		75.4	75.5	75.6	75.3	73.8	72.0	70.9	68.5	66.4	66.0	64.6	63.6
Natural increase of population, thousand		968	779	577	333	104	-207	-734	-870	-832	-818	-737	-705
Rate of natural increase of population (per 1000)	6.8	6.7	5.3	3.9	2.2	0.7	-1.5	-5.1	-6.1	-5.7	-5.3	-5.2	-4.8
–birth rate (per 1000)		17.2	16.0	14.6	13.4	12.1	10.7	9.4	9.6	9.3	8.9	8.6	8.8
–death rate (per 1000)		10.5	10.7	10.7	11.2	11.4	12.2	14.5	15.7	15.0	14.2	13.8	13.6
Life expectancy at birth, years	70	70	70	70	69	69	68	65	63.9	64.6	65.9	66.7	

* - year beginning

Sources: The Commonwealth of Independent States in 1997, p.430; The Commonwealth of Independent States in 1998, pp. 428–429; Statistical Survey, N2, 1999,p.10; N1, 1998, pp.7–8; N1, 1997, pp.7–8; Socio-Economic Situation in Russia, NXII, January–December 1997, pp. 291,295; Russian Statistical Annual 1996, pp. 36, 71–72; 1994, pp.17, 38–39, 43, 55, 60–61; Russia Demographic Annual 1996, pp. 486–489; 1997, p.103; Population of Russia—1994,pp.17,33; Countries – Members of the CIS, 1992, p. 328.

to coincide with the economic transition.[2] In the coming decades Russia will face depopulation. According to the official forecast depopulation in the best scenario stops in 2002. In 2010 the population is expected to recover to the present level of 147 million. By 2015 it will increase slightly to 147.2 million. In the worst scenario, which in our view is more probable, depopulation will continue until 2015 when the total will be 138 million.[3]

Progressive political and economic decentralization: The Soviet economic and political system was characterized by an extremely high degree of centralization. Economic agents and quasi-political elements were subordinated to the center within a strict hierarchy. An appropriate metaphor for the system was a "single factory."

After the break-up of the Soviet Union, ethnic, regional, ideological, religious, economic, and other contradictions that had accumulated over decades were relatively peacefully accommodated by the establishment of 89 political and economic entities at the sub-federal level within the Russian Federation. These units had existed in the Soviet system, but then they had only had an administrative meaning.

Under current arrangements each national and regional unit elects its own president or regional governor with similar powers, governing practices, and parliament. Economically strong regions, which in practice means those with access to export resources, and politically mobilized regions (as a rule on ethnic basis) follow independent economic policies. The emergence of a new ruling class at the sub-federal level allowed the former communist and Soviet *nomenklatura* to infiltrate smoothly into newly created local power structures and enhance their numbers. Those employed in administration (excluding police and juridical and penitentiary systems) in 1990–1998 increased by a factor of 1.65; by the end of the period they accounted for 4.7% of the total labor force.

Degeneration of the inherited economic system: By the beginning of the eighties the Soviet economy had exhausted its development potential. Thereafter, it was kept afloat by exports of oil and gas and after the mid-eighties by rapid accumulation of foreign debt. The first independent estimates of economic performance showed that Soviet (and also Russian) GNP started to decrease in 1986/1987. Official Russian statistics register negative growth rates since 1991 and no attempts to revise the old series have been made as yet.

The official data show that in 1998 Russian GDP was 57% of its level in 1990 (see table 2). The drop in production spreads over all sectors with the exception of finance and credit. It is especially deep in construction, industry, and transport and communications. In terms of the components of final demand, the largest reduction was registered in investment—in 1998 it was only one-fifth of its 1990 level.

As Russia's population in 1998 hadn't changed from the beginning of the decade, GDP per capita fell in proportion to the decrease in output. The fall

2. Vishnevskiy A. *The Demographic Potential of Russia*, pp.103–105.
3. Expected Population of the Russian Federation until 2015, p.2.

**TABLE 2: Results of socio-economic development
in the nineties (1990=100)**

	1990	1992	1995	1996	1997	1998
GDP	100	81	62	60	60	57
–Agriculture	100	88	68	65	66	58
–Industry	100	77	51	49	50	47
–Construction	100	59	40	34	32	29
–Transport and communications	100	79	52	49	48	46
–Trade	100	93	86	87	92	90
–Finance and credit	100	123	148	146	158	145
–Other	100	86	70			
GDP per capita	100	81	63	60	60	57
Gross domestic investment	100	51	31	25	24	22
Employment	100	96	88	88	86	84
–Agriculture	100	104	100	95	89	90
–Industry	100	93	75	72	65	62
–Construction	100	87	69	65	63	56
–Transport and communications	100	97	90	90	88	83
–Trade	100	97	114	116	148	158
–Finance and credit	100	123	204	199	194	183
–Other	100	96	95	100	96	96
Average wage*	100	64	45	51	53	49
Unemployment (%)						
–official	...	0.8	2.8	3.5	3.1	2.6
–ILO definition	...	4.8	8.5	9.6	10.8	11.9

* - wage due

Sources: National Accounts of Russia in 1991–1998,p.15; Russian Economic Trends. Monthly Update, 7 October 1999, table 5; The Commonwealth of Independent States in 1998, pp.429–430; Socio-Economic Situation in Russia, January–December 1997, p.7; Review of Russian Economy, III, 1997, pp.109–110; II, 1998, p.35; Russian Economic Trends, I, 1997, p.124; Statistical Handbook 1996. States of the Former USSR, pp.380, 383, 385–387 and table 9.

---

in numbers employed was less than the drop in production, i.e. there was negative labor productivity growth. Only the industry and construction sectors lost more than one-third of their labor forces. Employment in trade, finance and credit, and administration actually increased. Nonetheless, for the first time since the thirties Russia faces significant unemployment. The number of officially registered unemployed reached its maximum in 1996, and fell significantly in 1997 and 1998. But measured by international standards, the rate of unemployment continues to rise and in 1998 reached 11.9% of the economically active population.

The real average wage in the first half of the nineties dropped by more than 50%. In 1996–1997 and in the first half of 1998 it recovered slowly, but following the economic collapse in August, 1998, wages fell again to give a year-long average of 49% of their level in 1990.

Institutional and social transformation: The liberalization and privatization shocks caused an almost immediate cleavage of the quasi-egalitarian Soviet society—which basically had been divided into the *nomenklatura* and the rest

TABLE 3: Dynamics of inequality in the nineties

	1990	1991	1992	1993	1994	1995	1996	1997	1998
Share of quintile in total income									
Lowest 20%	9.8	11.9	6.0	5.8	5.3	5.5	6.2	5.9	6.3
Second 20%	14.9	15.8	11.6	11.1	10.2	10.2	10.7	10.2	10.5
Third 20%	18.8	18.8	17.6	16.7	15.2	15.0	15.2	14.9	14.9
Fourth 20%	23.8	22.8	26.5	24.8	23.0	22.4	21.5	21.5	21.0
Fifth 20%	32.7	30.8	38.3	41.6	46.3	46.9	46.4	47.5	47.4
Gini coefficient	0.23	0.26	0.289	0.338	0.409	0.381	0.375	0.375	0.379
Adjusted Gini coefficient		0.341	0.370	0.439	0.465	0.450	0.481	0.470	
Income of the richest 10% to the poorest 10%									
official	4.4	4.5	8.0	11.2	15.1	13.5	13.0	13.5	13.4
adjusted		8.9	12.4	15.0	21.5	18.7	25.3	23.3	
Population with income below the minimal subsistence level									
million	...	17	49.8	46.8	33.2	38.8	31.6	30.7	35.0
as % of total population	...	11.7	33.5	31.5	22.4	24.7	21.4	20.8	23.8
Population with income below the physical survival level									
million	...	1.4	7.0[1]						26.4[2]
as % of total population	...	1.0	4.8[1]						18[2]

1. December 1992.
2. Population in the extreme poverty, December 1998.
Sources: Russian Economic Trends, March 11,1999,tables 6 and 16; Izvestia, 26 January 1999,p.1; Shevyakov A. Improvement of Methodology of Measuring of Level of Living, p.9; Statistical Review, N2, 1998, p.13; N1, 1997, p.12; Review of Russian Economy, II, 1998, pp.58–59; II, 1993, pp.40,93; Socio-Economic Situation in Russia, NXII, December 1998, pp.260,268; Russia–1997. Socio-Demographic Situation, p.169; Russian Statistical Annual 1996, pp.116,118; Russia–1993, Economic Conjuncture, p.82.

---

of population—into proto-classes. An important indicator was a sharp differentiation of household income levels (see table 3).

Even according to official data, the Gini coefficient increased from 0.23 in 1990 to 0.379 in 1998. An adjusted Gini coefficient rose from 0.341 in 1991 to 0.470 in 1997.[4] The ratio of the average income of the richest 10% of population to the average of the poorest 10% increased from 4.4 to 13.4 according to official estimates, and from 8.9 to 23.3 in the adjusted data.

In 1992–1993 the income of one–third of Russia's population was below the minimal subsistence level. Between 1994 and the first half of 1998 the below-subsistence population share decreased to one-fourth. However, after the collapse in August, 1998, it started to increase rapidly, rising to 38.2% in January,

---

4. Correction of the official data is necessary because in the official budgetary samples, groups with different levels of income are represented disproportionately. Low income groups in the samples are "over-represented" while high income earners are "under-represented." For a detailed adjustment methodology see: Shevyakov A. *Improvement of Methodology of Measuring of Level of Living*, pp.1–9.

1999, for a total population of 56 million. By December 1998 around 18% of the population or more than 26 million people lived in extreme poverty.

2. External liberalization

In 1992–1996 Russia fully liberalized external transactions, first on the current account and then on the capital account. The macroeconomic problems that prompted these steps are easy to describe. The major reason for liberalization of balance of payments was "hard currency strangulation."[5] In the late sixties and especially the seventies the former Soviet economy caught a specific form of "Dutch disease." Seemingly unlimited expansion of oil and gas production produced a rising inflow of easy petrodollars which became the driving force for investment and intermediate and final consumption. The supply of energy and the increasing inflow of hard currency largely explain Soviet economic dynamism in that period. With the exhaustion of rich oil deposits and the end of the easy petrodollar era, the Soviet (and Russian) economy passed into a trajectory of degeneration.

An unavoidable series of internal and external shocks of an economic, social, and political nature resulted in a considerable loss of production. Studies date the beginning of the production decline to 1986–1987.[6] With a short interruption in 1997, when GDP increased an insignificant 0.8%, the decline continued over a dozen years. The GDP decline in the nineties mirrors drops in oil output and hard-currency export earnings (see table 4). The linkage is especially close for the period 1991–1995 until export earnings were restored and the post-Soviet, Russian economy found new mechanisms of adjustment in the form of arrears or non-payments for intermediate inputs, mostly energy-related.

The primary reasons for liberalization of the balance of payments, however, were not strictly macroeconomic, but rather grew from the worsening crisis of the state budget. All-out price and institutional liberalization of the national economy that began in 1992 resulted in a collapse of the public finances.

Dismantling the Soviet Union's public monopoly on foreign trade and privatization of oil, metallurgical, and other resource-intensive export industries as well as lifting of controls over alcohol and tobacco markets led to severe erosion of the tax base and in turn to a drastic reduction in state revenues. By 1997 receipts of the consolidated state budget declined to 26.8% of GDP, compared to 41% in 1990 and 48% in 1985.[7] In 1998 total revenues declined

---

5. On macroeconomic effects and implications of "external strangulation" see: Taylor L. *Economic Openness: Problems to the Century's End*, pp.37–42 .

6. See: "Ekonomika i zhizn," N40, October 1992,p.13; *Ekonomist*, N5, 1992, pp. 22–23.

7. "State of the Monetary and Credit System and Payments in the Economy in 1998," pp. 5–6 and table 1 Supplement; Sinelnikov S., Anisimova L., Batkibekov S. et al. *Problems of Tax Reform in Russia: Analysis of the Present Situation and Perspectives of Development*, p.8. Figures for 1985 and 1990 are for the former Soviet Union, but are fully representative for the Russian Federation.

Table 4. Russia's macroeconomic aggregates in the nineties*

	1990	1991	1992	1993	1994	1995	1996	1997	1998
GDP growth rate, %		−5.0	−14.5	−8.7	−12.7	−4.1	−3.5	+0.8	−4.6
Increase of crude oil production, %	−20.5	−13.6	−11.3	−10.2	−3.5	−2.0	+1.7	−1.0	
Overdue crediting arrears, % of GDP			6.7	24.6	22.2	22.8	29.2	45.8	
Goods trade balance									
(outside the CIS), US$ billion	−10.7	6.4	5.5	10.7	16.1	21.5	27.7	17.6	17.4
–export of goods	71.1	50.9	42.4	43.7	53.0	65.7	71.3	70.4	59.1
–import of goods	81.8	44.5	36.9	33.0	36.9	44.2	43.6	52.8	43.3
Goods and non-factor services									
trade balance (total), US$ billion				17.6	20.5	23.0	17.4	17.4	
Current account bal., US$ billion									
Official	−4.5	3.5	4.2	6.4	8.9	7.8	12.0	4.0	2.4
Adjusted					0.3	2.9	−8.1	−14.3	−12.7
Inflow of foreign capital, US$ billion									
Total					6.7	6.7	25.7	43.8	18.0
– foreign direct investment		0.2	−0.1	0.7	0.6	2.0	2.5	6.2	2.2
– portfolio investment			0.2	0.1	−0.01	0.1	8.9	17.3	8.0
– other					6.1	4.6	14.3	20.3	7.8
Govt. share in inflow of foreign capital, %							49	75	

* - 1990–1991: balances of payments prepared by the IMF and official statistics, transactions with the Soviet republics are not covered; 1992–1993: official balances of payments, transactions with the CIS countries are not covered; 1994–1998: official balances of payments cover all transactions with the outer world. For understandable reasons, including the methodological ones, macroeconomic statistics on Russia for 1990–1993 are of extremely poor quality

Sources: Kommersant-Daily, 14 May 1999,p.9; Zhukov.S. Russia and World Capital Markets, IMEMO, 1999, table 1; Zhukov S. Russia: Economic Growth and Imperatives of Globalization, table 2; Sarafanov M. The Grave Will Correct,p.16; National Accounts of Russia in 1989–1994, p.55; Russian Economic Reform. Crossing the Threshold of Structural Change, p.53; The Commonwealth of Independent States in 1998, pp.56, 258; Russian Statistical Annual, 1994, pp. 11, 238, 276, 320.

---

further to 24.5% of GDP, with tax receipts falling to only 20.3%. Tax revenues of the federal budget declined to 9.5% of GDP in 1997 and 8.8% in 1998.[8] Its inability to collect taxes sufficient to guarantee a minimal level of centralized expenditures and to perform basic functions of the state forced the government to rely heavily on foreign sources of finance.

There are just four main channels to generate foreign currency: a positive balance on foreign trade, foreign direct investment (FDI), credits and loans, and portfolio investment. For Russia, the first three were effectively closed.

The rise of world prices of raw materials and metals in 1995–1997 apparently allowed a positive balance on foreign trade. Export earnings returned to their historical levels of about US$70 billion per year (see table 4). In 1996–1997 the reported trade surplus was about US$20 billion per year. Nonetheless, the official balance of payments presents a cumulative value of export contracts *signed*, not actual payments by trade partners. If non-returned export earnings—

---

8. Ibid.

one of the most widespread schemes for capital flight—are excluded, Russia's current account was positive in 1994–1995 only. Subsequent negative balances were $8.1 billion in 1996, $14.3 billion in 1997, and $12.7 billion in 1998.

A poor investment climate, unfavorable geographical location, low quality of the labor force, unfinished adjustment of absolute and relative prices, and related factors make the Russian economy unattractive for foreign direct investment.[9] In recent years the gross inflow of FDI stabilized at about $2–2.5 billion per year. The record inflow of $6.5 billion in 1997 is fully explained by the privatization of the national telecommunications industry.

From the Soviet Union, Russia inherited a huge foreign debt. Until agreements with the Paris and the London clubs to reschedule the Soviet debt were reached in 1996–1997, the country muddled from one technical default to another. Problems with foreign creditors were repeatedly solved in an ad hoc manner. These maneuvers eased debt service obligations, but minimized possibilities to receive substantial fresh credits and loans.

Under such circumstances, the only possible way to attract foreign capital was via portfolio investment. To this end, the Ministry of Finance launched ruble-denominated short-term bonds known as GKO-OFZ. In 1995 the GKO-OFZ market was opened to non-residents.

The monetary authorities introduced a host of measures to create guarantees for speculators in the GKO-OFZ . First, in 1995–1998 (before the catastrophe in August, 1998) the ruble was subjected to a "dirty float." At the beginning of each year the central bank announced upper and lower bounds on ruble fluctuations against the dollar. An exchange rate band or corridor was included in annual memoranda on macroeconomic policy submitted to the IMF.

Second, the largest local investor in GKO-OFZ was the Savings Bank (largely controlled by the central bank), which accumulates the lion's share of personal savings. A crash of ruble-denominated money instruments would mean the immediate collapse of internal savings mobilization; for this reason it was considered to be a low probability event.

Third, non-residents were allowed to hedge investment in ruble-denominated financial instruments by signing forward contracts with Russian banks. The latter took obligations to buy rubles at a fixed exchange rate. Some of these contracts were signed by the Central Bank.

Fourth, interest rates on the GKO-OFZ were kept at a very high level.

These measures in combination with rising world oil and metal prices and the reaching of agreement with foreign creditors on the former Soviet debt sent positive signals to global investors. In the first half of 1998 volume on the GKO-OFZ market reached 36.8% of GDP. At least one-third of the market was controlled by non-resident capital. Parallel financial markets emerged rapidly. By March 31, 1998 stock market capitalization rose to 18% of GDP or

9. For a detailed analysis of entry barriers for FDI see: Zhukov S. *Russia: Foreign Investment and Perspectives of Economic Growth.*

US$81 billion in absolute terms—around 60–70% of the stock market was controlled by foreigners.

Social impacts of external and internal financial liberalization were contradictory. In the short run, the large inflow of foreign capital led to rapid appreciation of the ruble. Wages and salaries expressed in nominal dollars increased, especially if compared to the dismal years of 1992–1995. Ruble appreciation generated a consumer import boom. Middle-income groups, first in the large cities, benefited substantially. Emergence of a Russian "middle class" became the show window for market transition. Low-income households and pensioners also benefited from ruble appreciation and low inflation. Arrears on wage and pensions continued to grow, but current payments became more regular.

But the real winners from the liberalization were a tiny group of the new post-Soviet *nomenklatura*, who organized the pyramid of GKO-OFZ. Sophisticated schemes allowed this group to attain control over export earnings (in effect a rent on natural resources) and redirect the resulting financial flows in favor of cronies.

The financial bonanza driven by hot speculative capital and increasing foreign debt lasted for about two years. In August 1998 the bubble exploded. It is usually assumed that the Asian flu triggered the Russian catastrophe. However, detailed analysis of the balances of payments, public debt, and state budget shows that the crash was deeply rooted in the Russian economy per se.

In the first half of 1998 cumulative payments to non-residents on the internationalized part of the internal debt and on foreign debt reached 37% of the federal budget receipts, 18% of exports, and 4% of GDP (see table 5). Meanwhile the external current account in January–June, 1998 was negative and amounted to US$5.1 billion.

On August 17, 1998 the government was forced to devalue the national currency, return to a freely floating exchange rate regime, and effectively default on the GKO-OFZ. By July 1999 the nominal exchange rate had reached 24.4 rubles per dollar compared to 6.2–6.5 before the crash. Consumer inflation rose to 70.8% in September–December, 1998 and to 16% in January–March, 1999.[10] Neither wages nor pensions were indexed to the price increases.

The crash of the financial bubble left the economy with at least two severe crises. First was a new crisis of foreign debt. Second was a new budgetary collapse. In 1998 Russia's foreign debt rose to 19% of GDP from 7% a year before, and amounted to 59% of exports. In the first half of 1998 cumulative debt service accounted for 37% of total federal budget receipts.

For years to come Russia will be caught in a debt trap. In 2000–2008 annual payments on foreign debt due amount from US$13 to US$19 billion.[11]

---

10. Information on Socio-Economic Situation in Russia, p.41; *Russian Economic Trends*, 11 March 1999, table 8.

11. *Segodnya*, 23 July 1999, p.5.

TABLE 5: Russian economy and foreign economic relations

	1994	1995	1996	1997	1998	1998 IH
Total foreign debt[1]						
as % of GDP	44	33	29	28	55	
as % of export[2]	159	129	124	120	173	
Russia foreign debt						
as % of GDP	4	5	6	7	19	
as % of export[2]	15	19	25	31	59	
Actual servicing of foreign debt						
as % of GDP	1.7	1.8	1.7	1.7	3.3	2.7
as % of export[2]	6.0	7.2	7.4	7.5	10.4	12.3
as % of federal budget receipts		15.2	15.6	14.3	33.2	25.1
GKO-OFZ outstanding as % of GDP	2.0	4.6	10.8	14.9	23.8[3]	36.8
Payments on GKO-OFZ to non-residents						
as % of GDP			0.4	0.8		1.3
as % of federal budget receipts			3.6	6.3		12.1
Cumulative payments on foreign debt and GKO-OFZ						
as % of GDP		2.2	2.5		4.0	
as % of export[2]		9.2	10.8		18.0	
as % of federal budget receipts		19.2	20.6		37	
as % of current account balance		69	278		[4]	
Stock market capitalization						
as % of GDP[5]					8	18[6]
US$ billion					18	181

1. Former Soviet and Russian foreign debt.
2. Goods and non-factor services.
3. January–August 1998.
4. In the first half of 1998 balance of current account was negative.
5. Year end.
6. As on 31 March 1998.

Sources: Kommersant-Daily, 14 May 1999,p.9 and 19 November 1999,p.9; Finansovaya Rossiya, N43, 19–25 November 1998,p.2; The Central European Economic Review, Vol.7, N3, April 1999,p.18 and Vol.6, N5, June 1998,p.20; Russian Economic Trends, Monthly Update, 11 March 1999, tables 11, 13 and 16; Zhukov S. Russia: Foreign Investment and Perspectives of Economic Growth, tables 2 and 10; Zhukov S. Russia: Economic Growth and Imperatives of Globalization, table; Yasin Ye., Gavrilenkov Ye. On Problem of Russia's Foreign Debt Regulation, Voprosy Ekonomiki, N5, 1999, p.71.

Internal social costs of these external payments will be dramatic. The problem is not just technical, but institutional as well. It is unrealistic to expect cohesive (if any) social policy from a bankrupt state. Even less should be expected from the new capitalist class that has emerged from the transition.

Together with external liberalization, the overall reshaping of Russia has produced powerful redistributive mechanisms, namely, inflation and privatization. In its turn redistribution has led to emergence of a dual economic structure and the "shadowization" of national economy and society.

Dual economic structure

Absolute price levels and relative prices (and production costs) in the Soviet economy were strikingly different from prevailing world levels. An economic system created to support forced industrialization and scientific progress was subordinated to the needs of heavy, mostly military industries. Extremely low prices of energy and electricity discriminated against raw material sectors—they constituted the backbone of the Soviet economic system. In January 1990, for instance, the internal wholesale price of a metric ton of crude oil was 26 rubles or US$15.20 at the heavily overvalued official exchange rate. Natural gas was equally cheap, and the wholesale price of one ton of coal was 12.2 rubles or US$7.10.[12] In December 1991 a ton of crude oil at the market exchange rate cost only 0.4% of the average world price.[13]

This system functioned in a rather stable manner for about fifteen years beginning from sometime in the late sixties, but was destroyed in the eighties by the global oil shocks. The Russian (=Soviet) oil and gas industry as well as electricity (a major consumer of primary energy resources and supplier of intermediate inputs for all economic sectors) were crucially dependent on imports of modern technologies, equipment, and steel pipes. Rising investment requirements of the import-dependent oil and gas sectors, which could not operate in the old system of absolute and relative prices any more (with exhaustion of "easy deposits" and transfer of production to Siberia and to the Far Northern territories), forced the subsequent transition.

Even more crucial was the fact that in the late sixties and early seventies when world oil prices were moving upward, the Soviet fuel industry became the economy's largest source of hard currency export earnings. They were used to finance increasing imports of machinery and equipment, intermediate products, and consumer goods. For a short time, an increase in the physical volume of oil and gas production and exports combined with the parallel rise in world oil prices to create some dynamism in economic development. But economic growth based on mineral exports and fantastically low internal energy prices demanded constant increases in energy production and stable export earnings. Unsurprisingly, later decreases in world oil prices and an inability to maintain levels of production of mineral resources turned into a catastrophe for the Soviet (=Russian) economy.

With a sharp drop in world oil prices and a rise in the costs of energy production, the only way to ease the burden on the raw material sector was through a substantial cut in internal demand and complete re-orientation toward world markets. A forced increase of artificially low energy prices became inevitable—it was the only means available to overcome the market disproportions accumulated within the national economy for several decades.

---

12. See: *Russian Economic Reform. Crossing the Threshold of Structural Change*, pp. vii, 267.
13. Auslund A. *Russia: Birth of the Market Economy*, p.195.

TABLE 6: Index of price increases in various industries
(Dec. to Dec., Dec. 1991=1)

	1997 to 1991	1995 to 1991	1997 to 1995
Electricity	11,425	7,419	1.54
Fuel industry	9,066	5 887	1.54
Transport (freight)	7,684	6,247	1.23
Petrochemicals	5,825	4,004	1.32
Construction*	5,212	2,673	1.95
Ferrous metallurgy	5,129	4,274	1.20
Chemicals	4,310	3,592	1.20
Construction materials	4,204	2,940	1.43
Machinery and metal working	3,483	2,639	1.32
Non-ferrous metallurgy	3,352	3,032	1.10
Food industry	2,896	2,194	1.32
Wood, timber, pulp and paper	2,405	1,988	1.21
Grain production	2,206	1,212	1.82
Cattle and poultry production	1,642	966	1.70
Payable services to population**	1,552	853	1.82
Light industry	1,144	867	1.32

*—prices of capital construction
**—purchasing prices
Sources: The Commonwealth of Independent States in 1997, pp. 443–444.

Internal consumption was cut in two ways. One was curtailment of supplies to the former Soviet republics. A few years earlier, energy supplies to the COMECON countries had already been reduced. Second, internal prices of energy resources shot up. These moves permitted an increase in the physical volume of export to external markets and partially offset the drop in export earnings caused by falling world oil prices.

Naturally, in an economy with a dense network of forward and backward linkages—in 1992 intermediate consumption accounted for 58.5% of total output[14]—a change in the key internal price triggered intensive restructuring of absolute and relative prices (and costs). Leaders in price run of 1992–1997 were electricity and the fuel industry (see table 6).

In 1992–1997 the wholesale price of electricity rose more than 11.4 thousand-folds, and the price of fuel went up 9.1 thousand-folds. Transportation tariffs (freight) and prices of chemicals, construction, and ferrous metals increased more than 5 thousand-folds. Agriculture, light and food industry, and payable services to the population were left out of the self-supporting price run.

Such significant differences in price dynamics largely explain the direction of structural change in the transition economy. These changes cannot be attributed to such usual explanatory factors as variation in productivity and/ or extensive use of labor and capital. Our very crude calculation shows that

14. See: *National Accounts of Russia in 1989–1994*, pp.151–153.

differentials in changes of relative productivity (output per worker) between industries in 1990–1998 were insignificant (see Supplement, table I).

Rather, structural shifts in the Russian economy in the nineties resulted almost exclusively from changes in relative prices and shifts in the distribution of profits and mixed income between economic sectors. The major beneficiaries were two groups of industries. The first comprised the fuel industry, electricity, and metallurgy, which were discriminated against in the Soviet economy in favor of heavy and military industries. Second came trade, financial and some other services, which benefited from the liberalization and all-out external opening.

Because of the data limitations we can only calculate the structure of GDP, the cost structure of value-added (or VA), and industrial shares in total profits and mixed income in current prices. For GDP we also present very tentative estimates in constant prices (see Supplement, table II, III and IV). However, even these limited data point to some important conclusions.

First, for the economy as a whole the shares of wage income and profits and mixed income in VA are nearly equal. Their combined share exceeds three-fourths of the total VA. Consumption of fixed capital accounts for less than one-fifth of VA. In the trade and financial sectors more than three-fourths and four-fifths of their respective VA levels go into profit and the mixed income component. The relative importance of profits and mixed income increased significantly in industrial VA as well. Second, in industry the contribution of fixed capital to the generation of VA fell from 27.8% in 1989 to only 16.9% in 1993. That share is less than that of the economy in general. Third, the cost structure of VA in transport and communications and construction has changed insignificantly. Fourth, due to the overall redistribution of the nineties the lion's share of profits and mixed income comes from trade, the financial sector, and some sectors of industry and services. Finally, indirect information indicates that the rise of the share of profits and mixed income in industrial VA is explained by the relative expansion of the fuel industry, electricity, and metallurgy.

Summarizing, we return to the conclusion that current structural shifts in the make-up of GDP and changes in the factor composition of value-added are caused by a powerful process of redistribution. This in turn has been triggered by sharp changes in relative prices and the all-out external opening of the national economy.

Broadly speaking Russian industries can be divided into two sectors. The first is adjusting with a degree of success to the new economic environment. The second comprises degenerating and agonizing industries. The fall in production has been spread over the entire Russian economy, but the relatively better adaptability of the first sector is explained by the fact that the new price and demand configuration allowed it to gain and/or suffer less from the overall reshaping.

Such structural shifts were easily predictable. Recalculation of the Russian input-output table for 1991 into world prices reveals that with the new relative prices industries separate into VA creators and destroyers. Table 7 compares the structure of profits in internal and world prices. Negative value added (precisely profits) is generated in agriculture, chemicals, and light industry. In the first variant of recalculation they are joined by food and coal industries. The latter is also unprofitable in the old Soviet prices.

At world prices, the bulk of VA is generated in the fuel sector and some other industries based on natural resources and raw materials. In other words, the Russian (=Soviet) economy is a striking example of a natural resource rent economy. Since the late eighties it has spasmodically moved towards international standard absolute and relative prices (and costs), causing increasing dualism within the inherited economic structure.

Shifts in structures of employment follow the same general directions (see table 8). The relative share of successfully globalizing industries is increasing, while degenerating sectors lose labor in relative and absolute terms. In 1992–1997 the share of electricity in total employment rose from 0.79% to 1.49%; fuel industry, from 1.16% to 1.72%; metallurgy, from 1.83% to 2.34%; finance and credit, from 0.5% to 1.2%. Shares of machinery and metal-working, light

TABLE 7: Industry breakdown of profits in Russian economy in 1991 in internal and "world average" prices (%)

	Internal Prices	World average prices* I variant	II variant	III variant
Agriculture	14.0	−10.1	−9.7	−9.4
Industry	66.5	92.4	91.4	91.7
−electricity	2.8	22.6	20.8	18.6
− fuel industry	9.1	50.6	47.9	45.4
= oil and gas	9.2	50.5	47.6	45.0
= coal	−0.2	−0.02	0.2	0.3
= other	0.1	0.1	0.1	0.1
− ferrous metallurgy	3.2	4.5	4.2	4.0
− non–ferrous metallurgy	2.5	3.7	4.0	4.2
− chemicals and petrochemicals	5.2	−1.8	−1.5	−1.3
− machinery and metal working	24.4	4.5	4.8	4.9
− wood, timber, pulp and paper	3.3	8.1	8.4	8.7
− construction materials	2.5	3.3	3.9	4.5
− light industry	10.1	−2.3	−2.2	−1.9
− food industry	2.0	−2.1	0.9	3.5
Construction	6.2	5.5	5.5	5.6
Transport and communications	6.6	7.6	7.4	7.3
Trade	6.1	4.1	4.2	4.2
Other	0.6	0.5	0.5	0.6
Total	100	100	100	100
− Electricity and fuel	11.9	73.2	68.7	64.0
− other natural rent based indus.	20.8	89.6	85.0	80.9

*—Recalculations were done in the variants under different assumptions.

Source: Pitelin A, Popova V., Pugachev.V. Intra-sectoral Analysis of Rusian Economy in World Prices, pp.67–68.

TABLE 8: Industry's breakdown of employment (%)*

	1989	1990	1991	1992	1993	1994	1995	1996	1997	1997 as of 1990	1998
Agriculture, forestry and fisheries	13.4	13.2	13.5	14.3	14.6	15.4	15.7	14.4	13.6	88	14.1
Industry	31.2	30.3	30.4	29.7	29.4	27.1	25.6	24.8	23.0	65	22.2
- electricity		0.79	0.85	0.96	1.05	1.10	1.20	1.30	1.49	162	
- oil and gas			0.32	0.38							
- coal		1.16	0.67	0.77	1.39	1.34	1.35	1.66	1.72	127	
- other fuel			0.07	0.06							
- ferrous metallurgy		1.13	1.03	1.16	1.24	1.15	1.16	1.56	1.39	106	
- non-ferrous metallurgy		0.70	0.62	0.75	0.85	0.80	0.88	1.00	0.95	116	
- chemicals and petrochemicals		1.63	1.60	1.64	1.74	1.57	1.55	1.63	1.54	81	
- machinery and metal working		13.93	13.87	13.14	12.48	10.93	9.90	9.63	8.67	53	
- wood, timber, pulp and paper		2.59	2.61	2.50	2.58	2.39	2.21	1.79	1.56	52	
- construction materials		1.58	1.86	1.88	1.72	1.62	1.56	1.26	1.10	60	
- light industry		3.30	3.24	2.78	2.67	2.49	2.13	1.73	1.48	38	
- food industry		2.23	2.50	2.52	2.45	2.42	2.41	2.25	2.16	83	
Construction	11.8	12.0	11.5	10.9	10.1	9.9	9.6	8.9	8.7	63	7.9
Transport and communications	7.9	7.7	7.8	7.8	7.6	7.8	7.8	7.9	7.9	88	7.6
Trade, public catering, material supply and distribution	7.9	7.8	7.6	7.9	9.0	9.5	9.9	10.3	13.5	148	14.5
Finance, credit, insurance and pensions	0.5	0.5	0.6	0.7	0.8	1.1	1.2	1.2	1.2	194	1.2
Administration	...	2.4	2.3	2.1	2.3	2.4	3.0	4.2	4.3	154	4.7
Other	27.3	26.1	26.3	26.6	26.2	26.8	27.2	28.3	27.8	101	27.8
Total	100	100	100	100	100	100	100	100	100	86	100

*—figures in the table are tentative estimates. Official data on distribution of labor force by industries is lacking.

Sources: Labor Market in the CIS Countries, p. 260; The Commonwealth of Independent States in 1997, pp. 431–432; The Commonwealth of Independent States in 1998, pp. 429–430; Russian Statistical Annual 1996, pp. 84, 90; National Accounts of Russia in 1989–1994, pp. 99, 178; Statistical Handbook 1993, p. 507.

and food industry, and construction materials are on the contrary falling. More important is the fact that employment in the successfully globalizing industries increases in absolute terms, while in the degenerating industries it is falling.

Such large changes in relative positions of industries and the rapid social segmentation of a previously homogeneous (by income) population have led to socioeconomic differentiation. In the Soviet economy labor income accounted for three-fourths of the total. Combined with social transfers, wage and salary income provided more than 90% of total income (see table 9).

During the transition the relative importance of labor income decreased significantly. Still, in the first half of 1998 it accounted for 47.4% of total money

TABLE 9: Sources of household income in 1987–1998 (%)

	1987	1988	1989	1990	1991	1992	1993	1994	1995	1996	1997	1998
Wages and salaries	76.8	76.2	74.0	74.1	59.7	69.9	58.0	46.5	40.7	41.9	39.3	42.4
Social transfers	14.9	14.6	13.5	13.0	15.5	14.0	17.2	17.4	12.4	14.2	14.9	13.3
Entrepreneur and other income	8.3	9.2	12.5	12.9	24.8	15.0	19.1	31.8	40.5	38.6	13.0	16.5
Sales income											27.1	22.2
Property income						1.1	5.7	4.7	6.4	5.3	5.7	5.6
Total income	100.0	100.0	100.0	100.0	100.0	100.0	100.0	100.0	100.0	100.0	100.0	100.0

Sources: Russian Statistical Annual 1996, p.118; *Statistical Review*, N2, 1998, p. 13; N1, 1997, p. 12; *Review of Russian Economy*, II, 1998, p. 27; Socio-Economic Situation in Russia, NXII, December 1998, p.263; *Indicators of Economic Activity in "Household" Sector*, pp. 24–25; *Russian Economic Reform. Crossing the Threshold of Structural Change*, p. 318.

income, exceeding all other sources. In the transition economy a large part of labor income is camouflaged as other income sources, thus its true share in total income is higher than indicated in the official statistics. Mass polls held in 1994–1997 repeatedly showed that wage and salary income accounted for 65–70% of total income.[15] The implication is that for the bulk of the population increasing income differentiation is explained by rising inequality in wages and salaries.

The distribution of labor income by deciles is presented in table 10. It reveals an intense redistribution during the transition years. In the period September 1991 – May 1996 the ratio of income of the 10% highest earners to the lowest 10% increased from 8.40 to 23.97. There is sharp and rising inequality between the second and ninth deciles, the ratio of their respective incomes widened from 3.34 in September 1991, to 6.31 in April 1994 and 6.32 in May 1996. During this period the combined share of the lowest three deciles in total wages and salaries declined from 13.5% to 8.0%. The share of the highest three deciles on the contrary rose from 52.3% to 62.5%. This rise almost exclusively went to the 10% highest income earners.

One of the reasons for such sharp and increasing inequality is the widening gap in average wage and salary payments in different industries, implying a redistribution of the total wage fund between sectors. At the same time *inter*industry differences in wage and salary payments cannot explain such a sharp rise in inequality. *Intra*industry differentiation in payments is an equally and sometimes more important explanatory factor of inequality.

More generally, Russia's inherited economic structure is splitting into successfully globalizing and degenerating sectors along intraindustry, enterprise, and even sub-enterprise lines. There exist many degenerating producers within each relatively well-adjusting sector (due to unfavorable location in remote areas, bankruptcy of suppliers and consumers, inability to export because of weak bargaining positions of the management, and numerous other factors).

---

15. *Russia—1997. Socio-Demographic Situation*, pp.139–140, 257.

TABLE 10: Labor income distribution by deciles of wage and salary earnings

Decile	1	2	3	4	5	6	7	8	9	10
Gaps in wage and salary income (income level of the lowest 10%=1)										
September, 1991	1	1.57	1.97	2.32	2.69	3.08	3.58	4.24	5.25	8.40
April, 1994	1	1.95	2.24	3.75	4.77	5.89	7.26	9.35	12.31	23.37
April, 1995	1	2.03	2.92	3.87	4.95	6.20	7.81	9.96	13.41	26.41
May, 1996	1	1.95	2.79	3.66	4.67	5.81	7.18	9.09	12.32	23.97
Share of decile group in total wage and salary income (%)										
September, 1991	3.1	4.6	5.8	6.8	7.9	9.0	10.5	12.4	15.3	24.6
April, 1994	1.4	2.7	3.9	5.2	6.6	8.1	10.0	12.9	17.0	32.2
April, 1995	1.3	2.6	3.7	4.9	6.3	7.9	9.9	12.7	17.1	33.6
May, 1996	1.4	2.7	3.9	5.1	6.5	8.0	9.9	12.5	16.9	33.1

Source: On Differentiation of Wages of Employed at Enterprises (in Organizations) in the First Half of 1996, pp.71–72

Often the line dividing "globalization" from "degeneration" faces an enterprise, in which case its success depends on the ability of management to restructure it into profitable and obsolete units. In general, besides some enterprises that depend exclusively on export demand, the overwhelming majority of Russian producers exist simultaneously in both "globalizing" and "degenerating" sectors.

From 1994 to the first half of 1997, due to the noticeable increase of world oil prices as well as to its continuing reorientation towards external markets, the fuel industry reached a somewhat stable plateau. Despite the appreciating ruble, export earnings allowed it to earn profits in national currency sufficient to support its own development. The stabilization of the two key prices—the crude oil price and exchange rate—gave temporarily relief to the entire economy. Some industries even partially restored positions lost during the period of high and sectorally uneven inflation. In 1995–1997 leaders in the price run were construction, agriculture, and payable services to the population (see table 6).

Unfortunately, stability of the plateau proved to be short-lived. A sharp drop of world oil prices started in the second half of 1997, in a prelude to the collapse in August 1998. This time a new inflationary round was triggered by maxi-devaluation. It again allowed the fuel industry to increase its profits in national currency terms. We anticipate that the new inflationary surge will be shorter and less intense compared to the one in the first half of the nineties. First, the large-scale devaluation increased ruble profits of oil and gas sector sufficiently to ensure their own development. Second, further catching up of energy prices to world average levels could finally kill the inherited industrial structure, which had already largely failed to adjust to the pre-August, 1998 price levels.

4. "Shadowization"

Analysis of structural changes in production, employment, and the distribution of income would be incomplete without considering the phenomenon of the shadow economy. The shift of a substantial part of production and consumption outside official recognition is a salient feature of the Russian transition. According to official statistics up to 20%– 25% of GDP is being created in the shadow sector.[16] Some radical estimates raise this figure to 40%.

The methodology used to evaluate shadow activities is not fully transparent and in some cases arouses reasonable skepticism. However, the fact that shadowization is not just a statistical phenomenon, but a powerful process with broad economic and societal implications, cannot be seriously doubted. In terms of scale and intensity of influence on the economy and social sphere, shadowization can be compared to collectivization of agriculture and socialist industrialization in the twenties and thirties or militarization in the sixties and seventies.

Shadowization is based on ambiguous privatization, arrears, and dollarization. Shock changes in relative prices, the transformation of property relations, often in a disguised form, and full-fledged external liberalization led to de facto establishment of a "three-currency" monetary system. Besides the use of rubles, economic transactions in the Russian economy are being facilitated by quasi-money rooted in the arrears and hard currency, mostly American dollars (see table 11).

Arrears, initially thought to be a temporary phenomenon of the transition economy, are in fact expanding. By the end of 1997 overdue credit arrears of enterprises reached 28.3% of GDP and were twice official M2. In 1998 they increased to 45.8% (!) of GDP or about three times the ruble money mass. Just a few years ago in the beginning of 1994 they accounted for only 6.7% of GDP and were three times smaller than the official M2.

Initially arrears appeared as a defensive reaction on the part of the production system. It had become non-competitive in terms of the new relative prices (and costs) and had lost traditional demand in the form of purchases by the state. Unable to pay for raw materials and intermediate inputs, producers began to rely heavily on accumulation of arrears. The situation has not significantly changed since 1992. Regular write-offs of arrears accumulated in the real sector by successive governments in 1992–1999 sent producers clear signals that the authorities were also ready to maintain the system.

Gradually an increasing number of profitable enterprises have also moved under the roof of arrears. That was rational and expectable behavior as arrears allowed firms to receive resources and intermediate inputs free. Also, artificially created unprofitability allows enterprises to avoid paying taxes.

There exists a macroeconomic hypothesis, not supported by exact proofs, that the dynamics of overdue credit arrears of enterprises has a statistically significant negative correlation with "net errors and omissions" in Russia's

---

16. *National Accounts of Russia in 1989–1996*, p.16.

TABLE 11: Alternative measures of money mass in Russian economy

	January 1, 1999	January 1, 1998	January 1, 1997	January 1, 1996	January 1, 1995	January 1, 1994
1. GDP, trillion RR	2684.5	2586.4	2256.1	1630.1	610.7	162.3
2. Overdue crediting arrears of enterprises, trillion RR	1230.6	756.1	514.4	362.0	150.5	11.3
2:1, %	*45.8*	*29.2*	*22.8*	*22.2*	*24.6*	*6.7*
3. Official ruble M2, trillion RR	452.5	374.1	295.2	220.8	97.8	34.6
3:1, %	*16.9*	*14.5*	*13.1*	*13.5*	*16.0*	*21.3*
3.1. Official ruble M0(cash), trillion RR	187.8	130.0	103.8	80.8	36.5	13.3
3.1:1, %	*7.0*	*5.0*	*4.6*	*5.0*	*6.0*	*8.2*
4. Hard currency M2, trillion RR		325.0				
4:1, %		*12.1*				
4.1 Hard currency M0(cash), trillion RR	404.6	240.0				
4.1:1, %	*15.1*	*9.3*				
5. Ruble and hard currency M2, trillion RR		699.1				
5:1, %		*27.0*				
6. Ruble and hard currency M0,(cash), trillion RR	592.4	370.4				
6:1, %	*22.1*	*14.3*				
7. Gross M2(2+3+4), trillion RR		1,466.1				
7:1, %		*56.7*				

Sources: Economic Conjuncture of Russia in January–March, 1999,pp.53,63; Balance of Payments of the Russian Federation in 1998, Supplement, table 1; The Commonwealth of Independent States in 1998, p.439; Russian Economy in 1997. Tendencies and Perspectives, p.22; Socio–Economic Situation in Russia, NI, January 1998, pp.17,169; Russian Economic Trends, Monthly Update, 7 May 1998, chart 3; 30 January 1998, table 7; Review of Russian Economy, 1997, NII, pp.83–84; Russian Statistical Annual 1994, pp.9,269,276.

balances of payments.[17] If the hypothesis is correct, it means that payments between Russian enterprises are done via off-shore accounts in foreign tax havens.

Shadow transactions between economic agents within the Russian economic system are being helped by its overall dollarization. In 1997 the volume of hard currency in cash, circulating in Russian economy, was 1.8 times bigger than ruble M1 and amounted to 62% of ruble M2. The relatively high share of cash rubles in the total official money mass additionally helps many transactions to escape registration and taxes.

Given the size of the unreported economy, it is evident that the absolute money income of the population is higher than is statistically registered. For instance, adjusted account of the "household sector" in the social accounting matrix shows that a substantial and increasing share of labor income avoids reporting. In 1993 unreported wage payments accounted for 13.5% of the officially registered wage fund or 5.3% of GDP. In 1994 the corresponding figures rose to 20.8% and 8.5%, and in 1995 to 31.5% and 10.4% respectively[18]. Crude estimates from the Russian-European Centre of Economic Policy are

17. Gavrilenkov A., Kosarev À. *On Foreign Trade Statistics and Evaluation of Tendencies in Balance of Payments of the Russian Federation*, p. 9.

comparatively modest. They state that actually paid wages and salaries in 1995 were 7.9% higher than the official figure. The discrepancy rose to 15.5% in 1996, 19.8% in 1997 and 18.3% in the first quarter of 1998.[19] These indirect estimates are supported by results of some polls.

In all cases mixed income flows—not pure wage income—are implied. A strict split of unreported income into wage and entrepreneurial components is not possible. In the chaotic Russian economy in many cases it is more profitable and convenient to receive a part of entrepreneurial profits in cash via wage payments. More widespread is the practice of camouflaging wages as interest income on bank deposits and insurance premiums, as both are not taxed.

In any case, substantial underreporting of income allowed some authors to arrive at favorable assessments of the social situation in Russia. Results to date of the economic transition also look brighter. However, these conclusions fail to recognize that shadow incomes are distributed more unevenly than official ones.

In 1997 a research group headed by S. Aivazyan made an attempt to quantify the scale of unreported income and also estimated its distribution among different income groups using a sophisticated econometric approach.[20] The results permit a more adequate understanding of the peculiarities of the transition and social stratification in contemporary Russia. The methodology rests on common sense and deep understanding of the institutional and structural features of the present economic system.

It postulates that the standard mathematical apparatus employed to distribute the population into income groups is not appropriate for the present Russian situation. The log-normal distribution used to classify the population into quintiles and deciles works more or less correctly in stable economies. However, for Russia with its shocking jump in socio-economic differentiation and sharp shifts in sources and structure of incomes a log-normal distribution gives distorted results. In a first stage one has to split the population into groups, which are homogeneous by income characteristics, so that the distribution of income *within* a group can be described log-normally. In a second stage, these homogeneous groups are "mixed" to receive standard decile characteristics. For the splitting and mixing procedures, bootstrap analysis, the Monte Carlo method, and qualified expert estimates are used.

This technique showed that 54% of personal income escapes official registration.[21] By both sources and structure of income, Russia's population has split into five homogeneous groups.

The first, with the lowest income, is made up of the unemployed, sporadically employed, non-working retired persons, stipend receivers, and low-paid

18. Indicators of Economic activity in "Households" Sector, p. 25.

19. *Review of Russian Economy*, II, 1998, pp. 27–28.

20. Aivazyan S. *Model of Formatting of Russia's Population Distribution by Size of Per Capita Income*, pp.74–86.

21. Ibid, p.80.

blue-collars workers. The second group is represented by the employed in the budgetary and service sectors. The third includes wage and salary earners in the relatively successful fuel industry, ferrous and non-ferrous metallurgy, electricity, financial and banking services, and prospering traders. The fourth group comprises main shareholders and the highest managers from the fuel industry, metallurgy, and banking and finance. Low and middle levels of state bureaucracy, highly paid managers, low and middle personnel of the shadow economy, and a tiny share of intellectual and creative elite (=professionals) also belong to this group. The highest level of the state bureaucracy and heads of the mafia and the shadow economy make up the fifth group.

Relative shares of these five socio-economic groups in the total population, cumulative income, and respective per capita average incomes are presented in table 12. In October 1996 the first group with an average monthly income per capita of 350 thousand rubles (US$64) accounted for 39% of Russia's population. Its share in total cumulative income was 11.3%. At the opposite extreme were the fourth and the fifth groups with average monthly per capita incomes of US$2,210 and US$22,100 respectively. The combined share of these two groups in the total population was 4%, yet in the cumulative income it was 42.4%.

TABLE 12: Homogeneous income groups: shares in total population, cumulative income and average per capita dollar income (October 1996)

	Population, %	Income, %	Per capita income, US$
Fifth group	0.03	3.0	22,100
Fourth group	3.97	39.4	2,100
Third group	17	23.1	302
Second group	40	23.2	129
First group	39	11.3	64

Source: Aivazyan, p.80; Russian Economic Trends, 11 November 1998, table 16.

The adjusted distribution of Russia's population by income deciles is presented in table 13. The data flatly contradict the popular myth postulating the emergence of a middle class in wake of the transition. Russia-USA comparisons by quintiles show that if in America the combined share of the second and the third quintile groups in the total income reaches 26.5%, in Russia the same share is only 16.25%. The Russian fourth-quintile's share in cumulative income is 16.89%, well below the American level of 23.5%.[22]

The Gini coefficient is 0.556 and the share of the highest quintile in total income is 62.14%. Such sharp inequality places Russia in much the same position as Brazil (the corresponding figures in 1995 were 0.601 and 64.2%), Zimbabwe

22. *World Bank Development Report 1998/1999*, p.199 and table 13.

TABLE 13: Russia's population differentiation by income groups

Decile	1	2	3	4	5	6	7	8	9	10
Gaps in income (income level of the lowest 10%=1)										
October, 1996	1	1.31	1.40	1.81	1.97	2.78	3.07	5.21	7.64	22.82
Share of income group in total income (%)										
October, 1996		2.04	2.68	2.85	3.70	4.02	5.68	6.27	10.62	15.58	46.56

Source: Aivazyan, p.84.

(1990: 0.568 and 62.3%), Colombia (1995: 0.572 and 61.0%), Mexico (1995: 0.503 and 55.3%), Chile (1994: 0.565 and 61.0%), South Africa (1993: 0.584 and 63.3%) and other highly inegalitarian developing economies.[23] In none of the transition countries of Central and Eastern Europe has income inequality reached an intensity and scale comparable to that of Russia.

After the burst of the speculative debt bubble in August 1998, inequality in income distribution sharpened further. The share of income received directly in hard currency increased significantly from the lowest to the highest income strata. Massive devaluation hit first of all low-income ruble recipients, decreasing their real incomes significantly. Through mid-1999 the decrease had not even been partially compensated by indexation of nominal incomes in rubles. Average money income in the first and the second groups fell to US$20–25 and US$35–40 respectively. In other words four-fifths of the total population of Russia receive about US$1 per day. At the same time high-income earners, who receive a large part of their income in dollars, benefited from the devaluation.

5. Segmentation of the labor market

Increasing dualism of the economy and its progressive shadowization strongly affected the structure of the labor market. It has split into five overlapping segments: formal employment, hidden employment in the modern (=monetized) sector, hidden employment in non-monetized agriculture, officially registered unemployment, and hidden unemployment.

Such a configuration is not totally new for Russia. During Soviet times rural and a large number of urban residents, including those in the largest cities, were massively engaged in the production of potatoes, vegetables, and animal husbandry. Production was consumed within the household sector itself.

Crude estimates of absolute and relative sizes of the five major segments of the labor market are presented in table 14. As we have already noted, Rus-

---

23. Ibid, pp. 198–199. For some countries Gini coefficient and quintile distribution was received on the expenditure basis.

sian employment data are poor. Even data on labor force distribution by indus-trial branches are lacking. Thus, only incomplete quantification is possible.

The deep contraction of economic activity in 1986–1998 made a signifi-cant part of formally employed labor excessive. Partial unemployment, amount-ing to 4–5 million people or 6–8% of the total formal employment, can be treated as a minimal estimate of the excess labor supply. A maximum estimate can be drawn assuming that production and employment fall proportionally. Under this assumption, excess formal employment amounts to about 20 mil-lion people or 30% of the total employed. In reality the relationship between production and employment levels is not linear. Experts on the Russian labor market estimate that excess formal employment in 1997 was 12–14 million,[24] roughly equal to the average of our maximum and minimum estimates.

At the same time from 9 to 12 million people or 15–18% of the total labor force are connected to the sector of hidden employment.[25] This sector pro-vides jobs to formally employed workers and employers, both registered and unregistered unemployed, retired persons and youth under the working age, as well as to legal and illegal workers from the CIS and abroad.

Indeed, labor market segmentation is still more complicated due to wide-spread secondary and multifold employment. Up to 35–40% of the Russian population have additional employment besides a basic formal job.[26] A spe-cial survey taken in 1997 revealed that 49% of those polled had one additional job; 32% had two jobs; 14%, three jobs; and 3%, more than three jobs.[27]

Excluding the agricultural sector, the bulk of hidden employment is gen-erated at the interface between the national and world economies. Rather conservatively it can be estimated that more than two-thirds of hidden em-ployment is generated by shuttle import trade conducted by physical persons, retail trade with legally and illegally imported goods, and a wide range of personal services rendered to the high income groups benefiting from liber-alization and external opening.[28]

A special feature of hidden employment is a relatively high level of pay-ments compared to those for formal employment. Sporadic jobs often pay well (by local standards), especially in comparison to wages in the degenerat-ing sectors in the formal economy. Also, hidden employment is free of non-payments and arrears.

---

24. Russia—1997. "Socio-Demographic Situation," p. 88; *Vremya*, 5 November 1998, p.3.

25. The low figure was received in the representative poll of the working population. The high estimate is given by one of the leading experts on the Russian labor market T. Maleva. See: *Vreamya*, 5 November 1998, p.3; Perova I., Khahulina L *Evaluation of Income from Unregulated Addi-tional Employment*, pp.29–31.

26. *Russia—1997. Socio-Demographic Situation*, p.128.

27. Ibid, p.124.

28. More radical estimates put number of engaged into shuttle import only at 10–15 mil-lion—*Vremya*, 22 January 1999,p.4. This estimate looks exaggerated to us, but the problem is that reliable data are virtually nonexistent.

TABLE 14: Employment by socio-economic sectors[1]

	1992	1993	1994	1995	1996	1997	1998
Absolute numbers, million							
Formal employment	72.0	70.9	68.5	66.4	66.0	64.6	63.6
- minimal excessive employment (annualized number of partially employed)	...	3.3	4.8	4.5	5.8	4.1	...
- maximal excessive employment[2]	10.9	15.0	19.7	19.8	20.8	19.1	20.2
Hidden employment in modern sector[3]						9–12	
Economically active population	76.0	75.2	74.0	72.6	73.0	72.5	72.2
Official (registered) unemployment	0.6	0.8	1.6	2.3	2.5	2.0	1.9
Hidden (unregistered) unemployment	3.0			4.7	4.3	5.4	
Structure, %							
Formal employment	100	100	100	100	100	100	100
- minimal excessive employment (partially employed)		...	4.7	7.0	6.8	8.8	6.3
- maximal excessive employment[2]	15	21	29	30	32	30	32
Hidden employment in modern sector[3]						14–19	

1. Figures used by Maleva and Sinyavskaya differ slightly from the data in tables 1 and 2. To make the two series comparable we adjusted them on the basis of tables 1 and 2.
2. Figures calculated under the assumption that output per worker achieved in 1990 remains unchanged.
3. Transactions in modern sector rest on ruble, hard currency and various quasi-money means of payment.

Sources: Maleva T., Sinyavskaya O. Social Sphere,p.45; Vremya MN, 5 November 1998,p.3, sources to tables 1 and 2 and our estimates.

The multifaceted structure of the labor market partially eases social conflict. In the medium to long run, however, it contributes to the proliferation of marginal groups. About 12–14 million excess workers in the formal sector have been hanging on for the last decade. Enterprises with a major overhang of excess labor basically have no chance for revival. Excess labor just prolongs the agony of noncompetitive producers, and at the same time blocks the establishment of a market-type industrial organization. From the other side, new labor entering the market finds attractive niches in the hidden employment sector. The problem is that it has no serious future prospects.

6. Conclusion

The transition in Russia has been accompanied by a profound split of the economy and society in general into two disparate sectors. One is the global sector, comprising those activities which gained (or lost less) from the ongoing restructuring of relative prices and which have integrated successfully into the global economy. The other is the degenerating sector, unable to function with the new price proportions and demand configuration.

The increasing dualism of the economic structure implies sharpening inequality in the distribution of monetary flows. Given that the most acute, however often disguised, source of inequality lies with the distribution of assets and natural resources, true socioeconomic disparity in contemporary Russia is much more pronounced than is reflected in statistics of monetary flows. Privatization of a few efficient enterprises and the parallel process of shadowization are the key mechanisms ensuring redistribution of incomes and assets in favor of tiny high-income groups.

Crude estimates show that the global sector provides employment to 20–25% of the labor force and guarantees a satisfactory level of living to 15–20% of Russia's total population. About 50 million of the "excess employed" and up to 110 million of the rest of the population comprise the opposite pole of poverty and deprivation.

Enormous gaps in incomes and lifestyles, typical for people belonging to the opposite sectors, are only part of the problem. The rest is due to the fact that profits generated in the global sector continuously leak out of the country. The underlying causes include the extreme openness of the economy and overall dollarization of the financial sphere, combined with a lack of public control over flows of physical resources and money. Under the circumstances, the post-Soviet ruling class is well positioned to accumulate personal wealth in hard currency outside the national banking system.

According to official data, the share of personal savings used to purchase hard currency increased from 3% in 1992 to 84% in 1997 (see table 15). Data adjusted for shuttle imports, tourism, and migrant remittances reveal a less pronounced but still impressive dollarization of personal savings. The lion's share of saving comes from high-income groups. Meanwhile, even inaccurate polls, which tend to camouflage the real priorities of the wealthy, reveal that rich families generating about 60% of all personal saving place up to 30% in accounts in foreign banks.[29]

The temporary increase of world oil and metals prices in 1995–1997 slowed the shock increase in inequality. A positive and significant foreign trade balance, restructuring of Soviet debt, financial injections from the IMF and the World Bank, and a massive inflow of short-term private capital allowed inflation stabilization. For a short period these and related factors spurred a speculative regime of growth led by imports and accumulation of foreign debt.

Appreciation of the ruble in real terms as well as higher nominal wages and hard currency inflows temporarily stabilized the social and economic situation. Real income increases and parallel growth of cheap imports ensured relative stability and social peace. However, the collapse of the speculative debt bubble on August 17, 1998 immediately ruined the fragile regime of economic growth and social tranquility.

If the tendencies in the wake of the crash continue, the Russian economy will split completely into separate globalizing and degenerating sectors. Naturally, the splitting process will take a rather long period of time, as transitory socioeconomic forms of production and employment emerge. If world en-

---

29. Ibid, pp.268–269.

Table 15. Personal savings in Russia in 1990–1998

	1987	1988	1989	1990	1991	1992	1993	1994	1995	1996	1997	1998 IH
OFFICIAL DATA												
Savings as % of money income	6.3	7.1	8.3	12.6	29.4	18.9	23.4	28.7	23.9	25.2	25.6	27.0
Structure of savings												
Banking deposits	87	88	90		64	25	26	22	21	16	4	5
Cash rubles	8	7	5		33	72	39	16	15	6	7	12
Buying of hard currency (cash)	2	2	2	–	–	3	34	62	63	75	84	78
Bonds and stocks	3	3	3	–	3	0	1	0	1	3	4	5
ADJUSTED DATA												
Savings as % of money income						17.8	18.2	14.8	9.4	10.3	8.5	
Structure of savings												
Cash rubles						76	34	30	37	14	20	
Net buying of cash hard currency (buying minus selling)							–3	15	26	10	38	53
Banking deposits, bonds and Stocks						27	51	44	53	48	27	

Source: The Commonwealth of Independent States in 1997, p.469; Socio-Economic Situation in Russia, NVI, January–June 1998, pp.208–209 and NXII, January–December 1997, pp.278,280–281; Grigoriyev L., Nikolaenko S Personal Savings of Population, p.5; Kashin Yu. Financial Actives of Population (Savings): An Approach to Evaluation of Level of Living, p.49; Russian Economic Reform. Crossing the Threshold of Structural Change, p.319.

ergy and metals prices remain low the global sector, suffering from underinvestment and depletion of productive assets, is doomed to shrink like Balzac's *Peau de Chagrin*. Its capacity to support a certain level of employment will also diminish.

The mechanism of arrears, a degree of centralized budgetary financing of education, health and budgetary subsidies to communal services, and subsidized prices on bread and other basic food products may prevent the final division of the economy and the society into poles of poverty and relative well being. Production activities which are ineffective in the new configuration of final demand and production costs may receive sufficient resources via arrears and budgetary injections to prolong their existence. Similar mechanisms ease the burden placed upon the impoverished and low-income strata of the population. But in the medium and long run the redistributive potential of arrears and budgetary expenditures is limited.

Privatization of state enterprises, the decentralization of foreign trade, and the shift of nearly all profitable activities into the shadow economy have deprived the government of traditional sources of revenue, undermining budgetary finance. At the prevailing official exchange rate the Russian federal budget in 1999 is only US$20 billion. This level of revenues makes support of education, health, and social services—all created in the Soviet time to serve the entire population free of charge—impossible. As four-fifths of the population are poor and very poor, massive commercialization and privatization of social services are not useful. Hopes to transfer pension funds to the private sector are futile, as most Russians face increasing difficulties even in supporting their current levels of consumption.

The worst outcome of liberalization is that the arrears and massive price movements have destroyed essential economic information. Producers have no objective bases for the development of medium- and long-term strategies. Soviet-style industrial organization has been obliterated and a market-based system has not been created. The Russian economy is trapped in a vicious and narrowing circle.

The sudden world oil price jump in early 1999 significantly eased "hard currency strangulation" for the contemporary Russian economy. High export earnings and decreasing imports, reduced by the maxi-devaluation, made the foreign trade balance strongly positive. Inflows of hard currency via the current account substituted for portfolio investment and IMF/World Bank credit injections. In parallel to the new default on sovereign debt, Russian commercial banks and private corporations also defaulted massively, minimizing the outflow of hard currency. At the same time, the Central bank increased the mandatory surrender of hard currency for exporters. They now must sell 75% of earnings at special auctions. Through higher export duties, the government succeeded in enlarging budgetary revenues. Relatively high export earnings allow oil and gas producers to keep internal energy prices low.

As a result of these and related policy changes, Russia's GDP in 1999 is expected to rise 1–2%. Even stronger growth is forecasted for 2000. It is difficult to predict how long a restoration of the Soviet model of growth, which rested on inflow of petrodollars and low internal energy prices, will last this time. The restoration gives the economy a temporarily relief, but does not solve any of the inherent problems.

REFERENCES

Aivazyan, S. (1997) "Model of Formatting of Russia's Population Distribution by Size of Per Capita Income" (in Russian), *Ekonomika i Matematicheskie Metody*, Volume 33, Issue 4, October–December, pp.74–86.

Auslund, A. (1996) "Russia: Birth of the Market Economy" (in Russian), "Republika," Moscow.

Center for Economic Conjuncture (1999) *Economic Conjuncture of Russia in January–March, 1999* (in Russian), Government of the Russian Federation, April.

Center for Economic Conjuncture (1993) *Russia—1993. Economic Conjuncture* (in Russian), Issue 1, Government of the Russian Federation, February.

Center for Economic Conjuncture (1999) *State of the Monetary and Credit System and Payments in the Economy in 1998* (in Russian), Government of the Russian Federation, April.

Central Bank of the Russian Federation (1999) *Balance of Payments of the Russian Federation in 1998* (in Russian).

The Commonwealth of Independent States in 1998 (digest of provisional statistical results) (1999) Moscow: MSK CIS.

The Commonwealth of Independent States in 1997. Statistical Annual (1998) Moscow: MSK CIS.

The Commonwealth of Independent States in 1998. Statistical Annual (1999) Moscow: MSK CIS.

Countries—Members of the CIS. Statistical Annual (in Russian) (1992) Moscow: Finansy i Ingineering.

Economika i Zhizh (in Russian) (1992) N40, October.

Economist (in Russian), N5, May 1992.

Expected Population of the Russian Population until 2015 (Statistical Bulletin) (in Russian) (1998) Moscow: Goskomstat RF.

Finansovaya Rossiya (in Russian), (1998) N43, 19–25 November.

Gavrilenkov Ye and A. Kosarev (1998) "On Foreign Trade Statistics and Evaluation of Tendencies in Balance of Payments of the Russian Federation" (in Russian), paper presented at the conference "Problems and Perspectives of Economic Policy in Russia," "Bureau of Economic Analysis" Fund, Moscow, 2–3 July.

Grigoriyev, L. and S. Nikolaenko (1998) "Personal Savings of Population" (in Russian), paper presented at the conference "Problems and Perspectives of Economic Policy in Russia," "Bureau of Economic Analysis" Fund, Moscow, 2–3 July.

"Indicators of Economic Activity in 'Households' Sector" (Materials of the State Statistical Committee) (in Russian) (1998), *Voprosy Statistiki*, N1, pp. 24–25.

Information on Socio-Economic Situation in Russia, January–March 1999 (in Russian) (1999) Goskomstat RF.

Institute of Economic Forecasting and Center of Demography and Human Ecology (1994) *Population of Russia—1994* (in Russian), Second Annual Demographic Report, Moscow, Evrazia.

Institute of Economic Problems of the Transition Period (1998) *Russian Economy in Tendencies and Perspectives* (in Russian), Moscow, March.

Institute of Socio-Economic Problems of Population (1998) *Russia—1997. Socio-Demographic Situation* (in Russian), Moscow.

Izvestia, Moscow, 1997–1999.

Kashin,Yu (1998) "Financial Actives of Population (Savings): An Approach towards Assessment of Level of Living" (in Russian), *Voprosy Statistiki*, N5, pp. 43–51.

Kommersant-Daily, Moscow, 1995–1999.

Labor Market in the CIS Countries (in Russian) (1998) Moscow: MSK CIS.

Maleva, T. (1998) "It's Easier for Authorities not to Notice the Labor Market" (in Russian), *Vremya*, 5 November, p. 3.

Maleva, T. and O. Sinyavskaya (1998) "Social Sphere" (in Russian), paper presented at the conference "Problems and Perspectives of Economic Policy in Russia," "Bureau of Economic Analysis" Fund, Moscow, 2–3 July.

National Accounts of Russia in 1989–1994 (in Russian) (1995) Moscow: Goskomstat RF.

National Accounts of Russia in 1989–1995 (in Russian) (1996) Moscow: Goskomstat RF.

National Accounts of Russia in 1989–1996 (in Russian) (1998) Moscow: Goskomstat RF.

National Accounts of Russia in 1991–1998 (in Russian) (1999) Moscow: Goskomstat RF.

"On Differentiation of Wages of Employed at Enterprises (in Organizations) in the First Half of 1996" (in Russian) (1996) *Infomatzionno-Statisticheskiy Bulleten*, N13, November, Moscow: Goskomstat RF.

Perova, I. and Khahulina, L. (1998) "Estimate of Incomes from Unregulated Additional Employment" (in Russian), *Monitoring Obschestvennogo Mneniya*, N3, Moscow: VTZIOM, May–July.

Pitelin, A., Popova, V. and V. Pugachev (1994) " Intra-sectoral Analysis of Russian Economy in World Prices" (in Russian), *Ekonomika i Matematicheskie Metody*, Volume 30, Issue 1, January–March, pp. 61–75.

Review of Russian Economy II (in Russian) (1994) Moscow: Progress—Universitet.

Russia Demographic Annual 1997 (in Russian) (1997) Moscow: Goskomstat RF.

Russia Demographic Annual 1996 (in Russian) (1996) Moscow: Goskomstat RF.

Russian Statistical Annual 1998 (in Russian) (1998) Moscow: Goskomstat RF.

Russian Statistical Annual 1996 (in Russian) (1996) Moscow: Goskomstat RF.

Russian Statistical Annual 1994 (in Russian) (1994) Moscow: Goskomstat RF.

Russian European Centre for Economic Policy (various years) *Review of Russian Economy* (in Russian), Moscow, II, 1997; III, 1997; II, 1998.

Russian European Centre for Economic Policy (1997) *Russian Economic Trends*, Quarterly Issue I.

Russian European Centre for Economic Policy (various years) *Russian Economic Trends*, Monthly Updates, 30 January 1998; 7 May 1998; 11 November 1998; 11 March 1999; 7 October 1999.

Sarafanov, M. (1999) *The Grave Will Correct* (in Russian), Moscow, N25, 5 July, pp. 15–19.

Segodnaya, Moscow, 1997–1999.

Shevyakov, A. (1998) "Improvement of Methodology of Measuring of Level of Living," *Economic Inequality and Poverty: Dynamics and Interregional Comparisons* (in Russian), Moscow, mimeo.

Sinelnikov, S., Anisimova, L., Batkibekov, S. et al. (1998) "Problems of Tax Reform in Russia: Analysis of the Present Situation and Perspectives of Development" (in Russian), Moscow, Eurazia.

Socio-Economic Situation in Russia (in Russian) (1997) NXII, January–December, Moscow: Goskomstat RF.

Socio-Economic Situation in Russia (in Russian) (1998) NI, January, Moscow: Goskomstat RF.

Socio-Economic Situation in Russia (in Russian) (1998) NXXII, December, Moscow: Goskomstat RF.

Socio-Economic Situation in Russia (in Russian) (1998) NVI, January–June, Moscow: Goskomstat RF.

Statistical Survey (in Russian) (various years) N1, 1997, NN1–2, 1998, N2, 1999, Moscow: Goskomstat RF.

Taylor, L. (1988) "Economic Openness—Problems to the Century's End," Helsinki: WIDER, April.

Vishnevskiy, A.A. (1998) "Demographic Potential of Russia" (in Russian), *Voprosy Ekonomiki*, N5, pp.105–122.

World Bank (1996) *Statistical Handbook 1996. States of the Former USSR*, Washington, D.C.

World Bank (1993) *Statistical Handbook 1993. States of the Former USSR* (in Russian), Washington D.C.

World Bank (1992) *Russian Economic Reform. Crossing the Threshold of Structural Change*, Washington D.C.

Zhukov, S. (1998) "Russia: Foreign Investment and Perspectives of Economic Growth" (in Russian), *Developing Countries and Russia. Ways of Integration into the Modern System of World Economic Relations*, Moscow: Institute of World Economy and International Relations, pp.75–103.

Zhukov, S. (1999) "Russia: Economic Growth and Imperatives of Globalization" (in Russian), *Mirovaya Ekonomika i Mezhdunarodnuye Otnosheniya*, N1, January.
Zhukov, S. (1999) *Russia and World Capital Markets* (in Russian), Moscow: Institute of World Economy and International Relations.

SUPPLEMENT

Table I. Relative productivity (value added per employed, total economy=1)

	In prices of 1990			In prices of 1995		
	1990	199	1998	1990	1995	1998
Agriculture, forestry And fisheries	1.26	1.22	1.12	0.48	0.46	0.45
Industry	1.26	1.22	1.39	1.18	1.13	1.32
Construction	0.80	0.65	0.60	1.11	0.92	0.85
Transport and Communications	1.30	1.08	1.08	1.85	1.50	1.52
Trade, public catering, material supply and distribution	0.78	0.80	0.62	1.88	1.98	1.53
Finance, credit, Insurance and pensions	1.60	1.64	1.84	1.25	1.28	1.45
Other	0.65	0.83	0.87	0.53	0.71	0.68
Total	1	1	1	1	1	1

Sources: The Commonwealth of Independent States in 1998, pp. 429–430; Statistical Handbook 1996, pp. 383,386; Russian Statistical Annual 1998, pp. 50, 179; National Accounts of Russia in 1989–1998, pp. 31–38,40.

Table II. Industry's breakdown of value added (%)

	Current prices				Constant prices Prices of 1990			Prices of 1995		
	1990	1992	1995	1998	1990	1995	1998	1990	1995	1998
Agriculture, forestry and fisheries	16.7	8.3	7.1	5.8	16.7	18.3	16.6	6.3	7.1	6.4
Industry	38.3	35.7	29.6	29.1	38.3	31.5	30.9	35.7	24.6	29.2
Construction	9.6	8.2	8.7	7.2	9.5	6.1	4.81	3.3	8.7	6.8
Transport & communications	10.1	8.6	12.0	11.4	10.1	8.5	8.2	14.3	12.0	11.5
Trade, public catering, material supply & distribution	6.1	19.7	20.1	20.3	6.1	8.2	9.0	14.6	20.1	22.2
Finance, credit, insurance & pensions	0.8	5.3	1.6	0.4	0.8	2.0	2.1	0.7	1.6	1.7
Other	18.4	14.2	20.9	25.8	18.4	25.4	28.4	15.1	20.1	22.2
Total	100	100	100	100	100	100	100	100	100	100

Sources: The Commonwealth of Independent States in 1998, pp. 429–430; Statistical Handbook 1996, pp. 383,386; Russian Statistical Annual 1998, pp. 50, 179; National Accounts of Russia in 1989–1998, pp. 31–38,40.

Table III. Cost structure of value added by industries (%)

	1989	1990	1991	1992	1993	1994
AGRICULTURE						
-wages	25.5	42.9	31.9	39.3	36.7	34.7
-consumption of fixed capital	16.6	16.0	6.7	24.4	22.5	39.1
-net profit and mixed income	53.1	35.8	61.2	35.3	39.7	25.5
-taxes	4.8	5.3	0.2	1.0	1.1	0.7
INDUSTRY						
-wages	45.5	45.3	38.7	36.8	38.2	37.1
-consumption of fixed capital	27.8	25.6	11.2	15.5	16.1	24.6
-net profit and mixed income	18.7	20.5	48.5	43.9	42.4	36.5
-taxes	8.0	8.6	1.6	3.8	3.3	1.8
CONSTRUCTION						
-wages	70.1	72.8	70.0	83.0	69.0	63.2
-consumption of fixed capital	6.3	18.8	6.3	17.8	15.3	17.1
-net profit and mixed income	23.0	2.3	23.0	−1.2	14.9	18.5
-taxes	0.6	6.1	0.7	0.4	0.8	0.7
TRANSPORT AND COMMUNICATION						
-wages	56.0	58.2	51.8	51.4	54.2	49.3
-consumption of fixed capital	13.3	12.5	20.7	21.6	21.6	27.0
-net profit and mixed income	26.8	27.7	27.4	26.1	22.3	22.5
-taxes	3.9	1.6	0.1	0.9	1.9	1.2
TRADE						
-wages	67.4	71.3	23.8	7.3	16.0	19.0
-consumption of fixed capital	14.2	13.5	2.4	1.1	2.8	3.3
-net profit and mixed income	14.6	13.5	73.7	91.6	80.5	75.9
-taxes	3.8	1.7	0.1	0.0	0.7	1.8
FINANCE AND INSURANCE, ETC.						
-wages	43.0	58.8	23.6	11.9	17.9	25.3
-consumption of fixed capital	13.5	11.8	0.3	0.2	0.4	1.9
-net profit and mixed income	40.5	29.4	76.1	87.7	81.2	69.6
-taxes	3.0	0.0	0.0	0.2	0.5	3.2
TOTAL ECONOMY						
-wages	50.2	52.4	45.3	37.4	43.1	
-consumption of fixed capital	21.3	20.0	10.7	13.0	16.5	
-net profit and mixed income	22.3	22.3	43.2	48.0	38.7	31.9
-taxes	6.2	5.3	0.8	1.6	1.7	

Sources: National Accounts of Russia in 1989–1994, pp.31-35.

Table IV. Industry shares in net profits and mixed income (%)

	1989	1990	1991	1992	1993	1994	1995	1996	1997	1998
Agriculture	40.0	26.7	18.0	7.3	9.3	7.8	9.5	9.7	8.7	8.0
Industry	32.5	35.0	43.3	34.2	37.9	38.7	27.7	27.8	25.6	26.0
Construction	3.8	1.0	5.3	−1.8	4.5	6.3	6.2	5.8	5.8	5.5
Transport and communications	10.9	12.4	6.6	5.9	6.9	9.1	11.6	12.3	12.4	10.0
Trade	3.2	3.7	17.3	45.6	29.4	27.8	27.9	28.0	26.8	31.8
Finance and insurance, etc.	1.3	1.1	3.2	6.9	7.9	6.2	1.0	−1.1	−0.8	−1.6
Administration and defense	1.3	1.8	1.1	0.3	1.0	1.9	2.7	1.9	3.0	3.0
Other	9.0	20.6	9.4	4.7	10.0	10.1	15.3	16.1	19.1	17.5
Imputed financial intermediation	−2.0	−2.3	−4.2	−6.7	− 6.9	−7.9	−1.9	−0.5	−0.6	−0.2
Total	100	100	100	100	100	100	100	100	100	100

Sources: The Commonwealth of Independent States in 1998, pp.429–430; Statistical Handbook 1996, pp.383,386; Russian Statistical Annual 1998, pp.50,179; National Accounts of Russia in 1989–1998, pp.31–38,40.

9

South Korea: Economic and Social Consequences of Globalization

JONG-II YOU *and* JU-HO LEE

Introduction

Globalization of the economy is producing new opportunities for many, but it also poses serious risks. To the extent that globalization generates new problems, it requires new policy responses. Whether globalization can serve to reduce poverty and raise the living standards of the majority of the people is not entirely clear. If we look at the rich countries and those that have successfully raised incomes, they have actively, if strategically in some cases, participated in the world markets. At the same time, globalization based upon neo-liberal policies has resulted in worsening income distribution and poverty in many countries. At any rate, social policy response remains a critical component in deciding the outcome of the globalization process.

It is popular to think of globalization as a natural and inevitable product of technological advancement. But the experience of highly liberal and integrated markets across much of the world during the late 19th century and the early 20th century suggests that globalization is not just a technologically determined phenomenon. It is a consequence of policies that promote or at least do not deter cross-border flows of goods and services, finance, people,

*The original version of this paper was prepared for the project on "Globalization and Social Policy" led by Lance Taylor, Center for Economic Policy Analysis, New School University. We are thankful to the useful comments we received from him, John Langmore and others at the CEPA conference held in January 1999.

ideas and information. Liberalization policies can in principle be restricted to domestic economy, but in practice the centerpiece of economic liberalization policies tends to be precisely the liberalization of trade and capital flows. In effect, therefore, liberalization provides a policy environment that, in conjunction with the technological environment, serves to advance globalization.

This paper looks at the South Korean experience with economic globalization (South Korea will be referred to simply as Korea hereafter). Only a while ago, the Korean economy was the envy of the developing world. Its success was scrutinized by numerous analysts. Although diverse opinions exist, most agree that the secret of Korean success was a judicious mix of the state and the market. The exact mix of the state and the market, however, has gone through some changes. In particular, there has been a steady, albeit gradual and patchy, move toward liberalization since the early 1980s.

The impact of liberalization on the labor market and social policy is not easily observable in the Korean case due to the very gradual nature of the liberalization process. Liberalization in Korea took a serious turn only a few years ago with a series of measures to liberalize its capital accounts. The end result was the catastrophic financial crisis of 1997–98. No doubt the crisis will have profound effects on the labor market and social policy for years to come. In this paper, we review the overall developments in the political economy of Korea since 1980, with a focus on the connections among liberalization policies, the macroeconomic and labor market developments, and the social consequences.

The rest of the paper is organized as follows. In section 1, we look at the political economy of liberalization in Korea; how it happened, why it happened and why it went wrong. The following section describes the macroeconomic developments in the era of liberalization. Section 3 takes a closer look at the labor market. Changes in wage inequalities will be discussed here. The next section examines the problems of social policy in Korea. Finally, conclusions and recommendations will be given in section 5.

1. Political Economy of Liberalization in Korea

A Brief History of Liberalization

Although there was a major policy shift toward liberalization in 1964, the extent of liberalization was rather limited. With the "Big Push" toward Heavy and Chemical Industry in the 1970s, government control of investment was strengthened, giving rise to the term Korea, Inc. Steady moves toward liberalization began only in the 1980s. Macroeconomic imbalances resulting from the over investment in HCI began to take its toll in 1979 when the economy slowed down amidst rising inflation. The troubles deepened as a result of severe external shocks—the steep rises in the world real interest rate and the oil price—in that year. On top of all this, there was a political turmoil following the assassination of President Park. The economy tumbled to an unprecedented negative growth in 1980, when General Chun staged a coup and took power.

Under Chun's administration the economic policy emphasized stabilization, and a move to liberalization got under way. Particularly, trade liberalization was emphasized as a part of disinflation policy. Unlike trade liberalization in the 1960s, a continuous progress was made this time. However, it was not a drastic one-shot liberalization. Mindful of its impact on the balance of trade, the government took a gradual multi-stage approach. Strategic protection of selected industries such as agriculture and automobile industry continued. One estimate of the degree of import liberalization incorporating both tariff protection and quantitative restrictions indicate that it steadily rose from about 66 percent in 1980 to about 88 percent in 1990 (Kim, 1994). It is commonly argued, however, that the actual effects of liberalization were less than these numbers would indicate. Like in Japan, various non-transparent regulations are utilized to protect consumer goods markets.

In the 1980s the government also began to liberalize the financial system that had been tightly controlled. Following the announcement of financial liberalization plan in 1980, commercial banks were successively privatized and new commercial banks and non-bank financial institutions were allowed to enter in the following years. There were also partial measures to deregulate the interest rate and to move toward universal banking. In addition, a gradual opening of the financial market was introduced. However, financial liberalization measures were taken in such a piecemeal and gradual manner that the government controls over the financial industry remained little affected (Amsden and Euh, 1990). The single most important factor in this is that the government retained the power to appoint the top managers of the commercial banks even after they were privatized (Jung, 1991). The desire to maintain the credit control as a policy instrument for various microeconomic policies as well as the natural reluctance of the bureaucracy to relinquish its power meant that true autonomy of bank management, especially in loan decisions, was never a serious possibility. Meaningful financial liberalization was limited to non-bank financial institutions (NBFIs) that have grown rapidly.

The liberalization rhetoric was notched up during the Roh administration (1988–1993) and even further during the Kim Young Sam administration (1993–1998) that adopted *segyehwa*[1] as its guiding principle. Under the US pressure trade liberalization began to affect even such "sacred" areas as agriculture, finance and strategic manufacturing like automobiles from the late 1980s. The conclusion of the Uruguay Round negotiations and the launching of the WTO in 1995 accelerated this move toward dismantling the last pockets of protected industries. Of particular significance was the opening of the rice

---

1. *Segyehwa* literally means globalization, which is a phenomenon rather than a policy. *Segyehwa* policy is therefore a bit of a misnomer. The government resorted to the Korean word in order to distinguish it from globalization as such. It was meant to include not only economic liberalization policies but all types of policies to bring Korea up to global standards, including early education in English.

market and the markets for financial services and retailing.

Financial liberalization measures in the 1990s were much more comprehensive and substantial. They included interest rate deregulation, abolition of policy loans, greater managerial autonomy of the banks, relaxation of entry barriers to financial activities, and capital account liberalization (see Table 1). These measures proved disastrous. They failed to achieve the desired outcome of a competitive and sound financial system. Despite many liberalization measures, both the bureaucrats and the bankers found it difficult to change the age-old behavior of government-directed finance and primitive credit risk management. Capital account liberalization and relaxation of entry barriers to financial industry served to create much greater financial risks, but the moral hazard bred in the government-controlled financial system persisted. The government, moreover, failed to apply prudential regulations and supervision that became all the more important as a result of liberalization. Nonbank financial institutions were especially poorly supervised. In the end, the mismanagement of financial liberalization culminated in the catastrophic exchange crisis of 1997 (Radelet and Sachs, 1998; Chang, Park and Yoo, 1998).

Liberalization in Korea took a radical step in the wake of the IMF bailout in December 1998. The IMF-mandated reforms included a full-fledged opening of the financial markets, including selling-off troubled commercial banks to foreign banks and abolishing the Foreign Exchange Management Act. Inward foreign investment, both portfolio and direct, has radically been liberalized, and the import diversification policy (effectively, a ban on some Japanese imports) is to be dismantled. In addition, such standard liberalization measures as labor market reforms, privatization and deregulation are proceeding in earnest.

Impetus for Liberalization

What are the sources of the impetus for liberalization? Broadly speaking, three main sources can be identified. The first and probably the most important is the change in the balance of power between the state and the private sector that the economic success engendered. The very success of the government-led industrialization undermined its structural basis, namely a strong state and a weak private sector. Decades of rapid growth produced world-class-sized firms, prosperous middle class, and an assertive working class. While different groups took different positions concerning specific liberalization measures, it can be said that the increased strength of the private sector vis-a-vis the state has been the fundamental factor in the slow but steady move toward economic liberalization and political democratization since the 1980s (You, 1995). While the middle class that acquired discretionary spending power favored trade liberalization, the business sector in general championed financial liberalization.

The second main source of the impetus for liberalization is the external

TABLE 1: Major Financial Liberalization Measures in Korea during the 1990s

1) INTEREST RATES DEREGULATION (IN FOUR STAGES : 1991 TO JULY 1997)
–By 1997, all lending and borrowing rates, except the demand deposit rates, were liberalized

2) MORE MANAGERIAL AUTONOMY TO THE BANKS AND LOWER ENTRY BARRIERS TO FINANCIAL ACTIVITIES
–Freedom for banks to increase capital, to establish branches, and to determine dividends payments (1994)
–Enlargement of business scopes for financial institutions (1993)
   : continuous expansion of the securities business of deposit money
   : freedom for banks and life insurance companies to sell government and public bonds over-the-counter (1995)
   : permission for the securities companies to handle foreign exchange business (1995)
–Abolition of the limits on the maximum maturities in loans and deposits of banks (1996)

3) FOREIGN EXCHANGE LIBERALIZATION
–Adoption of the Market-Average Foreign Exchange Rate System (1990)
–Easing of the requirement for documentation proving the deal (i.e., non-financial) demand in foreign exchange transactions (1991)
–Setting up of foreign currency call markets
–Revision of the Foreign Exchange Management Act (1991)
   : changing the basis for regulation from a positive system to a negative system
–Introduction of 'free won' accounts for non-residents (1993)
–Allowance of partial Won settlements for the export or import of visible items (1993)
–Foreign Exchange Reform Plan (1994)
   : a detailed schedule for the reform of the foreign exchange market structure
–A very significant relaxation of the Foreign Exchange Concentration System (1995)

4) CAPITAL MARKET OPENING
–Foreign investors are allowed to invest directly in Korea stock markets with ownership ceilings (1992)
–Foreigners are allowed to purchase government and public bonds issued at international interest rates (1994), equity-linked bonds issued by small and medium-sized firms (1994), non-guaranteed long-term bonds issued by small and medium-sized firms (Jan. 1997), and non-guaranteed convertible bonds issued by large companies (Jan. 1997)
–Residents are allowed to invest in overseas securities via beneficiary certificates (1993)
–Abolition of the ceiling on the domestic institutional investors' overseas portfolio investment (1995)
–Foreign commercial loans are allowed without government approval as far as they meet the guideline established in May 1995
–Private companies engaged in major infrastructure projects are allowed to borrow overseas to pay for domestic construction costs (Jan. 1997)
–Liberalization of borrowings related to foreign direct investments (Jan. 1997)

5) POLICY LOANS & CREDIT CONTROL
–A planned termination of all policy loans by 1997 is announced (1993)
   : a step-wise reduction in policy loans to specific sectors (e.g., export industries and small and medium-sized firms)
–Simplifying and slimming down of the controls on the share of bank's loans to major conglomerates in its total loans

pressure or the forces of globalization. Direct pressures were applied mainly but not exclusively by the US that tried to force market-opening measures on the countries with which it was running bilateral trade deficits since the mid-1980s, leading to gradual opening of the markets for cigarettes, automobiles, agricultural products, financial services, and so on. Of greater significance was the broad globalization trend in the world economy as manifested in, for instance, the Uruguay Round negotiations. With its economy highly depen-dent on exports, Korea had to take steps to be in the mainstream of these developments. The decision to apply for a membership in the OECD was noth-ing but a decision to embrace globalization wholeheartedly. Creating an envi-ronment for freer capital movement and international investment was the *quid pro quo* of Korea's accession to OECD. There was a vocal opposition to applying for a membership, pointing to the dangers of capital account liberal-ization given the backward state of the domestic financial industry. But the government was determined to go ahead with its *segyehwa* policy.

The third source is the internal economic changes that the success of the government-led growth has brought about. The growing complexity of the industrial structure and the inevitably increasing integration of the economy into the global markets made the bureaucratic coordination and control increasingly ineffective or inefficient. An indirect evidence for this is the continuous rise in the incremental capital-output ratio over the years (Kim and Hong, 1997). The bureaucratic control of the economy produced enormous concentration of economic power into the hands of *chaebol* and a deeply flawed financial system. This led to a broad consensus on the need to reform, although it may be pointed out that the US-educated economists played an important role in setting economic liberalization as the priority agenda of reform.

Although it was a severe economic crisis of 1979–80 that prompted the move toward liberalization, it is fair to say that the impetus for liberalization can ultimately be traced to the economic success of the illiberal *dirigist* policy regime. Both the internal changes and the external pressures had a lot to do with the economic success. In particular, the large current account surpluses in the years between 1986–89 invited trade frictions with the US that was put-ting pressure on Korea to open up its markets. Furthermore, this translated into excess liquidity under the system of tight foreign exchange control which required all foreign exchange to be surrendered to the central bank and se-verely restricted uses of foreign exchange. The difficulties of monetary con-trol led to relaxation of foreign exchange control, which in turn made it difficult to control investment.

That the economic success rather than a failure provided the underlying force behind liberalization perhaps explains the very gradual and piecemeal nature of the liberalization process in Korea. The good side of this was that there was a strong dose of pragmatism in the liberalization process, but at the same time it created ample room for the vested-interests groups to intervene in and disfigure the process.

Liberalization Gone Awry

In the wake of the financial crisis in Korea, its economic institutions have been thoroughly discredited. From the reliability of government statistics and corporate accounts to the soundness of the financial system and the efficiency of corporate governance system—particularly, the *chaebol* system—all were deeply questioned. Korea's labor market institutions were also found lacking in flexibility. At the heart of the weak institutions, it is claimed, is the moral hazard in lending (Krugman, 1998). In the process of guiding industrial development by active industrial policies, the Korean government ended up extending implicit government guarantees to the financial institutions and the large corporations, and this encouraged excessive lending and risk taking, feeding into a financial bubble (Kim, 1998). And the laxity in prudential regulations and supervision of the financial institutions allowed the risky bubble to develop unchecked.

No doubt this view misses many important aspects of the Korean crisis. The moral hazard story is also contested as an accurate description of the reality that prevailed in Korea (Chang, 1998). More than anything else, the instability of the international financial system itself—as manifested in the international lending boom in East Asia and the subsequent panic—was an important part of the problem and aggravated whatever moral hazard problems that existed in the domestic economy. It is nonetheless true that there were serious domestic weaknesses, which had been causing a string of major bankruptcies before the onset of the currency crisis.

The irony is that the mainstream view of the Korean economy has ascribed its successes to the free market policies: competition, openness and neutral incentives. This interpretation sits uneasily with the view that the rampant moral hazard created by government industrial policies caused the present financial crisis. It was in fact the revisionists who argued that Korea's secret to success was the industrial policy implemented by selective protection and government control of finance. They argue that liberalization policies pursued in the 1990s weakened the institutions of bureaucratic discipline, making the economy more vulnerable to bubbles and panics (Chang, 1998; Lim, 1998). In this view, the moral hazard amplified by the government interventions in Korea used to be checked by the bureaucratic control over the financial institutions and large corporations, but liberalization policies have, by dismantling the control, exacerbated the moral hazard problems. The rapid rise of overseas borrowing and investment as well as the relaxation of the entry barriers to strategic industries that led to over-capacity are cited to support this view.

The problem with the revisionists is that they highlight only the positive side of the industrial policy and downplay its problems. To begin with, it was a severe economic crisis of 1979–80 that prompted the move toward liberalization. This casts doubts on the implicit assumption that all would have been well had liberalization not taken place. Furthermore, as discussed earlier, the very success of government-led growth produced changes in political and economic environment that made liberalization inevitable. The decline of the potential growth rates in the 1990s is also a sign that the past success could not be continued without modifying the institutional mechanisms. With growth largely dependent on input accumulation and little on increasing efficiency with which given resources are used, the law of diminishing returns had begun to set in (Krugman, 1994).

If it is accepted that a shift from bureaucratic discipline toward a greater reliance on market discipline was necessary, one could place blame on too slow and incomplete liberalization. In spite of all the liberalization measures, it is quite evident that the market discipline on investment allocation and firm survival has not been adequate. This is, we would argue, a problem stemming not from the speed or comprehensiveness of liberalization but from the distortions present in the process of liberalization.

Especially problematic was the liberalization of the cross-border financial flows without installing proper safeguards and supervision. The consequence was a rapid accumulation of foreign debt, particularly short-term debt, and a growing list of highly risky financial investments. While the government bears a large portion of responsibility for this, at a deeper level it reflected the increasing influence of the *chaebol* sector on economic policy. They were the driving force behind the capital account liberalization measures that would allow them to borrow freely cheaper funds from abroad to feed their expansionary ambitions. They also gained control of much of the non-bank financial sector and pushed for more deregulation in domestic finance, many of them ending up creating huge financial messes.[2]

The winding down of industrial policy was also mishandled because of *chaebol* influence on the government. The infamous Samsung Automobile case is illustrative. The liberalization impetus led the government to allow Samsung to enter the auto industry, reversing its earlier decision against Samsung. This exacerbated the over-capacity problem. The Samsung auto project, even without the industry-level problem, was nonsense, as its plant was to be built on reclaimed land that needed massive fortifying in a calculated move to give political benefits to President Kim Young Sam. Had the government truly liberalized its industrial policy, Samsung would have at least chosen a different site. This case is a tragedy born out of partial liberalization and the corrupt relationship between the *chaebol* and the government.

Chaebol firms became stronger under the policy of liberalization in the 1980s, and by the beginning of the 1990s strong enough to challenge the government in many ways (Yoo, 1997). Even though they were championing the cause of liberalization and deregulation, their position was not a coherent liberalization at all. They pushed for liberalization to gain greater freedom of business, but wanted to keep their unfair advantages they enjoyed. Maintain-

---

2. In 1990 the top-five *chaebol* groups had 36.5 percent of the shares of life insurance companies, 26.3 percent of the shares of the securities companies, and 12.8 percent of the shares of the merchant banking companies (Yoo, 1994).

ing restrictive regulations on inward FDI while turning permissive in cross-border borrowing and outward FDI, for instance, can only be explained by the influence of *chaebol.* Sometimes utilizing their collusive ties with politicians and bureaucrats and sometimes leveraging their enormous influence on the economy (so-called "too big to fail"), *chaebol* groups did much to distort the liberalization process and at the same time created vulnerabilities in the financial system.

2. Macroeconomic Developments and Income Distribution

Overview of the Macroeconomic Developments in the Liberalization Era

The first half of the 1980s was a period of stabilization and recovery from the crisis of 1979–1980. The government pursued disinflation with restrictive monetary and fiscal policy on the one hand and forceful policies to reduce wage costs and financial costs on the other.[3] Aided also by the recovery of rice production in 1981 and the falling oil price, the inflation rate declined rapidly from 29 percent in 1980 to only 7 percent in 1982 and to the 2–3 percent level during 1983–86 (Fig. 1). In order to tackle the large current account deficits and the foreign debt problem (Korea was the fourth largest debtor country

FIGURE 1: GDP growth and Inflation, 1980–97

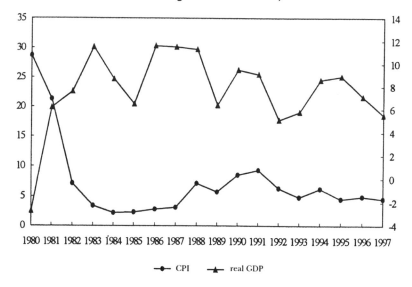

━●━ CPI   ━▲━ real GDP

---

3. However, it must be noted, the government gave a push to the economy by expansionary macroeconomic policies in the second half of 1980 after seeing the plunge of aggregate demand in the first half of the year. This pattern was repeated in 1998.

among developing countries), the government devalued the Won by 36 percent in 1980 and took care to maintain external competitiveness. It is notable that the much-maligned HCI program paid off at this time, contributing mightily to easing the balance of payment problems and the structural change of the exports. Helped by the successful stabilization and a timely fiscal stimulus in 1981, the economy recovered quickly, though the overall growth performance of the first half of the 1980s was mediocre by Korean historical standards.

The period between 1986 and 1988 is known as a period of "Three-lows Prosperity." The three lows include the low world interest rate, the low oil price and the low value of the Won. The most significant was the real effective depreciation of the Won that resulted from the nominal exchange rate depreciation against the dollar, the decline of domestic inflation and, most importantly, the Yen-*daka*. The steep appreciation of the Yen after the Plaza agreement helped improve the competitiveness of Korean industries competing against Japanese goods in third markets. The result of the favorable international environment provided by the three lows was three consecutive years of about 12 percent annual growth and large trade surpluses that amounted to 4 to 8 percent of GDP (Fig. 1 and Fig. 2). This was the first time ever that Korea enjoyed substantial and continuous current account surpluses. Thanks to the hyper-rapid growth, the unemployment rate declined from 4 percent in 1985 to slightly above 2 percent in 1988.

The year 1987 marked a watershed in the transition from authoritarian to democratic rule. Having achieved peaceful democratization on top of extraordinary economic success, the nation was overflowing with confidence when it

FIGURE 2: Current Account and Real Effective Exchange Rate, 1980–97

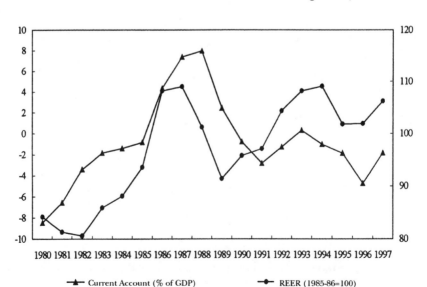

hosted the Seoul Olympics in 1988. But the seeds of trouble had already been sown. The political change quickly translated into an equivalent change in labor relations. Labor repression of the authoritarian era gave way to confrontational unionism (see You, 1995). Steep rises in nominal wages averaging 22 percent during 1988–90 followed, just when the excessive monetary expansion brought about by the large current account surpluses of the three-low years was rekindling the inflationary impulses in the economy. Inflation started to pick up, reaching 7 percent in 1988 and accelerating to over 9 percent in 1991, while a speculative boom in real estate developed. To make matters worse, the Won appreciated against the dollar under U.S. pressure by 24 percent between 1986–89. The consequent appreciation of the real effective exchange rate turned the current account surplus into a deficit by 1990 (Fig. 2). The government responded with restrictive policies in 1991, causing a reduction in inflation and lackluster growth performance in 1992–93 (Fig. 1).

President Kim Young Sam's government (1993–98) pursued an expansionary macroeconomic policy purportedly to support the ill-fated reforms discussed in the previous section. Helped by the expansionary policy, the economy recovered to high growth rates in 1994–95. However, by 1996, the economy once again began to slow down and serious macroeconomic imbalances began to develop. First, there was a large terms of trade shock, particularly the collapse of the price of memory chips in 1995–96, that did a great damage to exports. Second, there was real appreciation of the currency as capital flowed in following liberalization of the capital account. Finally, there was excessive investment, including notable instances of misguided and excessive investments by *chaebol* firms, which created severe financial difficulties.

Macroeconomics of the Financial Crisis

The immediate cause of the financial crisis of 1997–98 was the rapid build-up of foreign debt in the preceding years. Since important capital account liberalization measures began to be implemented in 1993, financial institutions and private corporations went on a borrowing binge. Especially alarming was the rapid increase in the short-term debt. During the period between 1993 and 1996, short-term debt held by financial institutions increased from $11.4 billion to $39.0 billion, while the increase for private enterprises was from $7.8 billion to $22.0 billion. The long-term debt by these sectors also showed about a two-fold increase in the same period. As a consequence, the total foreign debt at the end of 1997 stood at the astonishingly high level of $154.4 billion, which is almost five times of the total foreign debt at the end of 1990, $31.8 billion.

It is apparent that the rise in foreign indebtedness is closely tied to the capital account liberalization. But, what was it financing? Part of it was used, to be sure, to finance the current account deficit caused by a combination of the terms of trade shock and the real appreciation. The counter-part to this was the increasing gap between domestic saving and domestic investment.

Exhibiting a typical consequence of liberalization, the private saving rate declined from 33.7 percent in 1993 to 30.6 percent in 1996, while domestic investment boomed to increase from 35.1 percent of GDP in 1993 to 38.4 percent in 1996.

A decomposition of demand growth is shown in Fig. 3.[4] From this we can see that the government sector has consistently restrained demand growth and that the foreign sector in general kept pace with the output growth except during the "Three-low" boom. Investment demand, in relation to savings, has been leading the demand growth for most of the period. However, it is notably high in the years leading up to the crisis. This decomposition exercise shows that the chief culprit of the financial crisis must be found in over-investment financed by a rapid build-up of foreign debt.

However, the problems generated by capital account liberalization went further than the reduction of the saving rate, real appreciation and excessive investment due to capital inflows. A large part of the capital inflows was being used to finance outward direct and portfolio investment. Encouraged by the *segyehwa* policy and taking advantage of the relaxation of the capital flow restrictions, overseas investment became popular sport among large Korean firms. As shown in Fig. 4, the outward FDI rose from $1.3 billion in 1993 to $4.7

FIGURE 3: Foreign Direct Investment: 1980–98

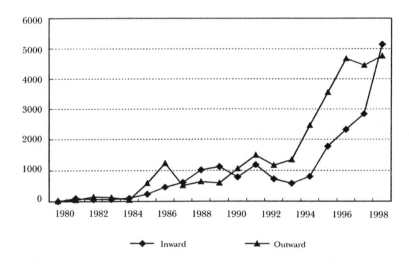

4. Considering an economy that imports only inputs and no finished products, the output, X, can be expressed as injections, divided by leakages as follows:
$$X = C + I + G + E = (I + G + E)/(s + t + m)$$
where s, t and m are private savings, taxes and imports scaled by output. Expressing this in terms of the "own" multiplier effects, we have
$$X = a_1(I/s) + a_2(G/t) + a_3(E/m),$$
where $a_1 = s/(s+t+m)$, $a_2 = t/(s+t+m)$ and $a_3 = m/(s+t+m)$.

FIGURE 4: Portfolio Investment: 1980–98

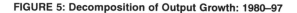

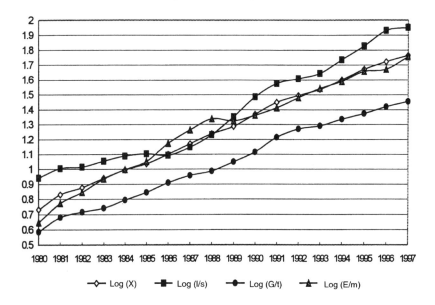

FIGURE 5: Decomposition of Output Growth: 1980–97

billion in 1996, overwhelming the inward FDI flow. Many of the overseas direct investment projects proved to be costly, but the financial institutions, particularly the merchant banks with no experience in international finance, played an even more dangerous game of adventurous financial investment abroad. Foreign portfolio assets rose from only $0.5 billion in 1993 to almost $6 billion in 1996 (Fig. 5).

Although the large current account deficit began to shrink as the real exchange rate gradually depreciated in 1997, it was too late for Korea to escape the wave of Asian currency crises that started from Thailand in mid-1997. Internally, a string of major corporate bankruptcies piled up huge non-performing loans in the financial system, inviting a credit crunch. Externally, the rapid accumulation of short-term foreign debt left the country vulnerable to a run on its currency. By November 1997, the attack on the Korean Won was in full force and Korea had to go to the IMF.

Korea at this time experienced the first-ever true change of government by election, and the new Kim Dae-jung government began to implement the IMF-mandated reform and restructuring. In 1998 the economy was in deep recession, recording an almost 6 percent decline in GDP and a rise of the unemployment rate to above 7 percent. However, helped by the record current account surplus, Korea piled up foreign exchange reserves of more than 40 billion dollars at the end of 1998 from less than a billion dollars at the time of the crisis. Furthermore, the financial market has stabilized and the economy is exhibiting a strong recovery in 1999.

Liberalization, Growth and Income Distribution

Due to the gradual nature of liberalization in Korea, it is hard to identify its effect on growth and income distribution until the early 1990s. Up to this point there was no discernable worsening of income distribution as a consequence of globalization. If anything, the most significant change in income distribution took place in the years following the democratization of 1987, and that was the significant rise in the labor share of income (Fig. 6). Two factors seem to account for this. One is the fall of unemployment, reaching full employment for the first time.

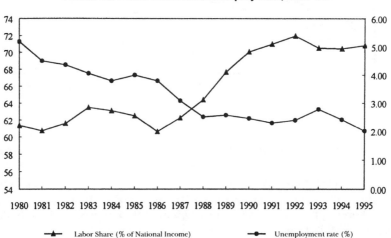

FIGURE 6: Labor Share and Unemployment, 1980–95

The other is the sudden rise in union strength in the aftermath of the collapse of the authoritarian regime of labor repression.

There is another notable fact regarding the labor share of income. Although Fig. 6 shows the trend only from 1980, the same series goes back to the mid-1960s and exhibits little change in the labor share of income over the long term until 1987. Remaining below 70 percent, the labor share of income in Korea was quite low by international standards. The counter-part to this is the high share of profits, to which high rates of capital accumulation have been ascribed (You, 1998).

The substantial increase in the labor share of income since 1987 signified a change in the nature of the growth process. Previously, growth was profit-led and investment-led. This was to change to a wage-led, consumption-led growth. Such signs appeared at first, but it was something that could be sustained only if followed by appropriate changes in the institutional mechanisms of savings and investment. Despite the decline in the profit share, however, the corporations went on to invest at very high rates. This translated into a rise in corporate indebtedness. The corporate sector debt to GDP ratio rose from 1.09 in 1988 to 1.63 in 1996. Traditionally a high leverage ratio within a firm can leave it highly vulnerable to unfavorable shocks.

The failure of the transformation of the growth process can be explained in another way. The previous input-driven growth needed to be transformed into productivity-driven growth. The decline in the growth rate of the labor force as well as the decline in the profit share of income implied that rapid growth based on accumulation of inputs would be difficult to continue. However, the firms failed to generate sufficiently high rates of productivity growth. The *Chaebol* groups responded to the steep increases in wages and unionization by subcontracting and outsourcing rather than improving productivity (see below). Subcontracting was used as a means to reduce labor costs, since there was a large wage differential between big *chaebol* firms and smaller subcontracting firms. With the latter's survival dependent on orders from the *chaebol* firms, their profits were squeezed. Instead of developing into a technically progressive and innovative sector, subcontracting firms were just fighting to survive on the margin while the productivity gap between them and the *chaebol* firms increased further in the 1990s.

The impact of liberalization and globalization on growth and distribution in Korea is closer to the typical story in the period since 1993 when a series of liberalization measures for capital account transactions were implemented. Initially, increased capital inflows and consequent real appreciation of the currency helped to raise growth rates. Soon, however, current account deficits and accumulation of external indebtedness followed. The problem was made worse because the large capital inflows caused the government to be complacent and fail to adjust to the terms of trade shock. Although it is doubtful that a drastic collapse of growth as has happened was inevitable, at least a significant slowdown of growth was bound to happen. This experience once again demonstrates the difficulties of managing capital account liberalization.

Under the IMF program in 1998, Korea experienced a recession of unprecedented severity. Even though growth resumed in 1999, the adverse impact on income distribution would linger on much longer. This is discussed below.

3. Labor Market Developments and Wage Distribution

Wage Inequality

It is well known that Korea has successfully reduced wage inequality while achieving rapid economic growth. Three observations and qualifications are in order regarding this success story. First, the steady improvement in wage distribution in the 1980s and up to early 1990s stopped around 1992, and is likely to have been reversed since the outbreak of the financial crisis in 1997. Second, the chief reason for the reduction in wage inequality was the continued rise in the share of college graduates in the labor force. However, since 1992, the persistent shift in the labor supply toward a more highly educated workforce has failed to narrow wage inequality. Third, in spite of the overall improvement in wage distribution, the wage differential between large and small establishments has widened rapidly and converged to that of Japan, which is well known for its dual labor market.

Fig. 7 shows the changing trend in overall wage inequality. The Gini Coefficient in 1981 was .355, it decreased continuously to .287 in 1992, and has since stabilized (Fields and Yoo, 1998). The ratio of the bottom decile wage earner to the top decile wage earner has steadily risen since it hit its lowest point in 1992. The wage differential by education level also shows a similar pattern. The wages of those who graduated from junior college, high school, middle school or below rose steadily relative to those of college graduates before stabilizing around 1992. Recent studies show that the change in the educational wage differential up to the early 1990s can be attributed to the rapid increase in college graduates in line with the expanded college enrollment quotas (Kim and Topel, 1995; Lee and Kim, 1997). This decline in the educational wage differentials was the main factor behind the improvement in overall wage inequality.

It is important to note that the narrowing of the wage differential by education stopped in the early 1990s. Although the rate of expansion of college education has remained as high since the early 1990s, it has not led to an improvement of the educational wage differential. The overall wage distribution has also ceased to improve. We suspect that it is caused by a structural shift in labor demand resulting from liberalization. Given the steady increase of the ratio of college graduates among labor force from 6.7 percent in 1980 to 12.5 percent in 1988, 17.5 percent in 1993, and up to 23.4 percent in 1998, the sudden pause of the downward trend in the college premium must be associated with demand shocks in favor of the highly educated. There are some indications of such an increase in the demand for the highly educated

FIGURE 7: Wage Inequality: Gini Coefficient and Ratio of 90th Percentile
Wage Earner to 10the Percentile Wage Earner

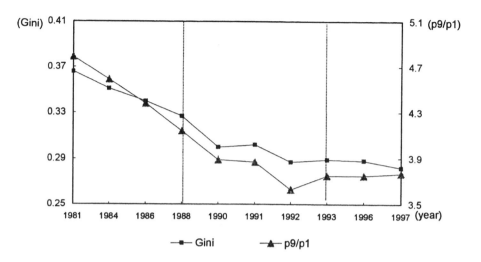

Source: Fields and Yoo (1998)

since 1992. During the period from 1992 to 1996, the increase in employment in finance, insurance, real estate and business services amounted to 30.2 percent of the total employment increase during the same period. This compares with only 18.4 percent during the period from 1988 to 1992.

Along with the decline of the wage premium for college graduates, the wage differentials across gender and industry have also declined since the 1980s. As shown in Fig. 8, however, the size wage differential in the manufacturing sector has steadily grown since 1980. The average wage at small establishments of 5–19 employees declined to 51 percent of that of large establishments with 300 employees or more in 1996 from 66 percent in 1980. This relative decline has been taking place throughout the 1980s and 1990s, except for a slight reprieve during 1988–1993. The picture hardly changes even if we control for the composition of workers in terms of gender, age and education level.[5] The anomaly of worsening size wage differential in the midst of overall improvement in wage distribution in the 1980s is closely tied to the peculiarities of the industrial structure in Korea.

---

5. The average wage in establishments with 10 to 29 employees declined from 93 percent of that in establishments with 500 employees or more in 1980 to 70 percent in 1989. It rose again to 81 percent in 1992 and then stabilized (Lee and Kim, 1997).

FIGURE 8: Size Wage Differential of Manufacturing Establishments:
Relative to Large Establishments (300 or more employees)

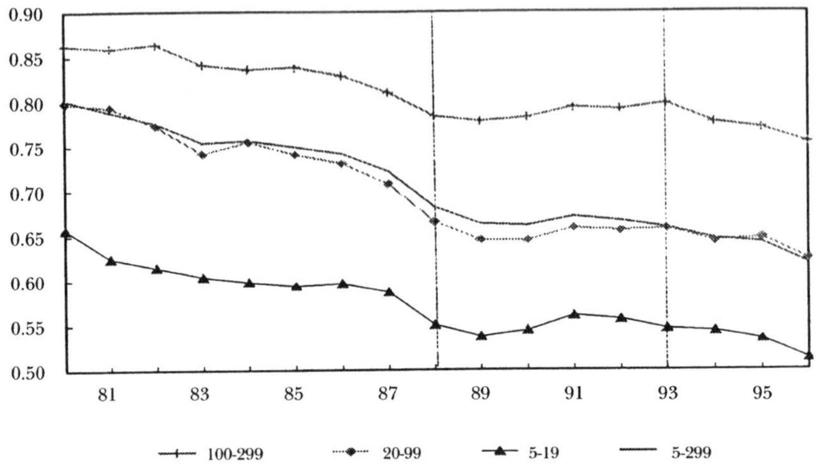

Source: Report on Mining and Manufacturing Survey, National Statistical Office, Republic of Korea, each year.

Chaebol System and the Enterprise Unions

The wage differentials between large firms and SMEs are directly linked to the problems of *chaebol* and enterprise unionism. A developed-country equivalent to enterprise unionism in Korea exists only in Japan. Labor unions in most developed countries are organized at the industry level or at the national level. But in Korea, labor unions are organized at the company level so that it is very difficult for Korean labor unions to bargain at the industry-wide level. Consequently, the strategy of taking the wage out of competition is ruled out.

The union organization rate in Korea is strongly correlated with firm size. In the case of companies with 10–29 employees in the manufacturing sector, the unionization rate is 0.9 percent, and 5.4 percent at companies with 30–99 employees. Compared to these figures, the unionization rate is as high as 62.1 percent at companies with 5,000–15,000 employees, and 76 percent at companies with more than 15,000 workers.

The industrial scene in Korea is dominated by large firms belonging to *chaebol* groups that enjoy economic rents in the product market and easy access in the financial market, not infrequently aided by government regulations and/or implicit protection. Most of these firms are unionized and pay substantial wage premiums. It seems fair to say the wage premium of large companies is made possible by the economic rents acquired by *chaebol.* The enterprise unions in large companies are sharing these rents with the firms.

Given the steady growth of *chaebol* during the 1980s, the hypothesis of rent sharing between *chaebol* and the enterprise unions seems to offer an explanation for the increase in the size wage differential. However, it does not render a plausible explanation of the stabilization in the size wage differential during the period between 1988 and 1992 when union organizing and strike actives were at their peak in Korea. One important observation that offers a clue to this puzzle is that *chaebol* firms began, in a massive way, to resort to subcontracting with SMEs in order to evade active unionism during this period.

The ratio of subcontracting firms among SMEs has continuously increased from 23.2 percent in 1981 to 63.2 percent in 1992.[6] In particular, the period between 1988 and 1992 saw the most noticeable increase in the share of subcontracting firms from 36.5 percent to 63.2 percent. This active subcontracting strategy steeply increased labor demand by SMEs and therefore their wage levels. This is why the size wage differential was stable during this period despite the huge wage increases in large firms due to rent sharing. We elaborate this point by looking into the size structure of manufacturing establishments below.

Size Structure of Manufacturing Establishments

The size structure of manufacturing establishments has changed significantly since the 1980s. The workforce in the entire manufacturing industry reached its highest number of 3.1 million in 1988 from 2.0 million in 1981, declining to 2.8 million in 1992. Within the manufacturing sector, the employment share of large establishments has shrunk since 1980, as seen in Fig. 9. Employment in large companies comprised 48.9 percent of the manufacturing workforce in 1981, declining to 30.8 percent in 1996. While a similar pattern is seen to a lesser degree among medium-sized companies with 100–299 employees, the trend is the complete opposite for the smaller companies employing less than 99 employees. The latter firms have experienced a large increase in their workforce.

Within this overall shift of the size structure, three stages can be distinguished. The first stage is the period of 1980–1987. During this time, the size wage differential widened. The employment share of large establishments slowly decreased, while that of small companies employing 20–99 workers substantially increased. The second stage, 1988–1992, saw the stabilization of the size wage differential and a drastic increase in the employment share of small establishments, particularly those with 5–19 employees. Therefore, a natural explanation for the stabilization of the size wage differential is the steep increase in

---

6. A firm is defined to be a subcontracting firm when more than 80 percent of its total sales consist of sales to other firms, with less than 20 percent of its sales going to end consumers.

FIGURE 9: The Composition Ratio of Manufacturing Employment

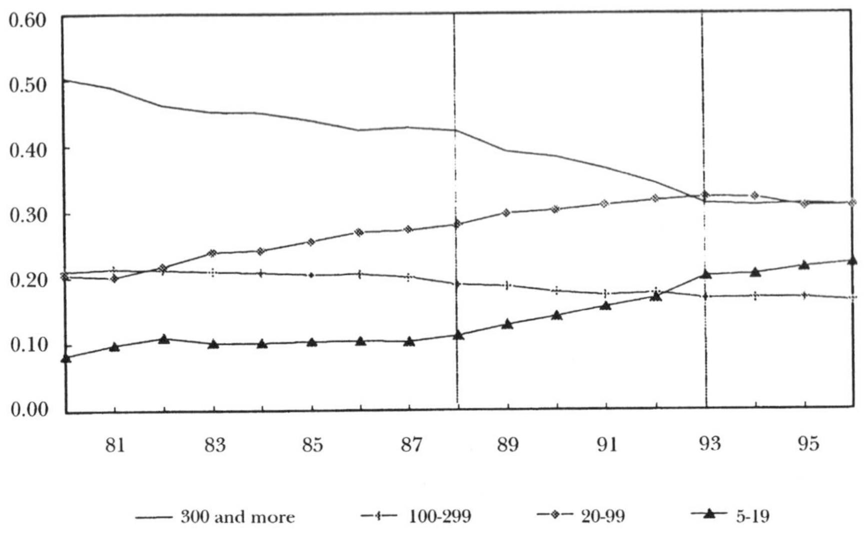

Source: Report on Mining and Manufacturing Survey, National Statistical Office, Republic of Korea, each year.

the demand for labor by small firms and the consequent rise in the wages paid by these firms. Further evidence for this is seen in the changes of the labor shortage rate. During 1988–1992, the labor shortage rate for SMEs was exceptionally high, exceeding 10 percent.[7] The third stage refers to the period between 1993 to the outbreak of the financial crisis in 1997. The wage differential between large companies and SMEs began to widen again during this time, while the overall size distribution of workers changed little. The employment share of large companies no longer decreased in the period of four to five years before the financial crisis, marking the end of the reallocation of labor between large companies and SMEs.

During the whole period, the ratio of subcontracting firms has continuously increased. In particular, the second stage, in which the employment share of small companies drastically increased, saw the most noticeable increase in subcontracting firms. Large companies were taking advantage of the relatively low wages of union-free SMEs by subcontracting with smaller companies. The changes in the size structure were, to a large extent, initiated by the large firms in their pursuit of union avoidance strategy.

---

7. Ministry of Labor in Korea conducts a survey on labor shortages of establishments with ten or more workers, asking about the number of employees needed to be recruited.

The changes in size structure of Korean manufacturing establishments can be compared to the Japanese case, where the issue of the duality between large companies and SMEs has long been raised. Table 2 shows that the wage differential between large companies and SMEs in Korea reached a level similar to Japan.[8] The difference is that in Japan, the wage differential remained stable, whereas in Korea it widened considerably. Of even greater concern is the productivity differential across firm size in Korea. In Japan, the productivity differential between large companies and SMEs showed little change between 1981 and 1995, while in Korea the differential widened substantially from 51 percent to 38.9 percent during that period.[9] It is also interesting to note that the employment share of large establishments (300 or more employees) in Korea has approached a level similar to that of Japan.

The widening productivity differential reveals a crucial weakness in the structure of Korean industries. Much of the SME sector in Korea has served mainly as subcontractors for *chaebol* firms and is unable to compete in the world market because of low productivity. This results in an unstable industrial structure that relies very heavily on *chaebol* firms. Such an industrial structure not only increases the vulnerability of the Korean economy to external shocks but also adversely affects the wage distribution. This problem

Table 2. Size Structure of Manufacturing Establishments: Korea and Japan

	KOREA		JAPAN (unit: percent)	
	1981	1995	1981	1995
Wage Differential Between Large Enterprises and SMEs[1]	78.9	64.3	62.1	63.7
Productivity Differential Between Large Enterprises and SMEs[2]	51.0	38.9	50.2	48.8
Employment Share of Large Enterprises (more than 300 employees)	48.9	31.1	28.1	28.1

1. Average Wage of SMEs as a Percentage of Average Wage of Large Enterprises (300 and more employees).
2. Average Labor Productivity of SMEs as a Percentage of Average Productivity of Large Enterprises (300 and more employees).
Source: Census of Manufactures, Ministry of International Trade and Industry, Japan, each year; Report on Mining and Manufacturing Survey, National Statistical Office, Republic of Korea, each year.

---

8. The Census of Manufactures of the two countries are very similar except that the Japanese census includes establishments with four or more employees whereas the Korean census contains those with five or more employees.

9. The widening of productivity differential between large firms and SMEs occurred steadily since 1980 except for the boom period between 1986 and 1988.

calls for appropriate competition and industrial policies. The low wages of SMEs should no longer serve as a major source of competitiveness for *chaebol* firms. For this, the enforcement of the Fair Trade Law must be strengthened and the support for SMEs must be increased, by fostering, for instance, the regional infrastructure of technological and human resource development for SMEs.

Economic Crisis and the Labor Market

It is fair to say that Korea did not experience major labor market difficulties in the process of globalization before the financial crisis in 1997. The long-term trend has been one of falling unemployment, rising wage share and improving wage distribution, although, as we noted above, the *chaebol* problem has grown worse. However, the outbreak of the crisis was followed by a sudden increase in unemployment and poverty, a drastic fall in the labor share and rising income inequalities.

The unemployment rate in 1998 reached 6.8 percent, the highest rate ever since 1967. Furthermore, the pattern of unemployment and job loss has not been neutral. The unskilled were the hardest hit by the financial crisis. During the 1997–98 period, jobs for production workers and laborers were reduced by 12.7 percent whereas professional and managerial jobs increased by 1.3 percent. The share of college graduates among the unemployed decreased from 23.3 percent in 1997 to 19.5 percent in 1998. Among different industries, construction and manufacturing have experienced the largest job loss, each losing 21.3 percent and 13.2 percent of jobs in 1998. This uneven impact worsened inequalities and aggravated social problems.

Poverty also exacerbated after the crisis. According to the Korea Development Institute (KDI), the proportion of households below the poverty line has almost tripled from 2.4 percent in the third quarter of 1997 to 7.5 percent in the third quarter of 1998. Although other institutions such as the Korea Statistical Office and the World Bank reported diverse estimates on the proportion of households below the poverty line, they all reveal similar skyrocketing, about two and a half-fold increase, of the poverty ratio.[10]

The recent government survey on income distribution among urban working households reveals a significant worsening of income distribution in 1998 (Table 3). The average income of the top (tenth) decile income earners rose by 4 percent, whereas that of the bottom (first) decile income earners declined by 22.8 percent. While all other income classes experienced

---

10. By the estimates of the Korea Statistical Office, the proportion of households below the poverty line increased from 1.9 percent to 4.9 percent during the period, whereas the World Bank estimated the increase from 8.5 percent to 22.9 percent. The large differences in the estimated levels of the poverty are mainly due to the different definitions of the poverty line.

**TABLE 3: Change in Urban Household
Monthly Income Distribution: 1997–1998**

(unit: won, percent)

Decline 1	2	3	4	5	6	7	8	9	10
1997									
avg. 729,243	1,164,951	1,435,441	1,667,593	1,900,159	2,155,964	2,460,398	2,847,124	3,419,821	5,089,836
1998									
avg. 562,741	1,005,431	1,255,177	1,481,475	1,703,445	1,951,006	2,252,089	2,628,348	3,193,028	5,294,871
Increase									
rate −22.8	−13.7	−12.6	−11.2	−10.4	−9.5	−8.5	−7.7	−6.6	4.0

Source: National Statistical Office (1998, 1999)

a decline in their incomes, only the top decile income earners saw an increase in their average income. This is probably due to the high interest rate in the first half of 1988. For the same reason, if households headed by employers and self-employed are included, the worsening of income distribution could be even more pronounced. Whether these recent developments will lead to a permanent reversal of the favorable long-term trends remains to be seen.

The practice among large Korean companies of generally not recruiting experienced mid-career workers is an important factor in the future development of the Korean labor market. This practice is closely related to the *hobong* (seniority wage) system, an economy-wide compensation scheme that ties wages to age and experience. Big companies are reluctant to recruit mid-career workers because they have to pay high wages according to seniority. This characteristic of internal labor market explains the virtual absence of a labor market for mid-career workers in large companies. As a result, those who are laid off from big companies in the process of restructuring that the financial crisis has necessitated will have difficulty finding employment in other big companies with comparable pay. This creates a concern that long-term unemployment may emerge as a chronic problem in the future.

The financial crisis also provided a major impetus for institutional changes toward a more flexible labor market.[11] Redundancy layoff that was previously scheduled to take effect in 1999 was immediately introduced after the crisis. Workers in large firms cannot enjoy *de facto* life-time employment any more.

The prospect of wage inequality does not seem bright, either. Four or five years before the crisis, the wage inequality had already reached its lowest point.

---

11. See You (1997) for a discussion on labor market flexibility in Korea.

The reduction in wage differential by education had stopped, but the widening of wage differential by size had resumed. In 1998, the average nominal wage decreased by 2.5 percent while the average real wage fell by 9.3 percent. The size wage differential also widened further. The average nominal wage in SMEs decreased by 2.5 percent in 1998, whereas that in large firms was reduced by only 1.1 percent. At the same time, the wage cuts fell more heavily to production workers. In the manufacturing sector, production workers' wages decreased by 4.1 percent compared to a 2.0 percent reduction of non-production workers' wages.

4. Developments in Social Policy

Social Expenditure

Unlike many Latin American countries where a fiscal squeeze forced cuts in social expenditure after financial crises, the crisis of 1997–98 provided a momentum for expanding social expenditure in Korea. This difference reflects not only that the traditionally conservative fiscal policy of the Korean government left ample room for deficit spending in a time of crisis but also that Korea had given very low priority to social policies before the crisis.

After the transition from authoritarian to democratic rule in 1987, the central government expenditure on social services in Korea gradually increased from 5.0 percent of GDP in 1980 to 7.8 percent in 1997. In particular, government expenditures in housing sharply expanded in the late 1980s and early 1990s with the implementation of the plan to construct two million government-sponsored housing units. In the mid-1990s, the expenditure on education also increased as the government committed itself to raising it to 5 percent of GNP. Despite the increases in social expenditures, they represent a relatively meager proportion of GDP by international standards. Social service spending by the Korean government amounts to around 7 percent of GDP. This fares badly even in comparison with Southeast Asian countries like Indonesia and Malaysia, which spend around 11 percent of GDP, not to mention the spending of advanced countries.

The composition of social expenditure shows that the portion spent on health care and social welfare is much lower than that of developed countries (See Table 4). The expenditure on education appears high. This is because most of the educational expenditure is centrally financed, leaving local governments with unusually small budgets for education. National defense expenditure is very high, given that Korea's compulsory draft system reduces personnel expenditures to far below the opportunity cost. High government subsidies to farmers resulted in large expenditures on agriculture, forestry, and fisheries. These expenditures have contributed to the government's reluctance to expand social policy aggressively.

**TABLE 4: Government Expenditure by Function:
Consolidated Central Government**

(unit: percent)

	Korea	U.S.A	Japan	Germany	Italy
Education	19.6	1.8	6.0	0.8	7.4
Health	0.7	19.7	1.61	6.8	9.7
Social Security & Welfare	12.2	28.8	36.8	45.3	35.1
Housing & Comm. Amenities	2.5	2.7	13.8	0.6	1.1
General Public Services	5.1	8.4	2.4	8.2	6.9
Defense	16.3	15.9	4.1	6.4	3.2
Public Order & Safety	5.8	1.3	1.2	0.3	–
Rec., Culture., Relig., Affairs	0.9	0.3	0.1	0.3	0.8
Economic Affairs & Services	21.6	5.2	3.3	9.7	12.0
Fuel & Energy	0.8	0.3	–	0.1	–
Agric., Forestry, Fishing, Hunt	6.6	1.0	1.1	0.9	1.2
Mining, Manuf., & Construct	2.4	0.1	1.6	1.4	2.2
Transportation & Communication	10.0	2.4	0.3	4.2	6.3
Other Economic Affairs & Serv.	1.8	1.5	0.3	3.1	2.3
Other Expenditures	15.4	15.7	30.6	11.6	21.4
Of which; Interest Payments	2.5	15.3	–	5.1	14.5
Total Expenditure	**100.0**	**100.0**	**100.0**	**100.0**	**100.0**

Source: Government Finance Statistics yearbook, IMF, each year.

Major Problems in Social Policy

The low expenditure of the government is only a small part of the social policy problem in Korea. The social services sector has lagged far behind the other sectors of Korean economy because of the continuing legacy of the "growth first, distribution next" economic development strategy of the past. In particular, there are many problems in social policy regarding policy priorities, the government's role, and government capabilities.

Education

In Korea, expenditures on out-of-school private instruction are increasing in spite of the government's growing investment in education. Government statistics show that private instruction expenditures decreased in the years following the ban on private instruction in 1981. But by 1997, private instruction expenditures increased to 3 percent of GDP. In Korea, out-of-school tutoring begins even before elementary school as students prepare to compete for college admission.

Private instruction has serious implications for equal opportunity for education. Since its costs are borne by the individuals, those who are less well-off are deprived of the opportunity to obtain supplementary instruction. Given the serious nature of this problem, it has become a key policy issue. The problem seems largely attributable to poor education policies. The Ministry of Education in Korea has tightly regulated the admission procedures of the universities. The quota set by the government for university admission raises the labor market premium of university graduates.

Since college entrance is based mostly on written examinations, education in and out of the school is primarily aimed at nurturing test-taking skills. The reason why universities uniformly adopt the paper and pencil entrance examination is to ensure fairness in the admission selection, while any other method is considered subjective. In particular, the proposed admission method in which a teacher recommends students based on their school performance has not taken root, because the public does not consider this process sufficiently fair and objective. However, the responsibility for ensuring fairness in the admission selection process must reside with the universities. Instead of trying to be the guarantor of fairness, the government must reduce its regulatory role so that universities can experiment with various selection methods, accumulating necessary experience and building up reputation.

Moreover, the choices and voices of parents and students in schools have been very limited in the Korean education system. Korean private schools are not really private. In fact, so-called private schools are assigned students through a regional lottery system and the teachers receive salaries according to a nationwide schedule. Operating deficits of these private schools are fully subsidized by the government. School administration contains no element of parental initiative or participation at the local level. The decentralization of education in Korea is rather minimal as local education authority is financially dependent on the central government. The local education administration office is not headed by elected officers. The local educational board is dominated by career educators. Consequently, consumers have little influence on educational decisions. Hence, school education cannot meet the educational needs of the parents and students, leading them to seek private instruction.

In this regard, a disproportionately large burden of education expenses falls on the shoulder of the poor parents and students. Poor families in Korea suffer from both large costs of private instruction and low qualities of schooling.

Social Insurance

Social insurance has developed belatedly and gradually in Korea. Originally, social insurance benefits were granted to workers at big establishments. Universal health insurance emerged in 1989, while unemployment insurance became universal in January of 1999. The national pension plan also came to include the self-employed and the unemployed, making everyone eligible after April 1999. In addition, with disability insurance to be effective in 2001 for workers at companies with at least five employees, Korea will finally be transformed into a welfare society with universal coverage of major social insurance policies.

Despite the quantitative expansion, Korea's social welfare system suffers from important deficiencies. In the case of health insurance, coverage is extended to the entire population, but applied to only a small portion of the total medical expenditure. Total medical expenditure has been on the rise mainly due to the problems of the supplier-induced treatment of medical services. Rising medical expenditure is an unavoidable side effect of mandatory health insurance given the information asymmetry between patients and service providers. However, inadequate health care policies in Korea have made the problem more serious.

Universal health insurance covers less serious illnesses such as the common cold but does not apply to many forms of expensive treatment, including MRIs, for illnesses like cancer. Physicians prefer to provide services that promise a larger profit with prices not regulated by the insurance plan. The fee-for-service method in reimbursing the doctors encourages doctors to provide needless services. The formula for calculating the amount of reimbursement is also problematic. Compared to medication provision and check-up services, the reimbursement rate for skilled services such as treatment, advice, and surgery is very low, giving physicians incentive to prescribe a lot of medication and conduct excessive clinical tests. Health insurance is not the only area in which supplier-induced treatment is a problem. Unlike in other countries where doctors prescribe medication but pharmacists are in charge of selling them, pharmacists perform both roles in Korea. Hence, a pharmacist is also inclined to over-prescribe medication.

The poorer section of the population in particular falls victim to the problem of supplier-induced treatment both because of their limited financial ability and because of their disadvantaged position in the information asymmetry problem of health care.

Nor is the National Pension System free from problems. Low contribution rates compared to the benefit rates are creating a fiscal imbalance, and the inefficient management of the fund is adding to the system's fiscal woes. By 2023, the National Pension Plan is expected to go into deficit. The problem is worse in the case of the Occupational Pension Scheme, which covers civil servants, servicemen and teachers. It provides higher benefit rates than the National Pension Plan and there is no age restriction for pension eligibility. As seen in Table 5, the military pension was already exhausted in 1977 and has since operated on a fiscal deficit. The civil servants pension went into the red in 1998, and the entire fund is expected to disappear by 2003. As a result, the burden of making up for this shortage will fall on taxpayers.

Labor Market Policies

Before the economic crisis, the government put low priority on unemployment policies. The best unemployment policy was considered to be one that creates more jobs by accelerating economic growth. In addition, vocational and technical education and training were important policy tools for promoting economic growth. When the government was implementing the HCI drive in the mid-1970s, it made large-scale investments in technical high schools and vocational training centers. However, in the 1980s, the government shifted its

TABLE 5: Pension Scheme: Introduction, Deficit and Depletion

(unit: percent)

	National Pension Scheme	Occupational Pension Scheme		
		Civil Servant Pension Scheme	Military Pension Scheme	Private Teachers Pension Scheme
Introduction	1988	1960	1963	1975
Deficit*	2023	1988	1975	2015
Depletion*	2033	2003	1977	2022

* Note: Projections Made by Moon (1998).
Source: Moon (1998).

focus to strengthening the role of the private sector in vocational training by instituting a training levy system and by expanding the number of private two-year technical colleges.[12]

In Korea, the problems associated with vocational and technical education and training are more qualitative than quantitative. The linkage between education and training institutes and the industry is very weak. For example, there are virtually no functioning channels for the industry and labor to participate in major decision-making regarding vocational and technical education and training. In addition, the job qualification system is not effective in controlling the quality of vocational education and training. Particularly with regard to the utilization of information technology, the rigidity of Korea's education and training system has emerged as one of the biggest problems.

Employment services, both public and private, are not adequately provided. It is very rare that a job seeker finds employment through a public employment service center. In addition, private temporary work agencies were not active because of heavy regulations. Due to the low priority on unemployment policy, the Korean government has not built up the capability necessary to deal with unemployment problems. The government remained unprepared to respond to the sudden increase in unemployment following the outbreak of economic crisis in 1997. Labor market policy has so far not been well targeted and designed. For example, subsidies for the unemployed were in some cases diverted to housewives in adult education programs. In addition, the government has shown a tendency to resort to quick fixes instead of developing serious long-term programs.

---

12. Korea has basically the same education system as the American and the Japanese system, a 6-3-3-4 school year system. However, since the Korean education system places as much importance on vocational and technical educational institutions such as technical high schools and community colleges as its does on academic educational institutions, the Korean system has an element of the European educational system.

Redistributive Tax-Transfer Policies

Although labor market policies attracted attention since the financial crisis of 1997–98, the income transfer program for the unemployed has been overlooked. There is a growing need for unemployment assistance for the workers regardless of their employment history and contribution to unemployment insurance. Only 10 percent of the unemployed received unemployment insurance benefits in 1998, and 16 percent of the unemployed is expected to receive unemployment benefits in 1999.[13] The government responded to this problem by simply raising the number of people receiving public assistance to 500,000 in 1999 from 374,000 in 1997. Local government administrators determine if one is eligible for public assistance based largely on their own discretion, instead of a standardized nationwide means test, giving rise to instances of abuse.

Right after the outbreak of the economic crisis, the government abandoned the consolidated tax system for interest income. Those with large interest incomes had claimed that abolishing the system would help revitalize the economy by drawing out funds from the underground economy. However, this decision has not had the expected effects and only contributed to making the tax system more regressive. Coupled with the high interest rate in 1998, the abolishment of the consolidated tax system contributed to exacerbating the income distribution. Taxes on real estate property and transaction taxes imposed on acquisition, registration, and transfers of property, are too high compared to possession-related taxes like the property tax.

In the case of the income tax, horizontal inequality—especially between employees and the self-employed—is a problem. This is caused by widespread tax evasion by the high-income self-employed such as lawyers and owners of big restaurants. Outdated bookkeeping methods, inefficient and sometimes even corrupt tax administration, and society's acceptance of non-compliance all contribute to widespread tax evasion. Hence, the introduction of a more progressive taxation system as well as modernization of tax administration is an urgent issue.

Prospects of Social Policy Reform

In the process of globalization, Korea has been gradually increasing social expenditure in the 1980s and 1990s. But it has become more evident that the existing social policy framework has clear limitations for dealing with social problems. Despite the steady increase in government spending, education and medical expenses for individuals have increased even faster. There is also the

---

13. The unemployment insurance system in Korea pays out unemployment benefits for a four to six month period depending on the unemployed workers' employment history and their contribution to the fund for the specific period.

growing question of whether the government can cope with the problem of rapidly rising unemployment.

It is clear that the Korean government cannot ignore social policy as it did in the past. Objectives of development should be broadened to include the sound development of social services. Rather than simply increasing spending on social policies, the government must overhaul the system. Social policy will comprise the next round of reform issues following the financial sector and *chaebol* reform in the midst of the economic crisis.

The foremost issue in social policies is setting the right priorities. Redistributive income transfer programs should receive more attention. Korea has not had much experience in administering a means-tested support program for the poor. The redistributive tax policy must also be improved and developed in light of the economic crisis.

The government's roles in social policies should be redefined. These roles would differ according to different areas. In education, the government's excessive intervention has been a major problem. In health care, the government has been lax in regulating health insurance administration and monitoring providers of medical services, yielding to the influence of special interest groups. Therefore, a more balanced role of the government in social policy is required.

In redefining the government's roles for implementing social policies, the government should pay special attention to the participation of various social groups. It is necessary to create a system that encourages parents and teachers to participate in educational policy decisions, industries and unions to have a voice in labor market policies, and a more active role by non-government or religious institutions in social welfare policy.

Finally, it is very important to enhance the government's capabilities in creating and implementing social policies. In the health care sector, the government's capabilities in setting up and enforcing necessary regulations should be enhanced. In labor market and income transfer policies, the government must also upgrade its ability to set policy targets, design appropriate programs, and evaluate them after implementation.

5. Conclusions and Recommendations

Korea must be counted as one of the countries that has benefited enormously from active participation in the world economy. It does not mean, however, that participation in the global market place only brings benefits. Korea had its share of economic crises related to over-borrowing from abroad. There were crises in 1969–70 and again in 1979–80, but the crisis of 1997–98 was the most vicious. What made the latest crisis more virulent was the unprepared and mismanaged financial liberalization that exposed the economy to the speculative movements of capital.

This is not to say that all would have been well had the tight controls on capital movement been maintained. On the one hand, there was a real and growing need for reform, particularly in the *chaebol*-dominated industrial structure and the antiquated financial system. On the other hand, Korea was under irresistible pressures to liberalize its dealings with the outside world. The problem is that liberalization was dragged and distorted by powerful vested-interest groups. As a result, liberalization policies left the problems of the *chaebol* and inefficient financial sector hardly improved. Rather than improving, liberalization of capital flows allowed those sectors to engage in imprudent expansion and overseas ventures, aggravating the risks to the economy of the webs and flows of foreign capital.

The Korean experience once again demonstrates the need for caution in the process of liberalization. Unless liberalization is carefully staged and safeguards are properly installed, it risks huge setbacks in terms of growth and distribution. In particular, a country must have a good "financial safety net" and a good "social safety net" before it liberalizes its capital accounts. The former must include not only a sound domestic financial system that is backed by a deposit insurance scheme and a lender of last resort, but also proper monitoring and enforcement of prudential regulations. In addition, it is necessary to have in place a policy framework and instruments to deal with excessive capital inflows and sudden outflows. The social safety net becomes more important as the economy gets liberalized, since liberalization exposes people to greater risks of insecurities inherent in the market system.

The social consequences of the financial crisis are grim in Korea. On top of the steep decline in the average real incomes, there has been a drastic increase in joblessness and a sudden worsening of income distribution. Hardest hit by the crisis were the unskilled workers in terms of both wage cuts and job losses. As a result, in just one year after crisis, income inequality is significantly worse than before. And urban poverty, which had been minimal before the crisis, has emerged as a serious issue, driven by the emergence of homeless people in the parks and the underground passages of the big cities.

It must be noted, however, that some uneasy developments in income distribution began to appear even before the crisis. While Korea was in a fortunate position of experiencing improving distributional trends in terms of the wage share and wage inequality in the process of globalization up until the early 1990s, this favorable trend stopped then. In particular, the wage differential by education ceased to narrow in spite of the continuous quantitative expansion in higher education after 1993. This seems attributable to a structural shift in labor demand in favor of the more highly educated, which in turn was caused by liberalization and globalization of the economy. Around the same time, the worsening trend of size wage differential, which was arrested for about five years during which large *chaebol* firms engaged in massive subcontracting as a union avoidance strategy, resumed with *chaebol*-led investment boom. This experience shows that appropriate competition and industrial policies are required to cope with the tendency for liberalization policies to aggravate income distribution.

However painful the social consequence of the financial crisis, the response of the government to these problems was commendable in many ways. From the outset, shoring up the social safety net was considered a central part of the restructuring and reform program and was supported by a huge increase in budget spending. At the same time, the Tripartite Commission, consisting of representatives from labor unions, employer organizations and the government, was created to deal with the difficult negotiations concerning employment adjustment and other labor issues. Despite various limitations, it undoubtedly contributed to maintaining social stability and labor peace in the midst of massive deterioration in employment and social conditions. One crucial factor in enabling such an active social policy in the wake of the financial crisis was the absence of a fiscal debt problem. Prudent fiscal policies in more tranquil times proved extremely useful in terms of allowing a bold deficit spending for social policy in a time of crisis.

However, the government's ability to design and implement social policies emerged as a big problem. Because of the continuing legacy of the "growth first, distribution next" economic development strategies, Korean social policy was not geared toward addressing the mounting social problems created by the crisis. The existing social policy framework in Korea has clear limitations in dealing with the social problems associated with the financial crisis. Simply pouring more money into social policies without overhauling the system is unlikely to be successful. Accumulation of government capability in social policy should be a high priority. Korea should not ignore social policy as it did in the past. Objectives of development should be broadened to include the sound development of social services, particularly as the economy gets more and more integrated into the global economy.

REFERENCES

Amsden, Alice and Euh, Y. (1990) "Republic of Korea's Financial Reform: What are the Lessons?," Discussion Paper, no.30, Geneva, United Nations Conference on Trade and Development (UNCTAD).

Chang, Ha-Joon (1998) "Korea: The Misunderstood Crisis," *World Development*, vol.26, no.8.

Chang, Ha-Joon, Park, Hong Jae, and Yoo, Chul Gyue (1998), "Interpreting the Korean Crisis: Financial Liberalization, Industrial Policy, and Corporate Governance," *Cambridge Journal of Economics*, 22.

Choo, Hak-Chung (1992) "Income Distribution and Social Equity in Korea," KDI/ÇIER Joint Seminar.

Fields, Gary S., and Gyeongjoon Yoo (1998) "Falling Labor Income Inequality in Korea's Economic Growth: Patterns and Underlying Causes," OECD.

Hwang, Seong-Hyeon., and Joung-Woo Lee (1997) "The Problems of Income Distribution and Related Policy Issue in Korea," mimeo, Korea Development Institute.

Jung, UnChan (1991) *A Tract on Financial Reform*, Bubmunsa (in Korean).

Kim, Dae Il, and Robert H. Topel (1995) "Labor Markets and Economic Growth: Lessons from Korea's Industrialization, 1970–1990," in Richard Freeman and Lawrence Katz, eds., *Differences and Changes in Wage Structures*, Chicago: University of Chicago Press.

Kim, Joon-Kyung (1998) "Korean Experience with Policy Loans," mimeo, Korea Development Institute & Economic and Social Commission for Asia and the Pacific (ESCAP) of the United Nations.

Kim, Kwang Suk (1994) "Trade and Industrialization Policies in Korea: An Overview," in G. K. Helleiner, ed., *Trade Policy and Industrialization in Turbulent Times*, London: Routledge, pp.317–363.

Kim, Kwang Suk and Hong, Sung Duk (1997) *Accounting for Rapid Economic Growth in Korea, 1963–1995*, Seoul: Korea Development Institute.

Krugman, Paul (1994) "The Myth of Asia's Miracle: A Cautionary Fable," Foreign Affairs.

Krugman, Paul (1998) "What Happened to Asia?," mimeo, Department of Economics, Massachusetts Institute of Technology.

Lee, Ju-Ho, and Dae Il Kim (1997) "Labor Market Developments and Reforms in Korea," KDI Working Paper #9703.

Lim, Linda (1998) "Whose 'Model' Failed?: Implications of the Asian Economic Crisis," *The Washington Quarterly*, Summer.

Majumdar, Dipak (1998) "Size-Structure of Manufacturing Establishments and Productivity Differentials Between Large and Small Firms: A Comparative Study of Asian Economies," mimeo, University of Toronto.

Park Se-Il (1998) "Labor Market Reform and Social Safety Net, " mimeo, Brookings Institution.

Radelet, S. and Jeffrey Sachs (1998) "The Onset of the East Asian Financial Crisis," mimeo, Harvard Institute for International Development, Harvard University.

Woo Cheonsik and Ju-Ho Lee (1997) "Efficiency of Korean Education: Myth and Mission," mimeo, KDI.

Yang Bong-min (1998) "Health Insurance and the Growth of the Private Health Sector: Korea," mimeo, World Bank.

Yoo, Seong Min (1997) "Evolution of Government-Business Interface in Korea: Progress to Date and Reform Agenda Ahead," mimeo, Korea Development Institute.

You, Jong-Il (1995) "Changing Capital-Labour Relations in South Korea," in J. Schor and J-I. You, eds., *Capital, the State and Labour*, Edward Elgar.

You, Jong-Il (1997) "Globalization, Labor Market Flexibility and the Korean Labor Reform," *Seoul Journal of Economics*, Vol. 18, No. 41.

You, Jong-Il (1998) "Income Distribution and Growth in East Asia," *Journal of Development Studies*.

10

Turkey: Globalization, Distribution and Social Policy, 1980–1998

KORKUT BORATAV, A. ERINC YELDAN
and AHMET H. KÖSE

Introduction

In this paper we aim to analyze the impact of globalization on income distribution and social policies in post-1980 Turkey. Broadly defined, *globalization* is the process of the complete integration of the constituent parts of the world economy with each other and with international markets. In the terminal stage of globalization, nation-states as distinct economic identities pursuing national objectives are expected to disappear. What remains will be an integrated transnational economy where goods, factors of production and financial assets will be perfect substitutes wherever they are located (UNCTAD, 1997).

The world economy and its constituent parts are, currently, far from this ultimate stage. However, the past quarter of a century has witnessed decisive and apparently irreversible transformations in this direction. Successive steps of liberalization of trade and capital movements have resulted in integrating national economies with world markets for goods and financial assets. Consequently autonomous decision-making powers of nation-states in regulating domestic economies drastically weakened.

There are, however, missing links. International mobility of labor is strikingly less than it has been during the past century or even during the "golden

* A previous version of this paper was presented at the CEPA Conference on *Globalization and Social Policy*, New York, January, 1999. We are indebted to Lance Taylor, Ute Pieper, Gülay Günlük Senesen, Ahmet Ertugrul, and the conference participants for their comments and suggestions; and to Ebru Voyvoda for her indispensable research assistance.

age" of post-1950 capitalism. Hence, whereas the capacity of governments to effectively control capital at the level of the national/domestic economy has been undermined, nation-states are faced with a situation where they can only regulate labor and socio-economic variables, i.e. social policies. The search for competitiveness and the freedom of movement of capital generates strong pressures for minimizing the individual and social cost of labor at the national level. The resulting conflicts and contradictions are resolved at the level of the nation-state, sometimes obstructing the overwhelming forces of globalization. This is the analytical conceptualization within which the Turkish context is to be covered in the paper.

Turkey initiated its long-process of integration with the world commodity and financial markets in 1980. The successive stages of liberalization have been surveyed elsewhere [Yeldan (1995) and Boratav, Türel & Yeldan (1996; 1995)] and will be briefly overviewed in the next section. Since its early inception, Turkish adjustment program was hailed as a "model" by the orthodox international community and supported by generous structural adjustment loans, debt relief, and technical aid. Currently the Turkish economy can be said to be operating under conditions of a truly "open economy"—a macroeconomic environment where both current and capital accounts are completely liberalized. In this setting, many of the instruments of macro and fiscal control have been transformed, and the constraints of macro equilibrium have undergone major structural change.

The analytics of the two distinct (i.e. 1980–88 and 1989–98) phases of liberalization is the theme of Section 1. We address the modes of accumulation and surplus creation under both sub-periods separately, and investigate the culminating inherent tensions of disequilibria under each episode. Section 2, in turn, carries this analysis to micro aspects of adjustment and reports on the evolving patterns of employment, labor productivity, and overall informalization of the labor force. Responses to pressures of international competitiveness and the emerging patterns of income distribution are studied in Section 3. In Section 4, the preceding analysis is applied to size distribution of income and the incidence of post-liberalization adjustments on poverty. The incidence of globalization on public sector accounts and the state's changing role in the provision of public goods are narrated in Section 5. Section 6 concludes with an overview of the social policy implications of globalization.

1. Phases and Analytics of Macroeconomic Adjustment: 1980–1998

The post-1980 Turkish adjustment path can be partitioned into two broad phases: "1981–1988" and "1989–1998." The main characteristic of the first phase is structural adjustment with export promotion, albeit under a regulated foreign exchange system and controls on capital inflows. Over this period, integration to the global markets was achieved mainly through commodity trade liberalization. More importantly, both the exchange rate and direct export subsidies acted as main instruments for the promotion of exports and pursuit of macroeconomic stability. The period was also characterized by a severe suppression of wage incomes via hostile measures against organized labor. This "classic" mode of surplus creation reached its economic and political limits by 1988. Coupled with a new wave of populist pressures under approaching elections, organized labor succeeded in attaining significant increases in wages. Furthermore, beginning 1989, there was a major shift in the public expenditure accounts towards more socially desirable ventures. An overall increase in both the share and level of public salaries, and investments on social infrastructure enabled the working masses to attain improved living standards.

The post- 1988 populism could evidently be financed by taxing the bourgeoisie and moving towards a more "fair" tax system. Yet, the strategic preference of the state was the maintenance of its present stance towards evasion of taxable capital incomes and its lax attitude towards the so-called unrecorded private transactions. Consequently, the state apparatus turned into a bastion of privilege as it assumed a regulatory role in the creation and absorption of the economic surplus, while the fiscal balances have taken the major brunt of adjustment. The main macroeconomic policy response to the increased wage costs and the culminating fiscal deficits was complete deregulation of financial markets. With the advent of elimination of controls on foreign capital transactions and the declaration of convertibility of the Turkish Lira in 1989, Turkey opened up its domestic asset markets to global financial competition. In this setting, the Central Bank lost its control over the exchange rate and the interest rate as policy instruments independent of each other, as these practically turned into exogenous parameters set by the chaotic conditions of financial arbitrage in the global markets. Thus, we regard 1989 as a crucial year in our analysis, segmenting the post-1980 economic development patterns of Turkey. Given this broad division, we further characterize each phase by three sub-periods, each roughly encompassing mini business cycles of growth, crisis and post-crisis adjustment. We base our detailed analysis of the macro aggregates utilizing data tabulated in Table 1-1.

Structural Adjustment, Export-Oriented Growth and Exhaustion 1981–1988

Turkey attempted to overcome the 1977–79 foreign exchange crisis with a series of reforms destined to integrate it with the world markets. The currency was left to a downward slide, and price controls were lifted. Substantial support for export manufacturing was granted, involving tax rebates, duty free import allowances and subsidized credit.

Probably the most significant economic policy characteristic of the 1983–87 period was the suppression of wage incomes. This had the dual effect of both reducing domestic demand in favor of creating an "exportable" surplus and also cutting labor costs. The share of wage-labor in private manufacturing value added receded from 27.5% to 17.1%; and in public manufacturing from

TABLE 1-1: Phases of Macroeconomic Adjustment in Turkey, 1980–1997

	Post-Crisis Adjust. 1981–82	Export-Led Growth 1983–87	Exhaustion 1988	Unregulated Financial Liberaliz. 1989–93	Financial Crisis 1994	Post Crisis Adjustment 1995–97
I. Production and Accumulation						
(Real Rate of Growth, %)						
GDP	4.2	6.5	2.1	4.8	−5.5	7.2
Agriculture	0.6	0.8	7.8	0.1	−0.7	1.3
Manufacturing	7.9	8.6	1.6	6.0	−7.6	9.8
Commerce	7.7	9.1	3.5	5.4	−7.6	8.7
Financial Services	2.5	2.6	4.4	0.5	−1.5	3.0
Fixed Investment:						
Private	−5.3	12.3	12.6	11.5	−9.1	13.6
Public	0.2	10.3	−20.2	4.3	−34.8	9.0
Manufacturing	−5.1	2.1	−4.8	6.3	−4.7	6.7
As % Share of GNP:						
Savings	17.7	19.5	27.2	21.9	23.0	20.7
Investment	18.3	20.9	26.1	23.7	24.4	24.8
Public S. Borrowing Req.	3.7	4.7	4.8	9.1	7.9	7.9
II. Distribution and Prices						
Inflation Rate(CPI)	33.2	39.5	75.4	66.4	106.3	83.2
Depreciation of TL/US$	45.0	39.7	66.0	50.4	170.0	68.9
Real Interest Rate						
on Government Bonds[a]	—	—	−5.8	10.5	20.5	24.9
Real Wages Growth Rate:						
Private Manufacturing[b]	0.4	−1.5	−5.7	10.0	−30.1	0.0
Public Manufacturing	−0.4	−5.9	−7.8	20.3	−18.1	−6.8
Average Mark–up Rate in						
Private Manufacturing (%)	31.0	32.6	38.0	39.6	47.0	41.1
III. Internationalization						
Man. Exports Growth[c]	19.7	12.5	14.0	5.1	18.0	6.3
As % Share of GNP:						
Imports	14.0	15.9	15.8	14.6	17.8	22.7
Exports	8.5	10.8	12.8	9.1	13.8	13.0
Current Account	−2.7	−1.9	−1.7	−1.3	−2.0	−2.6
Foreign Debt	27.1	37.8	44.8	35.1	50.1	42.7

a. Annual average of Compounded Interest Rate on Government Debt Instruments deflated by the whole sale price index.

b. Private manufacturing labor data pertain to the enterprises employing 10 and above workers.

c. Annual growth rate in manufacturing exports (in millions US $).

Sources: SPO Main Economic Indicators; Undersecretariat of Foreign Trade and Treasury Main Economic Indicators; SIS Manufacturing Industry Surveys.

25% to 13%. In this process, the average mark-up rate in private manufacturing has increased from 31% to 38%.

During this period, exports rose by 19.7% per annum in dollar terms and the real gross domestic product, following the low-point of the 1978–80 depression, rose by 5.4% per annum. However, the performance of fixed investments did not follow this pattern. In the private sector, gross fixed investments initially contracted by 5.3% in 1981–82, and increased by 12.3% during 1983–87. Decomposition of this path reveals that only a small portion of this amount was directed to manufacturing. The rate of growth of private manufacturing investments has been on the order of only 2.1% per annum. This resulted in a significant anomaly as far as the official stance towards industrialization was concerned: in a period where outward orientation was supposedly directed to increased manufacturing exports through significant price incentives and subsidies, the share of manufacturing investments declined substantially.

Given this background, we characterize schematically the main mechanisms of macroeconomic equilibrium with the aid of Figure 1-1. This figure portrays the dynamics of the Turkish economy under the export promotion and commodity trade liberalization episode, 1980–1988.

Low savings along with stagnant investments, high fiscal costs and tax evasion, and an oligopolistic structure set the stage portrayed in Figure 1-1. Low savings generation and meager investment demand resulted directly in disequilibrium in macroeconomic conditions along channels (1) and (2).[1] Along the fiscal operations, costs of export subsidization together with revaluation of foreign debt in domestic currency due to continued real depreciation led to excessive pressures on public expenditures. Given the extent of the informalization of the economy and consequent tax evasion, the fiscal gap widened (along channels [9] and [14a]), and necessitated increased demands for deficit financing through foreign borrowing (14).

Export subsidization (3), together with the decline in wage costs (7) and the discretionary devaluation policy (8) were the characteristic policy responses of the period which enabled the surge in export revenues. It has to be noted in this context that one of the components of wage suppression in this period was continued price inflation, enabling both the wage squeeze to generate an exportable surplus (channel [10]), and also inflation tax revenues for the state (channel [16]). Implemented under a regime of vigorous currency depreciation supplemented by direct export incentives, inflation policy did not seem to lead to any loss of competitiveness of Turkish exportables.

Rising export earnings and foreign debt accumulation constituted the main mechanisms for financing trade liberalization and the import demand along channel (13). This mechanism entailed, however, significant inner con-

---

1. Yeldan (1995) and Akyüz (1990) argue that the faltering investment performance of the economy under the 1980s is the end result of a marked re-distribution of national income towards rentiers exhibiting strong preferences towards conspicuous consumption patterns with low propensities to save and invest.

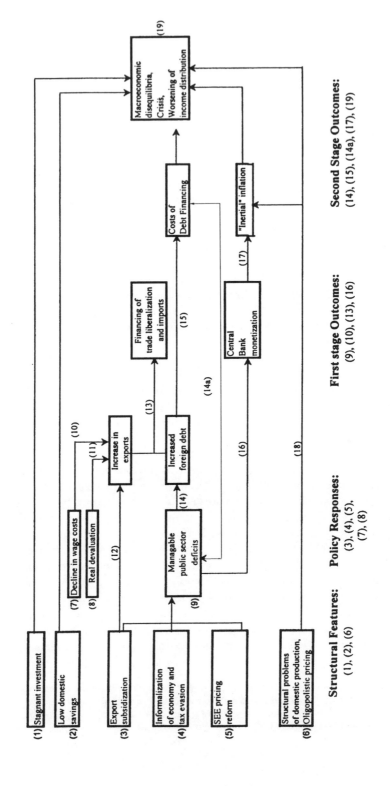

FIGURE 1-1: Macroeconomic Dynamics of the Turkish Economy under Export Promotion and Trade Liberalization (1980–1988)

Structural Features:
(1), (2), (6)

Policy Responses:
(3), (4), (5), (7), (8)

First stage Outcomes:
(9), (10), (13), (16)

Second Stage Outcomes:
(14), (15), (14a), (17), (19)

flicts since foreign exchange was "earned" by the private sector, and foreign debt servicing was carried by the public sector. This duality necessitated implementation of specific mechanisms for the transfer of foreign exchange from the private to the public sector, and as Ekinci (1998) attests, constituted the main conflict in the accumulation patterns of the period. Ekinci interprets the export subsidization policy as one of the means of resolving this conflict. No doubt, the same tension was observed to be a continued component of the trade and fiscal gaps faced in the post-1989 period as well, and would reveal itself in the resolution of the increased public deficit financing through short-term foreign capital inflows at the cost of excessive real rates of interest and increased volatility of investments and production.

Increased foreign debt, in turn, called for increased costs of debt financing (15), and constituted an important source of macroeconomic disequilibria (19). This process, complemented by channels (1), (2), (17), and (18)[2] signaled that the underlying modes of macroeconomic adjustment would reach its limits both economically and politically. We highlight 1988 as the limiting point of this episode, and interpret it as the year of "exhaustion."

Return to Populism, Capital Account Opening, and Crises, 1989–1998

All economic indicators of 1988 signal a stagflationary macro environment. The rate of growth of GDP was only 2.1%, and the inflation rate accelerated to 75%. Real wage earnings hit their lowest point, but then recover quickly beginning in 1989—the starting point of the new populist phase. Real wages in manufacturing increased by 90% from 1988 to 1991. Thus, the classical accumulation episode based on wage suppression had come to a halt by 1989.

Various counteracting mechanisms were invigorated to rationalize the increase in wage costs from the point of view of private industrial capital. The first policy response to the new macroeconomic environment was the advent of complete deregulation of the foreign capital transactions and declaration of the Turkish Lira as fully convertible in foreign exchange markets in 1989. This paved the way for injection of liquidity to the domestic economy in terms of "hot money" inflows. Such inflows enabled, on the one hand, the financing of rising public sector expenditures, and also provided relief on inflationary pressures by cheapening import costs.

The second mechanism was based on the imperfectly competitive market structures prevalent in the economy, and the consequent "costs-plus-mark-up pricing rules" on industrial output. We document the behavior of mark-ups against real wage *costs* and real wage *earnings* in private manufacturing industry[3]

---

2. On the extent of oligopolistic production structure of the domestic industry see Section II.B below.

3. *Wage earnings* are pre-tax and include overtime, fringe benefits and social security contributions by the employees, but excludes such payments by the employers. The latter are, however, included in compiling *wage costs*. (See SIS, *Annual Surveys of Manufacturing Industry*).

in Figure 1-2. Figure 1-2 portrays three sub-periods regarding the behavior of private mark-ups. Between 1980–84, the private sector industrial mark-ups follow the deflationary trend in prices with a downward adjustment. Following the first expansionary phase of 1984–1988, we observe a jump in this rate. We label this period as the classical export-led growth phase of the Turkish economy, which reached its limits in 1988. Starting in 1989, real wage costs increase abruptly. However, this does not cause a squeeze of profit margins in private manufacturing; on the contrary, they successfully trail the upward trend in real wage costs and reach a plateau of 47% during the financial crisis of 1994. Hence, during the 1990s, profits displayed significant upward flexibility via mark-up rates in response to increased wage costs.

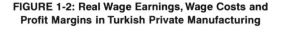

FIGURE 1-2: Real Wage Earnings, Wage Costs and Profit Margins in Turkish Private Manufacturing

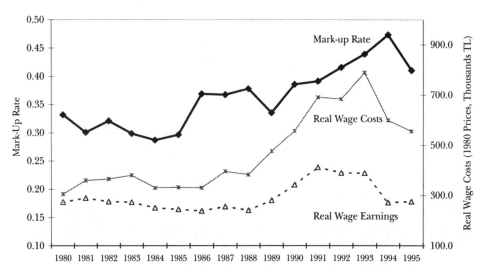

The third mechanism that enabled the private industrial capital to absorb the wage increases of the aforementioned period, was the pricing policy of the public sector. We calculate that the ratio of intermediate costs to wage costs declined from 11.8 in 1988 to 7.8 in 1990 and to 6.5 in 1991. This was mostly achieved with delayed restructuring of the public prices against an inflationary background, maintaining a surplus for the private sector.

A fourth defensive mechanism of private capital was labor-shedding. One of the major characteristics of the labor market adjustments throughout the 1990s has been widespread layoffs and an overall intensification of marginalized labor employment. Quarterly data on private manufacturing reveals that formal employment in medium to large enterprises employing 10+ workers fell by twenty five percentage points between the first quarter of 1988 and the last quarter of 1992. The outbreak of the 1994 crisis has taken an additional toll on formal employment in the sector bringing the index of private manufacturing employment to thirty points lower than its 1988 level (SPO, 1998). We document the extent of marginalization of the industrial labor force in further detail in Section 2-1 below.

Erratic movements in the current account, a rising trade deficit (from 3.5% of GNP in 1985–88 to 6% in 1990–93) and a drastic deterioration of fiscal balances (See Section 5) showed the unsustainability of the post-1989 model. This prolonged instability reached its climax during the fourth quarter of 1993, when currency appreciation and the consequent current account deficits rose to unprecedented levels. With the sudden drainage of short-term funds in the beginning of January 1994, production capacity contracted, followed by continued fall in industrial output throughout that year. Together with this contraction, the post-1994 crisis management gave rise to significant shifts in income distribution, and to an intensification of the ongoing processes of transfer of the economic surplus from the industrial/real sectors and wage-labor, in particular, towards the financial sectors. Likewise, dollar-denominated wage costs decreased substantially and enabled export earnings to rise. In this manner, Turkey has, once again, switched back to a mode of surplus extraction whereby export performance of industrial sectors depended on savings on wage costs. In fact, the disequilibrium could have only been accommodated by the massive (downward) flexibility displayed by real remuneration of wage-labor. The index of the real wage rate in private manufacturing fell by an aggregate of 29 percentage points between 1993.IV and 1996.II.

We can summarize the dynamics of the post-1989 macroeconomic equilibrium of the Turkish economy with the aid of Figure (1-3). The figure identifies the same sources of structural imbalances as in Figure (1-1), namely low savings capacity, large fiscal gap, and structural deficiencies in the production process along with an imperfectly competitive market structure. The resolution of these imbalances, however, disclosed quite different modes of adjustment following the 1989 opening of the economy to global financial competition. An important addition to the characteristics of the period was the wage explosion and the re-emergence of a populist stance against the background of intensified political struggle. In response to these structural features, we observe the state assuming an active role in the economic sphere, regulating the distribution of national output. The state carried out this task first through its enterprise system by a mandated policy of delayed price adjustments on the intermediates and the final wage and capital goods produced by the SEE's (Figure 1-3 box [3]).

Following the full deregulation of the capital account, the state actively participated in the domestic asset markets through its issues of debt instruments (channels [6] and [7]). This, together with the threat of currency substitution in the context of a convertible currency regime, necessitated high interest rates (channel [8a] and [8b])—the first vicious circle, and real appreciation (channel [9b]). The second vicious circle surrounding channels (9a), (9b), and (9c) is highlighted by double-sided implications among the three variables involved: short-term capital inflows (hot money), real appreciation, and high real interest rates. Real appreciation had been the prime cause of the rise of the import volume and the current account deficits. On the other hand, real appreciation had a direct positive effect on investment demand by reducing costs of imported capital goods and intermediates (channel [13b]). This positive effect was countervailed by the pressures of real interest rates (channel [13a]), the end result being increased volatility of investment demand. High interest rates gave way to inflationary pressures through increased costs of credit (channels [8b] and [13]); and fed speculative rentier type of accumulation (channel (12)) with consequent worsening of income distribution. The limits of this bonanza of "short term foreign capital-led growth pattern" was the eruption of the financial crisis in 1994 and the continued fragility and severe disequilibria that the domestic markets had to face in the late 1990s.

The relationship between the external accounts, production and the labor market can be understood by the analytical portrayal given in Figure 1-4. Demand for formal labor is given in the north-east quadrant. Labor market duality is depicted in the south-east quadrant by introducing marginalized labor as an indispensable complementary component. In the north-west quadrant we have two processes between output (accumulation) and the current account balance. The dependence of growth and accumulation of imports gives rise to the standard upward-sloping DD schedule. The aforementioned post-liberalization vicious circle generates an equilibrium of increased current account deficits and high real interest rates, with a consequent negative effect on accumulation. The end result is a negative relationship between accumulation and the current account deficit along the rr-schedule—higher CA deficits necessitate higher real rates of interest to attract foreign capital, which results in a contraction of investment. The equilibrium is given by the intersection of these processes, summarized by the DD and rr schedules.

The deregulation of the capital account leads to an appreciation of the real exchange rate, and leads to a structural increase of the real interest rate. We follow the post capital-account liberalization (1989–93) by shifting the rr-schedule out. Stimulated by inflows of short-term capital, the domestic economy experiences an expansionary swing together with a rise of the current account deficit. The delicate balance upon which this fragile growth path rests is broken by the build up of a confidence crisis and the sudden reversal of "hot money" flows beginning at the end of 1993. We portray the 1994 crisis as an abrupt shift of the capital-account schedule back to r"r". Furthermore, the aggregate demand schedule shifts downward indicating a decline in the absorption capacity of the domestic economy.

The 1994 crisis is a constrained equilibrium with lower investment demand, higher real interest rates, and a severe contraction of productive capacity. In the labor market, the post-liberalization response of private capital is revealed through shedding formal labor and increased marginalization. As

FIGURE 1-3: Macroeconomic Dynamics of the Turkish Economy under Full Financial Liberalization (1989–)

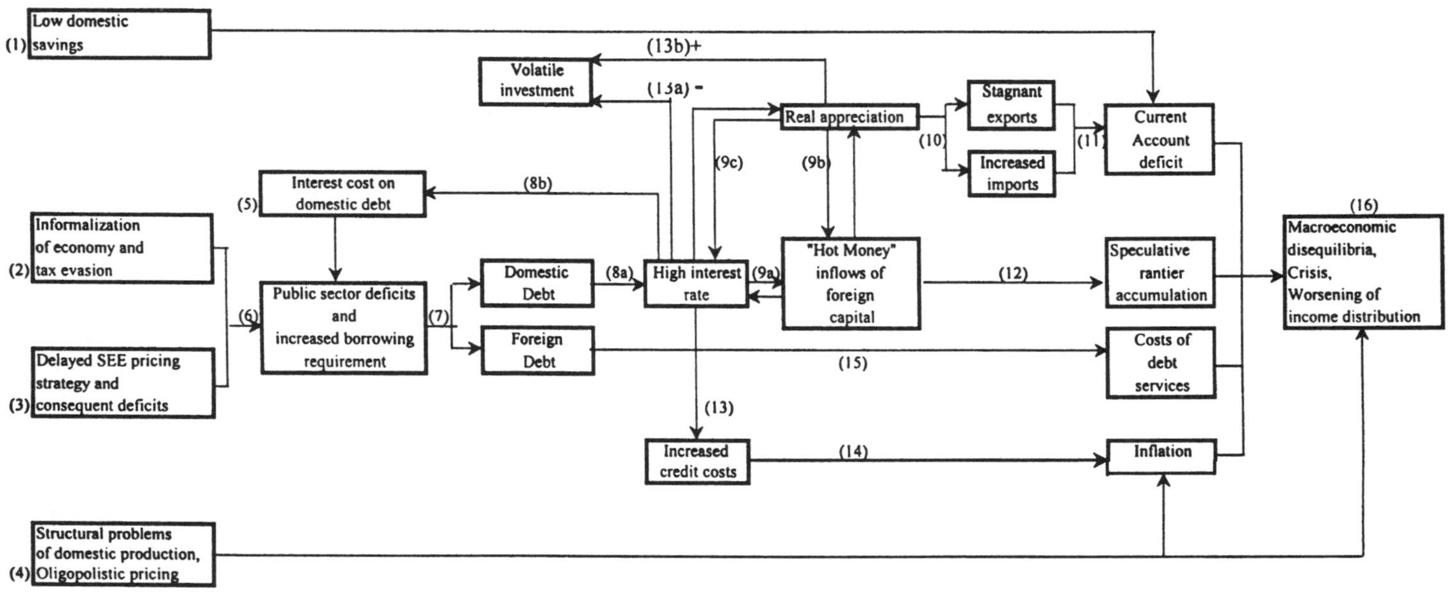

(1) Low domestic savings

(16) Macroeconomic disequilibria, Crisis, Worsening of income distribution

Current Account deficit

Speculative rantier accumulation

Costs of debt services

Inflation

Stagnant exports

Increased imports

(11)

(10)

Real appreciation

"Hot Money" inflows of foreign capital

(12)

(9b)

(9c)

(9a)

High interest rate

(15)

(13)

Increased credit costs

(14)

(13b)+

(13a) –

Volatile investment

Interest cost on domestic debt

(8b)

Domestic Debt

(8a)

Foreign Debt

(5)

Public sector deficits and increased borrowing requirement

(7)

(6)

Informalization of economy and tax evasion (2)

Delayed SEE pricing strategy and consequent deficits (3)

Structural problems of domestic production, Oligopolistic pricing (4)

Structural Features:
(1), (4),
wage explosion
return to populism

Policy Responses:
capital account liberalization
(3): keeping SEE prices low

First stage Outcomes:
(2), (6), (7),
vicious circle of
domestic debt: (8a), (8b)
vicious circle of capital
account liberalization: (9a), (9b), (9c)
(13a), (13b)

Second Stage Outcomes:
(6), (7), (8a), (8b) repeated
(10), (11)
(12), (14) (16)

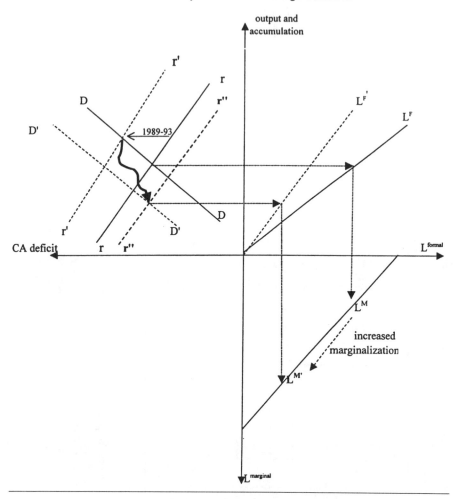

FIGURE 1-4: Dynamics of Accumulation,
Labor Market Equilibrium and Foreign Balances

also conceptualized in Amadeo (1996), this has the effect of tilting the formal labor employment schedule inwards to $L^{F'}$. Increased marginalization of the labor market, higher real rates of interest, and increased volatility of acumulation patterns become characteristic of the domestic economy under financial deregulation.

Clearly, the "reform fatigue and exhaustion" of the 1988 crisis, and the unsustainability of the post-1989 growth path which culminated into the 1994 crisis have had quite different macro dynamics in operation. Under both episodes, however, in spite of the official stance towards a policy of "reducing the economic role of the state," we observe continued use of the state's frontiers as a regulatory agent, overseeing the distributional conflict over the national product. In the next section, we study these adjustment dynamics and report on the distributional processes in more detail.

2. Impact of Liberalization on Industrial and Employment Structures

Structural Changes in Employment and Informalization

In this section we first provide a more detailed study of the impact of adjustment on employment, factor incomes, market structures, and technical productivity. Here our main focus will be on the manufacturing industry, as most reliable data are available mostly for this sector. We will, however, extend our analysis to the aggregate economy whenever data permit. The annual *Manufacturing Industry Statistics* of SIS is the most elaborate statistical database in that respect. However, it covers only public enterprises and the "formal/organized" category of labor in private establishments that employ more than 10 persons. Previous studies have in general argued that there is an extensive and accelerated usage of "marginal/unregistered" labor in the Turkish labor market (Yentürk 1997; Yeldan and Köse 1998; Bulutay 1995; Senses 1994, 1996). In this study, our operational definition of the "informal/marginal labor" category will be that part of the employed labor force which is not officially registered under any social security coverage and also is not entitled under the "self-employed or employer" status in the labor force statistics.

The SIS *Household Labor Surveys* document that as of 1996 the economically active population above 12 years of age is about 23 million and 23 % of that amount consists of "employer and self employed" (6,308,000 persons). As an operational hypothesis, we will regard this group as outside the wage-labor market, and conclude that the potential supply of wage labor in Turkish economy in 1996 was 16,611,000 persons. With this classification, we find that 58% of the total employed labor force is engaged under different wage relations (regular or informal). When employment is classified with respect to its "social security system" coverage, one observes that about 43% of total labor force is employed under the "formal/registered" category (6,553,000 persons). The rest (8,676,000 persons) is what we will refer as marginal labor.

A closer examination of labor employment in the manufacturing industry reveals similar trends of informalization during the 1980's. Our calculations reveal that the ratio of marginal labor to total employment in the manufacturing industry increased to 49 % (1,170,000) in 1994, and stabilized around 44 % (1,035,000) in 1995, from 41 % (700,000) in 1980 (Table 2-1). This phenomenon is observed to be even more acute in the private manufacturing industry. The number in informally employed labor exceeded the amount of formally employed labor in 1994, and was equal to 49% of total employment in private manufacturing in 1995. This form of employment is very extensive in traditional sectors like food processing, textiles, wood and furniture, and metal products, where small-scale enterprises have greater importance.

330   Boratav, Yeldan and Köse

Table 2-1: Employment Status and Average Real Labor Costs in Manufacturing Industry, 1980–1995.

	1980	1985	1990	1992	1993	1994	1995
Total Employment (in thousands)[1]	2150	2440	2741	3085	2766	3034	2942
1. Employer and Self Empoyed [2]	445	505	556	686	547	652	584
2. Total Labor Employment	1705	1935	2185	2399	2219	2382	2358
Formal (Registered) Labor [3]	1005	1186	1284	1254	1258	1212	1274
Public	287	276	250	228	214	197	170
Private, Employing 10+ workers	500	652	774	752	761	736	802
Private, Employing 1–9 workers	218	258	260 [4]	274	283	279	302
Marginal (Unregistered) Labor [5]	700	749	901	1145	961	1170	1084
Monthly Average Real Labor Cost, (1980, Thousand TL) [6]							
Public	39.000	26.727	45.328	79.738	72.501	57.150	55.349
Private, Employing 10+ workers	25.480	22.696	32.542	40.103	43.287	33.300	28.311
Private, Employing 1–9 workers	6.743	9.324	9.367	10.100	9.004	6.491	6.654
Weighted Average Formal Real Wage Rate (W^{AVG})	25.276	20.725	30.339	40.754	40.544	31.005	26.785
Memo:							
Small Private Firms (1-9 workers) Wages/W^{AVG}	0.267	0.450	0.309	0.248	0.222	0.209	0.248
Marginal Labor Wages/W^{AVG}	0.218	0.367	0.252	0.245	0.219	0.207	0.246

(1) SIS, Household Labor Force Survey (HLFS).
(2) SIS, HLFS: The values of 1980 and 1985 were calculated by taking into account the share of this group in total employment during 1992–1995.
(3) SIS, Annual Manufacturing Industry Statistics: Annual Average Number of Employed.
(4) Figure for 1990 is based on average estimates.
(5) Defined as the difference between total employment and formal employment.
(6) Deflated by the CPI.

Even though the extent of informal, marginalized employment is admitted to be a perennial feature of Turkish labor markets, we observe an intensification of this process especially after 1989—the era of post-financial liberalization. One important observation is the continued presence of small-scale production units in manufacturing. Across 1980–1995, one witnesses little change in the overall characteristics of the small-scale enterprises. As of 1995, 95% of enterprises in manufacturing employ less than 9 workers, and produce 7% of aggregate manufacturing value added. They employ, on the average, 24% of the formal industrial labor force, with an average wage of about one-fourth of the wages paid in "large" enterprises (*i.e.* those employing more than 10 workers). Average productivity in small manufacturing, likewise, reach only about a fourth of that of large enterprises. Furthermore, the real level of average labor product is observed to be almost stagnant throughout. In general, average wages fall as the share of small-scale production units increase

FIGURE 2-1: Patterns of Real Wage Costs in the Manufacturing Industry, 1980–1995

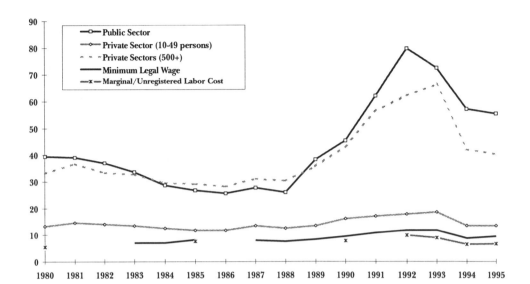

across a given sub-sector. In fact, Köse and Öncü (1998) provide evidence, for instance, that the annual average costs of labor in the small-sized private manufacturing enterprises (employing less than 9 workers) were held below the legal minimum wage floor throughout most of the 1980s and 90s.

In Figure 2-1 we document data on real wage costs of various labor categories employed in the manufacturing industries. The figure provides a close-up picture of the aggregate dynamics of the wage cycle in private manufacturing. Data disclosed in Figure 2-1 reveal that the post-1988 wage cycle experienced in small-medium private manufacturing followed quite a different path than the one observed in the public sector and the large manufacturing enterprises. The so-called wage expansion of the post-1988 period has actually been an episode shared mostly by the formal, organized ranks of the industrial labor force. Yet, the overall marginalization of wage-labor in the informalized sectors had been a prolonged pervasive characteristic of the industrial relations over the whole post-liberalization period. These processes led to a widening of the gap between earnings of different labor categories, and in turn led to an intensification of duality of the labor market.

Persistence of Oligopolistic Structures under Trade Liberalization

An important structural trait of the manufacturing industry of the post-liberalization era is continued intensification of the oligopolistic "costs plus mark-up pricing" behavior coupled with the maintenance of the level of concentration in the industrial commodity markets. Indeed, various studies on the market structure of the Turkish economy (Tekeli *et al.* 1982; Katircioglu 1990; Günes 1991, 1998; Kaytaz *et al.* 1993; Günes, Köse and Yeldan, 1996) indicate that there is a considerable tendency for monopolization in Turkish manufacturing industries. To document the extent of the oligopolistic structure of the sector, we tabulate in Table 2-2 the rate of concentration in the manufacturing industries that employ "10 or more persons," as calculated by the shares of the four largest enterprises in the total revenues of the sector (CR4). Accordingly, we classify those sectors with CR4 ratios above 50% to be "oligopolistic"; and those sectors with CR4 ratios between 30% and 49% as "monopolistically competitive." Finally, those sectors with CR4 ratios below 30% are classified to be "competitive." Furthermore, on a different spectrum we categorize the industrial sectors given their degree of tradability. We classify the sectors as trade or domestic-oriented on the basis of the ratio of the total trade volume (import and export) to the total production of the sector. Accordingly, the sectors are classified as traded if the ratio of total trade (export + import) to the total domestic production is higher than 50%.

On the basis of these data, one can make two direct observations on the market structures of the manufacturing industries: First, changes observed in the shares of production by the public and the private sectors do not have a decisive effect on the rate of concentration. As a result, it could be observed that there are both public (*petroleum refineries 353, tobacco 314*) and private (*glass and glass product 362, rubber products 355, printing and publishing 342*) dominated sectors with high rates of concentration.

In the same manner, it could also be deduced that reduction in the share of the public companies in the sector does not lead directly to an increase in the degree of competitiveness of the sector. In this respect, comparing the data for 1980 and 1985, one can see that there are sectors in which concentration rates (CR4) have declined parallel to a decrease in the share of the public sector (*iron and steel 371; beverages 313; paper and paper products 341*), whereas there have also been sectors (*chemicals 351, tobacco 314*) in which monopolization increased as a result of the same process.

The second observation is that the process of export promotion and overall trade liberalization since 1980 do not seem to have affected the structural characteristics of the manufacturing industry. This hypothesis is more visible when changes in the rates of concentration in the sector that is considered to be "open" by 1995 are examined. It is observed that over the post-trade liberalization episode, the rate of concentration has decreased only in *iron and steel 371,* and it was either kept constant or increased in the other sectors.

These observations reveal that, contrary to the expectations of orthodox theory, the process of trade liberalization has, in general, been insufficient to introduce the expected increase in competition in the industrial commodity markets. Effects of these developments on distribution and sectoral resource allocation can be better understood upon examination of pricing behavior. Given that prices in a monopolistic economy are to be set through a mark-up

Table 2-2:
Structural Characteristics of Manufacturing Sectors, 1980

Sectors	CR4	Mark-up Rates	Share of Labor Cost at Value Added	Share of Foreign Trade at Domestic Production	Share of Public Enterprises
COMPETITIVE SECTORS					
Domestic Oriented Sectors					
311	10.21	0.21	0.36	0.10	0.29
321	12.71	0.31	0.47	0.13	0.13
383	14.98	0.36	0.36	0.25	0.03
381	16.25	0.40	0.33	0.31	0.06
369	17.00	0.44	0.31	0.08	0.23
331	19.89	0.29	0.42	0.03	0.31
352	21.19	0.27	0.30	0.09	0.03
323	21.64	0.14	0.52	0.01	0.00
312	22.10	0.17	0.47	0.16	0.51
356	25.44	0.28	0.29	0.01	0.02
Trade Oriented Sectors					
322	21.33	0.21	0.42	0.66	0.01
MONOPOLISTICALLY COMPETITIVE SECTORS					
Domestic Oriented Sectors					
384	35.84	0.21	0.54	0.26	0.18
342	36.47	0.19	0.55	0.02	0.10
332	37.56	0.31	0.36	0.05	0.00
390	42.28	0.45	0.35	0.26	0.00
314	46.43	0.28	0.54	0.00	0.90
372	47.19	0.30	0.39	0.13	0.37
341	47.37	0.19	0.55	0.12	0.54
Trade Oriented Sectors					
382	33.44	0.25	0.48	0.53	0.22
351	49.20	0.47	0.23	0.74	0.50
385	32.16	0.42	0.33	4.85	0.00
OLIGOPOLISTIC SECTORS					
Domestic Oriented Sectors					
354	54.70	0.53	0.12	0.01	0.14
371	54.76	0.22	0.49	0.17	0.53
313	55.80	1.17	0.19	0.01	0.57
324	63.18	0.19	0.53	0.00	0.39
355	71.49	0.40	0.28	0.06	0.00
362	72.11	0.68	0.33	0.16	0.00
361	79.56	0.72	0.39	0.02	0.18
353	100.00	0.37	0.05	0.20	1.00

(continued)

Structural Characteristics of Manufacturing Sectors, 1985

Sectors	CR4	Mark-up Rates	Share of Labor Cost at Value Added	Share of Foreign Trade at Domestic Production	Share of Public Enterprises
COMPETITIVE SECTORS					
Domestic Oriented Sectors					
321	7.56	0.31	0.11	0.36	0.10
311	12.17	0.21	0.07	0.25	0.19
331	13.32	0.20	0.10	0.49	0.32
323	14.68	0.26	0.06	0.24	0.00
381	15.24	0.37	0.13	0.39	0.07
369	17.59	0.41	0.12	0.16	0.24
356	20.06	0.22	0.08	0.09	0.00
312	22.87	0.16	0.06	0.09	0.45
352	23.00	0.43	0.08	0.22	0.03
383	27.75	0.37	0.09	0.53	0.05
Trade Oriented Sectors					
322	14.71	0.25	0.08	1.69	0.00
MONOPOLISTICALLY COMPETITIVE SECTORS					
Domestic Oriented Sectors					
342	37.34	0.45	0.12	0.10	0.05
341	37.92	0.34	0.09	0.18	0.52
324	43.02	0.17	0.17	0.17	0.35
313	47.68	1.54	0.08	0.04	0.56
372	49.52	0.19	0.09	0.38	0.34
Trade Oriented Sectors					
384	34.37	0.28	0.11	0.52	0.08
371	39.01	0.21	0.07	0.57	0.40
351	34.98	0.22	0.07	0.97	0.39
382	39.22	0.24	0.13	1.14	0.20
385	34.48	0.26	0.14	9.61	0.06
OLIGOPOLISTIC SECTORS					
Domestic Oriented Sectors					
361	57.93	0.50	0.23	0.22	0.11
332	58.96	0.80	0.07	0.24	0.42
362	61.02	0.52	0.13	0.32	0.00
314	70.16	1.41	0.09	0.04	0.84
355	71.99	0.42	0.07	0.19	0.00
354	73.50	0.15	0.02	0.06	0.08
353	100.00	0.37	0.00	0.11	1.00
Trade Oriented Sectors					
390	51.14	0.64	0.10	0.63	0.00

Structural Characteristics of Manufacturing Sectors, 1990

Sectors	CR4	Mark-up Rates	Share of Labor Cost at Value Added	Share of Foreign Trade at Domestic Production	Share of Public Enterprises
COMPETITIVE SECTORS					
Domestic Oriented Sectors					
321	8.88	0.38	0.31	0.36	0.09
311	12.65	0.26	0.31	0.18	0.22
381	16.19	0.45	0.29	0.32	0.03
312	18.87	0.17	0.37	0.20	0.33
331	18.96	0.24	0.37	0.11	0.30
352	20.10	0.50	0.23	0.23	0.02
369	20.39	0.67	0.27	0.17	0.19
356	22.15	0.32	0.28	0.08	0.01
341	25.21	0.37	0.34	0.25	0.36
Trade Oriented Sectors					
323	24.76	0.21	0.34	0.63	0.00
322	5.74	0.29	0.28	0.80	0.01
MONOPOLISTICALLY COMPETITIVE SECTORS					
Domestic Oriented Sectors					
313	33.29	1.14	0.13	0.02	0.39
324	37.60	0.18	0.52	0.15	0.26
371	38.77	0.15	0.47	0.46	0.36
342	41.85	0.58	0.26	0.06	0.07
384	46.26	0.32	0.34	0.38	0.04
362	49.61	0.63	0.33	0.27	0.02
332	49.83	0.45	0.24	0.16	0.00
Trade Oriented Sectors					
383	31.48	0.43	0.27	0.55	0.01
390	32.43	0.57	0.29	0.77	0.03
382	43.22	0.44	0.28	1.04	0.09
385	41.25	0.48	0.35	3.81	0.16
OLIGOPOLISTIC SECTORS					
Domestic Oriented Sectors					
372	53.02	0.35	0.30	0.41	0.24
314	57.97	0.83	0.18	0.16	0.82
361	64.23	1.10	0.21	0.08	0.05
355	68.55	0.51	0.31	0.24	0.02
354	84.32	0.17	0.15	0.03	0.04
353	97.43	0.96	0.02	0.09	1.00
Trade Oriented Sectors					
351	53.53	0.40	0.26	0.89	0.41

(continued)

Structural Characteristics of Manufacturing Sectors, 1995

Sectors	CR4	Mark-up Rates	Share of Share of Labor Cost at Value Added	Foreign Trade at Domestic Production	Share of Public Enterprises
COMPETITIVE SECTORS					
Domestic Oriented Sectors					
322	5.31	0.28	0.22	0.45	0.01
311	14.11	0.36	0.22	0.36	0.15
312	17.39	0.06	0.76	0.34	0.16
381	17.64	0.48	0.19	0.43	0.03
369	19.10	0.69	0.19	0.19	0.06
352	20.63	0.61	0.17	0.38	0.01
356	21.63	0.39	0.17	0.32	0.01
341	24.61	0.41	0.21	0.44	0.22
Trade Oriented Sectors					
371	7.27	0.37	0.23	0.64	0.24
321	21.03	0.23	0.35	0.75	0.02
323	21.32	0.54	0.20	0.71	0.06
383	28.06	0.55	0.23	1.75	0.02
390	28.35	0.22	0.27	0.50	0.05
MONOPOLISTICALLY COMPETITIVE SECTORS					
Domestic Oriented Sectors					
331	32.65	0.37	0.23	0.23	0.10
313	33.84	0.66	0.14	0.06	0.19
324	38.62	0.42	0.24	0.44	0.09
332	40.65	0.50	0.19	0.30	0.00
Trade Oriented Sectors					
384	40.78	0.36	0.26	0.68	0.02
382	43.22	0.44	0.21	1.36	0.06
372	43.99	0.36	0.26	0.67	0.23
OLIGOPOLISTIC SECTORS					
Domestic Oriented Sectors					
362	57.54	0.72	0.26	0.35	0.00
342	58.81	0.26	0.24	0.07	0.03
361	61.04	1.00	0.18	0.12	0.06
354	61.23	0.52	0.12	0.00	0.13
351	61.29	0.54	0.16	1.14	0.44
314	69.22	0.63	0.21	0.26	0.61
355	76.22	0.70	0.21	0.41	0.02
353	98.33	1.14	0.02	0.13	1.00
Trade Oriented Sectors					
385	55.92	0.63	0.15	1.69	0.04

which maintains the rate of profitability, we find that the rate of mark-up rate which stood at 32% in the 1980's, increased to 47% in 1994, and stabilized at 41% by 1996. In the presence of this type of pricing, the relative position of wage-labor in aggregate value added will directly depend on the changes in real wages and/or changes in the mark-up rate.

Sources of Productivity Growth in Manufacturing Industry

We now turn to a disaggregated analysis of the technological processes of productivity surrounding the manufacturing industries in the post-liberalization era. Data limitations preclude such an analysis for the other sectors. However, we believe that many of the attributes of the industrial market are shared by the other sectors, and that much of the characteristics of industrial employment and technology provide illuminating lessons for the economy as a whole.

We follow a methodology developed in Syrquin (1986) and Pieper (1998) in their analysis of growth decomposition. We will try to decompose the sources of labor productivity growth in the Turkish manufacturing industry and categorize its sub-sectors into "leaders" and "secondary" activities.

We first make use of the definition of average product of labor as total value added, X, per labor employed, L. An increase in average labor product is subject to two processes: (i) due to advancements in total factor productivity, given total labor employed; and (ii) due to a fall in labor employment and intensification of remaining labor employed—labor shedding. Our calculations reveal that between 1981 and 1996 the average productivity of labor (value-added deflated by WPI) in large-scale Turkish manufacturing has increased by 87.4%. In order to study the sources of this increase we will search for the patterns of employment and production in the sub-sectors of aggregate manufacturing industry.

Defining average labor productivity as $Q = \dfrac{X}{L}$, and denoting level of production in the sub-sector i as x_i and labor employment, as l_i we get the following identity

$$(1) \quad Q = \frac{X}{L} = \frac{\sum_i x_i}{\sum_i l_i}, \quad \text{and} \quad q_i = \frac{x_i}{l_i}, \quad i = \{\text{subsectors of manufacturing industry}\}$$

taking the first differences of the above identity with respect to time we get:

$$(2) \quad \frac{\Delta Q}{Q} = \frac{Q_1 - Q_0}{Q_0} = \sum_i \left[\left(\frac{x_{i1} - x_{i0}}{x_{i0}} \right) \left(\frac{x_{i0}}{X_0} \right) - \frac{Q_1}{Q_0} \left(\frac{l_{i1} - l_{i0}}{l_{i0}} \right) \left(\frac{l_{i0}}{L_0} \right) \right]$$

Here, if we make use of the following notation,

$$\frac{x_{i1} - x_{i0}}{x_{i0}} = g_i \quad \text{(rate of growth in sector i's production)}$$

$$\frac{l_{i1} - l_{i0}}{l_{i0}} = n_i \quad \text{(rate of growth in sector i's employment)}$$

$$\frac{x_{i0}}{X_0} = \theta_i \quad \text{(share of output of sector i)}$$

$$\frac{l_{i0}}{L_0} = \lambda_{i0} \quad \text{(share of employment of sector i)}$$

we transform the equation (1) into:

$$(3) \quad \frac{\Delta Q}{Q} = \sum_i \left[g_i \theta_i - \frac{Q_1}{Q_0} \lambda_{i0} n_i \right]$$

Accordingly, equation (3) allows us to decompose the change in average productivity into weighted changes in output production and labor employment at the subsectoral level. A further manipulation of equation (3) enables us to write:

$$(4) \quad \frac{\Delta Q}{Q} = \sum_i \left[\theta_{i0}(g_i - n_i) + \left(\theta_{i0} - \frac{Q_1}{Q_0} \lambda_{i0} \right) n_i \right]$$

Here the first term in brackets signifies the weighted rate of growth in output in sector i in excess of its labor employment. The second term reflects the gains in aggregate productivity originating from re-allocation of labor across sectors. Equation (4) decomposes the changes in overall productivity into a weighted average of sectoral productivity shifts and "reallocation of labor employment" across sub-sectors of the manufacturing industry. Accordingly, the "reallocation weight" is made up of the difference between the output

and labor share of sector-i, $\left[\theta_{i0} - \frac{Q_1}{Q_0} \lambda_{i0} \right]$, and reflects the differences in produc-

tivity levels across the manufacturing sector. Following Pieper, we will identify those sectors which have a high value of this term as "leading sectors", and those which have lower scores as the "secondary" sectors within manufacturing. Thus, a "leading" sector is characterized by a relatively high value of its reallocation weight due to a relatively small labor share.

We report our findings in Table 2-3. Here we decompose the sources of growth within nine subsectors of Turkish manufacturing between 1981–1996. The first column of Table 2-3 gives the productivity gains of the individual sub-sectors in this period. We decompose these gains into two sources: (i) contributions from *pure productivity* gains (first term in brackets of equation [4]); and (ii) contributions to aggregate productivity gains *by reallocation of labor* (second term in equation [4]). Data reflect that the first five sectors with the highest productivity rate are the following:

1. Forestry products (335.0%)
2. Paper products (214.3%)
3. Machinery (161.9%)
4. Food processing (126.3%)
5. Pottery and soil products (104.2%)

It is very interesting to observe, however, that the net *contribution* of Forestry Products to total industrial average productivity through labor re-allocation is *negative* (-1.0%). The reason originates from the low share of the sector in industry (low value of θ_{i0}). It is surprising to find that the same result is obtained for four of the most productive five sectors identified above. This finding suggests that the sectors that have had high labor productivity increases have failed to act as the "leading" sectors in industry mostly due to their small shares within the industry itself. Thus they could not have given significant impetus to the rest of the manufacturing.

Our analysis identifies the following sectors with positive contributions to aggregate labor productivity via labor reallocation (and thus can be termed as a "leader"):

1. Chemicals (3.4%)
2. Metals (3.1%)
3. Food Processing (2.6%)

Here, it is interesting to observe that none of the fast exporters of the post-1980 export boom reveal themselves in the leading category. Our analytical findings document clearly the fact that the leading exporters of this period could not have assumed a leading productivity role. In particular, the leading export sector, textiles, is observed to generate a *negative* rate of productivity contribution with −28.9% from labor re-allocation, and +20.3% from pure productivity gains. This brings the *net* contribution of textiles to aggregate productivity to −8.6%.

These findings reinforce our previous assessments regarding the manufacturing sector at the macro level. With a meager investment performance in manufacturing, the so-called export-led growth episode seems to generate sizable cost savings and surplus transfer to the recipient sectors and did not necessarily

**Table 2–3. Decomposition of Total Labor Productivity in
Aggregate Manufacturing Industry, 1981–1996**

						Contributions to Aggregate Productivity due to:	
	Increase in Labor Producity	Increase in Output	Increase In Employment	Share of Sectoral Production in Aggregate Manufacturing	Share of Sectoral Employment in Aggregate Manufacturing	Pure Productivity Gains	Reallocation of Labor
Food Processing	1.263	1.005	−0.114	0.175	0.215	0.196	0.026
Textiles, Clothing	0.890	2.432	0.816	0.125	0.256	0.203	−0.289
Forestry Products	3.350	4.828	0.340	0.009	0.021	0.040	−0.010
Paper Products	2.143	2.209	0.021	0.024	0.035	0.053	−0.001
Chemicals	0.523	0.765	0.159	0.372	0.085	0.226	0.034
Soil Products	1.042	1.302	0.127	0.066	0.074	0.078	−0.009
Metals	1.019	0.435	−0.289	0.075	0.097	0.055	0.031
Machinery	1.619	2.129	0.194	0.151	0.211	0.291	−0.048
Other Manu.	0.975	2.446	0.745	0.002	0.005	0.004	−0.005

Memo: Total increase in labor productivity in aggregate manufacturing between 1981–1996 = 0.874.

generate gains in productivity. As such, the post-1980 export orientation could not carry over into productivity gains in the leading exporting sectors and could not be sustained as a viable strategy of "export-led industrialization." Lacking the necessary productivity investments, the export gains based only on price incentives and subsidies had exhausted their impetus by the end of the decade. In the next section we turn into a detailed analysis of the distributional dynamics of this structure.

3. Patterns of Adjustment: Competitiveness and Distribution

It was through its trade policy component, essentially *via* export orientation, that globalization generated strong impacts on income distribution. For firms and even for entire industrial branches improving competitiveness became a matter of survival, let alone development. This had direct and systematic consequences on income distribution. It is these aspects of globalization that will be investigated in this section.

Competitiveness Indicators of the Manufacturing Exporters

Promotion of manufacturing exports was the main policy objective of the structural adjustment reforms in 1980, and this priority lasted until the end of 1988. The export performance of the economy was impressive in the period 1980–88. Annual export growth rate (in terms of current US dollars) during this period reached 19%, and surpassed world export growth rate by a significant margin. The same rate declined to a modest 5.1% between 1989–1993; but picked up and attained 12.8% following the 1994 crisis. The contribution of the manufacturing sector to total exports of goods had approached 90% by late 1990s—a striking improvement compared with the 32% average of the second half of the 1970s.

   To study the microeconomic dynamics of this process we will first report on the productivity and competitiveness indicators of export manufacturing. If we denote labor productivity by LP, real exchange rate by RER^4 and real wage costs by Wr, competitiveness indicator (CI) is defined by $(LP*RER)/Wr$. If we define RER and Wr by deflating nominal exchange rate (En) and nominal wages (Wn) by WPI, this definition can be written as: $[(LP)*(En)/WPI)]/[(Wn/WPI)]$. After appropriate manipulation this definition is transformed into $LP*(En/Wn)$. The inverse of this expression is equal to the conventional "unit labor costs" (ULC) concept: $(Wn/En)*(1/LP)$, i.e. wages in dollar terms deflated by labor productivity.

---

4. RER is defined as the real price of the foreign currency and, hence, rising RER represents real depreciation of the domestic currency, and *vice versa*.

Rather than the conventional *ULC* concept we find its transformation in a decomposed version into *CI* as more useful in the sense that its components, i.e. *real exchange rate, labor productivity and real wages,* reflect the three different strategic variables corresponding to *exchange rate, industrial and incomes policies* which determine the country's (industry's) capacity to compete with the external world.

Table 3-1 is organized on the basis of the foregoing three determinants of competitiveness for the manufacturing industry. Their analysis enables us to identify the specific policy patterns affecting competitiveness of the sector, while the *X/GDP* ratios, in return, represent the outcome in terms of export performance.

Table 3-2 translates the findings in Table 3-1 into a schematic form for sub-periods. Declining real wage costs [negative *g(wr)*], rising real exchange

TABLE 3–1: Competitiveness Determinants in Manufacturing Industry, Average Annual Growth Rates for Sub-periods

	Wr,WPI	LP	RER	CI	X/GNP,%
1981–84	−5.2	−3.1	6.8	117.9	9.3
1985–88	3.9	13.8	5.2	194.2	11.7
1989–93	15.2	10.3	−4.6	113.9	9.5
1994–97	−2.4	−7.7	4.4	152.4	13.3
(1994–95)	−19.4	−2.0	−13.0	162.8	13.4
(1996–97)	5.3	−13.0	9.7	131.5	13.3

Notes: Calculations by the authors from SIS data (Manufacturing Industry Censuses for 1981–1994; Manufacturing Industry Surveys for 1995–97). *Wr:* Real wages: Annual wages per worker in manufacturing industry deflated by WPI. *LP: Labor Productivity:* Value–added (for 1995–97, gross output) per worker in 1981 prices. *RER: Real exchange rate:* 1 US dollar+1.5 DM deflated by WPI (hence, rising RER corresponds to real depreciation of TL). *CI: Competitiveness index=*(Labor productivity*RER)/Real wages, all in index numbers. *X: Exports.* The last six rows for the first three columns are annual growth rates between the terminal year of the specified sub–period and the terminal year of the preceding sub–period except for the 1981–84 in which 1981 is taken as the base year. The last six rows for the last two columns are average values for the covered sub–periods. 1994–97 and 1996–97 figures refer to 1994–96 and 1996 respectively when 1997 values are unavailable.

TABLE 3–2: Patterns of Competitiveness by Sub-periods

	g(wr),WPI	g(lp)	g(rer)	Δ(CI)	Δ(X/GNP)
1981–84	−	−	+	+	+
1985–88	+	++	+	+	+
1989–93	+	++	−	−	−
1994–97	−	−	+	+	+
(1994–95)	−	−	+	+	+
(1996–97)	+	−	+	−	−

Note: See Table 2–1. **g** denotes growth rates and D differentials in index numbers or percentage points. Periods covered in calculating **g** and D values are as in NOTE to Table 2–1. + and − represent positive and negative values. ++ in column two represent g(lp)>3.5%.

rates and labor productivities [positive $g(rer)$ and $g(lp)$] result in improved competitiveness [i.e. positive $\Delta(CI)$], and *vice versa*. In terms of performance, improved CI would be expected to raise the share of exports in GNP [i.e positive $\Delta(X/GNP)$]. A distinction between strong (i.e. in excess of 3.5% *per annum* denoted by ++) and moderate (i.e. positive, but below 3.5% denoted by +) productivity growth is also made. Table 3-2, then serves to differentiate between adjustment patterns in terms of competitiveness.

First, it is significant to observe that there prevails almost complete correspondence between changes in *CI* and export performance for all sub-periods. In terms of adjustment patterns, however, the "ideal" combination of changes in the *Wr, LP* and *RER* variables is [−, +, +] which is realized in none of the sub-periods. The most substantial improvement in *CI* takes place during the 1985–88 sub-period when the three relevant variables exhibit the [+, ++, +] pattern. Real wage growth was almost negligible and a high rate of growth of *RER* and *LP* contributed to the improvement in competitiveness. It should be recalled that the so-called "realistic" exchange rate policy, aiming at real depreciations was one of the pillars of the policy package of the 1980–88 years. The [−, −, +] pattern of the 1981–84 sub-period results in improved competitiveness when a mild decline in productivity is over-compensated by the erosion of real wages and substantial rates of real depreciations.

The most adverse combination (in terms of competitiveness) of the relevant variables would be [+, −, −]. In the Turkish case this would correspond to the late 1970s; but no such phase is observed during the 1981–1997 period. The 1989–1993 years, however, exhibiting the [+, ++, −] pattern comes closest: the wage "explosion" was accompanied by substantial real appreciation (with nearly 30% decline in *RER* from 1988 to 1993). The strong productivity growth was not sufficient to arrest the substantial and almost continuous erosion of *CI* during the five years following 1988.

In order to assess the strong performance of 1985–88 and 1989–93 sub-periods, one can further differentiate the two major factors beyond $g(lp)$ into a *dynamic* pattern based on investments, and a *static efficiency* pattern based on labor shedding, downsizing and intra-industrial improvements. In both phases we observe that manufacturing investment ratios are lower than the earlier period and the following sub-periods. However, employment growth is positive during 1985–88, but turns negative in the following sub-period. Strong wage growth and stagnant investment performance during 1989–93 directly enabled the manufacturing industry to raise productivity via labor shedding, i.e. via gains of *static efficiency*.

Relations and Patterns of Income Distribution

It will be shown in the following section that the majority of the poverty-stricken population is located within the ranks of wage-earners and peasants. Hence, changes in indicators of distribution on wage earners and terms of trade for agriculture (TOTA) are relevant both for an analysis of functional (class-based) income distribution; and for assessing whether the direction of change is equitable or not. It should be noted that the Turkish agrarian structure is based predominantly on a market-oriented peasant agriculture and, hence, *TOTA* corrected by labor productivity represents real income movements of farmers from their agricultural output and relative price movements *per se.* This is why we regard *TOTA* as the crucial indicator of distributional dynamics in the rural economy.

In Turkey, movements of *TOTA* since the late 1970s depict two phases: a dramatic decline by 45% from 1977 up till the end of 1988 (for 1980–88, see Table 3-3, Column 1) and an upward movement from 1988 through 1997, except for 1994. A comparison of *TOTA* with wage movements for the same years and for the main sub-periods (Table 3-4) suggests that there is a striking similarity between the distributional "destinies" of workers and peasants in Turkey. Even the apparent divergence between *TOTA* and *g(wr)* indicators for the 1994–97 sub-period is misleading. Once the average values of 1994–97 are divided into two equal segments, i.e. 1994–95 and 1996–97, divergence between *TOTA* and *g(wr)* disappears.

This phenomenon of "parallel wage and *TOTA* movements" is a reflection of the underlying role played by policy factors affecting workers and peasant-farmers in a common fashion. Broadly speaking, "populist" policy phases result in upward wage and *TOTA* movements. The reverse is observed in those years when stabilization, structural adjustment, and interests of private capital dominate policy making; and adverse incomes policies affect both wage-earners and peasants in a parallel fashion. An earlier study on the relative magnitude of support purchases by marketing boards and other subsidies supported this explanation.[5]

Table 3-3 further enables us to overview the distributional variables and to propose typical patterns for the sub-periods. In addition to *TOTA,* the table brings together three indicators: Annual changes in wages *g(wr)* and employment, *g(emp)* are accompanied by the differential between productivity and real wage growth rates, i.e. *g(lp)-g(wr).* A positive value for *g(lp)-g(wr)* implies, first a rising *gross profits/value added ratio* within manufacturing industry and, secondly, intra-industrial surplus generation and *vice versa.* Here, we move into *real wage earnings,* instead of *real wage costs* as an indicator of relations of distribution and, hence, use CPI as deflator in defining real wages instead of WPI as has been done in the preceding tables.

The presence of a permanent and almost violent wage cycle influenced strongly by the relative strength of social actors and by the political environment during the past twenty years is striking. In terms of real wage *costs,* a 44%

---

5. See K. Boratav, O. Türel and E. Yeldan (1996, Table 8). The correction of *TOTA* by labor productivity provides us data on agricultural income per employed person. Real farm incomes in this sense have declined by 45% from 1977 to 1989 and, thereafter improved by 47%. The 1996 level is still 18% below that of 1977.

TABLE 3–3: Distributional Variables by Sub-periods

	TOTA(1980=1.0)	g(wr),CPI	g(lp)–g(wr),WPI	g(emp)
1981–84	0.892	–3.5	8.2	3.1
1985–88	0.841	–2.0	9.3	3.1
1989–93	0.849	13.2	–10.5	–0.7
1994–97	0.993	–7.8	2.1	1.9
(1994–95)	0.893	–17.7	17.2	–0.3
(1996–97)	1.094	3.2	–22.6	6.3

TABLE 3–4: Distributional Patterns by Sub-periods

	D TOTA	g(wr),CPI	g(lp)–g(wr),WPI	g(emp)
1981–84	–	–	+	+
1985–88	–	–	+	+
1989–93	+	++	–	–
1994–97	+	–	+	+
(1994–95)	–	–	++	–
(1996–97)	+	+	–	++

Note I: TOTA is *terms of trade for agriculture* calculated from the ratios of implicit deflators for agriculture and for industry. Source: SIS, National Accounts. Column 2 is nominal wages deflated by CPI. See Table 3–1 for other columns.

Note II: *D TOTA* represents the sign of the differential between the average of the specified sub-period and that of the terminal year of the preceding sub-period. For 1981–84 the comparison is between the sub–period average and 1980.

"collapse" from the late 1970s up till 1985 is followed by a 158% "explosion" up till 1993 (most of which is realized in 1989–91) and another collapse of 62% in 1994–95. In terms of real wage *earnings* the same cycle (although trough and peak years are not identical) is represented by –42%, +95% and –37%. Wages/value added ratios are affected by the cycle despite the dominance of a downward trend thereof. Let us, once again, note that *TOTA* and wage movements are roughly parallel.

In the second part of Table 3-3 we study a schematic translation of these indicators. This enables us to move into *patterns*, this time of *distributional changes* and the characterization of the post-1980 sub-periods accordingly. We define an *egalitarian pattern* to incorporate simultaneous improvements in *TOTA*, real wages, wage shares and employment. In our notation, this would be represented by (+, +, –, ++) in the same order of the four variables covered in Table 3-4. Positive *TOTA*, *g(wr)*, *g(emp)* indicators may be accompanied by a non-negative value for $g(lp)$–$g(wr)$ which would be represented by (+, +, +, ++) in terms of our table. Let us label this as an *equitable pattern*. It signifies that popular classes are experiencing improvements in terms of the on-farm prices, wages and employment; but productivity does not lag behind the growth of wages. As long as surplus generation within industry is not transmitted into higher rates of capitalist consumption; but rather transformed into accumulation, employment creation and (*via* higher taxes) into public goods, such a pattern is usually considered legitimate and equitable. There are no sub-periods which fall either into the *egalitarian* or *equitable* pattern during the post-1980 years. There are however, brief *egalitarian* (i.e. 1989–90, 1996–97) interludes.

Trade-offs between real wages and employment generate different patterns. When positive *TOTA* movements are accompanied by positive $g(wr)$ and negative (or weak) $g(emp)$ we have a *possibly egalitarian (or equitable*[6] *)* pattern in favor of the employed workers, but against the unemployed urban groups. Findings in Section 4 for the post-1989 years in Turkey suggest a slightly different pattern when wage progression in the formal sector has accompanied rising employment in the informal sector—a combination which favors both groups of workers unless it also results in lower employment levels in the formal sector. Conversely, when positive *TOTA* movements are accompanied by negative $g(wr)$ and positive $g(emp)$ we have another *possibly egalitarian* pattern—this time discriminating against the previously employed workers, but in favor of the unemployed urban groups. If the employed and unemployed (marginal etc.) groups belong sociologically to the same social groups (e.g. the same households), the net distributional result of the wage-employment trade-off would depend on the relative size of the total wage bill and on the changes in real incomes of the related urban groups. Conventional neo-classical analysis treats them as distinct social entities with limited inter-group mobility, and, hence considers any trade-off which favors employment against real wages as an equitable movement. In the post-1980 years, such trade-offs have prevailed during the wage-boom/capital account opening phase of 1989–93 (against the unemployed, but in favor of wage-earners in the formal sectors).

Since average peasant incomes are substantially below urban wages and it is in the rural population that poverty is most widely spread, any combination of *TOTA* deterioration along with negative movements of either $g(wr)$ or $g(emp)$ must be considered a *partially inegalitarian/inequitable* pattern. Negative signs for the three indicators would represent a *totally inegalitarian* change. Such patterns have prevailed during the 1981–88 and 1994–95 years in Turkey. Both cases correspond to crisis (post-crisis) and orthodox stabilization phases.

---

6. "Egalitarian" vs. "equitable" labels depend on the sign of $g(lp)$-$g(wr)$ as explained in the text.

4. Poverty, Size Distribution of Income and Social Classes

Why Size Distribution?

The foregoing analysis of post-1980 distributional changes has been in terms of income types of specific social classes/strata. The distributional process *per se* consists of primary and secondary relations in which socio-economic groups, classes and the state are actively engaged. *Functional income distribution* or *income distribution between socio-economic groups* provide appropriate conceptual frameworks for studying the linkages which shape the distributional dynamics including the impact of economic policies. *Size distribution of income,* on the other hand, is the *statistical end result* of these relations of distribution.

However, once the analysis moves into the arena of poverty, information on size distribution of income becomes indispensable. This is because poverty is much more related to income *levels,* rather than income *types.* Hence, size (personal) distribution of income is the appropriate starting point in estimating the magnitude of the poverty issue. If poverty thresholds can be defined in terms of income levels for urban and rural households (or for other groups) and if we have frequency (i.e. "size") distributions of income or the same groups, the number of households living in poverty can directly be estimated.

In Section 3 above we have studied the behavior of real wage costs and remunerations, and agricultural terms of trade (*TOTA*) in Turkey under post-1980 liberalization. Given these findings, the following questions should be addressed: (i) What are the linkages between the observed wage and *TOTA* movements and size distribution of income and, more specifically, their incidence on poverty? (ii) How far have liberalization patterns affected inequalities among labor incomes? And finally, (iii) Apart from changes in the distribution of nominal incomes, have changing relative prices for consumers and farmers alleviated or aggravated the incidence of poverty? The following sub-sections will discuss these questions.

Income Types, Size Distribution and Poverty: Empirical Linkages

Empirical studies on poverty are scarce in Turkey.[7] Recent data on size distribution of income are available for 1987 and 1994. Information on the share of different income types within the total income of the lowest income brackets for total, urban, and rural households is available only for 1987. *Vulnerable income types* in 1987 are thus defined and presented in Table 4-1 and can be used as a

---

7. In the only recent study, Dumanlý (1997) on the basis of the 1987 size distribution data, the food basket corresponding to minimum calorie requirements and CPI index numbers, estimates the share of households living below the poverty line as 15%, 10% and 20% in Turkey, in urban and rural areas respectively. These percentages roughly correspond to our findings presented in Table IV-1.

**TABLE 4-1: Percentage Distribution of Income Types of Households:
The Lowest Two Income Brackets and Turkish Averages, 1987**

	The Poor: Turkey	The Poor: Urban	The Poor: Rural	Average Turkey	Average Urban	Average Rural
Wages	35.6	50.4	25.1	23.3	28.8	15.2
Farming	25.1	2.1	41.3	22.8	2.7	51.9
Trade & Services	6.8	9.1	5.4	20.3	24	14.8
Artisanal, Industry	2.1	2.7	1.8	8.2	11.3	3.7
House Rents	2.1	1.9	2.2	3.5	4.3	2.4
Interest & Dividends	0.7	0.8	0.6	1.8	2.8	0.4
Transfers, Official	12.1	16.8	8.8	8.1	10.2	5
Transfers, Abroad	0.5	1	0	1.5	1.8	1.2
Transfers, Other	3.2	3.1	3.2	1	1.1	0.9
Income in Kind	11.8	12.1	11.6	9.5	13	4.5
TOTAL	100.0	100.0	100.0	100.0	100.0	100.0

NOTES: Sources: State Institute of Statistics (SIS), *Income Distribution*, 1987. The lowest two brackets cover 0-99999 TL monthly incomes. This group covers 14.3, 10.4 and 18.5 percents of overall (Turkish), urban and rural households respectively and the income share of the same groups are 3.2, 2.3 and 4.6 percent of the overall (Turkish), urban and rural incomes. Rows 2–4 are defined as "entrepreneurial income" and official transfers include pensions and social assistance payments.

starting point of poverty investigations. The following observations are valid:

(1) Income sources of "the poor" differ from national averages (see Columns 1 and 4). Wages, agricultural "entrepreneurial" income and pensions constitute significantly higher shares in incomes of "the poor" than that of the "average" household. The incidence of poverty among the recipients of interest, dividend, rental and non-agricultural entrepreneurial revenues (which also incorporates revenues accruing to informal business) is much more limited. Two implications follow: (i) Adverse changes in real wages/salaries, in pensions and in agricultural terms of trade should, *ceteris paribus*, be interpreted as aggravating the incidence of poverty and, hence, inequitable. (ii) However, intra-group size distribution also matters and average changes of specific income types may affect different sub-groups (and, hence, poverty) in non-uniform manner. Therefore, further information on intra-group distribution is required.

(2) The old debate on whether higher agricultural, especially food crop, prices benefit or harm the rural poor seems to be settled in favor of the "beneficial impact thesis" in the Turkish case. Farming revenues of the agricultural poor exceeds their wage revenues (Column 3), and although poor farmers may also be buyers of food crops from the market, (i) as long as their agricultural revenues exceed their food expenditures, they benefit in net terms; and (ii) even if they are net "spenders," higher agricultural prices affect them less adversely than other non-rural social groups. This conclusion reiterates the earlier proposition on the equitable consequences of improvement in *TOTA*.

Poverty Impact of Relative Price Movements

We now report on the impact of relative price changes on the magnitude of the families below the poverty line. Two dimensions are involved. First, if relative prices of those consumer goods which occupy a major portion of the consumption basket of poor households (i.e. of food) deteriorate with respect to the overall price level (e.g. CPI) which had been used in estimating real wages, the size of the population below the poverty line may rise even with unchanged income levels. Secondly, if relative prices of those agricultural commodities which occupy a major portion of the output of poor rural households (i.e. of cereals and tobacco for the Turkish farmers) deteriorate with respect to the overall price level (e.g. implicit deflator for agriculture) which is used in estimating *TOTA* movements, the size of the rural population below the poverty line may rise even with unchanged *TOTA*.

TABLE 4–2: Poverty Impact of Relative Price Movements

	Cotton/ food	Sunflower/ food	Tobacco/ food	Wheat/ food	CPI/ food
1978/79	1.00	1.00	1.00	1.00	1.00
1983	1.25	1.44	0.77	1.17	1.01
1988	0.84	1.15	0.91	0.89	0.95
1993	0.65	1.42	0.41	0.92	0.91
1995	0.77	—		0.92	0.87

Notes: Data from SIS. In the first four columns the coefficients are the ratios between index numbers of prices receive by farmers and the "food" item of CPI (1978–79=1.00). The fifth column is self–explanatory. Values below unity represent poverty–augmenting relative price changes after 1978/79.

Table 4-2 provides hints on the poverty impact of relative price movements where food price component of CPI is used as the general *numerator* in assessing the impact. Values less than unity in the terminal year represent poverty augmenting relative price changes for consumers in general and for the relevant farming, since the end of the 1970s.

The last column compares movements of overall consumer prices with those of food prices. It turns out that relative price movements moved against consumers below the poverty line, i.e. households with a larger weight of food within their consumption baskets, by 13% between 1978/79 and 1995. Among farming households, poverty is more widespread among wheat and tobacco farmers than the cotton and sunflower farmers. Once again, farming households with the exception of sunflower growers have confronted lower prices received for their crops in terms of overall food prices. This last observation points at the inegalitarian impact of the widening of two sets of prices originating at the agricultural sector: (i) Poor consumers have been "taxed" by faster than average increases of food prices; but (ii) higher food prices have not been transmitted to (or have not been due to) higher relative prices for cereal/wheat farmers—the most numerous and poorest segments of the rural population. The overall impact of relative price movements have, thus, been in the direction of rising inequalities and aggravating poverty.

Wage Inequalities and Poverty

In which direction have wage patterns changed during the post-1980 years? What was the impact on poverty-stricken urban population? The discussion of these questions requires the prior clarification of a number of empirical issues.

A situation of constant average real wages is compatible with increased polarization at both ends of the frequency distribution for wage earners. That is why data on average real wage movements do not always have implications for poverty. On the other hand, a situation of constant average real wages for each sub-group of workers may also correspond to a situation of increased polarization of wage earnings when internal changes of the work-force from relatively higher-paid positions and activities towards lower-paid ones take place. Increased polarization corresponds to the aggravation of poverty if *suppression* of real wages at the lower brackets is part of the process. Finally, it would be helpful if data are available on the magnitude of non-wage revenues of lowest-paid wage earners.

Frequency distribution of wage revenues for the wage earning population (or for sub-groups thereof) is not available. Hence, questions on "which categories of wage earners are more vulnerable?" or "are vulnerable sub-groups growing larger?" can be tackled only indirectly. Two sets of appropriate data are available. The first set is from the *Survey on Employment and Wage Structure* of SIS and provides us with wage rates for specific sub-groups of *total* wage earners, yet only for 1994. We can infer some of the explanatory factors behind wage differentiation from this. We also have data from *Household Labor Force Surveys* of SIS on employment shares of the same sub-groups within *total* employment from 1988 onwards. Assuming that the ranking of different wage-earning groups has remained unchanged, the analysis of changes in the employment structure (e.g. whether the share of female workers has risen or not) provides information on changes in wage inequalities.

The second set of data consists of wage movements within *manufacturing industry* (i.e. by branches, private/public, small/large enterprises). Additionally, we have wage data for some years on a few non-manufacturing industries based on *Labor Statistics*. We can, thus, directly generate some indicators on wage differentiation. These two lines of analysis will be undertaken in what follows.

1. Diverse Factors Affecting Wage Inequalities

The SIS *Survey on Employment and Wage Structure* presents data on wage differentials on the basis of different socio-economic attributes and produces no surprises. It is among *female, young, uneducated, unexperienced, non-unionized* categories that poorly paid workers are located. Private sector wages are about half of that of the public sector. Unionization makes a great deal of difference. Wage rates for non-unionized workers are 44% below those under collective agreements. Female and young (i.e. below 20 years of age) workers earn 39 and 75 percent less than men and those at the prime of life (i.e. aged 35–54) respectively. University graduates earn 2.3 times more than workers with less than 5 years of education.

On the basis of these findings it can be inferred that higher employment of child and female labor, higher rates of turnover within the workforce (reducing seniority averages), declining unionization and educational levels, privatization and a declining public sector would be the channels aggravating the incidence of poverty within urban workers, and pushing average wages downwards.

During the past decade, public sector employment has declined, partly due to privatization. Although reliable data are not available, there is consensus among labor economists that unionization rates have recently been declining. The move towards increased flexibility of the labor market is likely to have raised turnover rates of the workforce. SIS surveys show that female employment has risen by three percentage points between 1988 and 1997. These are factors pushing for increased wage inequalities and, probably aggravating poverty. On the other hand, there are positive trend factors, e.g. gradual improvement of the educational levels and the age structure of the labor force, which operate in the reverse direction.

2. Differential Inter and Intra-Industrial Wage Movements

In Table 4-3 we present further data which enable us to compare wage movements and levels of relatively unorganized and informal workers (i.e. those employed in private, small enterprises and in clothing) with those in more organized and formal sectors (i.e. public and large enterprises, in mining and gas production).

The findings strongly suggest distinctions between two phases. The *first phase, 1981–88*, is distinguished by labor market controls imposed by extra-economic means. Reduced wage differentiation takes place by the erosion of wages of formal/organized workers much faster than other groups. Gaps between wages in private/public; small/large; organized/unorganized (i.e. mining, gas and electricity vs. clothing and trade) are reduced significantly. The *second phase* covers the wage explosion years of *1989–1993* and constitutes the complete reversal of the preceding pattern. The strong improvement in average wages was almost completely due to what was happening at the organized/formal sectors. Wage gaps between large/small and public/ private enterprises widen significantly and exceed the relative margins of the early 1980s.

Two interrelated questions can be addressed with respect to the comparisons of inter-industrial wage and employment structures. Has labor demand responded to changing inter-industrial wage structures and have changes in inter-industrial wage differentiation been caused by changes in employment? The direction of

TABLE 4-3: Relative Wage Movements by Industries, 1983–93
(Annual Wages per Worker; Industrial Average/Manufacturing Average)

	Priv./Public	Small/Large	Mining	Gas	Clothing	Trade, etc.
1981	0.63	0.26*	0.41	1982	0.67	0.47
1983	0.78		—	1.27	0.53	—
1984	0.84		1.1	1.31	0.54	—
1985	0.91	0.41	0.95	1.67	0.49	—
1986	0.91		0.97	1.53	0.58	0.89
1987	—		0.92	1.35	—	0.92
1988	0.91		0.87	1.23	0.59	0.79
1989	0.71		1.03	1.02	0.52	0.63
1990	0.73	0.29	1.18	1.9	0.47	0.65
1991	0.64		1.32	1.51	0.41	0.47
1992	0.59	0.25	1.4	1.35	0.39	—
1993	0.55	0.21	1.78	2.14	0.39	—
1994	0.47	0.19	—	—	0.4	—
1995	—	0.24	—	—	—	—

Notes: SIS, *Labour Statistics*, 1996 except for Columns 1, 2 and 5 which is from SIS data. The first column equals average private wages divided by average wages in public enterprises in manufacturing industry. The second column equals average wages in large (10+ workers) enterprises divided by average wages in small (1-9 workers) enterprises in private manufacturing industry. The rest compares average wages of the relevant branch to those in manufacturing The last column covers trade, restaurants, hotels and miscellaneous services.

causality is essentially a theoretical issue that will not be addressed here. Instead we shall merely overview the empirical wage/employment linkages for small-scale enterprises, for the "trade etc." sub-sector and clothing.

The predominantly export-oriented traded clothing industry has continued to expand its employment share during phases when its relative wage levels have been rising (1981–88) or falling (1989 onwards). Relative wages of the essentially non-traded *trade, hotels, restaurants and miscellaneous services* sub-sector have declined, accompanied by rising employment shares. The employment share of small-scale manufacturing, on the other hand, has remained essentially stable throughout the period despite ups and downs in the wage dispersion between small/large enterprises. Overall, it can be proposed that trend factors based on the dynamics of external/internal demand—to a large degree independently of wage movements—may have been effective in shaping employment patterns. Furthermore, essentially autonomous wage movements, independent of each other in the formal and informal segments of the labor market, have shaped changing dispersions of inter-industrial wage structures.

On the basis of the foregoing findings, a number of conclusions on inter-industrial and intra-industrial wage and employment movements can be proposed:

(a) The post-1980 period—when globalization and liberalization dominated the Turkish economy—has resulted in further opening the gap between the wages of high and low-paid segments of the urban working class.

(b) The dual character of Turkish labor markets shapes real wage movements of organized/formal and unorganized/ informal segments. The cycle of average wages is shaped by what is happening in the organized segment. This is not only due to the size of the organized sector, but also because wages there are much more volatile in both directions than those in the unorganized segments. If we distinguish large and small-scale manufacturing establishments, average real wage *earning* between 1980 and the peak year (1993) rose by 29% in the former group, but by a mere 2% in the latter. Real wages collapsed for both groups in 1994–95; but by 29% in large establishments and 20% in small-scale enterprises. Hence, when gaps between higher and lower-paid segments of the urban workers are opening (narrowing), it is due to the faster growth (decline) of wages in organized/formal sectors. In other words, both groups of workers usually experience parallel wage movements and there is no trade-off between their real wage levels. This signifies that a lower degree of wage dispersion does not, *per se*, have a favorable impact on vulnerable (poverty-stricken) groups of wage earners. On the other hand, it is more likely that during those phases when wage dispersion is rising, the number of wage-earners below the poverty line may be declining because these phases usually correspond to (i) real wage progression for all groups and (ii) rising employment rates for workers in informal/unorganized sectors.

(c) The preceding section argued that a more open trade regime affected wage movements through pressures on competitiveness. The linkage between inter- and intra-sectoral wage differentiation and globalization/liberalization is less direct. In Turkey it is, still, the dual character of labor markets and the relative bargaining power of social actors on wage settlements in the formal segments that shape trends in wage dispersion. Despite adverse developments, the formal, organized and medium-large sectors, particularly in manufacturing, mining and infrastructures still constitute the dominant segments of labor markets. An increasing scope of flexible arrangements in labor markets usually corresponds to phases of real wage progression for organized segments. Hence, during two decades of liberalization, trends in wage differentiation and their impact on poverty take place in a much more complex setting than that envisaged by neoclassical models and, therefore, the outcomes have not corresponded to conventional predictions.

We conclude this section with two final observations. The first is on the dichotomy between economic categories and social realities. The segmented character of *labor markets* in Turkey does not imply the segmentation of the *urban working class* into formal vs. marginal groups. It is members of the same households who shift from informal into organized activities as economic conditions change. Some sort of a gender or age-based division of labor also exists between formal/informal activities.[8] Hence, distributional trade-offs between

---

8. For empirical support see Boratav (1995).

organized vs. marginal industries should not be interpreted as implying conflicts of interest between two distinct segments of the urban social matrix.

The second observation is on micro (household)-level adjustment strategies. During periods when real wages or real prices for agricultural output are repressed, households, whether urban and rural, whether below or above the poverty line, undertake defensive adjustment strategies and attempt to preserve their real income levels. Urban households respond by strengthening their links with the agricultural and informal sectors. As for rural households, the typical defensive mechanism of poor peasants would be migration to the urban economy or moving into wage-labor (sometimes in non-agricultural activities) within the rural economy. The response of better-off farmers would be to shift investable resources outside of agriculture.

5. The Public Sector and Social Safety Nets

Deterioration of Fiscal Balances

It is during the post-1988 era that a drastic deterioration of the fiscal balances took place in Turkey. Public sector borrowing requirement (PSBR) as a ratio of GDP averaged 4.5 percent during 1981–1988, but rose to 8.6 percent for the 1989–1997 period.

In this context, it is important to note a fundamental change in financing of the PSBR. Data on the financing patterns of the PSBR suggest that, under the financially repressed conditions of the 1970's and early 1980's, deficit financing through central bank advances (monetization) was the predominant method. However, after removal of interest ceilings in a series of reforms throughout the 1980s,[9] the Turkish private sector faced a new element: real interest rates rising to unprecedented levels. While borrowers struggled to adapt to exorbitant real rates on loans, financial institutions and rentiers adapted swiftly to the new conditions and the government found it much easier to finance its borrowing requirements domestically through issues of the government debt instruments (GDIs). This also enabled successive governments to by-pass many of the formal constraints on their fiscal operations. Consequently, with the advent of full-fledged financial liberalization after 1988, the PSBR financing relied almost exclusively on issues of GDIs to the internal market—especially to the banking sector. The stock of domestic debt was only about 6% of the GNP in 1989, just when the liberalization of the capital account was completed. It grew rapidly, and reached 20% by 1997.

The underlying characteristic of the domestic debt management was its extreme short-termism. Net domestic borrowings, as a ratio of the stock of the

---

9. See Boratav, Türel and Yeldan (1996), Ekinci (1998), Köse and Yeldan (1998), and Balkan and Yeldan (1998) for a thorough investigation of the financial reforms over the 1980s and 90s.

existing debt, hovered around 50% before the 1990's. This ratio increased to 105% in 1993, indicating that each year the state had to resort to new borrowing exceeding the stock of debt already accumulated. In 1996, this ratio reached to 163.5%. Thus, the public sector has been trapped in a short-term rolling of debt, a phenomenon characterized as *Ponzi-financing* in the fiscal economics literature. For this scheme to work, however, domestic financial markets required the continued inflow of short-term capital inflows. Thus, the episode of hot money inflows should be interpreted, in the Turkish context, as the long arm of fiscal policy, overcoming credit restraints and monetary constraints of the monetary authority.

Currently more than 90% of the newly securitized deficit is purchased by the banking sector. Thus, the so-called deepening of the financial system in the Turkish economy has turned into a process of self-feeding cycles, ready to burst. High real rates of interest on the GDI's attract speculative short-term funds, and through the operations of the banking system, these are channeled to the treasury via bond auctions, which can thereby by-pass constraints imposed by the monetary authority. Except during financial crises, this is an extremely profitable process for the banking sector, and it is the capital account liberalization which makes it viable. The major brunt of the costs of this fragile environment, however, falls on the productive sphere of the economy, especially the traded sectors. High real interest rates and overvaluation of the domestic currency, as normal elements of the model, generate disincentives to exporters, productive entrepreneurs and contributes to a widening trade deficit.

Implications of the Rising Debt Burden: Adjustment Patterns

During the years when the Turkish economy was experiencing financial liberalization, inflation was accelerating. Average annual inflation (WPI) was 36.2% during 1981–84; but accelerated to 43.3, 62.3 and 90.6 percents during the 1985–88, 1989–93 and 1994–97 periods, respectively. With the diversification of investable assets under financial deepening, the most significant distributional outcome was an even faster acceleration of interest rates in nominal terms. While real returns on financial assets were registering an erratic, albeit rising pattern real interest rates on credits rose substantially. [See Önder, Türel, Ekinci and Somel (1993: Table 6.3)].

Regardless of the fluctuations in real interest rates, very high nominal interest rates generate trade-offs with other income categories. A rising share of interest payments from value added (and gross profits) crowds out the share of either net profits or wages or both. This is what is observed from the consolidated balance sheets of the largest industrial firms during the post-1980 years. Starting from a negligible share, the interest payments/gross profits ratio exceeded the 50% threshold after 1982 and inevitably generated downward pressures on wages. On the other hand, a countervailing process of investing in short-term financial assets on the part of large holdings incorporating banks or of those with better liquid positions is being observed in recent years.[10] However, this schizophrenic anomaly of firms acting partly as rentiers, partly as borrowers *cum* industrialists does not spread to middle and small producers.

A second distributional incidence of financial liberalization is on the fiscal system *via* the crowding-out impact of the debt burden. The continuing expansion of the public debt under conditions of accelerating inflation and rising interest rates results in expanding the share of interest expenditures within public spending and within GDP. Adjustment processes involving crowding-out effects on specific expenditure categories are the outcome. When welfare-oriented public expenditures are involved in the crowding-out processes, directly adverse distributional impacts follow.

Table 5-1 provides the conceptual and empirical framework for an analysis of these adjustment processes. The table succinctly discloses the magnitude of the problem. Shares of interest payments on the public debt (Int) within GDP (Y) are presented in the first columns of the table. It is observed that the Int/Y ratio has grown by a coefficient of 9.2 between 1981 and 1996. The rising share of public expenditures within GDP is not translated into a relative expansion of real public services, i.e. non-interest expenditures, as

TABLE 5-1: Fiscal Adjustment: Interest Payments, Major Expenditure Categories and Public Deficits (% of GDP)

	Int/Y	EH/Y	DSG/Y	EO/Y	Ig/Y	G/Y	Gr/Y	PSBR/Y
1981	1.1	3.2	11.5	4.1	3.9	20.0	18.9	4.0
1982	0.8	3.3	11.6	4.4	3.2	19.1	18.3	3.5
1983	1.5	3.0	10.0	4.3	3.4	18.8	17.3	4.9
1984	2.0	2.6	8.8	4.0	3.1	17.2	15.2	5.4
1985	1.9	2.3	7.3	3.8	2.9	15.4	13.4	3.6
1986	2.6	2.3	7.2	4.1	3.2	16.3	13.7	3.7
1987	3.0	2.6	7.8	3.8	2.7	17.1	14.1	6.1
1988	3.9	2.5	7.1	3.1	2.1	16.6	12.7	4.8
1989	3.6	3.3	7.1	3.1	1.7	17.1	13.5	5.3
1990	3.6	4.1	6.5	3.2	1.7	17.4	13.9	7.4
1991	3.8	4.5	8.6	4.0	1.9	21.0	17.2	10.2
1992	3.7	5.0	8.0	3.9	1.7	20.6	16.9	10.6
1993	5.9	5.1	9.7	4.1	1.8	24.7	18.9	12.0
1994	7.7	3.9	8.8	2.8	1.3	23.3	15.6	7.9
1995	7.4	3.5	8.6	2.5	1.1	22.2	14.8	5.2
1996	9.0	3.7	10.1	2.8	1.6	26.8	16.7	9.0

Notes: Y: GDP, Gr: Non-interest public spending; PSBR: Public Sector Borrowing Requirement.

10. Turkish car manufacturers suspended production and temporarily dismissed workers for a few months during the crisis period in mid-1994 and invested their working capital, i.e. wage funds on treasury bonds offering exorbitant interest rates. Their end-year balance sheets registered substantial losses on their productive activities, but even higher profits on their "auxiliary" (i.e. financial) activities. This is a typical case of interest-wage trade-off.

reflected by the Gr/Y ratio which declines from 18.6 to 15.8 from 1981–82 to 1995–96 although there are ups and downs in-between.

If fiscal austerity to control public deficits will be exercised in response or as a reaction to higher interest burden, certain categories of real government expenditures will, necessarily, be crowded out. Three "crowding-out patterns" (i.e on capital accumulation/infrastructure; on defense/ security/general services or on social spending) can be distinguished. After the return to the parliamentary regime, i.e. from 1984 onwards, it was to be expected that governments would be more willing to sacrifice the first two categories; rather than withdrawing from social spending.

(a) The first pattern involves letting higher interest payments to crowd-out public investments (Ig) towards sustaining the economic infrastructure (EO). This is clearly documented by the continual erosion of "EO/Y" and "Ig/Y" ratios. Declines of nearly 4 percentage points within GDP of the two expenditure categories take place between 1981 and 1996.

(b) The share of public spending on defense, security and general services (DSG) exhibits a definite declining trend between 1981–1990, but thereafter registers an upsurge, within GDP, essentially due to higher levels of security and military spending in response to the armed conflict in the South-East provinces. Allocational and (positive) welfare impacts directly follow, but there are also indirect distributional implications.

(c) Erosion of public spending on capital accumulation and maintenance of the economic infrastructure did not offset rising debt servicing. This may require drifting further into lowering the relative magnitude of social public expenditures. Spending on education and health (EH) is a major component of what we have labeled as social public expenditures. There is no unique trend throughout the period. Three phases can be distinguished in terms of EH/G and EH/Y ratios: an erosion which starts in 1982 and lasts up till 1989; progression up till 1993, and further erosion up till the terminal year. However, rising (in non-uniform manner) G/Y ratios during the same period have prevented the emergence of lower EH/Y values by 1996 compared with 1981.

It is clear that the orthodox stabilization/adjustment phase of 1980–88 had led to the erosion of real public expenditures and, in particular, social spending. Capital account liberalization has helped to stop and reverse this adverse trend. This signifies external savings in the form of short-term capital inflows crowding out public savings or, in other words, financing the expansion of public consumption during 1989–92. It is also significant to note that a stabilization of Int/Y ratios and falling Int/G ratios are observed up till 1992 essentially due to the fast expansion of real government spending.

Unfortunately this apparent "best of both worlds" (i.e. liberalization plus higher real levels of public services) of the post-1988 years proved to be unsustainable by 1993 and the 1994 crisis reversed the pattern of the preceding years. The acceleration of the debt burden in terms of "Int/Y" ratio together with fiscal austerity, transformed the fiscal system, once again, into a regressive transfer mechanism in favor of the holders of the public debt, i.e. private banks, individual or wealthy rentiers, and against the public at large *via* both regressive taxation and the inflation tax. Paradoxically, it is the progression realized during the so-called "irresponsible populism" of the ultra-liberal post-1989 years that, despite orthodox stabilization following the 1994 crisis, the capacity of the fiscal system to generate socially oriented public services is still not below the early 1980s.

6. Conclusions on Social Policies: Conflicts, Contradictions and Options

The Turkish Pendulum Between Orthodoxy and Populism

The foregoing sections depicted the distributional dynamics of the Turkish economy during a period, i.e. 1980–1998, shaped—as elsewhere—by globalization. A number of common features emerge. The first refers to the exogenous nature of distributional changes. Since the mid-1970s it is difficult to analyze distributional variables as endogenous changes responding to variations in externally determined or purely domestic macroeconomic variations. On the contrary, changes in income distribution turn out to be *exogenous shocks*, either in favor of or against labor—encompassing both urban wage-earners and peasant producers. Since the poverty-stricken population is predominantly located within the ranks of these two classes, the distributional pendulum can also be considered to involve changing relations between the poor and the rich.

What are the factors behind these distributional shocks? We tend to see the state apparatus as the main explanatory factor in influencing the strategic policy decisions affecting income distribution. This portrays, in one sense, the *distributional political cycle*. However, it would be erroneous to characterize distributional dynamics as a *purely political* process. Of course changing macroeconomic conditions (e.g. domestic and international expansionary vs. contractionary phases; opening-up to trade and to financial flows) as well as market parameters (e.g. supply and demand elasticities of labor and of agricultural output) constrain and influence the distributional process. Nevertheless, during the past quarter of a century, the overall process of adjustment which determines the final outcome has almost always started with a distributional shock affecting *both* wage and *TOTA* movements either upwards or downwards.

The favorable cycles in Turkey are *populist* phases. In understanding populism in Turkey, it may be useful to recall a well-known Turkish saying: "*Only God Almighty can give without taking.*" The Turkish populism has historically been a continual attempt of government to find ways and means of violating this common wisdom during changing balance of forces in favor of popular classes, i.e. how to accommodate distributional demands by "giving to labor/the poor without taking from capital/from the rich."

A typical case in point is the post-1989 years when the long (1981–88) phase of depressed wages and *TOTA* following the adverse 1980 shock inevitably had to come to an end. The "corrective" shock started when the Özal government was forced to concede a 141% wage rise to public sector workers when the rate of inflation was 75%. Substantial rises in civil servant salaries, in social spending from the budget, in farm subsidies followed suit. Private sector wages fell in line as well.

The "normal" (let us call it the "social democratic") adjustment in response to this distributional shock would have been by "taking from the rich", i.e. by a substantial increase of direct income and corporate taxation, a rescheduling of the domestic debt (i.e. some sort of a "wealth tax" on the holders of public debt instruments) and price controls (i.e. prevention of rising mark-ups in response to wage increases) on oligopolistic firms. However, the government opted for the "populist" adjustment, i.e. "giving without taking"... The "magic formula" for the implementation of the populist option in 1989 was the liberalization of the capital account. Capital inflows enabled the realization of rising rates of private consumption and public consumption (higher non-interest public spending) without any acceleration of the inflation rate. On the other hand high arbitrage gains for banks and higher mark-up rates for large-scale private manufacturing firms were also realized.

This "marriage" of populism with capital account opening differs from orthodox stabilization and earlier experiences with structural adjustment when regressive incomes policies was a necessary component of liberalization. Liberalization in this case does not meet the resistance on the part of organized labor and becomes compatible with democratic government. The experience may not be specific to Turkey. As elsewhere, the problem with this mode of "giving without taking", is its short-termism. Current account and/or public deficits sooner or later reach unsustainable levels. In the Turkish case it was the dramatic rise of PSBR to 12% of GDP in 1993, and the erratic reserve and current account movements which led to the sudden reversal of capital inflows in late 1993 culminating in the 1994 crisis.

Orthodox crisis-management of 1994–95 as in 1980–81 represent the "other side of the coin," i.e. the antithesis of populism. Here, the costs of adjustment are shifted almost totally on urban wage earners and the peasantry. In 1994, the 6% decline in GDP *plus* the primary surplus of the current account attaining 5% of GDP (i.e. 11%) constituted the macroeconomic cost of crisis-management. It is interesting to note that both the decline in real wages of formal sector workers (27%) and in the real incomes per employed person from agriculture (16%) exceed the macroeconomic cost of adjustment by significant margins. This implies that certain groups within the bourgeoisie may, actually, have benefited from crisis conditions in *absolute terms*. Currently, relations of distribution appear to have stabilized following the adverse distributional shock. However, a "corrective" shock, this time favorable for labor is always on the agenda.

All these involve a harsh and, for many households living in the thresholds of poverty, an inhuman response. There is, also, a longer-term solution which the Turkish bourgeoisie and international circles representing the Washington Consensus have been advocating consistently: *de-politicization* of the distributional process. This is part and parcel of the well-known structural adjustment program and, in the Turkish case, it involved moving towards flexibility in labor market arrangements and dismantling of pro-farmer interventions in agricultural markets. Taken as a whole, these so-called *structural reforms* aim at not only the elimination of *populist deformations* in the narrow sense of the term during the upward phase of the distributional cycle; but also of those *institutional* elements covering education, health and social security systems—the totality of which is usually referred to as *the welfare state*. Efforts towards *de-politicization* of the distributional process and the gradual *dismantling of the welfare state* have never attained their full objective. One major reason was that they were too ambitious in the sense that their full implementation would signify a total reshaping of the Turkish society. Society or social forces have either delayed or rejected the permanent changes in the relations of distribution. However, in the *welfare state* aspects of the "reform" program, significant, albeit gradual, changes have been taking place. These changes can be referred to as increased scope in the *market-based provision of public goods*, i.e. education, health and social security. A brief overview will illuminate the issues at stake.

The increasing scope of commercialization and/or private provision of education and health have been the dominant features of the period covered in this paper. Public spending on education and health services as a ratio of GDP has shown a downward trend up until 1989. On the other hand, between 1976 and 1983 the share of the private sector within total investment in education and health rarely exceeded ten percent. Hence the early 1980s, years of orthodox stabilization, represent a phase when the rate of human capital formation in Turkey had declined significantly.

Two developments reversed this adverse trend. From 1994 onwards, thanks to the generous incentives extended to private investors in education and health, entrepreneurs started to move into these sectors at a significant rate, and the private sector's share in total education and health investments reached the 50 percent benchmark by 1996–97. During the "populist" phase of the post-1988 years, public spending in the social sectors picked up and gradually approached the ratios of 1976–77.

These were, naturally, favorable developments. However, in terms of equity, it has certain adverse implications as well. An expensive, modern and, in certain respects, luxurious system of private health care—in part, supported by private health insurance schemes—is servicing the upper classes whereas the population covered by social insurance schemes is using the resources of an over-extended public health system. Public hospitals have, to an increasing degree, started to commercialize their services as well by significantly extending the implementation of users' fees. Thus one witnesses an increasing and striking polarization in terms of the quality and quantity of health services extended to different segments of the population. A similar pattern has been emerging in the area of education. An elite system of higher education has, since the early 1980s, been emerging, essentially based on private universities and, to an increasing degree, on private high schools. At state universities and high schools, *de facto* users' fees have increased substantially; government scholarships no longer exist in practical terms; and credits extended to students are based on commercial interest rates. Apart from a few select ones, the majority of state universities are considered to be involved in mass production of degrees, albeit in areas with limited employment prospects.

In short, a market-based provision of education and health is generating a dual system in human capital formation, contributing to further polarization between the children of the upper and lower echelons of Turkish society. Moreover, efforts to generate a primary surplus in the public budget has been a dominant feature of the new adverse cycle starting with the 1994 crisis resulting, once again, in the erosion of public spending in the social sectors.

Coming to *social security*, strong resistance on the part of the trade unions has, up until now, prevented the widespread implementation of privatization and commercialization of the component parts of the system. However, the sector faces very serious problems. Commensurate with the ongoing macroeconomic imbalances and the deterioration of public accounts, one witnesses a dramatic collapse of the fiscal accounts of the Turkish social security system. The system is characterized by a high level of evasion, low levels of pensions, and financial insolvency. [11] As of 1997, the combined cash deficits of the system reach 2.4% of GNP and it is expected to reach 10% by 2050 (ILO, 1995). Current actuarial balances of the system are in severe disequilibrium with 2.1 active registered employees per retired person. Estimates based on the 1985 census suggest, however, that the system can admit an actuarial rate of 9 to 1. Evidently, current problems of the Turkish social security system is independent of the so-called aging crisis faced by many OECD nations today; and instead, is directly related to the structural features, i.e. the scope of the marginalization/informalization of the labor market.

As narrated in more detail in Section 3, the responsibility rests with private sector employment patterns and the ongoing process of privatization has aggravated the problem. Based on 1996 data, the average of actively insured persons to total employment barely exceeds one third within the private sector. Based on SIS data, our calculations reveal that, in the private sector, those under 19 years of age constitute 14% of total employment, and 83% of these workers have no social security coverage. (Yeldan and Köse 1999). The absence of an age-limit for retirement induces middle-aged pensioners to join the labor force again, this time in uninsured status. This generates significant inducement on employers to shift their labor demand towards younger employees and workers accepting employment outside social security coverage.

Clearly, the current social security system is unsustainable and is in need of immediate reform. However, neither available private pension arrangements,

---

11. On current problems of the Turkish social security system, see Lordoglu (1999), Yeldan and Köse (1999), Teksöz (1998), Kenç and Sayan (1998), TÜSIAD (1997), Kenar, Teksöz and Coskun (1996), and ILO (1995).

nor the espoused securitization-based private financing schemes offer viable alternatives. Due to insufficient regulation and lack of formal supervision, the private health and life insurance sectors are characterized by cases of irregularities, high lapses, and unaccounted policy cancellations. Given the structural characteristics of the labor market, it is only fair to argue that a viable social security system reform cannot be meaningful without addressing the systematic evasion of employers due to the scope of the informalization of the labor market.

Concluding Reflections on the Societal Implications of Globalization[12]

The *societal impact* of globalization has gone beyond quantifiable variables, i.e. changes in income distribution and rising inequities in the social sectors, covered and analyzed in the foregoing sections. The dual processes of the liberalization of trade and of capital movements constitute *globalization* in its narrowly economic sense. On a broader perception, this economic duality necessitated "... a programme for destroying collective structures which may impede the pure market logic" (Bourdieu, 1998). In order to sanctify the power of the markets in the name of economic efficiency, this "infernal machine" requires the elimination of administrative or political barriers which limit the owners of capital in their quest for maximization of individual profit, which, in turn has been upheld as the supreme indicator of rationality (*ibid*). In the Turkish context, this economic duality appears to have also been accompanied by another duality—the dissemination of Western consumption norms and cultural patterns plus the internationalization of the Turkish bourgeoisie. Consequently, life styles of the privileged minority of the Turkish society during the past two decades have increasingly resembled, and even become almost identical with the upper classes of Western societies.

Finally, as elsewhere in the Third World, labor—as the internationally immobile factor—is imprisoned within the national boundary during a period when pressure towards the *de-politicization of the distributional process* and *the dismantling of the economic and social functions of the nation-state* is exercised. Hence, urban and rural labor in Turkey is losing its capacity to influence the state in areas that affect the destinies of the underprivileged. If present trends continue, the state apparatus will gradually transform itself into an institution, merely endowed with repressive functions. Alienation, social exclusion, political indifference, withdrawal into individualized survival strategies is likely to be the outcome for the majority of the population. This is fertile ground for flowering of obscurantist, reactionary, ultra-nationalistic ideologies and violence. Since the early 1980s, the unstoppable progress of Islamic funda-

---

12. This sub-section draws on Boratav, Türel and Yeldan (1996).

mentalism and fascistic political tendencies within the ranks of popular classes in Turkey can, in our view, be grasped only within this context.

While the destinies and even the interests of labor and the poor in the developed and developing world are de-linked or even opposed to each other, life styles and interests between the bourgeoisie in the North and the South have been converging. At least in the Turkish case, we rarely observe conflicting views on socio-economic policy options between the Washington circles, international finance and the dominant, influential segments of the relatively wealthier classes. It would not be an exaggeration to suggest that "national" and increasingly nationalistic working classes are currently confronting the "International of Capital". The class map of the nineteenth and early twentieth centuries is thus transformed into its opposite.

Let us therefore hope that the future, i.e. the twenty-first century, should not resemble the immediate past, i.e. the last quarter of the twentieth century. And it is our task as social scientists to contribute towards the realization of this aspiration.

REFERENCES

Akyüz, Y. (1990) "Financial System and Policies in Turkey in the 1980s," in T. Aricanli and D. Rodrik (eds.), *The Political Economy of Turkey,* New York: MacMillan.

Balkan, E. and E. Yeldan (1998) "Financial Liberalization in Developing Countries: The Turkish Experience" in Medhora, R. and J. Fanelli (eds.), *Financial Liberalization in Developing Countries,* Macmillan Press.

Boratav, K. (1995) *Class Profiles from Istanbul and Anatolia* (in Turkish), Istanbul: Yurt Yayinlari-Tarih Vakfi.

Boratav, K., O. Türel and E. Yeldan (1996) "Dilemmas of Structural Adjustment and Environmental Policies under Instability: Post-1980 Turkey," *World Development,* 24(2): 373–393.

Boratav, K., O. Türel and E. Yeldan (1995) "The Turkish Economy in 1981–92: A Balance Sheet, Problems and Prospects," *METU Studies in Development* 22(1): 1–36

Bourdieu, P. (1998) "The Essence of Neoliberalism," *Le Monde Diplometique,* December.

Bulutay, T. (1995) *Employment, Unemployment and Wages in Turkey,* Ankara: ILO/SIS.

Dumanli, R. (1997) *Poverty and its Dimensions in Turkey* (in Turkish), Ankara: SPO.

Ekinci, N. (1998) "Growth and Crisis Dynamics in the Turkish Economy" (in Turkish), *Toplum ve Bilim* No.77 (Summer), 7–27.

Güneş, M. (1991) "Concentration Criterias in Turkish Manufacturing Industry: 1985–1989" (in Turkish), *Research Symposium 91,* Ankara: State Institute of Statistics.

Güneş, M., A. H. Köse, and E. Yeldan (1996) "Concentration Trends in Turkish Manufacturing Industry in Accordance with IO Table's Sectoral Classification" (in Turkish), *Ekonomik Yaklaşim,* 8(26): 33–47.

ILO (1995) *Turkish Government Social Security and Health Insurance Project,* Ankara: Undersecreteriat of Treasury.

Katircioğlu, E (1990) *Concentration in Turkish Manufacturing and The Factors Determine Concentration: 1975–1988* (in Turkish), Istanbul: TÜSES.

Kaytaz, E., S. Altin and M. Güneş (1993) "Concentration in Turkish Manufacturing Industry" (in Turkish), *TMMOB Proceedings of the Congress on Industry* Vol. 1, Ankara: Chamber of Engineers.

Kenar, N.; A.T. Teksöz and A.H. Coşkun (1996) "The Social Security System and Reform Project" (in Turkish), *Hazine Dergisi*, August: 5–25.

Kenç, T. and S. Sayan (1998) "Transmisson of Demographic Shock Effects from Large to Small Countries: An Overlapping Generations CGE Analysis," Bilkent University, Department of Economics Discussion Paper, No. 98–5.

Köse, A. H. and E. Yeldan (1998) "Turkish Economy in 1990s: An Assessment of Fiscal Policies, Labor Markets and Foreign Trade," *New Perspectives on Turkey, No: 18, Spring.*

Köse, A. and A. Öncü (1998) "Anatolian Manufacturing Industry within the Context of World and Turkish Economy: Are we at the threshold of getting rich or getting poor" (in Turkish), *Toplum ve Bilim*, No. 77 (Summer).

Lordoğlu, K. (1999) "Informal Employment and The Social Security Problem" (in Turkish), *Iktisat, Işletme ve Finans*, February, No 14(155): 68–82.

Önder, I., O. Türel, N. Ekinci, and C. Somel (1993) *Public Finance, Financial System and Policies in Turkey*, Istanbul: Tarih Vakfi Yurt Yayinlari, Table V-1.3.

Pieper, U. (1998) "De-Industrialization and Social and Economic Sustainability: Cross-Country Evidence on Productivity and Employment," CEPA Working Paper, March.

Syrquin, M. (1986) "Productivity Growth and Factor Reallocation," in H. Chenery, S. Robinson, and M. Syrquin (eds.), *Industrialization and Growth: A Comparative Study* (1988) London: Oxford University Press.

Şenses, F. (1994) "Labour market response to structural adjustment and institutional pressures: The Turkish Case," *METU Studies in Development* 21(3).

Şenses, F. (1996) "Structural Adjustment Policies and Employment in Turkey," METU, Economic Research Center, Research Report No. 96/01.

Tekeli, İ., S. İlkin, A. Aksoy and Y. Kepenek (1982) *Türkiye'de Sanayi Kesiminde Yoğunlaşma*, Ekonomist Yayinevi.

Teksöz, T. (1998) "Simulation of Benefits from Money Purchase Pension Scheme for Turkey," unpublished MS Thesis submitted to City University, London.

TÜSIAD (1997) "Restructuring in Turkish Social Security System" (in Turkish), October.

UNCTAD (1997) *Trade and Development Report*, New York and Geneva: United Nations.

Yeldan, E. and A. Köse (1999) "Problems of the Turkish Social Security System and Their Impact on Growth and Accumulation" (in Turkish), İstanbul: Friedrich Ebert Stiftung.

Yeldan, E. and A. Köse (1998) "An Assessment of The Turkish Labor Market Against its Macroeconomics Policies," in T. Bulutay (ed.), *The Burdens Related with Turkish Labor Markets and Policies*, forthcoming, Ankara: State Institute of Statistics.

Yeldan, E. (1995) "Surplus Creation and Extraction under Structural Adjustment: Turkey, 1980–1992," *Review of Radical Political Economics*, 27(2): 38–72, June.

Yentürk, N. (1997) *Wage, Employment and Accumulation in Turkish Manufacturing Industry* (in Turkish), İstanbul: Friedrich Ebert Stiftung.

11

Zimbabwe: Economic Adjustment, Income Distribution and Trade Liberalization

ROB DAVIES *and* JØRN RATTSØ

1. Introduction: Issues and Overview

Zimbabwe's economic relations with the rest of the world have changed between extremes. The dramatic shift from import regulation under and after sanctions to full scale trade liberalization offers a unique opportunity for investigating policy-driven globalization.

Usually the economic motivation for such a historic shift is of long run nature. A protectionist regime has costs in terms of limited access to world market innovation and technology and limited competitive pressure in domestic markets. Reform is an attempt to take advantage of global technological progress and competition, although it is not clear that the dreams will come true. In this paper we focus on the short run aspects of liberalization, which are rather seen as obstacles to reform (Rodrik, 1994). Opening up for imports easily may crowd out more output than is gained in export product expansion, and the associated changes in income distribution involve losers who will protest the policy reorientation.

The conventional approach to the consequences of trade reform addresses the microeconomics of labor market adjustments and sectoral competitiveness. Allocation of production factors between sectors clearly is important to

Paper prepared for the project 'Globalization and Social Policy' led by Lance Taylor, Center for Economic Policy Analysis, New School for Social Research, and financed by The MacArthur Foundation and The United Nations. We are grateful to project participants and Trondheim seminar participants for comments and to Ragnar Torvik for CGE-model collaboration understand the experiences made in the recent trade liberalization in Zimbabwe. But the main story definitely looks macro. The key year is 1992, when the trade account was essentially fully liberalized. As confirmed by Table 1, output and investment contracted by about 8–10 %, the inflation rate doubled to above 40%, a consumption boom increased imports, and the trade balance moved into serious deficit. This performance must be understood against the unfortunate background of a coincidental drought, that must take much of the blame for the contraction. The worry is that the GDP never really has recovered. GDP per capita in 1996 is still at the 1992 level, well below the gradually expanding per capita GDP during the period 1985–1991.

TABLE 1: Macroeconomic Performance

	1990	1991	1992	1993	1994	1995	1996
GDP growth[1]	7.0	5.5	−9.0	1.3	6.8	−0.8	7.6
GDP per capita[1]	2196	2247	1982	1940	2003	1921	2002
GFCF							
Growth[1]	34.7	23.1	−8.5	7.9	5.3	−10.9	−1.3
Inflation[2]	12	23	42	28	27	23	21
Exports[3]	1750	1785	1530	1610	1947	2216	–
Imports[3]	1510	1700	1781	1512	1778	2128	–
Trad bal[3]	0	−245	−602	−89	−108	−164	–
Manufact[4]	139	143	130	119	131	113	117

1) National Accounts 1985–1997, CSO May 1998, Zim$, 1990–prices.
2) Same, consumer price index.
3) Merchandise exports and imports, trade balance including services, mill USD, ZIMPREST (Zimbabwe Program for Economic and Social Transformation) 1996–2000.
4) Index of volume of production of the manufacturing industries, 1980=100, Quarterly Digest of Statistics, CSO March 1998, Table 17.0.

A combination of factors messed up the price system also. While inflation jumped to an annual rate above 40%, nominal interest rates went up to about 30%. The inflation rate was gradually reduced towards 20% in the mid-90s, but the interest rate showed strong inertia. Consequently, real interest rates turned positive and quite large with depressing effects for investment.

As will become clear, limited data are available to describe the developments in income distribution. The broad agreement among observers, and backed up by numbers below, is that most wage earners took a big real wage loss with the inflation shock and have not recovered. The sources of this distributional shift are hard to sort out, but the new distribution looks like a permanent result of a change in economic policy regime.

We will take the two macro shocks, output contraction and inflation shift, as exogenous events in our analysis. The output contraction is associated with deindustrialization, which is a result of liberalization according to our previous CGE-analyses (Davies et al., 1998 and Rattsø and Torvik, 1998). The upward shift in inflation is the result of several factors. Econometrics can't help us too much in understanding this episode, but we have had some help from the investigation into the old inflationary mechanisms by Chhibber et al. (1989). The following aspects probably were important. First, the agricultural drought put upward pressure on food prices in particular. Second, trade liberalization contributed to output contraction (in importables) and a consumption boom (drop in savings). This combination of slow (or negative) output response and rapid (positive) demand response of course is a recipe for inflation. Third, the interest rate jump, itself a result of higher required return for financing the still increasing public debt, had a cost push effect on prices. Added to this were the price effects of reluctant, but definite devaluations of the currency. The paper addresses how the output and inflation shocks have worked their way through the economy, in particular concerning distribution and labor markets. The distributional shift is first and foremost the combined result of inflation and employment stagnation.

Broad evaluations of the reform have been written by Davies et al. (1992), Shaw and Davies (1993) and Skålnes (1995), but data have only recently become available for an evaluation of reform results. Gunning and Mumbengegwi (1995) have collected evidence based on firm level data, while Ncube et al. (1996) emphasise the regional context. This article is an expansion of Davies and Rattsø (1996), which supplies more evidence on adjustments and adjustment mechanisms.

The liberalization process is described in section 2, while section 3 offers a stylized theory of trade liberalization effects in Africa based on the Ricardo-Viner model. An expansion of the theory model is implemented as a CGE model for Zimbabwe, and deindustrialization effects of trade liberalization are calibrated in section 4. We begin the macro analysis by decomposing aggregate demand to identify changes in the short run adjustment mechanisms of the economy. Section 6 provides an econometric analysis of the role of wages in the macroeconomy. The estimation includes the wage formation process described by the wage curve and the consequences of real wage changes for aggregate demand. In section 7, disaggregated labor market data are applied to document changes in distribution and productivity. Concluding remarks are collected in section 8.

2. The Liberalization Process

Zimbabwe has a particular history of import substitution, against which the recent jump into globalization should be understood. International sanctions during the UDI (Unilateral Declaration of Independence) period represented forced protectionism. The international community did not recognize the settler regime and the United Nations introduced sanctions in 1968. The sanctions induced a period of import-substituting industrialization and economic diversification. Real GDP grew at an annual rate of above 7 % between 1965 and 1974, but later the escalating war of independence disrupted economic activity.

The sophisticated import control system built up under sanctions was continued by the new government after independence in 1980. The import regulations are described by Davies (1991) and Pakkiri and Moyo (1987). The post-independence boom (1980–82) was unsustainable on foreign exchange grounds, and the government resorted to administered foreign exchange allocation to control the current account deficit. This policy led to macroeconomic stability, but restricted growth. Green and Kadhani (1986) wrote the authoritative account of the early independent period, and Davies and Rattsø (1993) update the evaluation.

Since the mid-1980s, a number of institutional responses to deal with the linkage between import capacity and economic growth were introduced, basically aimed at export promotion. The measures were not without effect, and the relaxation of the foreign exchange constraint can be observed as rising growth rates in the last part of the decade. In view of the relative success of the modified protectionism, this looked like a long run solution of a government with socialist inclinations and rhetoric.

The government had a team of UNDP-funded Australian economists working on possible trade reforms for a couple of years, but still the policy announcement of the Economic Structural Adjustment Programme (ESAP) in the summer of 1990 came as a surprise (Government of Zimbabwe, 1991). It must be understood against the background of increased pressure to join the international trend of liberal economic reform. Outside Zimbabwe, both donors and the Bretton Woods institutions argued for liberalization and could add on funding. Inside the country, the powerful Confederation of Zimbabwe Industries changed its opposition to trade liberalization around 1987–88. Skålnes (1995) reports increasing concerns about the growth effects of regulation inside the ruling party ZANU (PF).

The program contains most elements of the orthodox Washington package, and trade liberalization has been the main area of action. Trade reform was designed to be gradual and implemented over the 1990–95 period, but implementation was accelerated compared to the original plan. The seriousness of the policy intentions was shown in October 1990, when raw materials and inputs to industries were put on a list of Open General Import License (OGIL). Industries in key sectors such as cement, textiles and mining gained free access to imported inputs. As discussed in section 3, we have shown that this first part of the program, emphasizing liberalization of intermediates, had very different consequences compared to the later stages. As early as late 1991, liberalization was extended to include imported final goods. At first the extension was part of the gradualist approach, and new items were put on the OGIL list. The Export Retention Scheme (ERS) introduced earlier in the year was broadened, and all exporters were entitled to retain 15% of export revenues in foreign exchange. Internal trade with ERS imports developed and an unofficial foreign exchange market was started up.

Later trade liberalization took on its own dynamics. In the summer of 1993, the process accelerated, with new extensions of the export retention and free trading of ERS entitlements. Individuals were allowed to open foreign exchange accounts, and a dual foreign exchange market developed with an official and an ERS exchange rate. Foreign exchange accounts were later extended to the corporate sector. External borrowing was allowed and exchange controls were relaxed (e.g. travel). The opening up for foreign capital flows was partly motivated by the high cost of domestic private credit. During 1994, the dual exchange rates were unified. All of these reforms have made Zimbabwe an extremely open economy, although some of the reforms have been reversed following currency crises in 1998—for example, the removal of foreign currency accounts for corporations. The only restrictions left on the capital account concern returns to investments made before independence and holding foreign assets abroad.

3. Trade Liberalization and Adjustment of Income Distribution: Theory

Trade liberalization changes the conditions of industry, and the consequent economic adjustment influences wages and profits, altering income distribution. The main structural change promoted is the shift from importables production to exportables. In large parts of Africa, the distinction between importables and exportables is closely linked to the separation between industry and agriculture/raw material production, which broadly mirrors the urban/rural divide.

Below, a simple model is outlined to discuss the implications of breaking down the protection of domestic industries. The framework is a compressed Ricardo-Viner model, concentrating on the interplay between importables and exportables. It is a simplification of the three-way disaggregation including nontradables, which has been used in many applied analyses since it allows simultaneous discussion of the foreign terms of trade and the real exchange rate. Rodrik (1994) and Rattsø and Taylor (1998) utilize the three sector framework to understand trade liberalization effects in more general terms. Rodrik (1998) has produced numerical simulations to quantify distributional implications of trade reform in a similar setup.

The labor force is distributed between the importables/industry sector and the exportables/agriculture sector. Exportables/agriculture is assumed to absorb the labor force not employed in importables/industry. From this dual economy perspective, the wage level is consequently determined by the marginal productivity of labor in exportables/agriculture. In the simplest form, the product real wage is constant and determined by subsistence. It seems more realistic to allow the real wage to fall when more labor is channelled into exportables/agriculture.

Protectionism is best represented as a tariff equivalent of a quota raising the price of importables above the world market level. This represents a rent that is determined by the size of the quota and domestic market conditions in importables.

Given ordinary supply and demand functions for importables, a small import quota drives up the rent and the employment in importables/industry.

Figure 1 describes the structural adjustment in the importables product market and the exportables labor market. Two motivations for having an import quota are easily derived from the diagram. With world market price P*, the excess demand for importables contributes to a trade deficit that is undesired or cannot be financed. The import compression implemented in 1983 after the post-independent boom, was introduced to control the trade deficit, and then acted as a macroeconomic policy instrument. An import quota also allows the country to move up along the importables supply curve as a way of industrializing. In the diagram, the import quota induces a higher domestic price of importables (tariff equivalent t) and generates higher profits, outlays and quota rents. In this setup, African protectionism has first foremost benefited capitalists in domestically oriented industries. Agriculture has been discriminated against by high prices of domestic inputs and overvaluation of the currency. When this holds true, trade liberalization should work progressively in terms of income distribution.

FIGURE 1: Trade Policy, Importables–Exportables Interaction

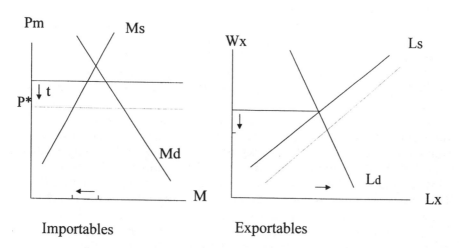

Importables   Exportables

Elimination of the quota drives down the domestic price of importables to its world market level, reducing importables profits and eliminating quota rents. Reduced importables production, that is deindustrialization in the African context, and a widening trade deficit, are to be expected. The drop in importables/ urban employment increases labor supply in agriculture/ rural areas and leads to a downward pressure on the wage level (if marginal productivity of labor is falling in employment). The distributional consequences of trade liberalization are a reversal of the redistribution obtained by protectionism. The hardest part to predict is the losers of the rents. In a centralized and strictly controlled import licensing system, there is no second-hand market for imports and the government absorbs the rent. In a less controlled system, rents may be taken by the owners in the importables sector, who consequently lose from liberalization. If importables/industrial wage earners are able to take a share of the rents (Rodrik, 1998), their loss will be bigger too. Trade liberalization in this African structure looks like a clear shift of income from industry to agriculture and from urban to rural areas.

The political economy of trade liberalization in Africa then should involve a strong rural/agricultural constituency as the driving force of the process. Domestically oriented industries and groups capturing quota rents are expected to oppose trade liberalization. This emphasis on functional income distribution may exaggerate the role of sectoral balances. As consumers, all gain from the improved availability of foreign goods, and this desire for world market access may dominate the political battle. In addition, even if the industrial sector is oriented towards the domestic market, firms would like access to foreign intermediates and technology.

Outside the model, if importables contraction is fast and exportables expansion is slow, nontradables and informal production activities may take a loss from the demand side. On the other hand, exportables expansion may be helped by additional mechanisms. Access to importables at lower prices may improve incentives to engage in exportables production—a classic argument about the export stagnation under protectionism. Deregulation of capital flows has a similar effect of raising the attractiveness of foreign exchange earnings. And firms in the importables sector that are made unprofitable, may shift to industrial exportables. These factors tend to shift the exportables labor demand curve outward, thereby contributing to higher wages. Rattsø (1999) has written an elaboration of this approach including a separation between upstream and downstream industries.

As mentioned in the introduction, the microeconomic framework has shortcomings. Macroeconomic balances also seem to respond to liberalization. The new availability of foreign goods tends to lead to a drop in private savings. High savings under protectionism have been forced postponement of consumption. On the real side, the drop in savings implies a consumption boom and an increased trade deficit, thereby threatening the credibility of the program. Monetary transmission mechanisms may include higher interest rates and possibly foreign exchange appreciation. The distributional implications of these macroadjustments are more complex and less distinct than those of the sectoral imbalances.

4. Liberalization and Deindustrialization: CGE Model Analysis

As outlined above, the Zimbabwe reform from quantitative import regulation to trade liberalization has changed significantly the conditions for production and distribution. The first liberalization measures during 1990–91 gave easier access to imported intermediates and raw materials, and an overall expansion of import dependent activities was expected. The delayed devaluation kept imported inputs cheap although some tariffs and charges were imposed. Opening up for free imports of inputs basically allowed the protected domestically oriented industries to expand and involved no structural change. Firms with the most restricted access to imports before the liberalization of course benefited most. No shift from domestically oriented to export activities was observed and the exports stayed on trend during 1991.

The extension of liberalization to final goods during 1991–92 changed the conditions for import-competing industries dramatically. They had been protected from competition for decades. The inflow of imported final goods made many domestically oriented manufacturing firms unprofitable. Imports have crowded out domestic production. The negative effect on industrial production was influenced by the 1992 drought with reduced agricultural income and demand and reduced access of inputs from agriculture to industrial processing. Other aspects of the adjustment process were important too. The interest rate shock associated with financial liberalization raised the costs of working capital, and the real wage reduction analyzed below reduced labor costs.

The coincidence of liberalization and drought motivates a counterfactual analysis of the liberalization process to separate out the effects of liberalization. A CGE model extending the theoretical framework above to include food agriculture, infrastructure and nontradables as separate production sectors have been used to quantify distributional shifts with liberalization. The starting point is a model representing the import compression regime at work through the 1980s, as analyzed by Davies, Rattsø and Torvik (1994). Import rationing allocates intermediates and investment goods, and also includes importables and food, and the domestic markets for importables and food are protected from international competition. Trade liberalization is analyzed as a regime shift imposed on the benchmark import rationing model eliminating controls. Full documentation is given by Davies et al. (1998) and more recently by Rattsø and Torvik (1998).

In this economy-wide setup, we can identify several expansionary and contractionary elements involved in a trade liberalization process. Expansionary effects include lower costs of intermediate goods and higher domestic content of investment goods. In addition, reduced savings rates mean more consumer demand out of a given income. The savings rates are calibrated to reproduce the GDP fall with drought, which implies a fall by about 15% points on average. The changing domestic markets imply that countervailing contractionary effects also are in action. The opening up of the market for importables crowds domestic producers out of the market. The old protection was efficient. The access to non-competitive consumer imports switches demand from domestically produced goods.

The model predicts that the combined final goods liberalization and drought contracted output, but expanded consumption. The trade liberalization implies expenditure switching from domestic to foreign goods that adds contraction to the drought. The expenditure switching from the future to the present when final goods imports are available explains the consumption boom. The model expects the main contraction to affect importables. A private consumption boom is expected even with the serious drought. The decrease in domestic demand produces a real exchange rate depreciation and exportables expansion, but this is dominated by the drop in exports related to agricultural markets and drought. Not surprisingly, the combination of drought, domestic contraction, import liberalization, and increased consumption has a major impact on the trade balance. So far the story is fairly consistent with the actual development described in Table 1.

To isolate the effects of the 1992 drought, we have constructed a counterfactual where agricultural output is 'normal'. Other assumptions are held constant; in particular we assume that the drop in savings rates calibrated fully represent a trade liberalization effect. Even with this drop in savings rate, the final goods liberalization without drought is contractionary. The combined intermediate and final goods liberalization is slightly expansionary. The previously protected importables sector is a key player in the adjustment process. In the old regime, both intermediate inputs and finished importable goods were rationed. When the sector got free access to intermediates, output expanded. When the final goods protection was removed, the loss of market share dominated increased consumer demand.

The CGE model tells a story of trade reform that generates structural adjustment away from non-tradable and importable goods towards exportables. The distributional consequences are moderate as long as the labor force follows this relocation. It is puzzling to us that intermediate goods liberalization is not more expansionary for manufacturing industries. After all, the intermediate rationing has been seen as the major factor explaining output stagnation after independence. It seems to us that domestic industries had adjusted to the rationing regime and were not ready for new expansion after the freeing of intermediate imports. This factor has consequently not been strong enough to avoid deindustrialization. The moderate income distribution effects predicted by the CGE model have been overtaken by reality. As shown above, inflation jumped and real wages fell quite dramatically. The inflation effect, which must be understood outside the real CGE model, also threatens the reallocation to exports. However, the lack of a nominal wage response to inflation obviously has helped exportables avoid the contractionary effect of real appreciation.

The CGE model analysis helps us understand the contractionary output and deindustrialization effects observed. But the distributional shifts have been much more dramatic than predicted by the CGE model. This motivates our emphasis on macro shocks in the rest of the paper, where we take the deindustrialization and the shift in inflation as given.

374 Davies and Rattsø

5. Changing Sources of Aggregate Demand

As a complement to the CGE model understanding of adjustment mechanisms, we turn to the short run determinants of economic activity linked to
aggregate demand components and parameters. Liberalization is expected to
change the working of the macro economy. In particular, as the economy opens
up, the foreign sector should begin to play more of a role in aggregate demand. Also the lifting of constraints may disturb the established savings-investment process as new economic conditions face savers and investors.
Applying the framework of Taylor (1998), we can identify different elements
of a possible shift in the structure of aggregate demand. The methodology is
presented in appendix 1.

The implementation of this decomposition using national account's data,
presented in Table 2, shows that the aggregate demand process certainly has
shifted with liberalization. The before-liberalization period 1986–90 is compared to the post-liberalization period 1993–97. The years 1991 and 1992 are
omitted, partly to avoid the 91–92 drought and partly to concentrate on the
post-reform rather than the transition period. The relative change in output
was similar in the two periods. The relative ranking of the contributions of the
three sectors to the overall change is about the same in both periods. However, there has been a shift in the demand injection from the public sector to
the foreign sector. After reform, the public sector has had a negative effect,
while the foreign sector has contributed to about 3.2 % points of the growth.

TABLE 2: Decomposition of Sources of Change in Total Output
Percent of Period Average Output

	Private	Government	Foreign	Interaction	Total
1986–90	3.4	0.9	1.7	−1.4	4.6
1993–97	4.0	−1.0	3.2	−1.4	4.8

	Private Sector		Government		Foreign Sector		Total	
	Invest	Sav	Exp	Tax	Exports	Imports	Inject	Leakage
1986–90	1.3	2.1	1.5	−0.6	1.9	−0.2	4.7	1.3
1993–97	0.9	3.1	−1.0	0.0	4.6	−1.4	4.5	1.7

The second part of Table 2 breaks these contributions into their 'stance'
and 'multiplier' or 'injection' and 'leakage' components. Before the reforms,
the bulk of the action came from the change in the savings parameter. If the
only change that had occurred had been the drop in the savings parameter,
total output would have risen by 2.1 % point because of the greater multiplier.
Although the overall impact of the private sector in the two periods is not very
different, the parameters imply that savings are more important and investment less important after reform. In the foreign sector the opposite is true.
The injection effect of export growth is much larger after reform (4.6 vs. 1.9

% point), while the rising import propensity has a much greater negative impact (–0.2 vs. –1.4 % point).

While the relative importance of the overall injection and leakage effects were roughly similar before and after the reform, within each sector they are very different. In the private sector the savings parameter effect rises. This is consistent with the view that a regulated economy induces forced savings, possibly by constraining consumption opportunities. Liberalization removes these constraints, causing the propensity to save to fall and the multiplier to rise. The reduced injection effect of investment after reform confirms the broad evidence that investment declines with reform. Although the government sector effects are small, they also are in accordance with observations elsewhere. As part of the reforms, government has attempted to reduce spending and taxation. The injection effect is consequently turned around after reform, while the reduction in taxation raises the multiplier. The foreign sector effects reflect the elimination of import rationing. Imports were previously kept low by import rationing, and liberalization has raised import propensities and reduced the multiplier. The injection effect is increased by exchange rate depreciation and other export stimuli.

6. Wages in the Macroeconomy:
Wage Curve and Wage-Demand-Linkage

In the introduction we have argued that macroeconomic factors are the main determinants of distributional shifts in Zimbabwe. In this section we use macroeconomic data to evaluate the wage formation process and the linkage between distribution and aggregate demand.

The first issue to be analyzed is the real wage consequences of inflation. The approach chosen is the estimation of wage curves following the tradition of Oswald (1996). The nominal wage level (W) is assumed to respond to the price level (P), productivity (Y/L) and macroeconomic fluctuation (capacity utilization CU). The econometric results are reported in Table 3. Most interestingly, the estimates show no wage response to inflation. This extreme nominal wage rigidity implies a sharp reduction of the real wage level with the rise in inflation. The results conform with the observation that wage earners in Zimbabwe have suffered a big loss in real wages. We are only able to detect stable short run effects on the nominal wage performance, since all long run variables are insignificant. No inertia are identified in the time adjustment of wages, but there is a trace of stability feedback to the evolution of the real wage.

The short run determinant of nominal wages is the capacity utilization. The wage level has an elasticity of about 0.6–0.8 with respect to capacity utilization. The drop in capacity utilization rate of about 12 % from 1991 to 1992 has contributed to a reduction of the wage level of about 8–9 %. The capacity utilization rate in 1997 is still below the 1990–91 peak. It follows that real wages have gone down because of both inelasticity to inflation and elasticity to

TABLE 3: Wage curve for Zimbabwe

	DlogW	DlogW	DlogW
Const	−2.42	−3.70	3.62
	(5.02)	(3.87)	(1.96)
$LogW_{-1}$	−0.34	−0.34	
	(0.24)	(0.23)	
$LogW_{-1}$ − $LogP_{-1}$			−0.13
			(0.18)
DlogCU	0.67*	0.57**	0.85**
	(0.34)	(0.24)	(0.32)
Log CU_{-1}	0.25	0.23	0.34
	(0.24)	(0.23)	(0.24)
DlogP	0.41		0.47
	(0.41)		(0.42)
Log P_{-1}	0.22	0.19	
	(0.19)	(0.17)	
DlogP + DlogYL		0.28	
		(0.25)	
DlogYL	0.11		−0.33
	(0.47)		(0.34)
$LogYL_{-1}$	0.46	0.60	−0.30
	(0.62)	(0.51)	(0.21)
LIBDUM	0.03	0.06	−0.03
	(0.10)	(0.06)	(0.09)
Rsq-adj	0.18	0.23	0.13
DW	2.62	2.53	2.53
Obs	21	21	21

Coefficients with standard deviations in parenthesis
Significance at 10% * and 5% ** level

capacity utilization. There is no additional shift in the wage path associated with liberalization (as tested with a liberalization dummy post 1992). Although few econometric anlayses of the wage process are available for comparison, the weak price indexation of wages is consistent with Chhibber et al. (1989).

The second aspect anlayzed is the possible consequences of the changing real wage for aggregate demand. We have already documented in section 4 that the linkage between demand components and economic activity has changed. Here we address the question whether the new distribution of income influences aggregate demand. The analysis concentrates on private investment (I), private and public consumption (CG), and the total.

The results in Table 4 show that the real wage has no effect on aggregate demand. There is no link between this measure of income distribution and the components of aggregate demand investigated. This may be explained by the procyclical real wage documented. The strong short-run responses to GDP variation may include the associated shift in the income distribution. The short run elasticity of both investment and consumption (and the total) with respect to GDP is well above 1. The estimated coefficients imply an unstable demand-determined macroeconomy. As will come clear below, we think that supply constraints contribute to stability.

To check the robustness of the result, the impact of the wage share has been estimated as an alternative to the real wage. The wage share comes out with a positive impact on investment demand. The result is hard to explain.

The dynamics of the consumption and investment functions represent adjustment inertia and a long run elasticity with respect to GDP of about 1. The time path of consumption has stronger inertia than investment, which is in accordance with conventional wisdom. Neither adjustment inertia nor long run relationships are detected for the total of investment and consumption. There has been no shift in the demand functions related to liberalization (as investigated by a liberalization dummy from 1992 on). Mehlum and Rattsø (1994) and Jenkins (1996) find significant effects of various measures of the import regulations, and confirm the present result that real wages are not important.

TABLE 4: Aggregate demand and real wage

	DlogI	DlogI	DlogCG	DlogCG	DlogI+CG	DlogIP+CG
Const	−0.35	−1.61	0.37	0.97	0.02	−0.13
	(3.00)	(2.04)	(1.44)	(1.28)	(1.20)	(1.07)
Log I_{-1}	−0.36*	−0.39**				
	(0.19)	(0.16)				
LogCG$_{-1}$			−0.47*	−0.52**		
			(0.23)	(0.21)		
Log I+CG$_{-1}$				−0.16	−0.19	
					(0.19)	(0.19)
DlogGDP	1.70*	2.68**	1.37**	1.32**	1.65**	1.76**
	(0.93)	(0.90)	(0.45)	(0.47)	(0.37)	(0.39)
LogGDP$_{-1}$	0.48	0.48*	0.30	0.42**	0.19	0.20
	(0.43)	(0.24)	(0.20)	(0.19)	(0.18)	(0.16)
DlogW/P	0.88		−0.21		−0.04	
	(0.92)		(0.45)		(0.36)	
LogW/P$_{-1}$	−0.17		0.12		−0.03	
	(0.53)		(0.28)		(0.20)	
DlogWS		1.92**		−0.17		0.19
		(0.80)		(0.44)		(0.35)
LogWS$_{-1}$		−0.01		0.26		0.10
		(0.47)		(0.27)		(0.21)
LIBDUM	0.08	0.24	−0.03	0.02	−0.06	0.01
	(0.27)	(0.23)	(0.15)	(0.14)	(0.11)	(0.11)
Rsq-adj	0.29	0.45	0.41	0.44	0.56	0.57
DW	1.47	1.49	1.96	1.96	2.12	2.22

Coefficients with standard deviations in parenthesis
Significance at 10% * and 5 % ** level

7. Labor Market Adjustments: Wage Structure

Most observers would agree that income distribution in Zimbabwe has widened since the reform program was introduced. Unfortunately, the data required to substantiate this observation do not exist. We have two sets of data to use. The first is an annual salaries and wages review of firms, undertaken by Price Waterhouse Coopers. This is intended to provide users with data on the trends in pay structures. It offers information on the pay for various grades of work but does not give any indication about the numbers of people in those grades. We can thus use it only to illustrate the evolution of pay structures, not income distribution.

We selected several grades by examining the data for highest and lowest paid jobs in different general categories. Our choice was partly influenced by continuity of data for the grades. In Table 5 we show the basic pay for median workers in 9 representative categories, expressed as a ratio of the pay of a security guard, one of the lowest paid categories. The most noticeable feature of the table is the escalation of executive pay relative to general salaries.

TABLE 5: Ratio of Basic Pay of Various Pay Categories Relative to median security guard

	1989	1993	1995	1997
Executive				
Chief executive	11.3	11.9	23.1	23.2
Technical/research executive	8.5	7.6	15.2	15.6
Marketing executive	8.1	6.9	14.6	15.1
Manufacturing executive	7.9	6.4	15.1	14.9
General				
Accountant—qualified 5–10yrs	6.3	4.7	7.8	5.1
Sales representatives—general (male)	2.5	3.0	3.1	2.2
Handyman	1.5	1.0	1.4	1.2
Security guard	1.0	1.0	1.0	1.0
Waitress/teamaker	0.7	0.7	0.7	0.7

Source: PE Consulting, Annual Survey of Salaries, various dates.
The growth rate is estimated by the slope of the line $lny = a + bt$ fitted to the nominal data deflated by the consumer price index for 1988–1996.

While all executive grades have experienced relative improvement over the full period 1989–97, general grades above security guards have had declining relative wages. Within the two levels there is no striking change to the structure. We could not find a significant trend towards a particular type of skill.

The rise in executive salaries is consistent with a number of explanations. Greater international mobility of these categories makes them a 'tradable' factor, so that liberalization raises their relative price as it does any tradable good. Greater reliance on collective bargaining in the context of the distorted structure of the Zimbabwean economy allows executives to protect themselves vis-à-vis workers. The creation of a more competitive, less regulated economy places a greater premium on managerial capabilities. We have not tested these alternatives, but they all suggest that we should not be surprised at the evidence.

The second source of labor market information is the sectoral employment and earnings data published by the Central Statistical Office. The reliability of these data has been increasingly questioned in recent years and it is recognized that the labor market surveys on which they are based fail to capture data from new firms. The following discussion should be read with this caveat in mind.

As with the decomposition of aggregate demand, we compare the pre-reform period (1986–90) with the post (1993–97), omitting the two transitional years. The data suggest a strong redistribution towards profits in the post-reform period. On average across all sectors, wages fell from 46% to 34% of value added. The real product wage fell by some 21% while output per worker rose by 6%. Such changes are consistent with the inflation driven redistribution we have identified earlier. Decomposing the 11 percentage point change in the wage share shows that 9 percentage points can be accounted for by changes in wage shares within sectors; the remaining two percentage points arise because of the changing composition of GDP. This is consistent with our earlier analysis that the redistribution mechanism is a macroeconomic one, impacting across all sectors, rather than a microeconomic one arising from a reallocation of resources.

8. Social Policy

To understand the post-reform approach to social policy, it is necessary to examine the approach taken in the 1980s. At independence in 1980 the new government made an attempt to narrow the inherited racial gap in living standards. Budgetary transfers were the main instrument used. On the expenditure side, education and health were the key elements of the social wage. The education system expanded rapidly, with non-fee paying primary education and heavily subsidized secondary education. Access to health care services was also improved. Free health care service was offered large parts of the population, including most industrial and all agricultural and domestic workers plus all communal farmers and unemployed. In this early period the application of the rules for determining free access was lax, so a large number of people benefited. Free immunization and other aspects of the improved preventive health care program also added to the social wage (Davies and Sanders, 1988). On the tax side, the post-independence tax structure was relatively progressive. Thus on both the expenditure and the tax side, the post-independence budgets improved income distribution and probably strengthened the improvements that were taking place in the primary distribution with the post-independence boom. Outside the budget, a legislated national minimum wage was the primary instrument used to address inequality. This, which was coupled with legislation preventing firing of workers, significantly increased in real earnings among the low paid. In rural areas agricultural support schemes were extended to previously excluded small-scale farmers.

It is significant that most of these efforts to redress social inequalities were directed at transferring income rather than restructuring wealth ownership. Although there was some effort made to resettle peasants on former white farms, these were minimal and largely irrelevant. Despite the government's socialist rhetoric, it acted as though the problem was a surface phenomenon rather than something which required structural re-organization of the economy to eradicate. Its approach was therefore more welfarist than social-ist. At the time, government argued that it was constrained from taking more radical solutions both by the independence constitution and by the threat from South Africa, although this argument has been disputed (see Davies, 1988). Rather the approach adopted revealed the essentially populist nature of the government. Visible contributions to welfare which can be attributed to government (such as provision of free education) are more politically desir-able than less visible and indirect ones (such as real wage growth), even though the latter may make a more significant impact. Furthermore, the willingness to tackle wealth distribution declined over time as the governing and bureau-cratic hierarchy began to emerge as an economic elite.

This preference of government was revealed further after 1983, when government policies became more concerned with stabilization, and the dis-tributional gains achieved started to be eroded. Although it was concerned with reducing the budget deficit, government defended the social wage through its budgetary allocations, so that real expenditure per head in education and health did not decline significantly (see Davies, Sanders and Shaw, 1992). Rather the cuts fell on capital expenditure. The minimal allocation for land redistribution and resettlement was the first budget vote to be cut. Outside the budget, government not only permitted the erosion of real wages, but used the minimum wage legislation to restrict rather than promote wage in-creases for the low paid. The consequent decline in the real wage not only offset some of the gains from the social wage but also undermined the ability of the poor to make use of these public provisions. For example, drop out rates at school started to rise, apparently as families were unable to carry the indirect costs of school children.

The initial announcement of the new policy stance in 1990 made men-tion of the possible consequences for disadvantaged groups. However, it was apparent that government was concerned with these mainly because of the potential for social unrest that they created, rather than because of the intrin-sic negative welfare consequences. The first draft of the document spelling out the reform program concerned itself only with the macroeconomic de-sign of the program. Specific discussion of the social dimensions was included at the insistence of the World Bank and the section dealing with this in the published document was written by the Bank. (Recall that this was the time when the Bank itself had begun to take social dimensions of adjustment more seriously.)

After 1990 attempts were made to control the fiscal deficit, for good macroeconomic reasons. But given the limited capacity to tax, spending has been held down and social services for a growing population have not been improved. User fees were introduced for the previously free education and health services. To cushion the poor from the some of these effects, the Social Dimensions of Adjustment (SDA) program was introduced in 1991. It established a Social Development Fund which provided financial assistance to households earning less than $400 per month to help them meet the increased user costs for education and health associated with ESAP. It also provided a small income supplement to offset the effects of deregulation of basic food prices. The SDF also provided introductory training courses and soft loans for retrenchees who had started new businesses.

The impact of the SDA was marginal, in part because of inadequate funding. The donor funding which had been anticipated in support of this program also fell short of expectations. However, although this funding was clearly insufficient, the SDA was also poorly designed and implemented. Administrative processes were slow and cumbersome. Allocations had a strong bias in favour of retrenched civil servants and against women. The SDA was also hampered by the effects of the drought, which both increased the number of people requiring assistance and also channelled resources away from the SDF into specific drought-related programs.

The Poverty Alleviation Action Plan (PAAP), drawn up in 1994 with the assistance of UNDP and other donors, was an attempt to address these problems. It was intended to tackle issues of structural poverty rather than simply to mitigate the effects of adjustment, as had been the case with the SDA. Its main component, which has drawn donor support, is the Community Action Project, which is intended to finance small grants and technical assistance for local communities through decentralized local government and community structures.

There has thus been some evolution in the approach to poverty alleviation since ESAP was introduced. The initial view—which was in keeping with government's revealed preferences in the 1980s—seemed to be that the negative effects would be transitory and therefore required only short term mitigation. It is now realized that the problems are more deep-seated—and not solely related to adjustment—and therefore require a longer term approach. However, while this change in focus improves upon the SDA, the PAAP suffers from a similar inadequacy of resources (UNDP, 1999).

The focus of social policy in the 1980s meant that the gains made were especially vulnerable to reversal through the macroeconomic processes outlined in this paper. Even welfarist transfers can have important structural impacts on an economy if they are sustained for a long time. As the endogenous growth literature has shown, a better educated and healthier population has significantly better growth prospects than a poorly educated and less healthy one. However, such improvements take time to bear fruit. Their erosion in the 1990s significantly undermine long term growth prospects for the economy.

9. Concluding Remarks

Globalization in the case of Zimbabwe is primarily policy induced, stemming as it does from liberalization of the trade and capital accounts of the 1990s. While the ambition of the liberalization was to stimulate competition and world market orientation, the experiences so far have not been very encouraging. GDP per capita in 1997 is still well below pre-liberalization levels. Income distribution has worsened, first foremost because of a shift in inflation with rigid nominal wages, but also because of stagnating output and employment.

The loss of real wages is not necessarily the result of liberalization. Other factors certainly have contributed to the shift in inflation. But we argue that liberalization changed the conditions for macroeconomic balance, and the underlying fiscal problem came into the open as inflation. Old regulations had kept private savings high; the new availability of foreign goods created by liberalization led to drop of savings and consumption boom. If this story is true, Zimbabwe is another example of the disadvantage of liberalizing when macroeconomic, in particular fiscal, balances are not under control.

Our contemplation of recent liberalization experiences in Zimbabwe has led us back to our previous evaluation of the first independence period (Davies and Rattsø, 1993). There are some striking similarities. When the first independent government took office in 1980, it attempted a redistribution with growth reform. Wage and fiscal policy was meant to stimulate demand, productivity and equal distribution. The reform ran into macroeconomic difficulties. The combined private savings deficit and government deficit were accommodated by foreign savings. Concern about accumulating foreign debt led to abortion of the distribution initiative and tightening of controls. The liberalization program of the 1990s led to similar adjustments of the savings-investment balance. The drop in private savings coupled with a continued government deficit once more necessitated inflow of foreign savings. There now are some signs of this causing reversal of the liberalization process, with the removal of corporate foreign currency accounts, increasing attempts by government to control basic prices and a gentlemen's agreement between the Reserve Bank of Zimbabwe and commercial banks to run a fixed exchange rate.

Although there are these striking similarities, our analysis also suggests that the adjustment mechanisms have been different. In the early 1980s, the inflation was kept low, real wages grew slowly, there was no obvious widening of the income gap and no deindustrialization. In the 1990s, the macroeconomic imbalance led to high inflation, real wage decline, sharp worsening of the income distribution, and deindustrialization. It is hard to avoid thinking that these new mechanisms of distribution are to the disadvantage of those at the lower end of the income scale.

Zimbabwe's experience highlights the dilemma faced by governments wishing to undertake rapid poverty reducing programs through budgetary processes (what we may call fiscal populism). Not only are such approaches vulnerable to reversal because of macroeconomic imbalance, but, to the extent that the imbalances arise because of the programs, they may be inherently self defeating.

Policy recommendations are not easy to make in this situation. Since our analysis suggests that the different adjustment mechanisms under the regulated economy shielded the poor more than those under the liberalized one, a reversion to the pre-1990 regulations may seem appealing. However, this conclusion is not warranted from our analysis in this paper, since we have not addressed the underlying sustainability of such a regime. Evidence from the 1980s suggests that it was not sustainable. Nonetheless, although a complete reversion is hardly a good idea, industrialization and equity do need a helping hand from the government. Tariff policy and other instruments should be used to promote industrialization.

Although there appears to be a trade off between macroeconomic imbalance and fiscal populism, there is clearly scope for government to improve this trade off by better prioritization of expenditures since not all of the macroeconomic imbalance can be attributed to the social expenditures. At the same time more attention needs to be paid to redistribution processes outside the budget.

REFERENCES

Chhibber, A., J. Cottani, R. Firuzabadi and M. Walton (1989) "Inflation, price controls, and fiscal adjustment in Zimbabwe," Working Paper 192, Country Economics Department, The World Bank.

Davies, R. (1988) "The Transition to Socialism in Zimbabwe: some areas for debate," in C. Stoneman (ed.), *Zimbabwe's Prospects: issues of race, class, state and capital in Southern Africa*, Heinemann, London and Basingstoke, 18–31.

Davies, R. (1991) "Trade, Trade Management and Development in Zimbabwe," in J. Frimpong-Ansah, S.M.R. Kanbur and P. Svedberg (eds.), *Trade and Development in Sub-Saharan Africa*, Manchester: Manchester University Press.

Davies, R. and J. Rattsø (1993) "Zimbabwe," in L. Taylor (ed.), *The Rocky Road to Reform: Adjustment, Income Distribution and Growth in the Developing World*, Cambridge: MIT Press.

Davies, R. and J. Rattsø (1996) "Growth, Distribution and Environment: Macroeconomic issues in Zimbabwe," *World Development*, 24 (2): 395–405.

Davies, R., J. Rattsø and R. Torvik (1994) "The Macroeconomics of Zimbabwe in the 1980s: A CGE-model Analysis," *Journal of African Economies*, 3 (2): 1–46.

Davies, R., J. Rattsø and R. Torvik (1998) "Short run consequences of Trade Liberalization: A CGE model of Zimbabwe," *Journal of Policy Modeling* 20 (3): 305–333.

384 Davies and Rattsø

Davies, R. and D. Sanders (1988) "Adjustment policies and the welfare of children in Zimbabwe, 1980–85," in A. Cornia, R. Jolly and F. Stewart (eds.), *Adjustment with a Human Face*, Vol. 2, Oxford: Oxford University Press.

Davies, R., D. Sanders and T. Shaw (1992) "Liberalization for development: Zimbabwe's adjustment without the fund," in G. A. Cornia, R. van der Hoeven and T. Mkandawire (eds.), *Africa's Recovery in the 1990s: From Stagnation and Adjustment to Human Development*, Houndsmill, Macmillan, pp. 135–155.

Government of Zimbabwe (1991) *Zimbabwe : A Framework for Economic Reform 1991–95*, Harare, Government publication.

Green, R. and X. Kadhani (1986) "Zimbabwe: Transition to economic crises 1981–1983: Retrospect and prospect," *World Development*, 14 (8): 1059–1083.

Gunning, J. and C. Mumbengegwi (eds.) (1995) *The manufacturing sector in Zimbabwe: Industrial change under structural adjustment*, final report on the round II RPED survey data, Free University of Amsterdam and University of Zimbabwe.

Jenkins, C. (1996) "Post-independence economic policy and investment in Zimbabwe, mimeo," Centre for the Study of African Economies, University of Oxford.

Mehlum, H. and J. Rattsø (1994) "Import compression and growth constraints in Zimbabwe," mimeo, University of Oslo and Norwegian University of Science and Technology.

Ncube, M., P. Collier, J. Gunning and K. Mlambo (1996) "Trade liberalization and regional integration in Zimbabwe," mimeo, AERC and Centre for the Study of African Economies, University of Oxford.

Oswald, A. (1996) *The Wage Curve*, Cambridge: MIT Press.

Pakkiri, L. and N.P. Moyo (1987) "Foreign exchange policies: The case of Zimbabwe," paper presented at IDRC Workshop on Economic Structure and Macroeconomic Management, Harare.

Rattsø, J. (1999) "Income distribution, growth and protectionism in Sub-Saharan Africa and the case of Zimbabwe," forthcoming in *Festschrift to George Waadenburg*, Rotterdam: Erasmus University.

Rattsø, J. and L. Taylor (1998) "CGE-modelling of trade liberalization in sub-Saharan Africa: An evaluation," mimeo, Department of Economics, Norwegian University of Science and Technology and Department of Economics, New School for Social Research.

Rattsø, J. and R. Torvik (1998) "Zimbabwean trade liberalization: ex post evaluation," *Cambridge Journal of Economics*, 22 (3): 325–346.

Rodrik, D. (1994) "Trade and industrial policy reform in developing countries: A review of recent theory and evidence," in J. Behrman and T.N. Srinivasan (eds.), *Handbook of Development Economics* Volume III, Amsterdam: North-Holland.

Rodrik, D. (1998) "Why is trade reform so difficult in Africa ?, " *Journal of African Economies*, 7: 43–69 (Supplement 1: June).

Shaw, T. and R. Davies (1993) *The Political Economy of Adjustment in Zimbabwe: Convergence and Reform*, Ottawa: North South Institute.

Skålnes, T. (1995) *The Politics of Economic Reform in Zimbabwe*, London: Macmillan.

Taylor, L. (1998) "Project on globalization and social policy. Revised methodology for country studies," mimeo, CEPA, New School for Social Research.

UNDP (1999) *Zimbabwe Human Development Report 1998*, Harare, UNDP/Poverty Reduction Forum/Institute of Development Studies.

APPENDIX 1: Decomposition of Aggregate Demand: Methodology

The basic structure of the aggregate demand model is:
(1) $X = Y + T + M$
(2) $X = C + I + G + E$
(3) $sX = Y - C$
(4) $tX = T$
(5) $mX = M$
where
X – 'output', GDP + imports
Y – private sector income
T – taxes net of transfers
C – private consumption
I – private investment
G – government purchase of goods and services
E – exports
and s, t and m are defined by equations (3)–(5).

When we solve out for X, the usual multiplier comes out:

$$(6) \quad X = \frac{1}{s + t + m}(I + G + E)$$

The model separates between shifts in the injections (I, G and E) and in the leakage parameters (s, t, and m). In order to see whether there have been such shifts, we need to decompose the sources of aggregate demand. To simplify the notation, we rewrite (6):

(7) $X = k\,Z$, where k is the multiplier in (6) and $Z = I + G + E$

Decomposition of (7) can be written as (8), where k_0 and Z_0 are initial or base year values:

(8) $\Delta X = k_0 \Delta Z + Z_0 \Delta k + \Delta Z \Delta k$

To facilitate an easy interpretation of changes in leakage parameters, we define

$$k_1^s = \frac{1}{s_1 + t_0 + m_0}$$

$$k_1^s = \frac{1}{s_0 + t_1 + m_0}$$

$$k_1^s = \frac{1}{s_o + t_0 + m_1}$$

to get

(9) $\Delta k = (k_1^s - k_0) + (k_1^t - k_0) + (k_1^m - k_0) + \xi$

where ξ is an error term arising because the decomposition is not exact.

The terms on the RHS of (9) show how the multiplier would have changed if only one of the leakage parameters had changed—the other two remaining at their previous period level. When we substitute (9) into (8), we can identify separately the contribution of each of the individual parameters to the changes in X. To make the results comparable with the Taylor (1998) decomposition, we distinguish between injection and leakage for each of the components of aggregate demand:

$$\Delta X = \underbrace{k_0 \Delta I}_{\text{Injection}} + \underbrace{Z_0(k_1^i - k_0)}_{\substack{\text{Leakage} \\ \text{Parameter}}} + \underbrace{k_0 \Delta G}_{\text{Injection}} + \underbrace{Z_0(k_1^i - k_0)}_{\substack{\text{Leakage} \\ \text{Parameter}}} + \underbrace{k_0 \Delta E}_{\text{Injection}} + \underbrace{Z_0(k_1^m - k_0)}_{\substack{\text{Leakage} \\ \text{Parameter}}} + \underbrace{Z_0 \Delta Z \xi}_{\text{Interaction term}}$$

Private Sector · Public Sector · Foreign Sector · Interaction term

Appendix 2: Econometric analysis of the role of wages in the macroeconomy

The wage curve is hypothesized to have this general form:

(10) $W/W_{-1} = F(P, CU, YL)$

where
W – nominal wage rate (wage per manyear)
YL – GDP per worker
CU – capacity utilization rate
P – consumer price index

The econometric formulation of the equation for the period 1975–1996 applies an error-correction model specification:

$DlogW = a\, logW_{-1} + b\, DlogCU + c\, logCU_{-1} + d\, DlogP + e\, logP_{-1} + f\, DlogYL + g\, log\, YL_{-1}$

The second relationship is a 'distribution schedule' is (where AD is aggregate demand):

(11) $AD = G(GDP, W/P)$

and new variables are:
WS—wage share
GDP—real gross domestic product
CG—general consumption, both private and public

The following error-correction models are estimated:

$DlogI = a\, logI_{-1} + b\, DlogGDP + c\, logGDP_{-1} + d\, DlogW/P + e\, logW/P_{-1}$

$DlogCG = a\, logCG_{-1} + b\, DlogGDP + c\, logGDP_{-1} + d\, DlogW/P + e\, logW/P_{-1}$

$Dlog(CG+I) = a\, log(CG+I)_{-1} + b\, DlogGDP + c\, logGDP_{-1} + d\, DlogW/P + e\, logW/P_{-1}$